Pilgrimage of Awakening

Pilgrimage of Awakening
The Extraordinary Lives of Murray and Mary Rogers

Mary V. T. Cattan

FOREWORD BY
Klaus K. Klostermaier

PICKWICK *Publications* · Eugene, Oregon

PILGRIMAGE OF AWAKENING
The Extraordinary Lives of Murray and Mary Rogers

Copyright © 2016 Mary V. T. Cattan. All rights reserved. Except for brief quotations in critical publications or reviews, no part of this book may be reproduced in any manner without prior written permission from the publisher. Write: Permissions, Wipf and Stock Publishers, 199 W. 8th Ave., Suite 3, Eugene, OR 97401.

Pickwick Publications
An Imprint of Wipf and Stock Publishers
199 W. 8th Ave., Suite 3
Eugene, OR 97401

www.wipfandstock.com

PAPERBACK ISBN: 978-1-4982-7909-3
HARDCOVER ISBN: 978-1-4982-7911-6
EBOOK ISBN: 978-1-4982-7910-9

Cataloguing-in-Publication data:

Name: Cattan, Mary V. T.

Title: Pilgrimage of awakening : the extraordinary lives of Murray and Mary Rogers / Mary V. T. Cattan ; foreword by Klaus K. Klostermaier.

Description: Eugene, OR: Pickwick Publications | Includes bibliographical references and index.

Identifiers: ISBN 978-1-4982-7909-3 (paperback) | ISBN 978-1-4982-7911-6 (hardback) | ISBN 978-1-4982-7910-9 (ebook)

Subjects: LCSH: Rogers, C. Murray, 1917–2006. | Rogers, Mary, 1915– 2006. | Sandeman, Heather. | Church of England—Clergy—Biography. | Christianity—India. | Hinduism—Relations—Christianity. | Abhishiktananda, Swami, 1910–1973. | Klostermaier, Klaus K., 1933–. | Title.

Classification: BX5199 M91 C37 2016 (print) | BX5199 M91 (ebook)

Manufactured in the U.S.A.   06/24/16

"Three Hills" by Everard Owen from *A Treasury of War Poetry*: George Herbert Clarke, ed. First Series. Boston: Houghton Mifflin, 1917; New York: Bartletby.com, 2002. Reprinted by permission of Bartleby.com.

"Grounds for Mutual Growth" by C. Murray Rogers is reprinted with permission from the *Journal of Hindu-Christian Studies*.

"The Need to Win" by Thomas Merton, from *The Way of Chuang Tzu*, copyright ©1965 by The Abbey of Gethsemani. Reprinted by permission of New Directions Publishing.

"Last night as I was sleeping," by Antonio Machado, translated by Robert Bly is reprinted by permission of Wesleyan University Press from *Times Alone: Selected Poems of Antonio Machado*.

Two letters to the editor of the *Times* (London), "Choice of Anglican Bishop of Jerusalem" by C. Murray Rogers [24.12.1973] and "Human Rights in Jerusalem" by C. Murray Rogers, G. Clive Handford, Edward Every, Adela M. Every [07.01.1977] are reprinted with permission of News Corp UK and Ireland.

Psalm 17, from *A Book of Psalms: Selected and Adapted from the Hebrew* by Stephen Mitchell. Copyright © 1993 by Stephen Mitchell. Reprinted by permission of HarperCollins Publishers.

"May Our Corner of the Earth Join Us," [pp. 382–83: 40 lines] from *Earth Prayers* by Elizabeth Roberts and Elias Amidon. Copyright ©1991 by Elizabeth Roberts and Elias Amidon. Reprinted by permission of HarperCollins Publishers.

"Deep Peace. . . ." [pp. 172–3] reprinted in full [30.1] and excerpted from [51.] *Earth Prayers* by Elizabeth Roberts and Elias Amidon. Copyright © 1991 by Elizabeth Roberts and Elias Amidon. Reprinted by permission of HarperCollins Publishers.

"A Prayer of Sorrow" reprinted by permission of the United Nations Environment Programme (UNEP).

For Mary and Murray's children:

Cheryl, Linda, and the late Richard Rogers

and my own children:

Deborah, Louisa, Sarah, and Andrew

who, like children everywhere, have both enjoyed and endured things done and left undone by their parents.

All this universe is in the glory of God, the God of love
... He is indeed the Lord supreme whose grace moves
the hearts of all. He leads us into his own joy and to the
glory of his light...

Concealed in the heart of all beings lies the Atman, the
Spirit, the Self; smaller than the smallest atom, greater
than the greatest spaces. When, by the grace of God, we
see the glory of God, we see beyond the world of desire
and then sorrows are left behind...

May God, who in the mystery of his vision and power
transforms his white radiance into his many-colored
creation, from whom all things come and into whom
they all return, grant us the grace of pure vision.

—Svetasvatara Upanishad

Contents

Foreword by Klaus K. Klostermaier | xi
Preface | xiii
Acknowledgments | xvii

1. Birth to Marriage 1916–1940 | 1
2. Fledgling Marriage and Ministry 1940–1945 | 21
3. Seeds of Transformation 1946–1951 | 28
4. Christians among Hindus: Encounters with Difference 1951–1953 | 37
5. A Family in Flux 1953–1954 | 56
6. Impossible Contradictions 1955–1956 | 69
7. Heather Sandeman: "One of Us" | 75
8. Lighting the Lamp of Jyotiniketan 1957–1958 | 81
9. Jyotiniketan—A Way of Life 1959–1965 | 98
10. In Love and Longing with India 1965–1967 | 124
11. A Deepening Journey of Light and Darkness 1966–1971 | 138
12. Jerusalem: Seeking Peace, Meeting Conflict 1971–1973 | 171
13. A Community of Resistance 1974–1980 | 194
14. Hong Kong: Growing into Weakness 1980–1986 | 227
15. Septuagenarians Looking Ahead 1986–1989 | 257
16. Canada: A Geriatric Escapade? 1989–1994 | 271
17. Young and Old Together in Canada 1995–1998 | 289
18. Complete Circle to England: "A Losing Victory" 1998–2006 | 304
19. Following the Light: Living into Death | 319

Epilogue | 333
Appendices | 335
Bibliography | 407
Index | 411

Foreword

A FLOOD-GATE OF PERSONAL memories opened up when reading Dr. Mary Cattan's account of the extraordinary lives of Murray and Mary Rogers: Jyotiniketan in the 1960s—stimulating interfaith discussions, deeply moving worship, preparing chapattis, and washing dishes. An exchange of letters from many parts of the world for over forty years till the very end . . .

Murray and Mary Rogers followed what they believed to be a personal call and they remained true to it in the face of tremendous obstacles. While married Anglican missionary couples were not unknown during the time of the British Raj in India, the kind of experiment which Mary and Murray Rogers undertook was quite unique. Wholly uncompromising in following their vocation, they were immensely flexible in adapting to outward circumstances, in the process interiorizing the cultures of India, Israel, and China.

Long and close association with the Rogers community gave Dr. Mary Cattan access to a great wealth of information. From her account it also becomes quite obvious that Murray and Mary Rogers had a heavy price to pay in personal suffering and anguish for following what they believed to be their calling: their own children could not understand why their parents had to be so different and make their lives so difficult!

Dr. Cattan combines in her work painstaking research with genuine empathy: the result is a fascinating book that deserves to find many readers!

Klaus K. Klostermaier, PhD
University of Manitoba, Distinguished Professor

Preface

> As ever, religious belief makes its claim somewhere
> between revelation and projection,
> between holiness and human frailty;
> but the burden of proof,
> indeed the business of belief,
> for so long upheld by society,
> is back on the believer where it belongs . . .
> There is no way to seek truth except personally.
> Every story worth knowing is a life story.
>
> —Paul Elie

This work has grown from a twenty-five year friendship with Murray Rogers and Mary Rogers. Our first acquaintance was made in 1979 in my home parish of Christ Church, Greenwich, Conn. It was Lent, and Murray had been invited by the church's rector to travel from Jerusalem where he and Mary were living to serve as "theologian in residence" for a few weeks leading up to Easter. As the mother of four young children in a marriage that had fallen apart, I was in the midst of my own Good Friday experience, with any sense of Easter light far over the horizon. My memories of his visit are cloudy; I cannot recall his words. From my place in the pew, I do remember him in the procession. It was not only his Indian garb and sandaled feet that caught my attention. I had a sense that he was walking to a different rhythm. From the place of my pain, I sensed holiness. For me, the old saying sometimes attributed to the Buddha was true: "When the student is ready, the teacher appears." For the first time I felt compelled to remain in my seat for the entire three hours of the Good Friday Service and then to come forward, kneeling, still a bit self-consciously, but devoutly at the foot of the looming rough wooden cross that had been erected for the day. Murray was there to greet each of us as we arose from that devotion, wordlessly reaching out and putting our hand to his forehead in blessing. Looking back, I can see that my own brokenness allowed me to receive the sense of hope and love that he conveyed, not only in his words, but in his demeanor, the look in his eye, and his movements.

But as a spiritual student and seeker, I was still young in my journey, not entirely ready for such a teacher. In diffidence, I held back, and until Murray and Mary arrived two years later for another Lenten visit, I had no contact. Then again, I was captured by his presence and, along with many others, became a regular at any teaching he would offer, eagerly jotting notes. Gradually, over the years, as he returned again and again to Greenwich and as I entered seminary as a student of spiritual direction, a spiritual relationship grew between us. I began to understand that his gift of friendship, whether to an ordinary suburban housewife like me or to an illustrious scholar or cleric was offered freely and wholeheartedly, with little distinction. As the years passed and I slowly imbibed his presence in his teaching, letters and visits, I realized how profound his spiritual impact on my life had become. My children too were touched; at one of my daughters' request, Murray came from England to officiate at her marriage on an island in Maine. Five years ago, to my utter amazement, I learned that my son's first child was named Murray.

In the final ten years of their lives, our relationships deepened. Since I had remarried and was negotiating the challenges of a blended family, it was apparent that marriage and family was the primary crucible of my spiritual path. Thus I was naturally curious about Mary and Murray's marriage and their life as the parents of three children. My training as a psychotherapist with intensive marriage and family training attuned me to their unusual family journey. Aware that with Murray often in the spotlight, their family story remained in the shadows, I wondered about that story. How could this remarkable couple have lived a life of near-monastic discipline in far-flung places and simultaneously raised three children? My diffidence dispelled, I began to ask questions and to receive responses that slowly revealed what could be shared.

It was clear that their story—complex, poignant and fascinating—was deeply worth knowing. Remarkably, it had not been told. For while each of them was willing to share certain details of their lives, neither had done so in any deliberate or methodical way. I indicated my willingness to be a part of that effort.

Murray in particular was willing and even eager. Following my visit to them in Canada in 1996, Murray typed a note to me: "I need your help if you can spare the time to give it to me. I'm all set with a tiny recorder to have a try at 'telling my little story'! Too many people have encouraged me to do so and I'm feeling rather a disgrace at not trying harder! As long as it can be in some way for the glory of God—and *not* of me—I want to give it a try." True to her nature and to her relationship with Murray, if Murray thought it a good idea, Mary was on board as well.

But it was not until the year 2000 when they had left Canada to live in Oxford, England, that we revisited the idea in earnest. By then I realized that the scope of their life story deserved a professional writer who had the expertise to organize their vast collection of papers, to reflect cogently on the significance of their lives, and to allow Murray's voice to be heard.

Happily there was just such a person—Judson Trapnell, PhD, a spiritual biographer and professor at the University of Virginia who could ensure that their experiences and contributions would be sensitively documented. In 2003 he completed an extensive series of interviews, not only with Murray, but with Mary and their sister-in-community, Heather Sandeman as well. With Prof. Trapnell writing a proper biography, I would focus my study on family relationships—those within their immediate biological family as well as their vast network of spiritual friends, all considered family.

By then they were well into their eighties. Murray was open to self-reflection, concerned with end of life questions, and desirous that shadow dimensions of his life be brought to light. "Truthfulness" preoccupied him. Particularly for their children, he yearned to leave a legacy of deeper understanding and desired an openness that might bring some measure of reconciliation to simmering resentments. Back in England where they were no longer geographically "family-at-a-distance" and where their children Cheryl, Linda, and Richard were each, in their own ways, attentive to their parents, a part of Murray longed for a deeper acceptance. "My children think I'm crazy," he joked, "and maybe I am!" For that hope of deeper understanding, he spoke to each of them about this work and urged them to be as open and "truthful" with me as they were comfortable. Cheryl and Linda, he said, would probably be willing; Richard, perhaps. "I'm afraid we failed Richard," he said sadly.

My connections with all three of them have been one of the great blessings of this work. Though Richard's life was cut short in his prime in 2009, he was generous with his time and his truth and shared delightful stories and insights. Cheryl and Linda responded not only truthfully and generously but open-heartedly.

Sadly, in those Oxford years, Mary's brilliant mind was gradually dimmed with dementia. Until near the end she remained a fount of information of people, places and happenings from years past. She was open and willing to share whatever she could, but the ability to connect with and articulate deep emotional truth was protected by a gentle but impenetrable shield.

It was a shocking loss when they received word that Judson Trapnell, their prospective biographer, with whom they had developed warm and respectful relationships, had died unexpectedly only months after their interviews with him. His widow returned the rough, untranscribed tapes to Murray.

Murray requested that I find a way to transcribe the tapes. That task completed (by a professional service), I returned the original tapes to him and, with his verbal permission and encouragement, retained a copy of the tapes for my own work.

Thus, with more resources and continued research and thought, I began to see the impossibility of limiting my exploration to any particular dimension of their lives. Everything was interconnected. Often brought to my knees by the complexity of the work, I now can echo Murray's own disclaimer about their lives: "*We* didn't make it happen. *God* did it!" Though I *can* lay claim to the short-comings and mistakes that certainly lie within my own work despite my efforts to remain faithful to both truth and complexity, I echo his disclaimer. Only with the help of the mysterious Holy Spirit (and numerous human cheerleaders) have I completed this challenging task. For that I am deeply grateful.

Murray and Mary Rogers with the author, Deseronto, Canada, 1996.

Acknowledgments

FROM THE VERY BEGINNING of this project, the help and support I have received from a wide spiritual community has been remarkable; it has seen me through to the end. It began with Murray Rogers himself, without whose encouragement and confidence I could not have told this story.

I am deeply grateful to the preeminent spiritual biographer, Shirley du Boulay. She merits special thanks for her reading of the manuscript at several stages. Her wise counsel and encouragement have been heartening all along the way. Shirley has been generous, not only with her time and patience, but in her hospitality. Not only is she a wonderful writer; she is a very good cook.

The work of the late Judson Trapnell, specifically his sensitive conversations with Mary, Murray, and Heather, recorded during the Lenten season 2003, has been an invaluable resource. I am grateful to his wife, Rose, who generously made the recordings available and added her own reminiscences of his experience with Jyotiniketan.

Gratitude goes also to the Rev. David Barton who, along with his wife, Susan Widgery, welcomed me warmly to their home in Oxford. David has been open as well with his time, insights, recollections, and resources. It was with David that early ideas for this work were first shared. He was unfailingly positive and encouraging. And, like Shirley, David is an excellent cook.

I am indebted as well to Andrea Andriotti, whose generosity and encouragement in sharing letters from Mary and Murray to their friend Raimon Panikkar provided an invaluable resource. Andrea and his life partner Agnes invited me to Tymawr Convent in Wales where, again, warm hospitality was offered. I am also deeply grateful to March Hancock, who kindly drove me from Oxford to Tymawr, allowing this sharing to happen.

The gifted writer and musician, the late Don Campbell, whose own spiritual life was enriched by his friendship with Murray, encouraged me with written resources as well with his words, "It is a ripe time to write about Mary and Murray's family." Sadly, he died in 2012.

I have been energized and delighted by the response from other friends of Jyotiniketan with whom I have corresponded, talked on the phone, emailed, and Skyped. Their enthusiasm and generosity in sharing their time, impressions, and memories has been a great gift.

Dr. Klaus Klostermaier, who generously lent his time, a scholarly eye, and a tender heart to read my work, gave me valuable firsthand clarification of the work of the Cuttat Group. It has been a special pleasure and honor to feel supported by such a very good friend of Jyotiniketan.

Also among them is Murray's friend of forty-seven years, the Rev. Michael David. I am grateful to him and to his daughter, Rebecca Rowland, who transcribed his memories and impressions.

I am grateful as well for good conversations with John Landgraf, their devoted friend, and for the reminiscences of Fr. Sergio Ticozzi. The late Bo Lozoff kindly shared an afternoon of reflections with me, and I am appreciative to Sita Lozoff for her warm sharing of memories and to Josh Lozoff for his wonderful photographs.

I offer thanks to good Christ Church Greenwich friends, Barbie and Chuck Goldschmid, whose memories and photographs are treasured. Will Duncan, Murray's young student, now a spiritual teacher in his own right, shared delightful stories; I am grateful to him.

I would also like to thank other good friends who shared stories, clarified information and offered encouragement: Jan Keny, Ruby Kells, Adelaide Winstead, Mary Valentine, and Sister Frances Dominica Ritchie.

Especially deep gratitude is due to those who shared life in Jyotiniketan with Mary, Murray, and Heather over long periods and were generous with me.

Particularly I thank Kate and Adam Campbell, who welcomed me several times to their Halifax home via Skype, sharing their Jyotiniketan experiences with deep sensitivity. Expressive and articulate, they have enriched my understanding of the Canada years immeasurably.

Dr. Verena Tschudin thoughtfully offered resources and knowledge on Jerusalem of the 1970s as well as insights on Jyotiniketan.

The Rev. Veronica (Vroni) Thurneysen, a close friend of Jyotiniketan for many years, offered important resources and insights, generously and trustingly, especially regarding Rosmarie. Her assistance has been invaluable.

The greatest appreciation of all goes to Mary and Murray's family.

Cheryl and André Poutier have been unfailingly responsive to my endless list of questions, generous in their openness, and warm in their friendship. André's thoughtful writings added an important dimension to my understanding.

Linda and March Hancock warmly welcomed me to their home in Barnes (London) and have been generous in their sharing. Linda's candid and spontaneous childhood memories enliven the story of life in Jyotiniketan. March's participation, both in his writing and in his practical help, has been deeply appreciated.

I hope Richard can know how much I appreciated his willingness to set aside his skepticism to talk with me. Riding his motorcycle from London to Oxford on a rainy day for our meeting, he offered his own candid and invaluable perspectives. He then answered my questions by email with unfailing good humor until our correspondence was cut short by his illness and death.

To my own family, too, I am grateful. Heartfelt thanks to Deborah, Louisa, Sarah, and Andrew and to their loyal spouses and wonderful children for their understanding and forbearance as, year after year, this research and writing continued. I know it has been a sacrifice for them. As this book nears publication, I offer a deep bow of gratitude to Deborah for her patient and meticulous proofreading. An English teacher par excellence, she has delightfully turned the tables on her mother, who, only yesterday, it seems, was proofreading *her* essays!

My friends, too, have been patient and helpfully curious, and I thank them for not giving up on me.

Finally, I am grateful to those who helped and supported me in my writing at Andover Newton Theological School. Thanks to the Rev. Dr. Mark Heim for his reading of my work and for his very helpful, knowledgeable observations. Thanks to my colleagues, the Rev. Dr. Penny Gadzini and Dr. Inge del Rosario, who remain among my most faithful encouragers. Most of all, to the Rev. Dr. Brita Gill-Austern, my heartfelt gratitude for her trust, patience, and unfailing empathy as I ever so slowly completed this manuscript. Without her waiting at the finish line, I might well have faltered.

1

Birth to Marriage
1916–1940

Three Hills

There is a hill in England,
Green fields and a school I know,
Where the balls fly fast in summer,
And the whispering elm-trees grow,
A little hill, a dear hill
And the playing fields below.

There is a hill in Flanders,
Heaped with a thousand slain,
Where the shells fly night and noontide
And the ghosts that died in vain,—
A little hill, a hard hill
To the souls that died in pain.

There is a hill in Jewry
On the midmost he is dying
To save all those who die.—
A little hill, a kind hill
To souls in jeopardy.

—EVERARD OWEN;
HARROW, DECEMBER 1915

IN A SENSE, IT was God who brought them together. Without their religious leanings, Mary Hole and Murray Rogers might never have laid eyes on one another at that meeting of the Student Christian Movement of Cambridge

University. Nor might that first spark have been ignited. But they did, and it was. It was 1935; she was twenty-one; he was twenty. It might have been a simple love story, or at least a conventional one.

But this was not the first time Murray had fallen in love, and in that complexity, this story unfolds. Seven years earlier, as he had gathered with friends 'round a fire at a church camp, a different flame of young love had been set burning in him. Most unexpectedly, as the immortal words from Isaiah were read, Murray experienced himself being addressed directly and intimately by God: "I heard the voice of the Lord, saying, 'Whom shall I send, and who will go for us?'" And, as Isaiah's reply resonated within him, he added his own small voice: "Here am I; send me." Young Murray had fallen in love with God.

Bright young Cambridge students, eager to step into the world, Mary and Murray could never have imagined the path their pilgrimage would take, the family they would create, or the multitude of lives they would touch. Nor could they have imagined the implications of that everpresent love affair with God: how they would be guided through the next seventy years, as Murray later noted, "always by God's marvelous grace, the reality of Him Himself, 'in whom we live and move and have our being.'"[1] Nor could Mary have foreseen the dedicated and complicated life she would be called to live as the wife of a man who ultimately wanted nothing so intensely as to be "burnt up in [God's] love."[2]

In the two decades before their meeting, both had already been powerfully shaped in the complex interweaving of British culture and the times, family, and religion that defined their world and their particular homes.

Charles Murray Rogers and Aileen Mary Seton Hole each were born to prosperous English families. As young citizens of the great British Empire, they entered a world in turmoil. In 1916, the year of Mary's birth, the brutal British quelling of the Irish uprising had taken place on Easter morning. With King George V on the throne and David Lloyd George as Prime Minister, Britain, with its vaunted navy, was intent on maintaining and extending its vast geographical hegemony. From Canada in North America, to Hong Kong in the East, East and West Africa, its empire was unrivaled. On the continent, it was fighting in the "Great War." The next year, shortly after Murray's birth, the Third Battle of Ypres had cost the British 324,000 men. That same year, Anglo-Indian troops occupied Baghdad, with a proclamation issued by the commanding officer: "Our armies do not come into your

---

1. Murray Rogers, interview with author, Oxford, England, 2005.
2. Murray Rogers, interview with Judson Trapnell, Oxford, England, 2003.

cities and lands as conquerors or enemies, but as liberators."[3] And while the British Raj was ostensibly in control of India, it was being challenged, not only by the Home Rule Movement, but by Mohandas Gandhi and his followers. Working on behalf of Indian peasants from his *Satyagraha Ashram* near the city of Ahmedabad, Gandhi, in those war years, had achieved his first victory through civil disobedience and had begun to employ fasting as a weapon against British power. In 1917 Sir Edwin Montagu, the British Secretary of State for India, acknowledging the unrest, promised reforms calling for gradual development of self-governing institutions. (Though when the war ended, Britain did not keep its promises, but further tightened its limitation of civil liberties with the despised Rowlatt Acts.[4]) Also in 1917 the British military defeated Ottoman forces, occupying Syria and Palestine. Soon after, the Balfour Declaration was issued supporting the "establishment in Palestine of a national home for the Jewish people . . . it being clearly understood that nothing shall be done which may prejudice the civil and religious rights of existing non-Jewish communities in Palestine." Four days later the Russian Revolution began.

Though not a part of Murray and Mary's conscious childhood memories, such was the ferment of the world as they lived their first years of life. Born only a bit more than a hundred miles apart, both were insulated within the privileged world that these political struggles were intended to perpetuate.

Murray was born on May 16, 1917. His birthplace was a house at the end of the only runway of Croydon, the City of London's first airport. Croydon was located between two World War I airfields and was part of a protective circle of small airfields around the city to shield it from Zeppelin raids. At the end of the war the two were combined into Croydon Aerodrome, which opened in 1920. Within the decade it became a place of international glamour, as long-distance flights arrived and departed for those who could afford them. Many heroic and pioneering flights came to Croydon, such as that of Amy Johnson, the first woman to fly to Australia and back again in 1930, and Charles Lindbergh, who made the first transatlantic flight from America in 1927. Murray recalled witnessing his landing: "We waited there for hours, a little band of us little boys. You can imagine we were thrilled. Then this tiddly little plane arrives, looking like a matchbox, and it became an even greater miracle that it had got over all that land and

---

3. The Proclamation of Baghdad.

4. The Rowlatt Acts were passed by the British Imperial government to help deal with increasing opposition from the Indian people. They included provisions that would allow arrest without a warrant, the silencing of the press, and the imprisonment of political activists accused of treason or sedition.

sea."[5] One wonders how such images of gallant and adventurous men and women flying off to distant shores may have stoked a small boy's yearning to see the world, or perhaps woven a fantasy of escape from what was often an unhappy home.

Other memories were fragmentary, as childhood memories sometimes are, but Murray attributed the haziness of his memories to the pain of his childhood. That time, he said, was "difficult to reflect on, because . . . it's too painful . . . It's puzzled me as to why, in those first years I asked so few questions. I just missed the chance, really, of knowing about my family. I knew I was living, and that wasn't very happy-making."[6]

The source of much of his unhappiness was his father's relationships within the family. According to Murray, Edgar Rogers was an ambitious man who had been disappointed not to be a part of the British Navy—somehow he hadn't made the grade—but did serve time in the Army. He had returned from the military to begin his career as a stockbroker and to make a good marriage. Murray's mother, Barbara, was a warm and attractive woman, whose family was also engaged in the commercial side of life—her eldest brother, Francis Berry, had made his mark as wine merchant to the royal family—so it would seem to have been an appropriate choice. Yet there was constant tension around money and ways of relating. Murray recalled his confusion in these words: "Father, you see, though he had lots of money, was always saying he hadn't any . . ." As the only son, he bore his father's expectations that Murray should emulate him with a career in either the Navy or finance. But the boy was diffident and retiring, more athlete than scholar, and he did not admire his father.

There were two older sisters in the household, Olive and Muriel, but contentment for Murray rested with his mother, whom he adored. As his father's wealth increased, the family was moved from the house near the runway (luckily, it seems, as the house was eventually destroyed in a fiery plane crash) to something considerably grander. It was "a wonder to all the neighbors . . . one of the first houses ever to have a furnace underneath for central heating. It had a hard tennis court . . . and a copse, little area of woodland, where he made a pond and brought water to the house—pretty ordinary things now . . . but in those days, they showed he was a very wealthy man."

Though the house may have brought satisfaction to Edgar Rogers, it was often the scene of emotional pain for Murray. "When he was in the house," Murray recounted, "I don't want to be unfair to the man—I'm sure he had a good heart—but he made life rather miserable for Mother. Mother

---

5. Interview with Trapnell.
6. Ibid.

was the person who loved us children. I always wanted to stand up for her and don't think I ever succeeded too much. I wept very easily . . . [and] she was being downed all the time; she was blamed for everything that didn't go right, and that hurt me a lot."[7]

There was happiness playing with cousins from his mother's large extended family, especially his cousin, Elizabeth—"playing railways, Hornby (electric) trains and farms, that part I loved."[8] But those carefree moments, and other pleasures of living a privileged and protected life in England, fraught as they were with conflict, seemed only to intensify his resentment. If his mother needed something, they could not afford it. But if his father wanted something, perhaps an extravagant holiday, his wishes would be indulged. Looking back, Murray explained, "The trouble was, who was I to say [that my father was wrong]? . . . I rejoiced in lovely family holidays in Switzerland, a very expensive place, particularly all those awful years of the late twenties and thirties, when masses of people were unemployed. [England] was terribly poor, [but] I didn't even notice. I was living in a little, shut-in place with lots of money and frequent arguments, often afraid, with a terrific sense of constraint, trying to make myself disappear . . ."[9]

Early on Murray's father seemed to have decided that his son was not the son he wanted. Murray recalled: "All I remember is that Father was so bored stiff with everything to do with me that Mother once remarked, 'If it was left to your father, you'd still be in Lower Kindergarten.'"[10] He added, "I mean, Father couldn't care less. He never expected me to pass anything, and he was too often correct."[11]

Murray attended Whitgift, a public day school (equivalent to a private school in the U.S.) in Croydon. Founded in 1596 by Elizabeth the First's last Archbishop of Canterbury, it provided the traditional rigorous academics, sports and comportment that upper crust British boys were expected to master. At school his lack of confidence made him vulnerable to further ridicule. "I can still remember now, we had the dreadful phrase, these small boys—or not so small—of calling people like me—quieter, more reserved types—'you little squirt.' I remember being called a little squirt, and because I must have *thought* I was a little squirt, it really hurt. I felt terribly inferior, and daren't speak up, except with an enormous amount of courage." Not surprisingly, Murray did not excel academically, living out his father's low

---

7. Ibid.
8. Ibid.
9. Ibid.
10. Rogers, interview with author.
11. Rogers, interview with Trapnell.

expectations. "I failed enormously many times . . . I'd [just] pass the necessary examinations and eventually got through, if you know what I mean . . . and when it came to leaving Whitgift, well, I'd succeeded in playing cricket and rugby for the school. That was at least something."[12]

The family's religious observance compounded his unhappiness. They belonged to a Protestant sect called "Strict and Particular Baptists" of the Anabaptist tradition. In brief, Anabaptists rejected infant baptism, believing that the condition for baptism was evidence of a "living" faith in Christ, indicating that one had been "saved." They were biblical literalists, called "Strict" on account of their closed position on membership and communion and "Particular" in their belief that Christ in his death undertook to save particular individuals, usually referred to as the elect. Thus Murray was not baptized as a child. Attending church with his family, his experiences seemed to reinforce his impression that he was inadequate, if not worse, in God's view as well.

Here too his Mother was his refuge. Murray recalled the Sunday service: "It went on for about an hour and a half. Forty-five minutes was the sermon, and half an hour of extemporary prayer . . . For music, we weren't allowed any instrument in the church, because that was of the devil. So we didn't have an organ, [or] a piano. All we had was a little tuning fork. I can see the man now. He used to go like that (hand gesture), then he would lead the singing . . . There was just no joy in it . . . God [was] a bore . . . Mercifully, Mother always [was] there; when I started nodding she drew me over, and I'd fall fast asleep on her knees. Well, that saved my life." Laughing, he exclaimed, "Otherwise, I'd have been a dedicated atheist forever!"[13]

When Murray was twelve, tension in the family mounted further when his mother gave birth to another sister, named for her mother. Barbara Rogers was in her mid-forties; little Barbara was born with Down Syndrome. At the time, babies such as Babs, as she was called, were dubbed "Mongoloid," with a layer of shame associated with beliefs that Asians, including Mongolians, were inferior to the white race. As a general practice, they were hidden away in institutions, ostensibly to give them the care they needed, but also to spare their families the embarrassment of their presence. As Murray remembered, "I could see it was an agony for Mother, and I may be wrong, but I had a horrid feeling that Father rather blamed Mother."

Babs was brought home. Not yet exposed to those attitudes of public shame, Murray recounts how he responded to the love of this little girl: "I was devoted to this little baby . . . When I was a small boy of twelve or

---

12. Ibid.
13. Ibid.

thirteen, I must have walked miles with the baby in my arms . . . She was awfully loving. You could see, she just responded to love. She loved music . . . and I could sit at the piano, and play, and sing, and she'd love it." But gradually, he grew more aware of the awkward embarrassment Babs brought to the family, and he became caught up in keeping her existence a family secret. "Hiding it, and you know . . . [telling others] to my shame now, that I had [only] *two* sisters."[14]

At thirteen there came a turning point. Tim Brook, a young schoolmaster at Murray's school, invited him to go to a boy's camp, run by an evangelical wing of the Anglican Church. Here is Murray's recollection:

> We had a jolly good time with games, walks, swimming when it wasn't too icy. There was a path to the sea near Brighton. And in the evening, a sort of meeting, in which one of the young undergraduates, fellows of twenty, twenty-one, twenty-two, would talk to us about the Christian faith, the Bible, and what not, and we'd pray. And then this evening came, and this man, I don't know who it was, read the Call of Isaiah, about God's glory, about the prophet feeling so inferior and inadequate, what could he do about it? And God came and in a flame solved all his problems of being such an awful sinner. Then comes the marvelous passage, verse eight, when God says, "Whom shall I send, and who will go for us?" And the prophet replies, "Here am I. Send me." Then a crazy thing happened. When he was talking, I just knew that God was saying it to me, and I was the prophet Isaiah for thirty seconds. And I said, "God, I'm here. I'd like to go."

After that, Murray said, his life changed. He began having some "quiet time" in the morning and started attending a fundamentalist Anglican church with a friend from school. His words capture something of the inner and outer shift:

> There must have been something secret inside me, I don't know where I got it—where it came from, so to speak. And so early on, I suppose because of that camp . . . when Jesus came to me, and God began to be alive to me—everything that happened was fun; it was lovely. It was like being at the camp. And the church, you see, it was enjoyable. I had my friends there. I didn't feel, as I did at home, being pushed all the time to be good, or as the Baptists made me—it was all very moralistic, you see . . . God

14. Ibid.

was like a headmaster with a cane. So the Anglican church, and *that* church, was a great sort of blessing.[15]

As Murray found a new sense of himself in this experience and moved into adolescence, he and a youthful mentor found one another. Derek Wigram, just out of Cambridge, was his Latin teacher (though Murray wondered aloud how much Latin he learned!) who enjoyed games of tennis with Murray on the Rogers family court. More significantly, Murray said, "he introduced me *really* to the real world around," including the somewhat left-wing Manchester *Guardian*. "I remember a tremendous argument with Father about that, because Father discovered a Manchester *Guardian* in his house. And this was *appalling*! Everything he stood for as a stockbroker . . . was against the Manchester *Guardian*, and he sort of rounded into me."

But Murray was ready to assert himself: "I said, 'I think, Daddy—I called him Daddy then—I've simply *got* to know about the world. It's no good just being shut up in this place.'" Summoning up a warning that was often repeated in the ensuing years, his father responded contemptuously, "Remember where the money comes from, you old blighter!"[16]

Little did his father know that even before Murray finished at Whitgift, he had already applied to the Church Missionary Society (C.M.S.) to make good on his commitment to God, "Here I am, send me." He was determined to know about the world and to begin his work. But officials of the Society told him to go to university first.

Describing his disdain for his father's preoccupation with money and social standing, Murray wryly commented, "Well, I'm not sure, were we *nouveau riche* or just *riche*"?[17]

Mary did not need to ask that tongue-in-cheek question. She came from a family whose lineage could be traced back to William the Conqueror, whose wealth was substantial and old, a family who carried the happenstance of their births with ease. She was born on April 6, 1916, in the little village of Edgefield, Norfolk, north of Norwich, the third child of Frank Binford Hole and Aileen Mary Seton Hole. Her sister, Marjorie, was three, and her brother, Bruce, was fifteen.

As it was the Edwardian era with its rigid class structures and clearly defined social mores, it was natural that an upper class family would have servants to take primary responsibility for the day-to-day care of the children and the household. So it was with the Holes. Among their several servants, one stood out: the indispensable Miss Sharp, who had lived with the

15. Ibid.
16. Ibid.
17. Ibid.

family since the newly married Holes arrived home from their honeymoon in 1898. Miss Sharp was clearly a servant, yet she was a central figure in the life of the family. It's likely that Mary spent nearly as many hours in her company as in that of her mother.

Mary's parents had been married eighteen years when Mary was born; their customs were well established. They lived a structured life-style, to which little "Mollie," as Mary was called, readily adapted. Providing love in the strict and formal ways of the times, her mother and father would receive their two little girls after supper every evening for precisely one hour. Then the children would curtsy and go upstairs with Miss Sharp to be put to bed. Physical warmth and affection were not natural parts of their expression.

Happily, Miss Sharp was later described by Murray and Mary's daughters as a "delightful person"[18]—"the lynchpin of the household,"[19] who was taken along on family holidays in Guernsey. And she lived with them for some seventy years, dying within six weeks of Aileen Hole, her longtime mistress. By then, beloved throughout the family, she was affectionately called "Old Snore."

Mary's most accessible early memory was having polio at age five. "Of course, in those days there was no remedy . . . but my mother was rather sensible and took me to an American osteopath right up near the Marble Arch in London. And I remember thinking as a small child, 'That's funny, he's . . . pounding my back! Why on earth? I thought it was my leg!'"[20] Fortunately, the polio's effect was limited—leaving one leg a bit smaller than the other.

Mary's father had inherited considerable wealth, some of it in prime London property on Jermyn Street. Educated at King's School in London, he began his career as a banker. But by the time Mary was born, he could afford to be fully engaged with his real passion, the evangelical work of his Christian faith. Thus, soon after her birth, the family moved to the Sydenham section of London, so Frank Hole could dedicate himself to his writing, to preaching, and to his little Christian bookshop near St. Paul's Cathedral.

In a sense, he became a giant of a man in that world—an evangelist *par excellence*—though Mary seems never to have focused on the reach or impact of his work. Excerpts from an address at his funeral service in 1964 give a flavor of the esteem in which he was held, especially by those sharing his Plymouth Brethren allegiance:

---

18. Linda Hancock, interview with author, Oxford, England, 2006.
19. Cheryl Poutier, telephone interview from Elancourt, France by author, 2007.
20. Mary Rogers, interview with Trapnell, Oxford, England, 2003.

> Frank Binford Hole was a man of God. His long life was marked by faithfulness, devotion, patience and hope. His memory is best honoured by remembering the massive pillars of the faith in which he laboured, lived and died. The conspicuous feature of his life was that he lived and laboured in the Christian Faith, and was constrained to do so by personal experience of the love of Christ. He had every opportunity to seek the ordinary satisfactions of life in a garish world. In possessions and intellect he was fitted to achieve such satisfaction: but early in life at the age of sixteen, he was met by the Stranger of Galilee and from that moment he 'endured as seeing Him who is invisible.'"[21]

His eulogist also noted: "He was entirely careless of human estimation of his work." So Frank Hole did not boast of his accomplishments at home; he simply lived his faith, and his children grew up steeped in the Christian Gospel and the rigid beliefs of the Plymouth Brethren.

The Plymouth Brethren movement began in Dublin in the 1820s and spread to Britain, where its first English gathering was in Plymouth, from which its name was derived. Its principles were in part a reaction to the Church of England and emphasized the need to return to the simplicity of the early New Testament church. Among them was a central notion that to ordain clergy was a sin against the Holy Spirit, as ordination failed to recognize that the Holy Spirit could speak through *any* member of the Church. Under the influence of John Nelson Darby, one of its most influential organizers, followers who adhered to his teachings were called Darbyites and embraced preaching of "dispensationalism": the belief that the true Church consists of only those saved from the Day of Pentecost until the time of the second coming of Christ, known as "the rapture." The alternative to being saved was, quite simply, eternal damnation. The reverberations of this teaching continue to echo throughout conservative Christianity to the present day. For exclusivists—those who believe there is only one true religion—study of the Bible was (and is) extremely important; for Plymouth Brethren believers, the consequences of incorrect belief were catastrophic. Thus, Frank Hole dedicated his life to this urgent mission: that the unchurched or the improperly churched be rescued from God's wrath, traveling, in his younger days, throughout England conducting "tent missions," later preaching in the West Indies and South Africa, and writing scores of books on scripture, many of which remain in print today. It was said in the family that he was an important resource for the young Billy Graham, helping him write his early sermons. His small volume, *Foundations of the Faith*, published in 1922, explicates meticulously

---

21. Blackburn, "Frank Binford Hole."

by chapter and verse his belief in the inerrancy of Holy Scripture. It concludes: "If one spoke be broken the strength of the wheel is threatened. If one stone of the arch be dislodged the stability of the whole is destroyed. If one foundation truth of Scripture be denied the faith of Christ is imperiled, its consistency broken up, and there is no knowing how far the mischief may spread."[22]

After publication, a sticker was added to the inside cover of the book which read: "The reader of this book is earnestly urged to keep his Bible at hand and to refer to it for every Scripture quoted. Only as he is led in a prayerful spirit to the Word of God itself can full profit be derived."

Other Plymouth Brethren beliefs that permeated family life forbade not only secular music, but any reading that was not entirely "true." Thus fiction was not allowed, and as a child, the stories Mary could read (or have read to her) could *not* have included the newly published (1914) translation of Grimm's Fairy Tales! Bible stories, or lives of the saints were standard fare to encourage a child's moral sensibility. Both at home and in church, the traditional division between the roles of men and women prevailed, as men took the "vocal" leadership roles, and women assumed supportive, "silent" ones.

Regarding intimacy, Victorian sensibilities reigned, with those attitudes reinforced by most churches. There were, of course, guides for parents. Among the best known was Dr. Beatrice Webb's *The Teaching of Young Children and Girls as to Reproduction*. First published in 1917 and in its twelfth edition twenty years later, it "stressed the need for hard exercise, team games and 'happy comradeship' to calm down the sexually aware teenage girl." It also advocated "plenty of 'homemade bread, cake, porridge, puddings' (but fish or meat only once a week, and tea and coffee as little as possible), a hard bed pulled up next to an open window, summer and winter, and cold water splashed regularly onto 'the parts' would all divert the sexual energy away from 'morbid excitement.'"[23] Sex was not a subject to be discussed in polite company, religious or otherwise, and even the utterance of the word "s—" was taboo. Sin and sex walked hand in hand. Properly understood, "conjugal relations" took place between husband and wife, primarily for procreation or in acknowledgement of a husband's baser needs. Outside of that context, it was unclean and simply not to be mentioned.

While Mary and Marjorie were taken by their parents to the Sunday Plymouth Brethren "meeting," she recalled that "we were otherwise sort of left to ourselves [religiously] . . . they didn't really push us into it." That seems not to have been the case with her older brother Bruce, who bridled within the Plymouth Brethren constraints. Evidently, his parents expected

22. Hole, *Foundations of the Faith*, 192.
23. Overy, *Twilight Years*, 154.

him, as the oldest or perhaps as a son, to fully embrace their beliefs. Unwilling to do so, a breach occurred between him and his family that was never fully repaired. His life ended tragically. In Mary's words, "I think he took life pretty hard over the question of a faith commitment . . . because he didn't come home . . . It was rather strange, and by the time that I was grown up at all, he was busy doing his war work . . . In about 1948, he and his wife were in a small plane, flying from Paris to London. It just happened to crash, and they were all killed. So I never really got to know him very well."[24]

It is easy to read between these understated lines and imagine the unspoken grief the family must have suffered over their "prodigal" son. But Mary seemed to have accepted that such adult matters were not her affair, and shows of emotion were inappropriate. Perhaps through this experience, her parents simply gave up trying to evangelize their remaining children, especially since they were daughters, and would eventually need to accept their husband's faith.

In any case, none of these were matters of serious preoccupation to young Mary; as a part of her *milieu*, they simply were taken for granted. Mostly, she was happily occupied with her studies. From an early age, Mary was an extremely apt student. After a few years in London, the family had moved to Bath, a lovely historic city in Somerset, where they occupied one of the elegant houses in the renowned Royal Crescent. There she attended school, continuing to excel in her studies. In 1933 she won acceptance to Girton in Cambridge, England's first women's college, and began her studies in classics and her athletic pursuits on the hockey team.

Murray arrived in Cambridge a year later, delighted to be away from home and more exposed to the wider world. The reader may recall that they met at a meeting of the Church Missionary Society. That was Murray's recollection; in all families, of course, there are conflicting accounts of events, reflecting different perspectives and personalities. So too it was for them, thus a second version of their meeting that probably came from Mary, rich and precise as it is in family detail, is offered as well. Ironically, according to this account, without a certain contribution from his father, Murray and Mary might not have met as they did.

For as much as Murray wanted to leave constraints of his family behind, in other ways, he continued to enjoy the advantages of his social status. His father, ever hopeful that his son would come to his senses, provided him with a membership at the exclusive Cambridge Union, renowned for its debates, illustrious speakers, and influential members, and Murray welcomed that privilege. That first year he also welcomed his older sister

---

24. Mary Rogers interview with Trapnell.

Muriel's suggestion that he meet one of her friends, who happened to be the vibrant young Mary. As the story goes, Murray's sisters Muriel and Olive both had spent holidays at a sort of "finishing school" in Italy, run by a pair of English ladies. Mary's family had sent her there as well to burnish her social graces and strengthen her social network. There Muriel and Mary had become friends. When both ended up in Cambridge, they renewed their friendship, and, predictably, Muriel introduced Mary to her younger brother Murray. So while Murray preferred to emphasize that he had met Mary at the SCM meeting and to downplay this painfully quaint version, wherever it was, Mary and Murray met through the web of connections within their upper class British families. It was, after all, a small, somewhat rarified world. They had much to share, as they came to know one another; the existence of his little sister Barbara did not come up right away.

Few details remain of their courtship, but it seems clear the two were drawn strongly to one another. One might imagine that their similar fundamentalist backgrounds and the intensity of Murray's passion to break away from that restrictive world was intriguing and even contagious to the studious Mary. Undoubtedly, Murray noticed that though Mary herself had never been to India, her family had a long history of government service there. Her father had traveled to distant shores as a missionary; to her a life abroad seemed natural. India intrigued him, and Mary did too.

As she and Murray pursued their courtship, Mary produced a distinguished Girton record. She excelled in Latin and Greek, and, despite her earlier encounter with polio, she was a tough competitor on the hockey field. "I played right inner," Mary recalled. "Now that I'm aged, I note how my feet are irregular; then it didn't bother me a bit!"[25] By 1937 when she graduated, she had become, in British academic lexicon, a "Double First," that is, with First-Class Honors in two subsequent parts of the vaunted Cambridge *Tripos* examinations. And in athletic lexicon, she was a "Hockey Blue," awarded only to those athletes competing at the highest level. She was a young woman of exceptional ability and promise.

Murray's mode of learning was very different from Mary's. Already he was dreaming of a way to serve God as a missionary, and finishing university was simply a hurdle he needed to cross. Though competent in academics, his passion was people. He learned from them; he reveled in them; he imbibed them. "I loved Cambridge, obviously, [but] in a way, I'd never been taught to think properly, from the earliest years. People, friendship, suffering . . . I wanted to belong to *people* . . . I was waking up, in those

---

25. Mary Rogers interview with author, Oxford, England, 2004.

Cambridge years . . . seeing what the British Empire was doing . . ."[26] And, it seems, to what God was doing with him. He was attracted to the God he could sense in people, to people who seemed touched by God, as he was. He was hungry for knowledge, not so much of books, but of God. The diffident little boy was finding his voice. Freed at last from his father's disapproving gaze, he could allow his passion for God and a wider view of life to be freely expressed.

As an undergraduate, Murray wasted no time in meeting the Rev. Evered Lunt, then the young chaplain of the Queens' College. To Evered he poured out his heart, sharing his conversion experience and his desire to become more deeply connected with the Anglican church. Baptism and confirmation would be the next step, and Evered, knowing of Murray's desire to become a missionary, guided him to work with the Rev. Max Warren for his formal preparation. Then the vicar of a local parish, Max Warren was soon to become the head of the Church Missionary Society (C.M.S.), to which Murray had already applied. With his faith experience affirmed by these similarly passionate men, Murray was baptized and confirmed in a church in London during his second year at Cambridge. His decision was met with warm support from his mother, but only disdain from his father.

Continuing to respond to his love of God, his newly freed passions could also lead him into deep water. Drawn to a Christian organization called CICCU, the Cambridge Inter-Collegiate Christian Union, Murray described how this could happen:

> CICCU was very fundamentalist, the low church sort of way I'd been converted, you see. So naturally, in the beginning of my first year I joined . . . because they were people who were very concerned with prayer and loving God and Jesus deeply. And I wanted that to be more true for me. And then I ran into the Student Christian Movement, the other Christian society, less evangelical—but the SCM was open to all thoughts, probably some of them quite wild, if you know what I mean. Nothing ruffled them. They felt that Christian faith was able to cope with everything, and we needed to face everything. If you had a question, you needed to ask, to try to fathom how that fitted into God's purpose and the biblical revelation. And of course, everything in me knew that I needed that, too. I wanted to be brave enough never to sort of run away into a huddle with the people who agreed with me. I wanted to be out there with all

---

26. Interview with Trapnell.

sorts of human beings. So I belonged to them, too, the SCM as well as the CICCU.[27]

Yet Murray's tolerance for the fundamentalist approach of his childhood, with its required doctrinal lists, membership limitations, and authoritarian figures was wearing thin. He continues his story:

> Now after about six weeks, the man who represented the CICCU in my college came to me, and said, "Murray, could we have a walk together?" That was a clear signal to me that there was some trouble. We went for a walk, and he said, "Is it true that you belong to the CICCU *and* to the SCM?"
>
> And I said, "Oh, yes, of course it's true, for this reason: that I want to love God as much as I think CICCU people want to love God, and the SCM people seem to be brave enough to ask all the questions. And I think it's possible for God to face all the questions. I don't want to have to hide away from [a question]; I want to think about it, and be helped to think about it."
>
> And he said, "Well, Murray, you can't. You've got to belong to one or the other."
>
> I said, "Well, sorry, but I'm not going to walk out of the CICCU. You can throw me out, if you want to. That's *your* responsibility. But *I'm* going to stay until you do so." And so, I was duly thrown out!

Though his ejection from the CICCU may have created a bit of controversy in Murray's Christian circles, he was not deterred. As he continued to be deeply involved in the SCM, he drew Mary in as well, reveling in ideas that were very new for them—ecumenism, the social gospel—perspectives considered quite left of center on the Christian spectrum. Gradually he was moving beyond the fundamentalist Anglicanism of his initial conversion.

There were more opportunities to experience the world, and Murray seized them. For two summers, he studied at the University of Madrid, finding himself on the streets the very day the Spanish Revolution began in 1936. He made new friends, drawn particularly to fellow students whose backgrounds were different from his. Atul Mukarjee, from Delhi, India, was one of those. The visits of Atul's parents gave Murray his first glimpse of a high-caste Indian woman, dressed in a sari, seated comfortably along with her husband on the floor. That image made a big impression on him. His world was quickly expanding.

Meeting the renowned C. F. Andrews also left a indelible impression. Murray's connection with him intensified his inner flame and clarified his

27. Ibid.

direction. Andrews, an Anglican priest, was taking some time away from his long career as a missionary in India to teach in England. For more than twenty years, he had worked alongside Mahatma Gandhi for Indian civil rights, both in South Africa and later in India, joining Gandhi in the effort to ban the untouchability of outcasts and for Indian independence as well. Through Gandhi, C. F. Andrews had become a deep friend to the renowned Indian poet Rabindranath Tagore. He had created dialogue exchanges between Christians and Hindus. Much beloved by the Indian people, he was given the affectionate name "Deenabandhu": Friend of the Humble. For just one year of Murray's time in Cambridge, Andrews was there, giving occasional lectures. Murray tells of listening to him, experiencing his presence: "You could just see what India had done for him, and you couldn't resist, sort of, *sharing* it. He just made me feel I *must* go to India [in a way] that linked up with old Isaiah, you see, 'Whom shall I send?'" Murray's courage continued to expand, as he took the bold step of inviting C.F. Andrews to tea in his Queens College quarters. "That was a wonderful occasion," he recalled, "just listening to him talk and asking him questions. A man who had lived so near to God, and so near to people . . . He sort of 'made my mouth water,' if you know what I mean. He gave *me* a great longing both for God and for dear people . . . He just sort of rubbed off on me . . ."[28] One wonders if Mary was there too to share that time.

Then came his third year at Queens' College. Mary's academic work continued to be outstanding, while Murray's was, one might say, passable. He and Mary were spending lots of time together, and they had gone on a brief holiday in Yorkshire, perhaps with a group from SCM. Suddenly there came devastating news. His beloved mother was dead at the age of fifty-two of cancer. Though he had known his mother was unwell, he had been shielded from the seriousness of her disease and from the immanence of her death. His memories of that time are fragmentary, mostly lost in a sea of grief. "I remember weeping my eyes out . . . I remember standing with my sister Muriel at her funeral . . ."[29] His mother had been his advocate, his refuge, his comforter, and now she was gone.

Just at that time were the crucial *tripos* honors exams, which the distraught Murray failed. An honors degree was out of the question. Fortunately, he had a close connection with his tutor who understood the circumstances. Permission was granted for him to continue on to get a more limited degree in three years. By then it was clear to Murray that he wanted to be a priest.

28. Ibid.
29. Interview with author.

Despite his father's disapproval, he would stay on in Cambridge for two more years at Westcott House, an Anglican Theological College.

Not surprisingly, the highlights of Murray's Cambridge years were connected with particular people, who not only inspired his learning, but who mentored him personally and became his heroes.

Until he met Evered Lunt (who would later become Bishop of Stepney), Murray's focus was on being a missionary, but not at all on being a priest. But as he came to know him, Evered became a living revelation, and Murray felt a call. As he later recalled, "Somehow his priesthood was something so precious, full of meaning for me, so wonderfully centered in Christ and not in himself. That probably set me off wanting to be a priest. It slowly happened."[30]

As Murray began to discern a call to the priesthood, Evered again pointed the way, this time to Westcott House, led by Evered's close friend, B. K. Cunningham.

B. K. Cunningham, the principal of Westcott House, was another mentor. Murray recalled his "tremendous sense of humor" and observed, "I find that the people who have influenced me most, or I've looked up to most, nearly always laugh a lot . . . They sort of take themselves lightly." Still a bit more evangelical than most of his fellow seminarians, Murray said B.K. would "pull his leg" for his little evangelical excesses. Then there was Charles Raven, the Regius Professor of Divinity, whom Murray recalled as "a *wonderful* man . . . a scientist, as well as a theologian. Every time [he] lectured, it was sort of on the edge of worship. At the end of a lecture, you finished up with wonder . . . . I used to go 'Wow! That's worth its weight in gold!'"[31]

Did Murray hear the news, just weeks before his ordination, that his teacher and mentor, Charlie Andrews, had died in Calcutta? Most likely he did, and surely he would have identified with an impression shared by someone present as Andrews had conducted a service just months before his death: "It was an unforgettable experience. From beginning to end one was caught up in an act of pure worship. He gave, not a sermon, but a meditation on love, and seemed to me to be the Beloved Disciple himself speaking . . . his face radiant with love and peace."[32] The determination to follow Andrews' footsteps was already firmly rooted in him, the experience of that radiant love drawing him magnet-like to India.

During these years, as he absorbed the basic teachings of the Anglican tradition, he had begun, little by little, to shed his low church ways and

30. Interview with Norma deKadt Nelson, Old Greenwich, CT, 1986.
31. Interview with Trapnell.
32. Chaturvedi and Sykes, *Charles Freer Andrews*, 316.

to embrace the possibility of confession, of simple symbolic acts of devotion, and of interpreting scripture with some sense of latitude. Indeed, the freedom and support he found at Westcott House and from Mary as well allowed his gifts to begin to emerge. Mary too had become an Anglican. In 1939 Murray finished his theological training and was ordained a deacon at Exeter Cathedral on Trinity Sunday.

Meanwhile, Mary had completed professional training at the Teacher Training College in Cambridge, followed by practice teaching Latin and Greek at a school near Cambridge. Her parents had moved from Bath to Cambridge, so she was able to live with them, while spending ever-increasing time with Murray.

With World War II underway, the sense of urgency to marry grew stronger. But as they began to envision their future together, circumstances seemed to conspire against them. One day, headed back to Cambridge in her sister's car to have lunch with Murray, Mary collided head-on with a lorry (truck). It was a bad accident; she had a broken jaw and frightening periods of amnesia. But after six weeks in the hospital, she was back in the classroom.

There were yet more hurdles. Technically it was forbidden for students in the ordination process to marry; Murray used his powers of persuasion to convince B. K. Cunningham he might be an exception to the rule. Pronouncing Mary "such a fine girl,"[33] Murray's spiritual mentor endorsed the match, making them the first ever in Anglican circles in Cambridge to receive such permission.

In 1939 the young couple became engaged, ignoring yet another potential pitfall. Still in the C.M.S. regulations (dating from 1889) was the rule proscribing marriage for a young missionary with C.M.S., at least until he had completed a few years in the field and "the spiritual and missionary qualities of the lady"[34] had been deemed acceptable. Murray was not exempt from this rule. As the time of the wedding approached, it was required by law that their banns be published and read in church for three weeks in succession, announcing their intention to marry and allowing anyone to put forth a reason why the marriage should not take place. Worshipping on one of those appointed Sundays, Mary and Murray noticed a close family member of the head of the Church Missionary Society sitting in a nearby pew. Heart-stopping moments ensued, followed by weeks of anxious uncertainty. Any objection from a C.M.S. authority could derail their plans. But nothing happened, and their plans moved ahead.

33. Interview with author.
34. Stock, *History of the Church Missionary Society*, 356.

Predictably, Murray's father continued to disapprove. In the midst of a festive engagement party, he is said to have confronted Mary's sister, warning her to keep Mary from marrying Murray, as she was *much* too good for him.[35] But in the end, Murray and Mary had their way. "I broke all the rules," Murray recalled, "and we ended up with each other. I couldn't quite get why she was doing so, but I was suitably delighted!"[36]

They were married in Cambridge, at the ancient Norman church of St. Bene't on August 3, 1940. The Rev. B. K. Cunningham of Westcott House performed the ceremony. Following a reception at the Garden House Hotel, the young deacon and his bride departed for a honeymoon in Devon.

The young bride and groom, Cambridge, 1940

35. Hancock, interview with author.
36. Interviews with author and Trapnell.

The wedding party back row left to right: Mary's elder brother Bruce, Murray's father Edgar, Mary's sister Marjorie, Murray, an unknown clergy friend, Murray's sister Muriel, Mary's father Frank Binford Hole. Front row: Bruce's wife, Murray's sister Olive, Mary, Mary's mother Aileen Mary Seton Hole.

2

Fledgling Marriage and Ministry
1940–1945

> Rise up, O men of God!
> Have done with lesser things!
> Give heart and soul and mind and strength
> To serve the King of kings.
>
> —William Pierson Merrill
>
> 1867 *Student Christian
> Movement Hymnbook*

As the war intensified, it might have been understandable if Mary and Murray, safe in Cambridge, were preoccupied with ordination and wedding concerns. Yet it could not have been possible to ignore the air raids, reports of battles, and endless lists of casualties. Even before Murray's ordination in Exeter Cathedral, special treasures there, such as the Great East Window and the Bishop's throne, had been removed and sent to the safety of cellars in Cornwall and Devon. On May 19, 1940, the very day he was ordained in that great sacred space, Winston Churchill made his first radio address as Prime Minister. His words included the following:

> Today is Trinity Sunday. Centuries ago words were written to be a call and a spur to the faithful servants of Truth and Justice: Arm yourselves, and be ye men of valor, and be in readiness for the conflict; for it is better for us to perish in battle than to look upon the outrage of our nation and our altar. As the Will of God is in Heaven, even so let it be.[1]

---

1. Churchill, *Winston S. Churchill: His Complete Speeches*, 6:223.

Within the city of Plymouth, located on the south coast of England, is Devonport, home to the royal dockyards and at the time one of the most important naval ports in Europe. St. Andrew's Parish Church is located nearby, in the heart of Plymouth; it was to St. Andrew's that Murray was called to minister. Shortly before Mary and he arrived, the city had been targeted with its first Luftwaffe bombs. Though most of the wartime targets of the German Luftwaffe were large, industrial cities, the strategic importance of the British navy meant that Plymouth was to be relentlessly bombed. By the end of the war, the Plymouth Blitz had reduced the city's population of 220,000 by nearly half. With nearly 1200 civilians killed and thousands more dispersed to the countryside, much of the city was left in rubble.

Mary and Murray moved into their quarters in an architecturally lovely Georgian crescent, similar in design to the elegant building where Mary's family had lived in Bath. But there were few similarities in lifestyle. The flat was comfortable but small, located in the heart of Plymouth, close to the church. Murray's salary as curate was less than Mary had earned as a beginning teacher. "We had a rule," Murray recalled, "that our main course for dinner could cost no more than 6p. Mary bought lots of fish heads, and we made do."[2] Perhaps it seemed their newly frugal life was only a wartime exigency, but this early test of the young bride's adaptability was a harbinger of what was to come.

Even then, Murray's father remained disapproving. Murray recollected a visit to the newly-married couple in Plymouth: "He came down, but he made it very clear that I'd been entirely irresponsible, marrying Mary ... before I had *much* more money. He was probably right, but by that time I said to myself, 'Well, Father, it just doesn't matter to me what you think. I mean, how can it? I can run my life, I'm grown up now, I'm twenty-three, twenty-four. I've talked to other people who advised me.' So I said to him, 'I hope—I believe I haven't been irresponsible, and I think God will look after us.'"[3]

The Rev. Clifford Martin was Murray's vicar and mentor at St. Andrew's. He was a strong, steady presence in perilous times, and Murray quickly became devoted to him. In the midst of preaching his first sermon, the sound of bombs erupted close by. Murray hesitated, frozen in place. "Keep going, Murray, keep going!" urged the vicar. And so he did. From then on, "there was no fluff in my sermons, when it was possible we'd be

---

2. Interview with author.
3. Interview with Trapnell.

blown up before the end!"⁴ Musing on those days, Murray said, "With a marvelous vicar, it was a wonderful time."⁵

With death all around, life must have felt very intense; day after day, the young curate found himself assisting in mass burials. In pauses between the bombings, his work was to tend to the living. He particularly remembered a woman who had lost her husband and two children and was crippled herself. "She helped me more than I helped her," he said. "She had great faith."⁶

Visits with sailors at a nearby club left an indelible mark on him. One day, chatting with men who were there for a respite, he recalled seeing a sailor, sitting alone, weeping, head in hands. Murray told the story:

> "What's the matter?" I asked him.
>
> "I can't go back, I can't do it again," the sailor replied.
>
> The man told of being in battle; the British Navy had sunk a German U-boat, leaving many German sailors in the sea, swimming in an oil slick. They were ordered by their captain to fire on them, like fish in a barrel, until all were dead.
>
> "Why couldn't we pick them up?" the sailor sobbed.⁷

As the Blitz continued throughout the winter, Mary and Murray coped with life in the midst of war. Soon familiar with the sound of bombs, they learned that if they heard a whistle sound, they were probably safe. They bonded with neighbors and, when the sirens went off, huddled together in shelters. When their building sustained a direct hit and caught fire, they grabbed a few belongings and ran for their lives. But the fire was contained, and life went on. "Mary was much better with the bombings than I was," Murray said.⁸

Mary's recollection confirms Murray's impression. Recalling the bombs sixty years later, she said, "I can feel it now, but really, it sort of did us good . . . The Spirit of people—it's rather strange how [with so much] anxiety, I got to know those neighbors so much better because they were more cooperating with each other."⁹ Under such extreme duress, they had their first experience of real community solidarity.

---

4. Interview with author.
5. Interview with Trapnell.
6. Interview with author.
7. Ibid.
8. Ibid.
9. Interview with Trapnell.

On the night of March 21–22, 1941, in some of the heaviest bombings of the Plymouth Blitz, St. Andrew's Church, where Murray served, was bombed and severely damaged. The entire roof was destroyed. The next day, someone attached a wooden sign to the door that read "*Resurgam*: I shall rise again." This bold affirmation soon became a symbol of wartime spirit, repeated across Europe at other devastated churches. For another month the bombings, the destruction, and the carnage continued.

At the end of that long, bleak winter in Plymouth, Murray was ordained a priest in Exeter Cathedral, again on Trinity Sunday. Then he and Mary returned to the wreckage of Plymouth, where they spent another year at St. Andrew's. The worst of the Blitz was over. In early summer 1942, they returned to Cambridge to take the next step on their journey and to await the birth of their first child.

Though Murray felt compelled to go to India, the war made it impossible to travel by sea. While he and Mary waited, it was suggested by C.M.S. that he be trained as a teacher to prepare to be the principal of a teacher training school in North India. Thus he enrolled in the London University Institute of Education, and he and Mary were given living space on the top floor of her family's spacious Cambridge house.

Designed for those going abroad, the course was satisfying. "It was a jolly good course, about social anthropology . . . about educational systems . . . the differences between the French colonies, the British ones, the Belgian ones."[10] When possible, Murray would join Mary in Cambridge.

Back in a fundamentalist household, he took considerable pleasure in tweaking his starchy mother-in-law. Sixty years later, Murray's version of an encounter with her still evoked chortles of delight in him:

> Mrs. Hole came home and said, "Murray, I can't tell you what I saw today!"
>
> And I said, "What's the matter, Mrs. Hole, what was it? What's so awful? Come on, Mrs. Hole, tell me what it was."
>
> So of course I thought it was somebody posing without any clothes or something like that . . . (laughs)
>
> She told me it was something being advertised in Heffer's Bookstore: the author was a respected Methodist minister who'd written a book about sex.
>
> So I said, "Well, he's a Christian, a good man."

---

10. Interview with Trapnell.

"Dreadful, *dreadful!*" she said. Eventually she told me the title; it was *The Mastery of Sex*. Poor soul, she was shivering all down her spine.

So I said, "Isn't it a good idea, Mrs. Hole, to master it? We've all got it, so we'd better master it!" And I added, because I'd read it, "It's a jolly good book!"

"Murray, don't mention it! Don't mention it!!" she said.[11]

Movies were verboten for Plymouth Brethren. Even the Anglican Church agreed that their effects were deleterious for young minds. Earlier in the 1920s, the Bishop of Birmingham, in his role as president of the National Council of Public Morals, had initiated an inquiry into the effects of cinema on schoolchildren. According to the resulting report, ". . . adult life was displayed as an endless round of 'flirtation, jealousy, robbery, unscrupulous intrigue and reckless assault, incessant excitement and wild emotionalism.' . . .The presentation of relations between the sexes . . . stimulated 'the sexual instincts and interest . . . prematurely and precociously.'"[12] Murray recalled that though no longer schoolchildren, "We weren't supposed to go to the cinema; we'd tell her we were going, and she didn't know what to do." Still, he continued, she was "marvelously kind. Very strict, yet very loving and very kind." He sensed that she would have liked to escape the strictures of her faith, yet as the wife of Frank Hole, it was out of the question. "We lent her a novel," Murray said, "some famous novel from the 1930s—a very good novel. She read it and loved the story. Then she mentioned it at the table. Poor Mr. Hole didn't know what to do. 'Dear Mother doesn't realize that it's a mere story,' he said. 'That it isn't true.'"[13]

Mary and Murray's first child, a daughter named Cheryl, was born in November 1942 in the Hole household. Mary was supported in childbirth and breastfeeding by a family retainer known as Nurse Rouse. Other servants stood by to care for the four-generation household. "Old Granny," Frank Hole's extremely elderly mother, who lived with the family as well, was tended like another child by Miss Sharp (aka "Old Snore"). According to Cheryl, "Old Granny" was the quintessential Victorian lady, who passed her elder days tatting intricate lace for the bathroom towels. In those waning days of her long life (she died at 105) she was remembered for her frequent complaint, "I'm sick of Mollie's baby!"[14]

11. Ibid.
12. Overy, *Twilight Years*, 152.
13. Interview with Trapnell.
14. Telephone interview with Cheryl Poutier from Elancourt, France, by author,

By the time Mary gave birth to their second daughter Linda in 1944, Murray had completed his course and practice teaching. Still biding his time, he was invited to join the staff of C.M.S. in London. Max Warren, who had prepared Murray for confirmation, then headed the organization. During that interlude, Murray absorbed his ideals and missionary thinking even more deeply. Though written nearly twenty years later, the following citation from Max Warren imparts a sense of the man:

> Our first task in approaching another people, another culture, is to take off our shoes, for the place we are approaching is holy. Else we may find ourselves treading on men's dreams. More serious still, we may forget that God was here before our arrival. We have, then, to ask what is the authentic religious content in the experience of the Muslim, the Hindu, the Buddhist, or whoever he may be. We may, if we have asked humbly and respectfully, still reach the conclusion that our brothers have started from a false premise and reached a faulty conclusion. But we must not arrive at our judgment from outside their religious situation. We have to try to sit where they sit, to enter sympathetically into the pains and griefs and joys of their history, and see how those pains and griefs and joys have determined the premises of their arguments. We have, in a word, to be 'present' with them.[15]

Still in 1945, there were no civilian ships to India. As they continued to wait, another opportunity arose. Because the education of rural blacks in the United States was often seen as a model for American missionaries in India, Murray was invited by the Agricultural Missions Incorporated in New York to spend a few months in the U.S. There, Murray could also generate support for his Miss-A-Meal program. Initiated during his time in London, the program encouraged participants to agree to forego one meal a week, donating the money saved to missionary work. His first stop was White Plains, New York, where he was a guest of Dr. John Reisner, head of Agricultural Missions, a stay most remembered by Murray for their attendance at an American football game. Then on he went to Tuskegee Institute in Alabama, where he spent a number of weeks and was influenced by some of the giants of Black culture of the day. Although George Washington Carver had just died, to Murray "he was more than alive in his spirit."[16] Carver, whose mission it was to "improve the lot of 'the man farthest down,'" the poor,

---

2007.

15. Warren, *Primal Vision*, 10–11.
16. Interview with Trapnell.

one-horse farmer,"[17] had, in the late 20s, inspired C. F. Andrews as well, when he had come to Tuskegee to write his book on Gandhi. Under the wing of a Black Tuskegee professor, Murray said he discovered firsthand what the "colorbar" meant. He also remembered being called "Dr. Rogers," which, as yet another manifestation of racial assumptions, he found awkward and embarrassing. It was Murray's introduction to the subtle and not-so subtle implications of racism, to its distorted assumptions and its crushing power.

At the end of 1945 the war ended, and as Murray returned to England, word came at last that he and Mary, Cheryl, and Linda, aged three and one, could sail on the very first ship taking women and children from England to India. As Murray's wife, Mary was also considered a part of C.M.S.— a missionary in her own right. She was ready to go. In her self-effacing, understated way, she recalled, "I was quite willing . . . My mother and her family had done quite a lot of work abroad, and it didn't surprise them at all. They didn't object . . ."[18] On January 12, 1946, the family began their three-week voyage from England to India. Though it happened to be the birthday of Murray's father, neither of them gave that event a second thought.

17. Tuskegee University, "Legacy of Dr. George Washington Carver."
18. Interview with Trapnell.

3

Seeds of Transformation
1946–1951

> Lust of possession worketh desolations;
> There is no meekness in the sons of earth;
> Led by no star, the rulers of the nations
> Still fail to bring us to the blissful birth:
> Thy kingdom come, O Lord thy will be done.
>
> —Laurence Housman, 1919;
> Hymnal 1940

Upon arriving in Khatauli in northern India, it did not take long for questions to arise concerning C.M.S.'s plan for an Anglican school. Finding the proposed site, Murray noticed there was a Methodist school nine miles down the road, and yet another missionary school not far in the opposite direction. "I wrote and said to the friends [at C.M.S.] in London, 'Well, isn't this crazy? Do we really need to have a separate Anglican teacher training college?' Mercifully, it was never born."[1] Young and inexperienced as he was, he already had an instinctual disdain for denominational divisions.

So instead he accepted an appointment from C.M.S. as chaplain to the Agricultural Institute of Allahabad University. As the only Christian Agricultural College in south Asia, the Institute drew students from Burma, Thailand, and Ceylon, as well as from India. Founded by Sam Higginbottom, a British-born American, it was viewed as an American college and was highly regarded.

---

1. Interview with Trapnell.

Murray, Mary, and the children moved into a so-called 'bungalow' on the banks of the Jumna River. Located close to its convergence with the Ganga, considered a very holy site for Hindus, it was, according to Murray, "lovely." He added, "Coming from rationing in England, it was living on the fat of the land. We hadn't had that at all, ever since we were married. That . . . was a bit of a surprise, because we were to come as missionaries—they even use the phrase in the literature sometimes—'sacrificing their all.' And we were sacrificing precisely nothing . . ." Their living quarters had been made ready by a senior missionary, and servants had been employed. He continues:

> Six servants, and we were told that we needed three more! Our sitting room was so big, I laughed with Mary, because we had the two girls and they had to call out to see whether we were in the room. I mean, a vast place. And all these servants to do different jobs. A bearer, another to do the washing, because the cook could *never* do the washing up! And then the person who sweeps the ground and looks after the toilets, the gardener, the night watchman, and the *ayah*, to look after the children . . . We were not supposed to do anything. I mean, when I went out to the garden in shorts, ready to do some gardening, people would rush up to me, saying, "Sir, don't! Sir, don't! We'll do it!"

Murray describes an aspect of his job: "There in the extension department, once or twice a week, we would get into a jeep—an agricultural animal person would be there, coming from our staff. Somebody else would be coming about plants, vegetables. We'd all get a little team of people, and we'd go out [to the villages], and we'd each try to add our bit of technical information to the whole."

His role was to serve as chaplain to the students and to bring the Christian Gospel to the people in the villages. "I was there," as he said, "to give; I was there to educate. I was there to be a priest . . . to help . . . I dressed like an Anglican priest, with dog collar and everything. I mean, that was me! And of course, as chaplain . . . I wanted them to know that God loved them."[2]

Their family was growing as well. In June 1947, in the cool of the hills above Dehra Dun, Mary gave birth to Richard, their third child. Faithful in her work as a traditional missionary wife, "framing and fashioning" a Christian family "according to the Doctrine of Christ," as Murray's priestly vows required,[3] she—and they—continued to live in the style traditional to British families in the Indian Empire, with many, if not all, the comforts of

---

2. Ibid.
3. *Book of Common Prayer 1928*, 687.

Cambridge. Though the heat in Allahabad could be unbearable, the family could retreat to cooler climes in the hill country for extended holidays. Mary loved being a mother, and their decision to send Cheryl, then about six, to Woodstock, an American boarding school, undoubtedly was difficult. Back in London, word reached C.M.S. of an exceptionally gifted young missionary couple, who could be expected to rise in its ranks.

But Murray was beginning to question the effectiveness of his work within the missionary structure. Not only had British class structures been exported to India, but the caste system, in place long before Britain arrived, reinforced a wall of separation between them and the people he and Mary had come to serve: "These were the poorest people in the world, pretty well. Poorest I've certainly met, anywhere. And you can't, when you're well-fed, living in an air-conditioned house with refrigerators, washing machines, plenty to eat—how can you go out to this village and to that village, and say to them, 'Dear people, God loves you. I just want you to know God loves you'? And they probably hadn't had any food for twenty-four hours. The words stick in your throat! It's an insult . . . And that's what I was supposed to be up to!"

He was disturbed as well by the political jockeying amongst the staff: "The spiritual condition of our college was an agony. I mean, everything was around money, and catching up, and doing better than the other person . . . All the staff members were trying to get scholarships to go to America, and they all wanted double increments, and if they got more degrees then they'd get more money, so there was much fighting . . ." Murray continues:

> There was a prayer meeting for the staff members every week; some of them, especially the ones I felt were the best human beings, never came near it. So as Chaplain I wondered: why was this considered a thing that you didn't touch with a barge pole? And I discovered that if you wanted to get a scholarship to America or somewhere abroad, you always had to show up at the prayer meeting. If you didn't, there wasn't a chance of your getting either a scholarship or a double increment. Obviously the powers that be were favoring the people becoming more and more Christianized, and more and more westernized with a bigger salary. Nearly everybody was aiming to be like the people who lived in the big bungalows.[4]

The prayer meeting, it seemed, was a sham, seen primarily as a tool for getting ahead. Learning that the charade of religiosity was so pervasive was deeply disillusioning to Murray.

4. Interview with Trapnell.

Yet what he was noticing was understandable in the context of British-Indian history. Although, in 1946, India was on the cusp of freedom, its people had lived under foreign domination for centuries. In the past hundred or so years it had been dominated not by an ordinary conqueror, but by a commercial trading company, the British East India Company. As Eknath Easwaran, a writer and teacher Murray would come to value deeply, notes:

> Sometimes in visible authority, often content to rule behind puppet regimes, [the Company] set about systematically draining the wealth of India into private hands. The fortunes made were staggering even to contemporary eyes; historians have observed that Great Britain's place in the Industrial Revolution was essentially financed by the loot of India.
>
> The economic burden of this on Indians was equally staggering . . . Within a generation, cities became nightmarish extremes of wealth and poverty . . . But most Indians lived in villages and there, consequences were worse. Forced to grow crops for export instead of local use and then taxed heavily for the privilege of doing so, hundreds of thousands of villages under Company control lost all capacity to sustain themselves . . . [5]

In 1857, a mutiny had occurred in the very area of North India where Murray and Mary later settled, convincing the British they must teach the Indians a lesson. The insurrection was ruthlessly put down,[6] and India was made an imperial colony: "the jewel in the Crown." As Easwaran says, "the British government stepped in to 'do things right.'" Little wonder that after nearly another hundred years of British rule, most Indians had lost all self-confidence and bought into the belief that they were inferior: "not fit to be masters in their own homes." Survival meant "aping the Englishman;" the "road to success . . . had to be by imitation of western ways."[7]

But to Murray, western ways were not the answer. Since Cambridge he had aspired to follow the path of C.F. Andrews. Perhaps in his teaching Andrews had woven ideas from a book he had written earlier in the century, part of a series entitled *Handbooks of English Church Expansion*. In it he had warned aspiring missionaries of attitudes that permeated the sensibilities of both English and Indians:

---

5. Preface to *Essential Gandhi*, xi.

6. With reports in the British press of atrocities against Europeans that outraged the public, the British army was deemed justified in adopting a policy to take no prisoners. Instead, captured flighters were lined up and shot. By many accounts, more than 100,000 Indians were killed in the uprising and its aftermath.

7. Preface to *Essential Gandhi*, vi-vii.

... A very definite theory is held as to what is expected of every Englishman in India, and in what manner English prestige and position are to be maintained .... [These ideas] run somewhat as follows:—"Never, under any circumstances, give way to a 'native,' or let him regard himself as your superior. We only rule India in one way—by upholding our position. Though you are a missionary, you must be an Englishman first, and never forget you are a Sahib.[8] You may do incalculable mischief if you lower the dignity of an Englishman, by allowing 'natives' to treat you familiarly or take liberties with you: they are the inferior race, and we hold India by the sword. Be kindly, by all means, but always be on your guard, and do not give away English prestige.[9]

In ways radical for his time, Andrews challenged these prevailing assumptions:

We must as missionaries, reverse the whole position and counteract the false impression of Christianity given. We must continually "give way to the native" if we are to show any humility worthy of the Name of Christ; we must try and lose our "superiority," and become servants of all, if we are to follow Christ; we must come to India with the one wish in our hearts, to break down all barriers of race, not to build them up. It may be realized, therefore, how very difficult the military atmosphere is for a missionary to breathe. For the missionary is very human, with warm English blood tingling in his veins; and the martial, conqueror's spirit, the pride of blood and race, the clannish feeling, are very hard to keep under due control, even when he comes out as a minister of peace and good will . . . [10]

Gradually, Murray became more and more uncomfortable with the behaviors he observed in the Institute, despite its good work in agricultural education. Even more troubling was the growing realization that he and Mary were complicit with the colonial attitudes decried by Andrews as they enjoyed their comfortable bungalow, with its mimicry of western lifestyle.

The ongoing political battle reverberated within Murray and Mary's experience as well. Gandhi's long non-violent struggle against British rule in India was reaching its climax. As early as 1909 Gandhi had declared: "I believe repression will be unavailing . . . The British people appear to be obsessed by the demon of commercial selfishness. The fault is not of men, but

---

8. *Sahib*: a term of respect given to a man of superior standing.
9. Andrews, *North India: Handbooks of English Church Expansion*, 166.
10. Ibid.

of the system . . . The true remedy lies, in my humble opinion, in England's discarding modern civilization, which is ensouled by this spirit of selfishness and materialism, which is purposeless, vain, and . . . a negation of the spirit of Christianity . . ."[11]

Needless to say, England did not discard modern civilization, and by 1942 Gandhi, still maintaining his friendship with the British even as he protested their policies, declared, "Whether Britain wins or loses, imperialism has to die. It is certainly of no use now to the British people, whatever it may have been in the past . . ."[12]

When freedom for India finally arrived in August 1947, Jawaharlal Nehru spoke from the newly formed Constituent Assembly in New Delhi. His speech included these words: "Long years ago we made a tryst with destiny, and now the time comes when we shall redeem our pledge, not wholly or in full measure, but very substantially. At the stroke of the midnight hour, when the world sleeps, India will awake to life and freedom. A moment comes, which comes but rarely in history, when we step out from the old to the new, when an age ends, and when the soul of a nation, long suppressed, finds utterance."[13]

Despite the rejoicing, for Gandhi the event was mixed with sorrow for the ongoing religious strife and the pain of dividing the nation between Muslims and Hindus, between Pakistan and India. He implored the nation to stop the ongoing violence. "Each of us should turn the searchlight inward and purify his or her heart as much as possible . . . You should think how best to improve yourselves and work for the good of the country . . . No one can escape death. Then why be afraid of it?"[14]

Gandhi's work continued. On January 25, 1948, at a prayer meeting, he was gratified by the news that in Delhi, there had been "a reunion of hearts"[15] between Muslims and Hindus. He greeted and bowed in reverence to those gathered, including a man sitting in the front row. Suddenly, without warning, the man retrieved a small pistol from his pocket and pulled the trigger. Gandhi was dead.

On receiving the news, Prime Minister Nehru's words again moved the young nation:

> The light has gone out of our lives and there is darkness everywhere and I do not quite know what to tell you and how to say

---

11. Gandhi, *Essential Gandhi*, 103.
12. Ibid., 303.
13. Nehru, "Tryst with Destiny."
14. Ibid., 318.
15. Ibid., 323.

it. Our beloved leader, Bapu as we call him, the father of our nation, is no more... We will not run to him for advice and seek solace from him, and that is a terrible blow not to me only but to millions and millions in this country...

The light has gone out, I said, and yet I was wrong. For the light that shone in this country was no ordinary light. The light that has illumined this country for these many years will illumine this country for many more years, and a thousand years later that light will still be seen in this country, and the world will see it and it will give solace to innumerable hearts....[16]

Though Mary and Murray would continue their work in Allahabad another three years, that light from Gandhi, already aglow in their hearts, grew brighter. They had never met him in person, yet through their connection with C.F. Andrews, their minds had been opened to Gandhi's work and thought.

Towards the end of their India assignment, as they anticipated their return to England, Murray received an invitation—"a wonderful bit of synchronicity—"[17] to meet a member of the Gandhian movement and a close friend of Gandhi. A.V. Thakkar Bapa, was an Indian social worker, who had dedicated his life to working with the aboriginal people and *harijans*[18] of Gujarat, a state in the northwest of India, where Gandhi himself was born. Hearing of Murray's discomfort with the lifestyle at the university, he invited him to spend a weekend in his little ashram in the slums of Old Delhi. A friendship developed and more weekend visits followed. He was, Murray recalled, "a magnificent character, frightfully well educated, lovely to meet."[19] Eventually there came a dialogue between the young Christian priest and the elderly Hindu man that had a profound impact on Mary and Murray's lives. "He was on to me," Murray said. "Very gentle, but absolutely devastating in his questions":

"Murray," he said, "you've probably had the chance to learn about Hinduism." I said I had, in Cambridge.
And he said, "Have you any idea why I love being a Hindu?"
I said, "No, I haven't really. I would love to know from you."
And he said, "You see, you come, and you think it's God's will for you to attack our religion. I know most of you do it very

---

16. Nehru, "We must hold together."
17. Interview with Trapnell.
18. *Harijans* were also known as "untouchables." They were considered outside the Hindu caste system, thus dubbed "outcasts." Today they refer to themselves as *"Dalits,"* meaning "broken" or "crushed."
19. Interview with Nelson.

politely, but that's what you're really out for, to make us into one of you Christians. And you simply don't understand."

Of course, I recognized it was the truth.

And he said, "You come here, you pretend you care about the poor, but you are living as rich people. Do you really think poor people can accept the advice of rich people? They never will." He continued, "For us Indians, if we want to have a major operation, of course we'll look for a Christian hospital, or good education, or for a good degree in agriculture, we'll come to the place you're working [the Agricultural College]. But if we want to know anything spiritual, ah, we won't go near you, because you really don't do this. We don't see those things as spiritual at all. It's just scientific and technical. You're jolly good at it!"

He was devastating, and I knew perfectly well I agreed with him.[20]

For Murray, this friendship and painful encounter was "a *huge* gift of God," and it led to another invitation—to visit Sevagram, Gandhi's ashram, for a full week. Although Gandhi was dead, his work was continuing, carried on by his followers. Leaving Mary and the children in their big bungalow at the Institute and going directly to Sevagram, Murray found himself in a community of about three hundred people, then headed by E.W. Aryanayakam. He was astounded with the contrast between Sevagram and the Agricultural College: "I find no servants, find everybody on the staff having the same amount of money, whether they've been there a year or seventeen years . . . They all share in all the work, from the kitchen, the cleaning out-of-doors, the agriculture, cleaning the loos, everything! All shared.

"That's where I began to think—now this is very peculiar. We in our Christian college seem incapable to inspire anybody to be even mildly Christian. And you have these Gandhians who evidently *enjoy* living that sort of community life."

His visit coming to a close, Murray recalled his departure: "Following my mother's noble advice, I went to see Sri Aryanayakam in his office to say thank you very much for having me . . . a very interesting week indeed! And he said, 'Good-bye, Murray-bhai.[21] We'll probably never see you again. You'll go back to your lovely little mission compounds, where you have all the money and all the power and the authority. We won't see you.' I didn't know what to say, I was so embarrassed.

---

20. Interview with Trapnell.
21. Murray-bhai means brother Murray.

"I stumbled out, 'Well, Sri Aryanyakam, you say you won't see me again. But I haven't been *asked* yet.' I just didn't know what to say, and then went off."[22]

Back at the Institute, as they were preparing for their return to England, an astounding letter arrived. It was an invitation to Murray to join the staff of the educational arm of Sevagram. After consulting with his Bishop, the Bishop of Lucknow and receiving his endorsement, the family returned to England, hoping and praying the Missionary Society (C.M.S.) would also allow them to accept the invitation.

Most of its members in London were against it, fearing, it seemed, that one of their missionaries might become a Hindu. Interviewed by the committee, Murray was warned of the dangers. His reply, he said, was something like this (though undoubtedly more diplomatic!): "Look, friends, we say that Jesus Christ is able to look after us. If he can't look after Christians living in a minority position with Hindus, I think he's not worth his salt! Of course I can see the danger, but I find it very appealing." Fortunately, he had the support of Max Warren, the head of C.M.S., who had prepared Murray for confirmation at Cambridge, and who asserted unequivocally that "this was the most wonderful opening that had ever been given to a C.M.S. missionary. He wanted me to say yes!"[23] Eventually the others were swayed, and with their reluctant blessing, plans were made for the family to return to India to establish a new home for at least one year in the Hindustani Talimi Sangh[24] at Sevagram.

---

22. Interview with Trapnell.

23. Ibid.

24. *Hindustani Talimi Sangh* literally translated: Center for New Education of Northeast India.

4

Christians Among Hindus: Encounters with Difference 1951–1953

> Christian missionary to Gandhi:
> "How are we to help outcasts?"
>
> Gandhi: "We must step down from our pedestals and live with them, not as outsiders, but as one of them in every way, sharing their burdens and sorrows."
>
> —WITHOUT CITATION

IN SEPTEMBER, 1951 MURRAY and Mary began an epistolary work of ministry to their friends. A Letter, the first in a series, was sent from Surrey, England, where they were staying with family on home leave. In the very first paragraph, they state an intention: "to steer a middle course between being too impersonal (which loses the spice of interest) or too personal thus becoming merely boring . . ."[1] Though the Letter's voice is plural, it seems to have been penned primarily by Murray, speaking for them both. Its focus is on his missionary work. Sidestepping the personal, it does not mention Mary by name. Nor does it mention the expectation that Mary was holding in her heart of a traditional English Christmas with her entire family. In the five years since their departure, Aileen Hole's health had failed, but within weeks, Mary anticipated, there would be a happy reunion with her beloved mother, and she would introduce her and her father to their three-year-old grandson Richard. It was when they were at sea, headed back to England, that

---

1. Letter #1. These circular letters will be cited throughout the text with the number assigned.

Mary received the crushing news that there would be no Christmas reunion. Her mother was dead. Mary's heart-broken weeping remains seared in the memory of the then six-year-old Linda. One can only imagine Mary's experience, returning to a very different household in Cambridge, her mother gone, the ever-faithful family retainer Miss Sharp dead as well, their funerals over, and Mary's father, Frank Hole alone. The sacrificial quality of the life she had chosen with Murray was clear. But their Letter carries no acknowledgment of those happenings or of Mary's grief. Might those "personal" details have been "boring"? Irrelevant? Or simply inappropriate to share in those times, in that place?

The Letter was a succinct and somewhat formal report of their five years in India, with reflections on what they had gleaned so far, and news of their anticipated life at Sevagram. Murray highlighted two ideas impelling their decision to leave the Agricultural Institute: first, the idea that Christian faith could help solve the problems of India; second, the need for Christian missionaries to "live within the situation rather than as spectators of the game." With the energy of an idealistic thirty-four year old, he envisioned bringing "a living, personal faith by whose dynamic *alone*, India will be enabled to solve the problem of freedom and order which besets the life of the country at present."

He described as well the "strands of concern" that guided their decision to join the ashram Gandhi left behind at his death: "Hunger and poverty and social injustice are the stuff of life, and the church cannot stand outside the situation any more than did that firebrand, the prophet Amos . . . In an Asia of growing nationalism . . . it is essential that the church shall not only have Indian leadership, but that its structure and institutional life should be such as can be borne by Indian resources of personnel and money. The great dependence on western money and leadership is a most serious handicap to the work and witness of the church; western standards of pay, status, [and] preferment are by no means necessarily Christian . . ."

Regarding Sevagram's approach, he wrote that he would work in Gandhi's so-called "new education": '*nai talim*', with the goal of local self-sufficiency at its core. It would be "centred around spinning and weaving and agriculture," said Murray, "but chiefly to be thought of as the culture which comes from living in community." He closed the Letter with an affirmation of his Christian faith, earnest enough to warm the hearts of his C.M.S. supervisors: "Our only reason for believing that [our work] can make any difference to the vast problems of India and of the church there is our conviction that history, Asian as much as European history, is in God's hands and that His love shown forth in Jesus Christ our Lord will be answered by the love and worship of people of every land including those of our adopted home, India. Asking for the prayers of friends, he signed the Letter with formality: "Yours sincerely, Murray Rogers."

This would be the first of forty-two Letters over nearly fifty years, tracing Mary and Murray's life together and their spiritual evolution. Though writing in the first person plural, ("As you can imagine, it will be an entirely new experience for my wife and me . . ."), Mary's voice is submerged in his. Only later do we learn that the letter-writing process was a collaborative one, with her poetic gifts lending clarity and sometimes even lyricism to the expression of his ideas. That his ideas were also hers—or so it seemed—went without saying.

Yet their roles continued to be different, very much in the manner of the times. Maintaining relationships in England and as much consistency in the girls' education as possible, Mary planned to stay in England with the children until they finished their term of school at St. Michael's School, in the neighboring village of Limpsfield, where they had been enrolled for their time away from India. Even for a temporary visit in England, "we *had* to go to school!" Cheryl recalled. They would sail to India some four months hence, when the school term and Christmas holidays were ended. This was just the first of many Christmases the family would be apart. At the end of the journey, Cheryl and Linda would return, of course, to St. Hilda's in the hills of South India.

Murray, meanwhile, would embark on an ambitious overland journey from London to Sevagram, via train to Baghdad, then by bus across Iran, Afghanistan, and Pakistan, and finally back to Allahabad and their new home. His purpose, he said, was "to do some study of the agrarian situation and of the church's work in relation to it in a number of countries . . . learning from men of many nationalities. I feel extremely fortunate to have such an experience ahead of me."[2] And what an adventure it would be for this curious and gregarious young priest.

Their second Letter, written from Sevagram three months after their separate arrivals, includes impressions from Murray's travel. Lessons in hospitality throughout the journey are taken to heart—from the "delightful Serb, a functionary of a communist state," who served him his first meal on the Simplon-Orient Express, to an Iranian Customs Officer who took him home for lunch. "The various lubricants to conversation and friendship in different countries deserve a letter to themselves!" he exclaims. "It was brandy in Jugoslavia, a spoonful of jam and a glass of water in Greece, and green tea in Afghanistan." He tells of traveling in Afghanistan with the Russian Mail, seated on a Dunlop rubber cushion brought from Cambridge

2. Letter #1.

"which came near to saving my life as we bumped for two days on the road between Herat and Kandahar." Summing up those experiences of human connection, he writes, "In a world where international communication consists so often in mutual recrimination across the ether, I found those human kindnesses, so often quite unnecessary, vastly encouraging."

But he was disturbed as well: "The sheer insecurity of life of millions of people—that's what struck me most all along the way." The plight of refugees in this post-war era—Greeks expelled from Turkey, Turks expelled from Bulgaria, Jews fleeing Baghdad, Palestinians displaced to camps in Jordan—left him shaken. Testifying to his visits to small Christian outposts along the way, Murray expresses measured but heartfelt hope, in the language of a true missionary evangelist: "For a Christian such a journey was extremely encouraging and almost as depressing; encouraging to discover so many people and pieces of work, generally small as regards size but not significance, where I saw the church really at grips with the world and using the Lord's weapons . . . Members of the Orthodox Church in Jugoslavia, [who] know the almost intolerable tension and the great invigoration of struggling to be loyal to Christ in a communist country . . . A little group of women [in a refugee camp in Amman, Jordan] bringing personal Christian service to bear on overwhelming misery . . . In Iran, at one of the centres of Moslem pilgrimage when [in a service of Baptism] two young men took the plunge after years of preparation and fearless witnessing . . ."

And in a comment that now seems prescient, he offers his view of Afghanistan: "The land of the Hindu Kush still seems remote . . . one of the very few remaining medieval states, but if history is anything to go by, what happens there between the Oxus and Indus Rivers will make a crucial difference to all of us in southern Asia, and if it does not sound conceited, that means you in Europe also."

There indeed is Murray's voice, polite, but outspoken—willing to challenge, hoping others will listen. Yet already it is a bit less formal, less authoritative, softer.

Then Mary's voice chimes in, describing their new home and adding her own details of domesticity:

> Our family is a small part of a community about 300 strong; we hope, as the days go by, to take a full part in the various work-teams and activities and so to become more fully members of it . . . For a foreigner coming to live here, the keynote of the life is self-support. The days start early, by 5 a.m. By that time you can hear the tinkling of the cowbells, one or two ox carts rumbling by and the sounds of the boys getting up in the hostel over the way. By 6 a.m. we have had our Bible reading and prayer. I have

fetched a little milk and am getting Richard's breakfast ready and Murray is off to prayers and breakfast in the Hall. Many people seem to acquire the art of sweeping by lamp-light—I find that none too easy but it's light by 6 and after that the daily household chores can be done.[3]

Having just spent five years tending her children in a comfortable bungalow with a multitude of servants, landing in Sevagram must have been a shock, however mentally well prepared Mary tried to be. Gone was the dining room, the gracious amenities of western living. More than fifty years later she recalled the "big, big dining hall," where all were seated on the floor around low tables, and the memory of adapting to harshly abstemious ways remained. Mary remembered the prohibition of any waste and its impact on their daily habits: "When people came round with a bucket of rice or a bucket of this, that, or the other . . . it was *absolutely forbidden* to let them give it to you if you weren't going to be able to eat it all."[4] Richard too, only four at the time, recalls his mother's help in making the transition: "It was a huge crime to leave anything, and when bananas arrived cooked, to be eaten whole [not ordinary bananas], my mother used to peel mine furtively leaving no trace of the crime." Everyone, even the smallest child like Richard had their assigned work. "My duty," he said, "was to carry a bowl of salt around to any who asked for it; I gather it provided entertainment—probably to me as well!—for people to call for salt from the furthest point from where I was to get me running around manically to get to everyone!"[5]

In that joint Letter from their new home, Mary is unfailingly cheerful, softening the apparent hardships with good-natured humor:

> We are already quite attached to our house. It is small and compact—two rooms, a small veranda, a kitchen and a bathroom, i.e. a place where there is a stone tank for storing water where we can wash our clothes, dishes, and ourselves. One of Murray's tasks is several trips to the well to fill up this tank. There is no tub, of course, but the Indian method of throwing water over oneself becomes quite preferable after a while. We're longing for the day when we acquire the technique of *dhobiing*[6] sheets and such like on a slab of stone—certainly our friends here get their

---

3. Letter #2.
4. Interview with Trapnell.
5. Richard Rogers, interview with author, Oxford, England, 2007.
6. *Dobhis*, who earn their living by washing for the higher caste, are part of the traditional *Dalit* (untouchables) in the traditional Hindu caste system. Tradition says that before they begin their work at the river, they first must bow to the washing stone.

clothes Persil-white by that method in a way we find hard to manage!

Mary's description of the mud and wattle house, with its bamboo and thatched straw roof is matter-of-fact, with hardly a hint of the enormity of the transition from their servant-filled bungalow. Though its stone floors require daily sweeping, "luckily," she continues, "there's not much dusting to do. With beds of the string variety that can easily be shifted, our furniture consists of camouflaged trunks, some shelves of bamboo and some rush mats. One of the most coveted objects is the Dunlop cushion, used by Murray in Afghanistan buses, whose double I now deeply regret leaving behind in England. We are getting fairly well used to using the floor though Richard's legs are the most amenable—mine less so!"[7]

Though they had kept the Dunlop cushion, they had been required to part with most other belongings. Mary later wrote of the simplicity of the lifestyle there and of the "reduction of needs" and "shedding of avoidable extras." Each person—man, woman, or child—"had his or her small tin trunk containing one change, or at the most two, of white homespun clothing (usually spun and woven by himself) plus a few basic necessities such as *thali*[8] and *katori*[9] and *lota*.[10]" Echoing Murray's amazement at the lack of hierarchical behaviors, she said, "It was impressive to see Sri Aryanayakam and his wife Asha Devi eating in the big dining hall, cleaning their allocation of rice before meals, joining the teams in the kitchen or in keeping the trench-latrines in good order, and receiving the same money as the other staff members."[11]

The experience was chastening. Ending the Letter, Murray's summary is more subdued, more humble than it was only seven months earlier, when he was writing from England, euphoric with C.M.S.'s endorsement of their plan to join Sevagram. Now he wrote: "As we try to see where our tiny contribution fits into the whole Purpose of God in history . . . we find it hard to say . . . where we are going, but we find it enough that the Living God knows where He is going; all this makes life most invigorating but not one little bit easy. Please pray for us when you have time. Yours sincerely, Mary and Murray Rogers"[12]

Being at Sevagram was a shock to Murray as well, but a shock of a different sort. Hoping for a different way of life, the differences he encountered

---

7. Letter #2.
8. *Thali*: a round metal plate with compartments for Indian meals.
9. *Katori*: a metal bowl.
10. *Lota*: a small metal container for water.
11. Interview with Trapnell.
12. Letter #2.

shook the foundations of his Christian assumptions. Suddenly he was surrounded with people, Hindu in their faith, who seemed full of the Holy Spirit. Murray named the qualities he could not help but notice: "humility, extraordinary compassion, humanity, devotedness, caring for others, ready to do work. There were no hours there—nobody worked from nine to six or nine to five-thirty. The whole of life was work. It was very ordered. But the unselfishness and," he repeated, "*the humility!*"

He continued ruefully, "Those fruits of the Spirit got me down quite a lot . . . because I don't think I've ever lived in a place where human beings, men and women and little children seemed to be happy and living on very little. Sharing everything, and not fighting." At the Christian Agricultural College, "we were *begging* people to come by increasing their salaries! . . . There was no challenge. Whereas at Sevagram, you were challenged up to the hilt. All that was pretty embarrassing for me and Mary."[13]

There were other challenges. He told of the committees that guided aspects of the community, each made up of members of all ages, even as young as four years old: committees for cleanliness, for food, for entertainment, for worship. Murray said he was chosen to be on the Worship Committee. "And therein hangs a tale!" he recalled. "I was thankful to be chosen, but then, oh, dear, what a pickle!"

God was worshiped, he explained, in the Gandhian way, with Hindu, Muslim, Christian elements. The Christian parts always included the Lord's Prayer. Murray told of an issue raised by one of the older members of the Worship Committee and recalled listening to his concern. For Hindus, said the older member, there were two parts of the prayer that were difficult to say. The first was asking God to "give us our daily bread." Murray interpreted their view: "Very difficult, because if we do our work and behave properly with the land, we will have our daily bread. And it seemed demeaning [for them] to ask God for something so ordinary." The other concern was the phrase, "Forgive us our trespasses," because it seemed to be at odds with the Hindu doctrine of karma. Again taking their perspective, he explained, "I mean, if I knock your head off, I reap the consequences. And it's no good saying God, please take that away. You've lost your head; you're dead! So what do you mean?" Lively discussions amongst the committee ensued, said Murray, and, as the only Christian, he tried, unsuccessfully, to persuade them of the merits of the Lord's Prayer. They asked instead, with *great* kindness, he emphasized, that he undertake to rewrite those offensive parts of the prayer. He recalls saying, perhaps to them, perhaps to himself, "'Well, brothers and sisters, this is remarkable. I never thought that I would be invited to

---

13. Interview with Trapnell.

work over what Jesus had given us!'. . . In the end I think I declined. But it was really very educative for me . . . It was an extraordinary time."[14]

His involvement with Gandhian education led him to Marjorie Sykes, who became their lifelong friend. Described by Murray as "a magnificent lady,"[15] she was a British Quaker and follower of Gandhi. Sevagram offered a year-long training course for western teachers to learn "Basic Education [*Nai Talim*]" in which she and Aryanakanji[16] were teaching, and Murray joined in as a very junior member of the staff.

In that context, another challenge arose. Murray noticed that some of the teachers, uncomfortable with what they were learning, raised questions or challenged its techniques. The response from the Sevagram people, he said, was to "lay down the law." No arguments allowed here: that's what we do, and that's what you'll do. They cited Gandhi, now three years dead. "A number of times I heard people say, 'Gandhiji said . . . !' And this was so sick-making to me." Not only did Murray react sharply to this authoritarian approach, but he deeply believed their understanding of Gandhi's beliefs were flawed. Murray continued: "By that time, asking people who knew Gandhiji . . . I'd discovered he had a terrific sense of humor. He enjoyed people disagreeing with him; he was a most open man . . . And here was his place for educating people about him doing just the opposite."[17]

In fact, even decades later, in Gandhi's writing, one finds evidence supporting Murray's view. An example follows: "I am not a perfect being. Why should you see eye to eye with me in my errors? That would be blind faith. Your faith in me should enable you to detect my true error much quicker than a fault-finder . . . Therefore, you should not paralyze your thought by suppressing your doubts and torturing yourself that you do not agree with my view . . . You should pursue the discussion . . . till you have the clearest grasp of all my ideals about it."[18]

It was heart-wrenching for Murray to experience this conflict with Aryanakanji and Marjorie Sykes, his close friends. "I just disagreed utterly, feeling you can't dragoon people into a system of education they don't believe in. You've got to win them over. A lot of them were won over, but some were not."[19]

In the meantime, Mary and Murray were grappling with another perplexing dilemma. Was this sort of education—spinning, weaving and

14. Interview with Trapnell.
15. Ibid.
16. Aryanakanji: The addition of *ji* to a name denotes both respect and affection.
17. Interview with Trapnell.
18. Gandhi, *Essential Gandhi*, 272.
19. Interview with Trapnell.

agriculture—suitable for their children? Richard, who was four, adapted readily, helping the other boys tend the cows or weed the vegetables while Mary did household chores. But for the older children, it was what Murray called "an impossible contradiction."[20] On the one hand, they were coming to believe that the western lifestyle, including its traditional education, ran counter to the Christian Gospel. On the other hand, they were reluctant to impose that belief—or any—on their children. Never would Mary expect her children to conform to their spiritual beliefs and punish them for following their own path as her parents had done to her older brother Bruce. Nor would Murray pressure his children to conform to his ideas of life, as he had been pressured by his father. Cheryl, Linda, and Richard each should be free to choose. Thus Mary and Murray's determination to live a life more congruent with the Gospel in India meant they would need to be separated from their children, and their children from them, for extended periods. Writing to "Friends" from Sevagram late in 1952, Murray says, "The matter of the children's education is difficult; a few western parents have thought it right to bring their children up . . . as Indian children. We do not feel we should do that, but western education in Asia is expensive and because of the climate it has to be boarding education."[21]

Murray and Mary, young and looking ahead in India

20. Ibid.
21. Letter #3.

Cheryl, Linda, and Richard c. 1949

As long as they opted for western-style boarding schools in India, they needed to depend on C.M.S. to pay for that education. While longing to live closer to their ideals by lessening their dependence on C.M.S., they could not make choices for their children that would limit their life options. Years later Murray reflected: "Mary and I always felt we had got to put them in a position where they could really choose themselves. If they had only been to (Gandhian) education, they could only have stopped in India."[22] Freedom of choice was a value both Mary and Murray held particularly dear, yet it seemed that securing their children's ultimate freedom of choice was utterly inconsistent with their desire to be free of western ties.

And so, accepting this "impossible contradiction," Mary and Murray, like most British parents of the era in India, had enrolled Cheryl and Linda in boarding school. St. Hilda's was located in Ootacamund, in the hills of South India, far from Sevagram. Except for vacations, Cheryl and Linda never lived with their parents there. Hence, part of Mary's routine, along with the sweeping and washing, was writing frequent letters to her young daughters. To her delight, she discovered that the mail coming to Sevagram was the fastest in India, a remnant from the days when Gandhi's letters and messages were top priority. For those months the speedy post eased the ache

---

22. Interview with Trapnell.

of missing her girls, and that summer the family was reunited for a holiday in the Nilgiri Hills nearby the school.

While Linda has little memory of St. Hilda's, Cheryl has recollections of those times as well as a desire to put them into perspective: "We traveled down to school in south India two days and two nights by train, accompanied by some adult or other. British children—not all, but many, were traveling somewhere. We were in boarding schools pretty young; that's how it was." For those who react with shock or disapproval that her parents sent them away so young she emphasizes the historical context: "One has to remember that it was the period when there were lots of Whites in India. There were missionaries, there were armies, there were tea-planters. It was the colonial times. In fact we were not very different in that epoch from many other people. Lots of us were boarders. We only knew our own life and took it for granted. Frankly, I don't remember giving it two thoughts!"[23]

In any case, the separation was softened that first year when, at the close of the summer holiday, there was a temporary opening for a teacher, and Mary happily jumped into the breach. For several months, while Mary taught Latin, Richard stayed with her, enrolled in St. Hilda's kindergarten. Murray returned alone to Sevagram.

Mary made friends easily at the school, among them a young Scottish teacher named Heather Sandeman. Heather was fascinated with the choices this young British couple were making in their lives. She too was drawn to the East, having been born in India, where her father was an officer in the British Army. When the teaching assignment was over, Mary and little Richard returned to Sevagram and resumed their life there, with promises to Heather from Mary that she would stay in touch. For her it was, "a wrench to leave and to switch back to this different Sevagram existence—straight from gerundives to ginning!"[24] Richard, it was reported, seemed equally at home in either environment, nearby his mother.

While Mary devotedly tended their simple home, Murray continued to struggle with his beliefs. The problems he had identified within the Gandhian "Basic Education" continued to nettle him. The difficulty, he said, was not, with its goals of productive work and self-sufficiency, that Indians be able to provide for their own basic needs of food and clothing. Those he found "true." As a system of education, he could appreciate, admire, and even strive to emulate its ideals and life style. Rather, the problem for him lay in the fundamental philosophy of *Satya* and *Ahimsa*—Truth and Non-Violence—and living in community, which seemed to take it beyond

---

23. Interview with author.
24. Letter #3. Ginning: the removal of seeds from cotton in preparation for spinning.

a system of education, allowing it to become an ideology. And as an ideology, a religious belief system, it seemed incompatible with Christianity, which for him was, of course, the one true religion. "Gandhianism, upon which it is based," he wrote, "is essentially a religious movement having its inspiration in the life and teaching of Mahatma Gandhi." He continued, "A Christian faced with such an ideology has to confess that he believes it to be one more humanist and idealist delusion, however much he admires and respects the work done by the followers of Gandhiji."[25] Affirming the values he saw in Gandhism like simple living and decentralization, he asked his readers and, implicitly himself, a challenging question: "Have we [Christians] the spiritual and physical guts to act in as revolutionary a way as these Gandhian friends, but with the Christian Faith as our dynamic?" Having shared his growing concerns with Mary along the way, Murray had come to a hard decision. They would leave Sevagram and try to live what was most worthy in Gandhianism in a Christian context. Together they shared the decision with their friends and he with his superiors at the C.M.S. as well. He acknowledged what they had gained: "It has been a privilege to live in a community so largely made up of those who are Hindu by faith; we are grateful for the real friends that we have made, for an existential understanding of their faith almost impossible to experience from the reading of books, and for the opportunities . . . in sharing with some of them our convictions as Christians and what our Lord means to us, for shared Bible study. Not many Christian westerners have the chance of living in a situation where they have no power springing from economic, social or religious advantage and this has given us a freedom in relationships which we are very loathe to lose."

On the other hand, he continues, "Being a Christian here also involves something of a crisis and a clash. The two ideologies, Gandhian and Christian, are poles apart, however frequently both use the same words and speak the same ethical language. Unless silence is kept by the Christian, a parting of the ways is inevitable and that is never pleasant."[26] Murray was not one to keep silent.

While Murray's voice leads the way and Mary seems to concur, it is hard to discern what her wishes might truly have been. Years later, Linda agreed that her views were underrepresented, even in their joint communications. "She was really extremely academic, but I now think that Mother over all of her years, way back, was so extremely stoical in many ways. She

25. Letter #3.
26. Ibid.

was so uncomplaining, always uncomplaining . . . But of course you have to remember . . . in those days . . . the wife just trotted off after the husband."[27]

In any case, the parting of the ways was difficult. Murray's own late-in-life reflections on the decision still contained puzzlement about the experience and an inability to understand his own dogmatic assertion that Gandhism and Christianity were "poles apart." He remembered: "When we left, in the end, I never felt so torn . . . There was so much of Gandhiji and his legacy which I found marvelous and thanked God for, and wanted to somehow continue in our little life . . . I didn't feel at all proud about leaving, but I felt I sort of had to."[28] Was it perhaps his own spiritual immaturity, the poles within himself that were not ready to be integrated? He was conflicted, wanting to be a follower of both Jesus *and* Gandhi. Yet his mind still tended to think dualistically, clinging to his young beliefs that unless he explicitly acknowledged Jesus as Lord, he was an apostate. It had to be this *or* that; he was not yet able to inwardly contain both. He told of writing a letter, sharing his concerns with Aryanakanji and the others. "They of course were very kind with me." When the news got back to the C.M.S. in England and the wider church in India, Murray said his supporters like Max Warren, saw his point, but others, like his bishop in India, believed he had not given it enough time and were disappointed he had chosen to be so outspoken, seemingly impetuous. They had been at Sevagram for less than a year. Where would they go? As yet there was no answer to that question.

Before long, an opportunity arose. Even in that short time at Sevagram, lasting friendships had been forged, not only with Marjorie Sykes, but with Banwari Lal Choudhri, a Hindu man, the head of a large family, who lived in a nearby village. During their stay, Choudhri had asked Murray to read the Gospels with him, and Murray had reciprocated, listening to him share his Hindu faith. It was a strong connection, one-to-one. When it became apparent to Choudhri that Mary and Murray were unsure where to go, he offered a remarkable invitation: Would they come live with him and his large traditional joint family in the nearby village of Raisalpur?

With prayer but little hesitation, Mary and Murray accepted the invitation. They found the opportunity to be part of a multi-generational family, inspired by Gandhian ideals, but without the dogma, compelling. "We weren't there to do anything special," recalled Murray, "but to really live and put our hands to anything we thought well to do."[29] They described the set-up in a Letter: "Our adopted family," they wrote, is a typical joint fam-

27. Interview with author.
28. Interview with Trapnell.
29. Ibid.

ily, "with mothers and fathers and children of three or four generations all living under the same roof and . . . organised as one working group." Before their arrival, "there were 150 souls in the Choudhri family, and we make it 155!"[30]

As the first Christian family ever to live in Raisalpur, they felt "welcomed into the heart of the Choudhri family." They were given their own little house, a one-room mud hut. There they could sleep and cook and share their own family prayers, yet spend time in the Choudhri family quarters and share some of their meals as well. Again their Letter describes their new home, located on the edge of the village near a communal well. At their request, writes Murray:

> Village friends knocked five small windows and a back door into this room and we enlarged our domain with the help of tin sheets above and bamboo matting around . . . At one end we have what we call "the dining room," a plain mud floor on which we put mats and thalis at mealtimes, at the back a bathroom and (in between) the kitchen with its mud grate and mud oven. In front on the left is the girls' room and on the right a similar bamboo matting room, used for guests or for my study. Daily sweeping and a weekly plastering of cowdung over the floors and courtyard keep the house clean and even attractive . . . Sanitation consists of a trench latrine in the field at the back . . .

He continues, describing their daily routine: "Mary and I are fully employed, and so are the children when they are at home from school!" Though Mary and Murray had help carrying the water and plastering the cow-dung, the other tasks were theirs. "Every other day we sweep the village road in front of our house—cleanliness and godliness not being universal convictions—wood is readied for cooking, lanterns cleaned as well as the latrine, washing, sweeping and . . . never-ending cooking done." In an understated acknowledgment of his extraordinarily patient and hard-working wife, he adds, "*And did Mary read classics for this*?! I sometimes think it's because she *did* read classics that she is able to do so much of the job of an Indian village woman without breaking."[31]

Apparently, Mary and Murray had received correspondence from friends concerned for their well-being. "Some friends of ours," he admitted, "whose views we respect, think that we are being unfair to ourselves and to our children." He addressed their concern with a counter-argument that for him "carries the day." Citing the extreme disparity of incomes between

30. Letter #4.
31. Ibid.

southeast Asia, Britain and the United States, he passionately contended that it is this disparity that makes wars between countries and "fodder for communists." He continued, "The Bible leaves us no doubt that this is God's business and therefore the church's . . . Only action will persuade (the masses) that God cares."

Admittedly, Murray mused, "The Church of England ordination vows appear somewhat distant . . . Yet if God's children in the villages are to hear the Gospel with their inner ears, I am more certain than ever that it is from *within* the situation . . . that God can speak through us." Indicating that he was learning to exercise discretion in proclaiming their Christian beliefs, he observed that most village people seemed to welcome their presence, though others were "slightly suspicious . . . knowing we are Christians and (that we) believe every man will only find freedom and fulfillment through conversion to Christ."[32]

Much as he may have aspired to emulate Charles Andrews whom he so admired, Murray was not ready to embrace the openness of his spiritual thinking. Writing to Gandhi in 1937, Andrews had shared his hope for the future: "I don't think it follows that we shall always be fighting as to whose 'Gospel' is superior . . . There is a precious element of goodness which we can all hold in common. St. Paul says: 'Whatsoever things are true, honest, just, lovely, and of good report . . . think on these things, and the God of peace shall be with you.' That seems to me to be a fine way towards peace in religion, without any compromise, syncretism or toning down of vital distinctions."[33]

While Andrews' hope was for *swaraj*,[34] Murray's hope still lay in the eventual conversion of all people to Christ. "Our claim is that only one revolution is radical enough, deep enough, all-embracing enough, the revolution which springs from God's eternal action in history in Jesus Christ."[35]

Coming from the radically egalitarian culture of Sevagram, their return to a traditional village still governed by a hierarchical caste system, was a big adjustment. They had learned something already of the strict rules for Hindu society. William and Charlotte Wiser, Christian missionaries in another area of North India, noted that those rules

> settled beyond all doubt the religious, social, and economic standing of every person. His birth fixes his station. And

---

32. Ibid.
33. Chaturvedi and Sykes, *Charles Freer Andrews*, 310.
34. *Swaraj*: Literally, self-rule, but more specifically here, Gandhi's belief in freedom in all spheres of life and independence from any sort of foreign rule.
35. Letter #4.

nothing he can do will alter the plan. We who are outside the order are amazed at the contentment of those within it, until we comprehend its strength and all-pervasiveness . . . On one occasion, when a high caste, unorthodox friend of ours spoke to a group of our villagers about the justice of granting some rights to untouchables, a high-caste villager spoke up, "Then why were we born farmers, barbers, tailors, carpenters, potters, and the rest?" This attitude, that each man has been created by God to fill a certain position in the great religio-socio-economic order, fosters contentment, or at least resignation.[36]

In their daily life in Raisalpur, Mary's presence eased the way for them to interact with village people. As a European woman, she would be called by the respectful term *memsahiba*,[37] applied only to Indian women of rank. Often she had the first opportunity to be invited into a home by another woman while Murray, the *sahib*, might speak only to the men. Gradually, as their connection to the Chowdhri family became known, their presence was more accepted; often it was assumed they could be of medical assistance. Sometimes called into a house where someone was ill, expectations brought them up short. They could, of course, offer basic homely remedies and suggestions for improved sanitation. "We explained," writes Murray, "that we were not doctors nor nurses and then it began to dawn on us that they were bringing the sick to us because we are 'religious people.' It has given us much to think about—and to repent of—that these Hindu friends appear to have a greater belief in the power of prayer . . . than we ourselves have."[38] One cannot help but wonder, was it the villagers' belief in the power of prayer, or some earlier experience with medical missionaries that created that assumption?

In those years Richard was an unexpectedly effective village emissary. Murray recalls Aryanakanji's affectionate teasing at Sevagram: "He's the best of the bunch of you three!" In Raisalpur he played happily with village children, who would crowd the house to share his little trains and his good-natured company. "I'll never forget," said Murray, what Richard once said to Mary when she was sending the visiting children home so the family could have their customary rest after lunch. "Richard (aged six) made the wonderful comment: 'Well, thank goodness for a little time to myself!'"[39]

---

36. Wiser and Wiser, *Behind Mud Walls,* 38.
37. *Memsahiba*: a term of respect for European women.
38. Letter #4.
39. Interview with Trapnell.

Cheryl and Linda had briefer tastes of village life during their school holidays. Linda recalls what she called "kerosene sugar"—sugar that tasted nastily of fuel for the lamps and undoubtedly tainted any special treat.

It was not an easy adjustment. While Mary and Murray's concerted efforts to learn Hindi helped, the village people remained reticent, raising a frustrating barrier to real friendship.

But still they persevered. Opening their daily noon worship to neighbors, a few of them came. When Christmas arrived, they invited everyone in the village to share their celebration, using the village barber to deliver the invitation, as prescribed by the *jajmani* system.[40] "Imagine our delight—almost bewilderment—when a crowd of 2,000 neighbors arrived! Stretching away down the road and sitting packed on the ground in our courtyard . . . gave us a Christmas we'll never forget!" Mary shared the Christmas story in the form of five tableaux created using their own three children and several others from the village. Their host, Choudhriji read the scriptures; a visiting Christian who had converted from Hinduism spoke, and sweets and guavas were offered.[41]

Then there was the Hindu wedding of a daughter of the head of the joint family to which they were invited. Overwhelmed by the intricacy and the length of the elaborate ceremony, Mary and Murray shared their impressions of the nearly weeklong event: "When we tell you that all the most important functions, such as the joining of hands and the walking around the fire, took place between midnight and 4 a.m. you can understand that it tested our powers of endurance in a way that our own weddings do not!" Then they added, "However fascinated and interested we were, we began to wonder whether we would ever understand a society so entirely unlike our own with roots running down into men's unconscious thinking . . . back into antiquity."[42] Their initial excitement at being in the midst of a joint family in a Hindu village seems to have been challenged.

As the year wore on, consumed with the daily routine, Mary again felt the need to return to South India to be near the children in school. Being there allowed her not only to practice her teaching skills but to find companionship and deepen her growing bond with Heather Sandeman. In her absence, Murray moved out of their quarters and into the very heart of the Choudhri joint family. He was given an upper room accessed by "perilous steps." From the window he could look down on the small courtyard: "There

---

40. Wiser, *Hindu Jajmani System*, 20. The *jajmani* system refers to the caste system with its rigidly prescribed roles.

41. Letter #4.

42. Ibid.

stood the water pots and tank, round which life revolves in the heat of the summer; there too some ten family members slept, with me just above on the tin sheeting which covered the animal shed." One can only surmise what lay between the next lines of his Letter: "Those were weeks of much sharing when I often used the prayer: 'Lord, make me aware.'"[43] Observing intimate family interactions up close, he noted their lack of privacy, as well as the dynamics described by the Wisers, cited earlier, "Husband and wife have little opportunity for a natural relationship, except in their courtyard or roof under cover of darkness . . . As it is, a woman performs her duty to her husband, satisfying his elemental needs, while she lavishes more and more of her love on her children."[44] Was this becoming true of his and Mary's relationship as well? Whatever he noticed gave him pause.

He joined his family for two cool, refreshing months in the Nilgiri Mountains before returning to their joint family with Mary and to a somewhat larger and more comfortable house. But then came the monsoons: "Dozens of our neighbors' houses were flooded," Murray writes. "One day when I had been out visiting a nearby village, I came home through a torrent of water—believe me, not of the cleanest variety—up to my chest."

After the floods came "the break for which we had prayed": the opportunity to be accepted in the village and to make connections with its people. When Community Project workers arrived to protect the contaminated village against cholera with inoculations, Mary and Murray joined the effort. "That was a sort of panic moment," said Murray. The people would not readily let him enter the house alone, but he and Mary could often be admitted together. "I'd not given any injections before then. I think I gave about eighty injections in a day and a half."

Now they had gained access to many homes and "were trusted in a most humbling way . . . Almost without noticing it," they wrote, "we began a Door-step Dispensary," with some two-dozen patients visiting daily between 7:30 and 10:00 a.m. The work of offering a mixture of caring, love, and prayer blended with preventive health advice and simple remedies was deeply satisfying. Nearby medical friends could guide them and even arrange hospital stays for those who needed it and were "willing to take the plunge" of entrusting themselves to professionals beyond the village. Many were not.

Yet another conundrum emerged as they observed the people in these times of suffering. Rather than the instinct to revolution he expected, he found passivity. "The quiet, ungrumbling way village friends cope with these

---

43. Letter #5.
44. Wiser and Wiser, *Behind Mud Walls*, 80–81.

difficulties is most impressive and, in a real sense, noble, but how we longed for disquiet, for a determination that such conditions must not continue."[45] They considered the sense of resignation nothing short of tragic. Certainly it was not an attitude Murray had met in himself.

Somewhere in the process, Murray later reflected, a part of him began to relax a bit. He and Mary maintained their close connections with Marjorie Sykes and others at a big Quaker center a few miles away. Perhaps Marjorie's strong but gentle model of openhearted Christianity softened him. Already he had realized he could not teach openly about Christ. But distracted, perhaps, by the daily life duties and crises, he also had ceased working so self-consciously to show Christ by his life. While hardly noticing at the time, very gradually, "the trying part fell off . . . and I suppose I became less earnest. That's what God did," observed Murray.[46]

Then, practically overnight, things changed in the Choudhri family. After a brief illness, the head of their part of the joint family died; his body was cremated at a nearby lake. Suddenly Mary and Murray were asked to leave so that the four remaining brothers, who had lived jointly, could divide the family and have more living space. So five months ahead of their planned departure, they hastily gathered their few belongings and left, "grateful for very much kindness from the Choudhri family and friendship from many others, yet sad at such a sudden leaving." Writing six months later from Kareli, Murray mused, "We almost said 'strange leaving' because many friends and neighbors thought there were other reasons for our being asked to go. About this we don't know and are not trying to find out. So much is different between cultures; . . . for all we speak of 'East meets West' we know there is much we do not understand. The brothers have now decided not to divide the family and we are in a new home."[47]

---

45. Letter #5.
46. Interview with Trapnell.
47. Letter #5.

5

A Family in Flux
1953–1954

> At times we have to stake our whole existence,
> and it is only by making these great and daring commitments
> that we can . . . know what life really is.
>
> —J. H. Oldham

Though the five months between their sudden departure from Raisalpur to their arrival in Kareli may have been painful and confusing, when they were over, Mary and Murray spoke simply of "months of wondering, of seeking, of waiting." At times, they said, "we have felt ourselves to be in the flow—getting on with the work—while at others it almost seemed we were meant to tie up by the bank and wait for further orders."[1]

But even before they left the Choudhri joint family, new ideas had been forming. In stirring tones that identify the voice as Murray's, these ideas were proclaimed in the last Letter from their mud house in Raisalpur: "We are called, we believe, to live right in the world, surrounded by the world's economics and politics, but so to live where God has put us that the Holy Spirit may break through . . . We hope and pray that God may lead other Christian men and women to join us in what might best be called a Christian joint family."[2]

Gradually over the next year, the desire to differentiate their life from that of the traditional missionary took on a more affirmative tone. "It is the claim of Christians that the Gospel comes with the power to make men one in Christ Jesus in that utterly new quality of fellowship which needed

---

1. Letter #5.
2. Letter #4.

the new Greek word '*koinonia*' to describe it. "There," Murray continued, "you have the specific (the remedy) for a divided society." With the sense that he had come to a spiritual "eureka" moment, he shared an urgent new sense of call: "We *must* discover this fellowship of 'belonging in Christ' in practical, down to earth terms of group living, working, and worshipping, if friends in this country are to say: 'This is the thing! These people are not just talking about freedom, friendship, love; they are caught up in the thing!'" Concerned above all with "personal meeting, personal relationships," their way of life would be one of vulnerability and simple living. "We love security as much as anyone but hope to have the guts to pray to be kept vulnerable," he added.[3]

Yet for all their radical rejection of the missionary lifestyle, the belief in an underlying battle for souls remained intact: "We are persuaded more than ever before of the inevitable clash between Christ, the world's Lord, and every other lord and -ism, not solely in relation to those who are not Christian or in relation to such evils as caste and color bar, but as certainly within us too." Echoes of childhood preachers still reverberate in their message: "There is a tremendous chasm between . . . the world's Saviour and the principalities and powers who are usurping His power in village India—and village England—and that challenge will result in a Cross as it eternally does . . ."[4] Though moved over the years by messages of peace and co-existence from C. F. Andrews, Mahatma Gandhi, and Quaker friends like Marjorie Sykes, Mary and Murray's vision so far remained one of spiritual warfare and the ultimate triumph of Christ's Gospel over all other religions, belief systems, and evils of the world. Thus, their life was to be an "experiment in group witness." They would live "as an enlarged Christian Family, discovering how properly to fulfill our responsibility towards our narrow families and to the wider family." What, one wonders, were their thoughts about their "narrow family"? Would they, with God's help, find a way forward with or for their three children? If that seemed a daunting task, still it was not primary. At least for Murray, "Our first and most difficult job will be so to work, live, and worship together that God's Holy Spirit may do something with us." That would be the key to "our neighbors being gripped by the Good News of Christ."[5]

But where? And how? At a loss for a specific location, they found temporary shelter back in Allahabad. Living on the edge of the Agricultural College, adjacent to a home for lepers, they reconnected with old friends

3. Letter #5.
4. Ibid.
5. Ibid.

and bided their time. At Christmas the children came for the holidays from St. Hilda's School in South India, along with their teacher, Heather Sandeman, by now a familiar family friend. Amidst the daily rounds, always the conversation and the prayer returned to the burning question: "What does God want us to do?" Others were invited and drawn into their quest. "A sort of prayer group" had evolved, and Heather, too, during that holiday visit felt herself being drawn to their vision. Friends, like Marjorie Sykes, Hepsie Smith, and M. M. Thomas supported their desire to be missionaries in some new way: "We were disillusioned, whatever good things happened through missionary organizations . . . the time had gone by; the Empire was gone . . . It was just out of date, thoroughly disliked by masses of Indian people, and we didn't know how we were to go."[6] As they consulted their bishop, the Rt. Rev. Christopher Robinson, Bishop of Lucknow, he too was drawn in, first as a part of their discernment process, then an active player. Through him and a serendipitous confluence of circumstances, possibilities began to emerge. Mary describes their vision, honed in response to their experience in Raisalpur: "We wanted a degree of independence from landlord or church supervision. We wanted to be in a village situation but were a little chary of being positioned in the centre of a village, having found in Raisalpur that the complete absence of quiet made it difficult to attempt any timetable of corporate worship and prayer. Also that there was a strong tendency to identify us with the caste among whom we lived, which produced a certain resentment when we showed signs of welcoming and being friendly to all, including the *Harijan* or (had they been there) the Muslims."[7]

Murray, always the consummate storyteller, years later delighted in recalling how it all happened—how he and Mary found themselves shaping their vision—transforming a small plot of land on the Ganges plain of northern India, in the state of Uttar Pradesh—India's poorest—outside the village of Kareli, and, in the process, being transformed themselves.

The Bishop, it seemed, sometimes sought counsel in the legal affairs of the diocese from a lawyer, Mr. A.B.L. Agnihotri by name. Agnihotri, Murray explained, had been put in charge of a large piece of land owned by another client, a British citizen living in France who was a descendent of the legendary Colonel Hearsey. Thus, in Murray's words, it was Agnihotri's responsibility "to look after the remnants of an old estate that had come down to (his client's) family from well over a hundred years (before). (As) you know, there were British men called soldiers of fortune who would fight for some Maharajah, or some prince in India. And this man—a Colonel

---

6. Interview with Trapnell.
7. Mary Rogers, written reflection, undated.

Hearsey—fought very much and very admirably, from the point of view of his master, who was the *Nawab*[8] of Awadh (or Oudh). In exchange he was given . . . two hundred villages by this prince, this *Nawab*, who owned everything—who owned everybody, I mean, everybody was sort of a slave. It was the old *Zamindari*[9] System."

Hearsey had received this enormous amount of land, between Bareilly and Ballia to Agra, as a prize for being a good soldier. "By the time we got there," Murray continued,

> it had been cut down to about forty acres, from being thousands and thousands of acres. At independence, you see, they were beginning to bring in the abolition of the *Zamindari* System, the big landowners, of which Hearsey was one. Now, there'd been a Miss Hearsey, his descendent, a remarkable lady who lived in that great big house with fifteen rooms. She lived—a single English lady—just like a queen, up until about '42 and the war. The stories of her—extraordinary! Kareli, of course, was of a part of her *zamindari*, where she was the chief figure. And of course, when she went into town—can you imagine it?!—three or four miles away, somebody would run (ahead), clearing the road of everybody. They all had to get to one side. The carts and everything. She was absolutely the *Maharani*! She was the queen! And she had this house of fifteen rooms, and she lived in the one that didn't have any windows in the very middle, beautifully cool, of course, wonderful to behold . . .

Murray, reveling in his narrative, digressed: "There's a story," he said,

> that once some crime had been committed around there, and the Englishman who was Commissioner of Bareilly and the district around sent out the police to look at Kareli, because they thought the thief, or the murderer, or whatever, had come from there. And when Miss Hearsey heard about it she was furious that the police had been anywhere near *her* village. And she called for her horse-drawn carriage, had the road cleared, and was driven in this carriage into town. When she got to the Commissioner's house, instead of behaving properly—writing a note or sending her card in to say, 'I would like to speak to you,' she

---

8. *Nawab*: A Muslim prince.

9. The *Zamindari* System, which originated during the rule of the Moguls in India (1526—c. 1850) was a way to rule vast tracts of land, raise armies, and collect taxes from the peasants. The rulers, or *zamindars*, were hereditary aristocrats with royal titles, such as *Maharaja*, *Raja*, or *Nawab*. Under British rule, the system was continued and remained until the departure of the British in 1948, when it was it was legally abolished.

> walked straight in to his office. Walked straight in, and said, "Mr. Commissioner, I hear you've sent your police into my village of Kareli. Let it never happen again!" Turned around, walked out, and went home. And I don't think he did. I mean, it was the British Empire and (everyone) quaked when Miss Hearsey got cracking. She was the last of that line.[10]

Catching himself spinning one of his extended anecdotes, Murray returned to the narrative:

> So to get back to where we come in, the great, great great nephew or something, of Nat Hearsey, who had done that military prowess that had got him all this land, was a Hearsey who was the Reverend somebody Hearsey, who lived in France, and was the Anglican Chaplain of Nice, you see. That's (how) we got to hear about it. That Anglican Chaplain of Nice had written to our Bishop, Christopher Robinson, and the Bishop had put him in touch with Agnihotri, the diocesan lawyer. So Agnihotri had heard from the Rev. Hearsey in Nice, who said, "I own this property . . . I want you, Mr. Agnihotri, to organize it, and to get someone to look after it." . . . We were hanging around, so this invitation came from Agnihotri, plus Christopher Robinson: Would we be prepared to go and live in the big house and be *chowkidar*?[11] To see that people didn't start plowing up bits of land and running away with it? (Which of course they got into the good habit of doing over the years since Miss Hearsey had been dead, since '42 or '43 and it was then '53. They'd had a real free-for-all, had a great time!) We hadn't anything else to do. So I told Mary about it, and we prayed about it, and we said, "Yes!"[12]

At first, they had been encouraged to take possession of the big house. But, as Mary said, "We replied quite firmly that we had escaped from bungalow life and really could not contemplate returning to it. We were wanting something completely different, poorer, more Indian." But they had noticed that the land on which the estate was set was promising. It was, Mary continued, "close to two villages, near both but not right inside either. It was a rural spot close to the poor but not too far removed from a city (Bareilly) and a big railway junction. We could very well imagine ourselves in small huts in one of the corners of this big estate."[13] Thus they agreed to move into

---

10. Interview with Trapnell.
11. *Chowkidar*: a caretaker.
12. Interview with Trapnell.
13. Rogers, reflection.

the big house but only temporarily, letting their interest in a small piece of the property be known.

By then Murray was well aware that he was the driving force in the family while Mary's heart was often away with her children. "It showed how brave she was," he said. "We got our poles from our beds, which was the only furniture we had, and bits and pieces, a couple of tin trunks. We arrived in Kareli junction and set up in this old house."[14]

The first months were spent just settling in, deciding which of the fifteen rooms would serve as a chapel and beginning regular worship. The house was in a state of abject neglect. Most of the thatch of the roof was gone, leaving all but a few rooms open to the sky. "In three of the fifteen rooms," Murray said, "lived civet cats—with a ghastly smell, strong and musty . . . cats being cats. Occasionally (in bed) there would be a sort of 'rain storm' from the cloth (mosquito netting) that was over our heads." Echoing and augmenting Murray's recollections are Mary's: "As they repaired the old house over our heads, we moved (from room to room) where the repair work was done. We had brought with us from Raisalpur our dismembered beds, ditto the bamboo and matting hut to erect over the trench latrine . . . and one fly-proof '*doolie*'[15] for food. We borrowed a table for washing up from the Hearsey relics and soon invested in a couple of benches about six foot by one foot high which still form our dining benches at which we eat, sitting cross-legged on mats on the floor."[16]

Unwittingly, they had stepped into the feudal past of India, where it was assumed by villagers that they would adopt the lifestyle and fulfill the role of the old *zamindar*. Despite the Zamindari Abolition Act of 1948, the system was deeply entrenched and reform happened slowly, or hardly at all, in rural India. Murray explained, "There was still the bazaar . . . and all the stores collected little bits of money, which they handed to the *chowkidar*, who was there sick in one of the side rooms of the house."[17]

Mary recalled Salig Ram, the *chowkidar*, with amusement and affection:

> He dressed as a Sikh, and maybe he was! . . . He was quite a 'bumbler,' but good at heart and even made us *chapattis* and ground our spices until we'd learned to do our own. His most remembered act was when Murray wandered into the village and, after a while, Salig Ram enquired from me where he had gone.

14. Interview with Trapnell.
15. *Doolie*: a screened food cupboard.
16. Rogers, reflection.
17. Interview with Trapnell.

On hearing, he buckled on his sword and dashed in pursuit, presumably to the rescue. We wondered whether the Hearsey Sahibs had merely summoned their subjects and never thought of setting foot in the village themselves. It was a bit surprising for one who had the new theology of Prayer and Presence much at heart to be followed into the village by a sword-rattling Sikh![18]

Murray embroiders the story of miscommunication and cultural confusion: "We didn't know that we were going to be given any land; we were just living there, getting to know the people a bit, and they, of course, were expecting us to be another Miss Hearsey!" He continues: "I remember within the first few days, some man arrived and said, 'Do you want a horse?' I said, 'Well, why should we have a horse?' And then I discovered that he was asking whether we needed a *dead* horse! So why did we need a dead horse? Because Miss Hearsey—we were supposed to be in the line, you see—always had a dead horse, every fortnight, for her dogs. She had thirty dogs! Either forty dogs and thirty servants or thirty servants and forty dogs. I mean, an extraordinary setup, and this whole carcass of a horse arrived to feed the dogs."

Before many months had passed, news arrived from the Rev. Hearsey in France. He had concluded he never intended to come to India and wanted to be rid of the land. "He just sort of washed his hands of the whole show," said Murray.[19]

Thus Agnihotri and the Bishop decided that four and a half acres could be given to Mary and Murray for their new life and work. At the suggestion of Bishop Robinson, the new joint family would be called "A Family of the Holy Spirit." Though still more vision than reality, "the Family" might soon be augmented by others; perhaps a few of their little praying group might join as full members. That was their prayer. But to begin, they were alone.

Rattling around in the big house, seeking the civet-free rooms, they prayed, they planned, and they read together. In particular, they were captivated by a small book titled *Life is Commitment* by J. H. Oldham, another British missionary. Asserting that life entails much more than the "objective world" of science and technology, Oldham wrote, "It is possible to have the deepest reverence for science and at the same time to believe that reality is richer, profounder and more mysterious than all that recent centuries have revealed . . ." He continued, "There are some things in life and they may be the most important—that we cannot know by research or reflection, but only by committing ourselves. We must dare in order to know." Citing

18. Rogers, reflection.
19. Interview with Trapnell.

Martin Buber and his predecessor, Ludwig Feuerbach, Oldham asserts, "The essence of man is found only in the community, in the unity of man with man." It is the nature of reality that "life is essentially dialogue" and in the "momentous nature of the choice" to dedicate oneself to this assertion—or not—man's very "humanity is at stake." Of course, Oldham admits, this "unity of man with man" is not easy to attain: "When we consider this real world of the encounter of persons, we have to start from the fact of contradiction and conflict, since this is inherent in the existence of distinct and separate individuals. As an individual person I see life from my individual perspective—from the perspective of the situation into which by no choice of my own I have been pitchforked. From that standpoint . . . I can apprehend . . . the entire world . . . When I meet another person I encounter someone who with equal right sees the whole world from *his* perspective. How are those two perspectives—or two billion perspectives—to be reconciled? That is the basic problem of human existence."

Oldham continues with an assertion that was coming to resonate deeply with Murray: "The truth is that it is only through the other person that I can myself become a person . . . By the very fact that he sees life from a different perspective every person is a source of enrichment for me. The greater the number of my relations with other persons, the deeper and more intense those relations are, the greater is my fullness of life."[20]

How validated Murray felt, finding such a clear articulation of his own evolving life experience, his natural inclinations and desires.

Between their prayers and their reading, reflecting on Oldham and Buber, they ventured forth into their new surroundings—Murray the eager extrovert, easily making connections; Mary, the intrepid introvert: curious, observant, supportive. And industrious as well: already in a corner of the old house she had established a little medical dispensary to serve villagers, just as she had done in Raisalpur. Gregarious, yet quietly so, Mary again found her way into village homes, offering friendship, lending a listening ear to the mothers, "sharing a little of their weariness and unending labour."[21] It is easy to imagine just how much credibility *her* presence contributed to *their* presence.

But how in the world could two Cambridge-trained Britons, talented and dedicated as they might be, transform an abandoned mango grove into a livable space for a joint Christian family?

Through unimagined new relationships, Providence provided. One day, Murray was called to the local hospital to provide pastoral care to a

20. Oldham, *Life is Commitment*, 21–37.
21. Letter #6.

Quaker couple whose baby had died soon after birth. Joining with the parents, Laurie and Kuni Baker, in their grief, Murray at first simply ministered with his presence. But he would come to know much more. He would learn that Laurie was British, and it emerged quickly that the two men shared a common source of inspiration. Murray would hear his story—how some years earlier he had experienced a chance meeting with Mahatma Gandhi. Noticing the shoes Laurie had made from discarded scraps, Gandhi had posed a question: Might the young architect dedicate that creativity to house the poor of India? Laurie had responded to that challenge with an unequivocal "yes," devoting his life to creating buildings in India that utilized indigenous designs and solutions, while his wife, whom he met and married in India, served the poor as a medical doctor.[22] Immediately drawn to one another's way of life, Laurie responded to Murray's request for help. Soon he had taken up temporary residence in the old house along with Mary and Murray and was transposing their vision into drawings: a small grouping of buildings nestled into the old mango orchard, and at the heart of the plan—a chapel.

Even before building the Chapel, however, basic physical needs had to be be met. Sanitation would be provided by trench latrines like those at Sevagram. Determined, of course, that they would not have servants in the traditional way, one day, as Murray set himself to the thankless work of digging one of those trenches, along came a young Muslim man of about eighteen—no doubt curious about what this western man was doing. Engaged in conversation by Murray, he said his name was Fidah Hussein, and he offered to help. Although Murray could stand on principle, digging alone in the hot sun was clearly a time for compromise, and he accepted Fidah Hussein's offer. That day began a long, loyal, and trusting relationship with a man—never a servant exactly—who was to be a godsend in their day-to-day household survival.

By October the first of several work camps had been organized with thirty-five university students recruited to clear the land of decrepit date palm and mango trees, create roads, and dig the foundations of the Chapel and living quarters. Laurie Baker's creative genius, known for preserving "the simplicity of the Quakers and Gandhian thought in his architecture",[23] provided the plan—a plan that "articulated a vision, suggested a revolution . . ."[24] To "Friends" in their latest Letter, they described the layout. "The chief axis runs from the rounded Chapel up an avenue to a large rough cross

---

22. Baker, "India and Gandhiji."
23. Singh and Warkhandkar, "Laurie Baker's Creative Journey."
24. Letter posted on Laurie Baker's website: lauriebaker.net/.

which stands in the centre of the Garden of Silence; to the left are the living quarters and to the right a small building for a library and study as well as a dispensary or health building . . . There is land set aside for fruit and vegetable gardens, poultry, etc."[25]

More work camps followed, and the dreams and blueprints slowly became reality. Mary and Murray's excitement could hardly be contained as they described the Chapel:

> We wish you could see the Chapel. It is a small building set among trees; each side has large doors and to the east behind the altar is glass through which we can look out upon the Cross and the scene of our labours. There must be no barrier separating our work of worship and prayer from our work on the land, in the dispensary and in the villages, and the bricks and mortar say so every time we go to pray. The entrance is always open—only a 2 ft. door exists to keep the dogs out—for the House of prayer must never be locked to keep men out, nor must it be locked in an attempt to keep God in. As you look east the chief colour is bright yellow and as you look west bright blue; there is more than enough dull and mediocre in the world and this is the place where heaven meets earth with many a reminder of the glory that shall be revealed.[26]

But symbolism alone did not suffice. Their worship and prayer had now taken on a distinct structure, woven into the strands of their life. It began their morning at 5:45, guided their day at noontime, and ended with the setting of the sun. "If we fail in this part of the day's work," they wrote, "if we are not people of prayer, people who are continually aware of the presence of power of Jesus Christ then every one of our other activities will go for nothing."[27]

Mary and Murray were in Kareli a full year before they wrote to their friends, attempting to explain all that had happened. The Letter opened with a self-deprecating disclaimer, in a style that would become familiar in Murray's way of sharing their life: "Dear Friends, Maybe you will turn to this letter from your morning newspaper in which the headlines speak of great fears or hopes of mankind . . . and it's almost an embarrassment to intrude with something so small as Kareli. Forgive the strain on your imagination as we share with you what's been happening to one of the smaller of small things."

25. Letter #6.
26. Ibid.
27. Ibid.

Then, briefly, they told of how he and Mary came to occupy the land: "The owner has given us part of one of the mango groves. That is where our work and our interest and our prayers are centred."

Careful readers of the Letter might have discerned some new perspectives taking shape, borne perhaps from their painful struggle to find direction. Oldham's writing seemed to have opened a new vista on their life, allowing them to acknowledge more fully the reciprocal nature of relationships, of the need to let go of control. "We Christians . . . have too often imagined the Gospel to be something we could control, distribute, organize . . . In so far as we have controlled it, it has ceased to be the Gospel; in so far as it has come to control us it has become the Power of God."

Oldham's prescription for the suffering of humanity was relationships—as many and as deep as possible—and this idea was catnip to Murray; his passion could hardly be contained: "We would hate you to think that we are involved in a stunt of simple living, of excessive asceticism, of hard labour. We are frankly out for a revolution in ourselves . . . a revolution in the lives and homes and relationships and agriculture and sanitation of our village neighbors—no part of life is excluded. How can men accept that revolution for themselves if it is hidden in us?"

Along with the outer vision, an inner vision was taking shape. Relationship extends not only to the Family of the Holy Spirit or to the village of Kareli; it included anyone interested in joining the effort in any way, There was some disappointment, perhaps, that none of their prayer group supporters had decided to join them in their endeavor as members of the "Family," but their enthusiasm for participation of friends was not dampened: "We need books for the library, money for the Health building, and the Community buildings, for poultry and for much else, but we do not think of our friends who receive this letter as necessary donors! We are indeed anxious to have your prayers and your understanding; letters also, involving criticism and comment . . . There is a representative character to our work; it is a shared responsibility, and we happen simply to be at the Kareli end."

Describing the year's events, the Letter tells of their first Quiet Day, led by an Anglican priest from Sri Lanka and of the "Blessing and Hallowing" of the Chapel by Bishop Robinson in early December.

Tucked unobtrusively into the sequence of events is one more highlight of that year, 1954. As Christmas approached, Heather Sandeman again had arrived with the children—this time not to visit, but to stay. She had been invited to join the new little community; her desire was to be with them as well. "Much to our joy," they wrote, "the Family ceased to be the Rogers family; this letter therefore comes from the three of us."

The change was not insignificant. "The three of us": a new capital-F joint Christian Family was now to be distinguished, it seemed, from the more "narrow" small-f biological family. Mary and Murray were members of both, the children belonged to the small-f family, and Heather had become a member of the capital-F Family. The Letter was signed: "Yours sincerely, Mary and Murray Rogers, Heather Sandeman."[28]

And how was this complicated arrangement to be lived out? In closing the Letter, perhaps it was Murray, determined to follow his call and his bliss,[29] who penned the words: "We are not too concerned with mapping out a future." The outcome of the capital-F Family would involve work, prayer, and discernment.

But what of the small-f family? Cheryl, Linda, and Richard, now twelve, ten, and seven, attending school together at St. Hilda's, had grown accustomed to a routine. For mid-year holidays, they joined the overnight train parties with other young boarding students, sometimes with Heather as their chaperone, traveling the vast distance from Ootacamund in the Nilgiri Hills in the South back north to the Ganges plain and their parents. Or, conversely, in the summer, their parents would arrive in the South for some relaxing days together in the hills. There were always invitations to stay with friends, and it was a lovely place, high above sea level, dotted with tea plantations, forests, and cool streams. Often Mary would linger there, while Murray returned to his work. Or Mary might arrive alone. The children loved those days, together with their "small-f family." Linda later recalled: "I think I quite enjoyed this funny little school. We always used to do the colonial thing about going into the mountains. I'm in *love* with mountains. I think my happiest memory with my parents was when we used to go up and stay in a little house built by a really good friend of theirs (Laurie and Kuni Baker)." Cheryl still cherishes memories of those holidays as well: "We had lots of giggles when we had prayers as a family, or saying grace. The three of

---

28. Letter #6.

29. Though in 1954 Joseph Campbell had not yet penned his famous phrase, "Follow your bliss," the phrase is descriptive of Murray's singleminded determination to respond to a sense of call within himself. In Campbell's televised conversations with Bill Moyers, later transcribed into a book titled *Joseph Campbell and the Power of Myth with Bill Moyers* and published in 1988, Campbell explained his choice of the phrase in his description of the hero's journey through life. The phrase was inspired by the compound Sanskrit word *Saccitananda*, formed from three smaller words: *sat* (being), *cit* (consciousness) and *ananda* (bliss or rapture). Though the phrase "follow your bliss" was often misunderstood, Murray came to embrace Campbell's intended use of it and its relevance in his life.

us would giggle, and Mother would join in. Father would get cross! But that never did any good."[30]

But their lives were about to change—radically. These times together, short-lived as they were, would become even more infrequent, and this Christmas, 1954, would be their final Christmas together as a family. After one last summer holiday in 1955, the children would leave India for a proper British education in England.

Was it Mary who insisted that a P.S. be added to that expansive Letter, so focused as it was on plans for the Family of the Holy Spirit? We cannot know for sure. Nor can we know of the long months of prayer and discussion, the heartache, pain, and perhaps quiet conflict stirred in that private decision made for their children. Publicly it culminated in the terse announcement, found in the postscript: "Here are a few personal bits of news. Heather . . . sails on May 15th for the U.K. . . . She hopes to return next year. The children are just finishing a very happy 3½ years at St. Hilda's School . . . Mary returns with them to England by next August to start them in school in September. Murray hopes to follow in March 1956 . . . We hope to meet many of you."

---

30. Interview with author.

6

Impossible Contradictions
1955–1956

> Sovereign ruler of the skies,
> Ever gracious, ever wise,
> All our times are in Thy hand
> All events at Thy command.
>
> May we always own Thy hand,
> Still to Thee surrendered stand,
> Know that Thou art God alone,
> We and ours are all Thy own!
>
> —John Ryland 1753–1825
> The Hymnal 1892

IRONICALLY, THE MEMBERS OF the Family of the Holy Spirit, the flesh and blood of this bold initiative in community living, spent the next year "in dispersion." Despite their passionate profession of the belief that "only through the other person . . . can I myself become a person," there were preparations that would keep them far from one another. Murray, on one side of the world, at first stayed behind and tended the small plot of land "between Bareilly and the Ram Ganga" with a succession of visitors, mostly able-bodied young men who could contribute to the site's development. Buildings were completed and the ground tilled for the first crop of wheat. Trees were planted, for shade and for fruit, and a field planted with lucerne grass for a pair of bull calves, recently received as a gift. "We go to the Chapel morning, noon and night; . . . this [life] is a training ground for finding glory in the common tasks of each day."[1]

Meanwhile, Mary and Heather were on the other side of the world, in England, each separately preparing *their own* soil for what lay ahead. Despite Murray's disclaimer of concern for the future, the two women did have reasons to be apprehensive.

In August 1955, as announced, Mary and the three children, now aged thirteen, eleven, and eight, again boarded a ship in Bombay for the long voyage back to England. Since she and Murray had firmly decided that the children would attend school in their home country, Mary was focused on obstacles to be cleared. Who would care for the children on their school holidays? Where would they go for Easter? For Christmas? With the voyage back to India requiring more than three weeks, certainly it was not possible to go home to their parents. The task of resolving these dilemmas fell to Mary.

For the first year, they were invited by Murray's Aunt Margaret and Uncle Sidney to stay in their home in Middlesex; with Mary in England to establish a temporary family headquarters, the resolution of those troubling questions could be postponed. Mary's first order of business was to enroll them in their respective boarding schools: Cheryl and Linda at Sherborne School for Girls, located in Dorset in the southwestern part of England, and Richard at Monkton Combe School near Bath. Murray would not arrive in England until March; Mary was the home base to which they could return on holidays, as they adapted to yet another new environment.

It was not generally considered a hardship for a boy to be sent to boarding school at age eight in England during those years—years when being strong, stalwart, and disciplined was particularly highly valued. After all, Britain had demonstrated the force of her national character during World War II; otherwise, she might well have crumbled under the assault of the German Blitz. Yet it is not a stretch to imagine that the parting between mother and child was painful, that both Mary and Richard had to practice their best stiff upper lip behavior, as least in public. Had Richard protested, and perhaps he did, it would have been to no avail. In those days, it was not unusual for the family of a young boarding school student to be in India; following independence many British families remained behind, loyally attached to their second home and to the comfortable life style they enjoyed there, while their children were boarded at schools in England. At the time it seemed only sensible: though separated from their families, children could receive a fine British education to prepare them for their place in the world, where British standards and power still held sway. And they

---

1. Letter #7.

were with friends, others with whom they shared vigorous sports on the fields, rigorous study, and firm discipline, backed by judicious use of the cane. Parents could be assured that they were well tended. This way of life was not viewed as odd in any way, but simply the way of the privileged class.

Mary and Murray's lifestyle in India, however, *was* unusual, and word had preceded the arrival of Cheryl and Linda to Sherborne that they might also be a bit odd. As Cheryl recollected, their housemistress seemed to anticipate that the Rogers family could be "sort of half primitive" and to imagine she might have to introduce the children to the knife and fork. When two well-mannered little girls appeared at Sherborne, she was taken aback, "surprised we didn't eat with our fingers!"[2] Cheryl and Linda, veteran boarders, made the transition unremarkably.

For another year, Mary stayed nearby her children in England, at the ready for school visits and holidays. Murray, as promised, arrived in England about six months after their parting at the docks in Bombay. En route, his visits to Egypt and Germany had nourished him, reinforcing his growing conviction that the spiritual life had ever so much to do with the political. Egypt was then deeply embroiled with Israel and its western allies over control of the Suez Canal. In an extended visit to a Coptic monastery in the Egyptian desert, Murray soaked in new perspectives. Murray wrote, "As the whole history of Christian community began in the area of Wady Natrun with St. Anthony, this is a place of pilgrimage for any of us who hear the same call as he did to life in community."[3] One young monk who called himself Father Antonios the Syrian made a particular impression in his depth and personal warmth; little did either of the new friends know that this young Egyptian one day would be called to lead the entire Coptic Christian world under the much revered name Pope Shenouda.[4]

Before England, he stopped in Berlin as well where he stayed in the family house of Dietrich Bonhoeffer. Arriving at last in England, he was bubbling with enthusiasm for all he had experienced on this latest journey, especially for the bonds of friendship—"of common interest and prayer" made with other dedicated Christians, who "are discovering the Spirit's

---

2. Interview with author.
3. Letter #8.
4. Pope Shenouda III served for more than forty years as Patriarch of the Church of Alexandria. Known and respected for his good relations with Islam, he promoted ecumenism within the Christian church as well. He was known for his teachings and writings on tolerance and forgiveness. In the year 2000, he was awarded the UNESCO-Madanjeet Singh Prize for the Promotion of Tolerance and Non-Violence. Pope Shenouda III died in 2012 at the age of 88.

presence . . . in the daily decisions of Christian obedience."[5] He was heartened and energized to find Jyotiniketan's vision of Family reflected in other communities. This was a life embraced by a wide variety of Christians, not just Anglicans. They seemed to be "Family" in a broader sense, through prayer and the Holy Spirit, leading them to discover one another, bringing them into relationship, into connection. He was eager to share it all with Mary, knowing she would embrace it as her own.

Surely Mary too was full of news of their children and their lives at school, and relief too at Murray's safe arrival. She would have shared events with him when the time was right; a keen observer of human nature, she delighted in the little details that would bring her children's routines to life. Singlehandedly, she had managed significant transitions and adjustments, competently, thoughtfully, and without complaint. But she would not dwell on the emotional stress; that was less mentionable, less relevant.

For this brief period, they could share holidays—Easter and summer—with their children. With their father now there, conversations often shifted to affairs of the world. These were months of growing international tension, culminating in President Gamil Nasser's nationalization of the canal and followed by a joint British-French-Israeli attack on Egypt. Crisis in the Middle East was a frequent family topic.

There were family affairs as well. Dutifully, Mary and Murray called upon Murray's ever-critical father, sometimes with the children. Edgar Rogers had remarried after the death of Murray's mother. Kathleen, his new wife, was thirty years his junior, a schoolmate of Murray's sister, Olive, presumably selected for her potential to care for him well into his old age. But, alas, poor Kathleen had suffered a stroke and died well before him. Their visits to him were unpleasant. Linda recalls her grandfather's loud warnings that he had spent his fortune living in hotels for years and certainly would have nothing to leave to any of them. And to Murray, who generally wore his priest's cassock wherever he went, Edgar would roar, "And why, in God's name, are you wearing that long frock?!"[6] Even Mary grew disgusted with his behavior; their visits grew perfunctory.

For Murray, there was also work to be done. As they remained missionaries under the aegis of C.M.S. and received regular financial support, he needed to report to superiors in London. Running the risk of their censure, fresh from Egypt, he brought the force of his personality to share his dismay at the use of British military power in that part of the world. Were not England's actions simply a reassertion of its domineering past to protect

---

5. Letter #8.
6. Interview with author.

its own economic interests against poorer nations? With or without their approval, as a member of C.M.S. he fired off an outspoken letter of protest to Lord Mountbatten, who had coordinated naval operations in the joint invasion with France and Israel. Murray later recalled Max Warren's exasperated reaction to his renegade spirit: "Murray, you are the *limit!*"[7]

At the same time, he conveyed his vision for the Family of the Holy Spirit, sharing his elation that Jyotiniketan was part of a wider Christian vision. With Max Warren still at the helm, Murray's hope that they would continue their support—spiritual as well as financial and practical—was not disappointed. C.M.S. was eager to support his work, unorthodox as it was. Indeed, they found him so persuasive that C.M.S. agreed not only to continue their support of him and Mary, but to include Heather as a third missionary. Their allowance would be larger.

He also met with a remarkable young man, John Watson, who also was caught by the contagion of Murray's spirit and enthusiasm. Agreeing to join them in Kareli "as a member of the Family," John, both a medical doctor and an Anglican priest, seemed to be the answer to prayer, a person who would enhance their work in the villages. "For this sort of life and work you cannot advertise," they wrote, "you cannot even ask people to consider coming; you simply have to pray and wait. For these past years we have been doing a fair amount of both, and we believe John is the answer."[8]

But much as he relished his warm welcome to England and his reunion with Mary, Murray needed to be on the move, taking action. Though heartened by his visits to Christian communities, he was deeply alarmed by postwar hardship in Europe. Everywhere he saw evidence of refugees, hunger, and human suffering. Following the summer holidays, he was off again, making new contacts for his Miss-a-Meal Fellowship in England with friends in Berlin. With his connection to C.M.S. affording him entrées, he continued to Switzerland to visit the Sisters of Grandchamps and to France to stay with the Brothers at Taizé and meet with the founder of that ecumenical community, Brother Roger Schütz. And finally to two communities founded by the Roman Catholic, Charles de Foucault, the Little Brothers and the Little Sisters of Jesus. Inspired by their commitment to the poor, their dedicated spiritual disciplines, and the contagious spirit of their communities, he reflected on their own spiritual "Family" as part of a larger web: "Superficially, this little community may look very individualistic, curiously unlike the usual type of Christian service in India, the idea of a few slightly mad enthusiasts; [but] these experiences outside our own little world have

7. Interview with Trapnell.
8. Letter #8.

made us more convinced than ever that we are one small and very immature part of a vast, interlocked response to God which Christians of many countries and traditions are being called to make. The responses are as varied as could be but we have all heard the same call."[9]

Murray, of course, was anxious to return to India, and he arrived back in Kareli alone, energized to bring his vision to reality. After so much waiting, so much confusion, everything seemed to be falling into place. There was much work to be done.

Mary's time of return to India came only when she felt enough at ease, some six months later, knowing her children would be well tended. For the time being, their substitute family in Britain would be the Martins, family friends who lived in Scotland. The Martins too had lived in India; they had enjoyed holidays together, hiking in the mountains. They were well known to the children. Granted, their home in Scotland was a good distance from their schools, but for now, it seemed a good accommodation. As Mary returned to her husband and to the mission they were to share, her children were never far from her mind. How torn her mother's heart must have been as she again boarded a ship for India, this time alone.

Such was the point and counterpoint between Mary and Murray in these years: Mary, from near or afar, attentive always to the small-f family, while Murray, irrepressible and uncontainable, ventured into the world, meeting people, seeking ways to support and enhance the large-F Family, always in the service of God's call. In that Letter again we hear Murray's voice, speaking for her and for Heather as well. When finally they were reunited in India and he could share his impressions and convictions with them in person, his words soon melded into their words, and all three embraced the vision. The small gifts given to him on his visits became *their* gifts: a little basket from Upper Egypt, a picture of Charles de Foucauld, an embroidered cloth from an Arab refugee camp in Jordan, a little cross from a Rumanian monk and others; all would be treasured over the years as "sacraments of unity" with other Christian communities.

But soon betwixt the point and counterpoint would be Heather. From two to three. From a married couple to a married couple plus one. And, God willing, more would join them. Dr. John Watson could make four.

Now what lay ahead? Could their vision of Family become a reality? What would be their "sacraments of unity" with one another? And what would be their stumbling blocks?

9. Letter #8.

7

Heather Sandeman: "One of Us"

> Have you not heard his silent steps?
> He comes, comes, ever comes.
>
> Every moment and every age, every day and every night
> he comes, comes, ever comes ...
>
> In sorrow after sorrow it is his steps that press upon my heart,
> and it is the golden touch of his feet that makes my joy to shine.
>
> —Rabindranath Tagore

AND WHAT OF HEATHER? She, too, during this time, was preparing for her new life as an integral part of the Family. She had departed by ship in May to enjoy a holiday with her family in Scotland and to spend time in spiritual discernment. Her challenge was daunting as well. Was she truly prepared to make a lifetime vow and to live in community with Mary and Murray and unknown others who, it was hoped, would also join them?

But first, it must be asked, "Who is Heather?" Over and over again for more than fifty years, friends and acquaintances, puzzled, posed that question. Each time it was asked, the answer from Mary and Murray was simply, "Heather is one of us, one of the community." Often, Heather's gentle, soft-spoken manner and her natural reticence seemed a disincentive to further questions, but with patience and persistence, Heather would allow herself to be known. For those who knew her, her quiet attunement to God's "silent steps" reflected Tagore's radiant reflection that serves as an epigraph for this chapter.

It is significant that she began her life in India. She was born in 1923 to a Scottish military family in Peshawar, near the Afghan border, in what is now Pakistan. The second child of three, Heather recalled a happy early life, with early morning pony rides and the arrival of a little brother. Her father would often take her and her sister Armine into nearby villages where the sounds of Urdu and Pashtu became familiar and where she began to relate strongly to the poor. As her devoted niece Elizabeth wrote,

> Her parents were atypical of many of their generation, preferring to spend free time not at the club, but as a family picnicking in the hills or playing in their homemade boat on the lake. Heather connected the love of her parents with the love of God and the enjoyment of creation; in her words, "God made the sky, the clouds, the great trees, the smell of pines and the dew on lupine leaves." Even at this early age she remembered her parents instilling the idea that God cared for those in difficulty. She determined that she was going to be friends with poor people when she witnessed a young boy being brought to the doctors with lockjaw too late to be saved.[1]

Sadly for Heather, when she was eight, she and her sister were sent back to Scotland to attend school. Devastated to leave India and her family, she hated the school that was run by the two elderly ladies who had also been her mother's teachers. She was one of just a handful of boarders. "It was a disaster,"[2] she said.

When her mother became ill with cancer, the entire family returned to Scotland. Heather recalled that her mother gave her a gift when she was eleven, as she was being confirmed in the Scottish Episcopal Church. It was a small book assuring her that "Jesus would always be near if she belonged to him."[3] For an anxious child, as Heather understandably had become, those words were precious assurance and comfort.

At seventeen, just before she entered St Andrews University, her mother died. For Heather it was another disaster that she managed by throwing herself into her studies in French and German and pretending to her friends that nothing at all was amiss. Always she prayed that Jesus was with her. Always within her was the longing to return to India, where life had been so happy.

1. Elizabeth Robin, funeral tribute, 2010.
2. Interview with author.
3. Ibid.

Upon graduation, in the midst of the war, Heather joined the FANYs.[4] Those were the groundbreaking days of the earliest computers, and Heather was trained in the crucial top-secret work of decoding enemy radio signals. Dispatched to Ceylon, she recalled the routine of working nights, sleeping during the day, of life in a secluded camp in the hills near Kandy, the ancient capital. Nearby in the Botanic Gardens was the headquarters of Lord Mountbatten, where he was to oversee the recapture of Burma from the Japanese. Particularly vivid in her memory was the night a message came though to a friend working next to her. Not in code, it was a desperate call for help from a soldier—hungry, with nothing to eat, nowhere to go in some distant war-torn location. It was none other than her friend's fiancé, calling for her. Thousands of miles away, there was nothing the woman could do to help.[5] Might Heather's keen recollection of this occurrence have been linked to her own helplessness at learning of the death of *her* intended in the war? Perhaps, but, if so, it was not Heather's way to dwell upon her griefs.

Following the war, searching again for a way to return to Asia, Heather was on a train from Scotland to London. Her ears perked up as she overheard a nearby conversation about Afghanistan. Joining in, she learned there was a family in Kabul who needed a teacher for their child. She followed up and was hired by the Squire family to share their household, while the father served as the first secretary of the British embassy. Soon thereafter Sir Giles Squire would become the British ambassador. "That train ride changed my life," said Heather. Returning to the part of the world she loved, she found a renewed sense of "being in God's hands."[6]

Heather was an energetic young governess and teacher, as ready to ride horses and to ski as to give school lessons to the children. The children's mother began each day with a half hour of silent meditation. Invited to join her, Heather acquired a lifetime practice of starting each day in silence, listening to God.[7]

After nearly four years in Kabul, Heather returned to her father's house in Scotland and resumed her teaching there. India was still her heart's desire, and it was not long before that desire was fulfilled with a contract to teach in the Nilgiri Hills of South India at St. Hilda's. Again she knew the happiness of

---

4. FANY (First Aid Nursing Yeomanry) was a volunteer women's military organization in Britain, founded in 1907. In World War II its members served in various capacities and in several theaters of war; today it has been renamed Princess Royals Volunteer Corps, but it is still best known by its original name. Its members still call themselves FANYs.

5. Interview with author.

6. Ibid.

7. Robin, funeral tribute.

being able to "go off in any direction in the woods for a picnic" and the sense of safety that she felt in India. She enjoyed her work, despite the low pay, which was "just enough to get along." To augment her funds she served as a chaperone for students on their long train rides home at the "end of term." That was also a way to visit different parts of India, and she often found herself in distant cities, staying in the elegant homes of the boarding students. Heather especially remembered one "very beautiful, unselfconscious, grey-eyed Muslim girl from a princely family in Allahabad" at whose home she stayed on one such trip.[8] But perhaps the most serendipitous assignment for Heather was to escort the school party, including the Rogers girls, home for a holiday. Boarding yet another life-changing train ride, Heather was stocked, as usual, with enough food for her all young charges and herself for the two-day, three-night journey. But this was not business as usual; this time she was invited to stay for the holidays. Already, of course, her friendship with Mary was well established; how drawn she was—and even a bit envious—to Mary's tales of living in Gandhi's ashram and in a Hindu joint family. She enjoyed Mary's children as well; she had taught both Cheryl and Linda. And four-year-old Richard? She remembered him from his very first day at St. Hilda's, his gregarious and charming self-introduction: "How do you do? I'm Wichard Wogers!"[9] When the invitation from Mary and Murray arrived, she accepted eagerly, with curiosity, but without expectation. "Somebody had told me they were starting a conference center, so I thought, that's not my line. And then I found, of course, [something] quite different."[10] Here, at last, was what she had longed for since her childhood: the opportunity to live and work among the poor of India. In addition, it was the chance to live with people whose lives were embedded in prayer.

Simultaneously, of course, Mary and Murray had been longing and yearning for others to join. Attracted both by their vision and by their flexibility, their openness to move as the Spirit beckoned, Heather still had doubts about making a lifelong commitment. Together they prayed and pondered. She recalled,

> The very nice bishop, Mr. Robinson from Allahabad, who was Murray's bishop for that part of India—he came, and I remember we had a retreat with him, and talked about it. He was very strong. He said, "I don't think you should take any promises because Mary and Murray have children, and if they don't settle down . . ."—and I knew that, but you know, it came home to me,

8. Interview with author.
9. Interview with author.
10. Interview with Trapnell.

that we must just go—step by step together, and he said, "I think that's the best way."

And I've always felt that—that in intention, we all, both they and I, felt it would be for life. But we also knew quite clearly that the children came first, and if they weren't happy, and hadn't got places, and they couldn't come to India for any reason, then they would have to go, leave India. And then I would have left them and started somewhere else on my own . . . [11]

Thus it was that Heather became part of the Family of the Holy Spirit. She would spend her first four months in Kareli, helping out at the work camps, wandering into the village with Mary, and joining in the daily worship. "Why I joined," Heather explained, "was that I very much wanted the daily worship. Murray had come and celebrated communion at the school when they'd been in the hills to see the children, once a year. I thought that he did it in a way that was really meaningful. And so, immediately that was our pattern." For Heather it was all enjoyable: "Having Mary, and they having lived in a village, in a way I felt secure that one wasn't putting one's foot in it in any way."[12] Even in those few short months before she sailed for England, she had begun to learn Hindi and Urdu, the two local languages.

With Mary planning a long stay in England to get the children settled in school, Heather would have the opportunity for an extended visit with her family as well. Already she had been four and a half years in India; never had it been her plan to join a religious community, even the most flexible. Happy as she was with Mary and Murray so far, the shift from professional contracts to a new and perhaps lifelong "Family" commitment gave her pause.

Thus, while Mary was preparing the way with her children, Heather was in Scotland with her family, picnicking in the hills, preparing the way inwardly to embrace a different Family. There were weeks in solitude as well, spent in a convent in worship, in silence, in prayerful discernment. Members of her family recall that this was not an easy choice for Heather, that the time of discernment was painful.[13]

But at the end of the time, she did not falter in her decision, and she was ready to return to India ahead of Mary. Along with her spiritual preparation, she needed practical preparation as well. Heather explained, "I realized to go among poor people and not speak their language . . ." would be useless. So before returning to Kareli, she enrolled in language school,

11. Ibid.
12. Ibid.
13. Robin, funeral tribute.

immersing herself in the study of Hindi and Urdu. Other practical matters needed attention. Financially, Heather had no resources, and now no means of support. Yet hearing that she would be considered a missionary by C.M.S. did not please her: "I didn't want to become a missionary . . . or to change anyone's religion." She recalled what she had learned from her father: "He was in the Indian Army, and he respected the Muslims. I remember them getting out of the bus and praying . . . It had never occurred to me that we were in any way superior . . . So I thought, well, missionary societies . . . that wouldn't be me. I wouldn't be honest to do it." Nevertheless, she agreed to sign on as "a local connection, or something," explaining, "I think C.M.S. realized they'd like to give more support to Mary and Murray in this way. And so they gave me the money, too, though I can hardly say I was a missionary!"[14]

At least for the time being, the practical matters were settled; the spadework was done. In November 1956, soon after Mary's arrival from England, Heather joined them in Kareli. The Family of the Holy Spirit was no longer in "dispersion," but together. Their work could begin in earnest.

---

14. Interview with Trapnell.

8

Lighting the Lamp of Jyotiniketan
1957–1958

> The spirit of light, never-born, within all,
> outside all, is in radiance above life and mind,
> and beyond this creation's Creator.
>
> —Mundaka Upanishad

INDEED, THERE WAS MUCH work to be done. It was, as they wrote, "a pretty hard and disciplined life together."[1] But always the work was guided by their sacraments of unity, their days and nights infused with a sense of "a light, shining in the darkness."[2] By August of 1957, their own small lamp, "burning all night near the roadside and visible to the wayfarers and cart travelers passing in and out of the village," was a "pointer" to a new name. To them the name "Family of the Holy Spirit" had begun to feel "too grandiose; . . . for our Hindu and Muslim neighbours it was simply a puzzle." Their new name, Jyotiniketan, meant "Place of Light." "We discovered," they explained in their eighth Letter, "in the Sanskrit there were two words for light, created light and uncreated light." *Jyoti*, uncreated light, "refers not to the sun or indeed to any form of light made by God or man," but to the Eternal. Therefore it followed, they continued—perhaps to reassure themselves, as well as their friends, that they were not wandering too far afield—, "Uncreated Light" could "properly only be used of Jesus Christ, our Lord."[3] And *ketan* meant place or abode. The new name seemed less presumptuous. "It made us feel just sort of little, little beings in the shade of Jyotiniketan—a

---

1. Letter #10.
2. John 1:5.
3. Letter #8.

bolt of light."[4] For them and their Christian friends, Jesus Christ was the hidden meaning, while for their neighbors, Jyotiniketan carried more familiarity and hospitality than the baffling "Family of the Holy Spirit." Hindu and Muslim friends seemed comfortable with the change, "and they began to come, inquisitive and wondering..."[5]

It was just what they had prayed would happen. Yet so much was at stake. The vulnerability and trepidation Murray felt with some of those early visits were intense:

> This [Hindu] man came; he had heard that some Christian people were living the life of an ashram, and he wanted to know a little about it. And he said, "Please, I just come, I like to come and sit in silence with you." And I really almost panicked, because you see, that's just like typically Hindu. He didn't want to ask me any questions. He just wanted to sort of take my temperature down there [pointing at his heart]. It's an awful thing! We sat in silence for a half an hour, maybe an hour. Then the man got up, and bent over very reverently in front of me, did *namaste*, said, "Thank you very much," and walked away. It's difficult enough to find the words to use, but when you have to [communicate] without using any, then you see, you're completely in the hands of God, which is no doubt very blessèd, but not entirely comfortable [laughs]. You like to keep a *little* control on things![6]

Without words, without questions to answer, with no access to his usual verbal panache, Murray was forced to be present at quite a different level.

It was 1958 when the word "ashram" first appeared in one of their Letters. Undoubtedly, that use of a Hindu term caused a stir amongst their Christian friends. What *were* they doing? To distant observers it may have seemed a sudden shift; in reality it was an acknowledgement of a deeper, slower movement within them and amongst them. Murray speaks of this gradual shift:

> Way back in Sevagram, Mary and I were speaking together about a way we might follow. What other way could we be [in India] as western Christians who wanted to live a Christian life? We were clear that the Christian life [we had encountered] wasn't being [truly] lived. We'd *got* to find another way.
>
> Then we discovered that for Hindus, for as long as history had ever been recorded in India... [the ashram] always had as a

4. Interview with Trapnell.
5. Ibid.
6. Ibid.

source some holy man or holy woman, who simply was wanting to love God more. Nothing else. People didn't set out to start an institution; they set out to love God more, and the thing had just happened. They lived very simply, and everybody joined in the work. It paid just enough to keep alive, and they all contributed to service, not the master necessarily, or the guru, but the disciples who were there to have a deeper drink of God. And traditional deep Hindus were never there to do anything. They were there simply to learn, to listen to their guru, and to listen to God . . . It didn't need a lot of money, because you just built little huts, and it was always understood—way, way back, six thousand years ago, that when the guru departed this life, crossed to the further shore, then if God raised up another person, it would continue. But normally it didn't. There was nothing to leave behind, because it just went back to the earth, or the mud . . .[7]

Echoing in their language as they interacted with Hinduism were strains of Quakerism: ordinariness, simplicity, listening, friendship. Surrounded and enfolded as they now were in the creative genius and living examples of Laurie and Kuni Baker and Marjorie Sykes, how could they not be affected?

Day by day, they were swimming in the calm, clear waters of Laurie and Kuni's Quaker spirituality. Quakerism was present in the physical layout of Jyotiniketan, in the simple, local materials, in the respectful way Laurie interacted with the local people. And it surrounded them in the deepening bonds of personal friendship nurtured with visits to the Bakers' home in the mountains.

Marjorie Sykes' strong, gentle Quaker faith had been a constant force in their lives since Sevagram. It was there, of course, that Mary and Murray had met Marjorie. More than a decade older than the young couple, her experience in India ran very deep. Yet there were certain parallels between them. Like Mary, Marjorie Sykes had graduated with first class honors from Cambridge. Soon after, in 1928, she had arrived in India to teach at a girls' school in Madras. Drawn to the Indian way of life, she became fluent in Tamil and soon was the principal of the school. It was there in Madras that her own spiritual evolution led her to join the Quakers. In 1939 she had been invited to become a part of Santiniketan, the experimental educational center of Rabindranath Tagore; it was at Santiniketan that she met and became friends with Charles Freer Andrews, the remarkable teacher and intimate friend of Gandhi who had so inspired Murray back at Westcott House in Cambridge. By the time Mary and Murray met Marjorie, she had

7. Ibid.

spent several years after Andrews' death holding the Andrews Memorial Chair at Santiniketan while writing his biography. One can only imagine the delight Murray and Mary experienced in their friendship with her at Sevagram, where she then served as Principal of Gandhi's Basic Education program. Not only did had she known well the beloved C.F. Andrews [Deenabandu]; she had known his mentor and friend Gandhi as well. How remarkable that this slight English woman, born of a middle class family in the coal-mining district of South Yorkshire,[8] would find herself in the midst of this constellation of brilliant spiritual stars: Rabindranth Tagore, C.F. Andrews, and Mahatma Gandhi. Despite Murray's painful disagreement with her over Sevagram's educational philosophy, their friendship endured. With her as a continuing mentor, the reflected light of those great men infused Jyotiniketan, and Marjorie's Quakerism seeped into their way of life. Her universalist perspective was articulated in her writings: "Early Quakers, Fox and Penn and Barclay and Penington . . . were sure that the same Inward Light which guided them also shone in the hearts of 'Heathen, Turk and Jew'; that the 'true ground of love and unity is in the Light and the Spirit'; that the humble, meek and merciful 'are everywhere one religion' no matter what 'outward livery' of religion they may wear."[9]

And what of the simplicity for which Quakers are known? Marjorie's understanding of simplicity was far from simplistic; rather it plunged quickly into unitive consciousness:

> Simplicity is not a negation; it is not a turning away from the rich complexities and relationships of this most marvelous world; rather it is the single eye which sees within this infinite diversity a deep and sustaining harmony . . . The simplifying dynamic, the simplifying energy, which helps us to know in what direction we should go is a commitment and a focus . . . I think that Jesus was asking us to shape our lives by the controlling purpose of the rule of God . . . to see how our lives fit into the real pattern and purpose of the life of the world . . . This is where the call to simple living does fit right into the whole question of the desperate needs and suffering in so many areas of the world. It is only as we learn to be real stewards of our share of the riches of the universe . . . that we can help toward preserving the wealth of the world for all its inhabitants.[10]

---

8. Dart, ed., *Transcending Tradition*, xi.
9. Ibid., 61–62.
10. Ibid., 5, 7.

All through their time with the Choudhri's joint family in Raisalpur, through their dark days of uncertainty in Allahabad, unable to see how *their* lives fit into the real pattern and purpose of God, Marjorie was there, prayerful and supportive in their waiting.

It was not easy then, nor was it easy as they began their life in Jyotiniketan, for Mary and Murray to fully embrace her deep faith. Her life reflected her belief: that "true simplicity is a light-hearted freedom from the anxiety that 'looks before and after and pines for what is not.'"[11] Even as they bravely began to use the word "ashram," distancing themselves from the traditional Christian missionary movement, Murray later admitted, there was fear: "To begin, I think we were still, yes, tarred with the western brush. It took a lot of years, in a way, to live and to trust—to trust that one is living something when one doesn't see any results. One feels that one's got to show results, as Christians. That [we're] doing a good thing . . ."[12] Surely it was anything but simple, especially for Mary, to feel she could "shape her life by the controlling purpose of the rule of God," when it meant her three children were growing up in England, so very distant from her daily life and concern. But their job, Mary and Murray insisted, "is to be a Christian family living an ordinary life, doing ordinary work in an ordinary Indian village."[13] Inadvertently, the complicated and disconcerting use of the big-F Family designation had just disappeared. They were an ordinary Christian family; the inclusion of Heather and the separation from their children just went without saying.

They pressed on with their ordinary work. For Murray at this stage it was completing building activities; by August 1957, following Laurie's plans, they had completed their chapel, kitchen and adjacent dining room, an open sleeping porch, and a common room, along with sleeping and living quarters for the community. Their dispensary, built of mud and thatch to serve the medical and nutritional needs of the village was makeshift; plans were in mind to construct a more permanent building as well as a building for their growing menagerie of farm animals: a pair of bullocks, a cow, and some chickens. In addition, the Letter added, "There is one other building we have put up lately, namely Shanti Bhavan, or House of Peace. This is a little bamboo and straw building which is set aside for silence. We ourselves are trying to keep one day a month silent by turns, and we believe visiting

---

11. Ibid., 6.
12. Interview with Trapnell.
13. Letter #8.

friends may well find days of complete quiet in the presence of God a real strength to them . . . "[14]

The heavy labor was supplied once again by members of the Student Christian Movement, who had been regular contributors to the development of the site since the beginning. They worked as well on a village road. "Certainly our neighbours saw for the first time what 'the gift of labour' means, and it was with difficulty that they could believe our student friends were not paid!"[15] Thus, much was accomplished in the warm relationship and sense of adventure shared between the students and the community: labor willingly exchanged for physical and spiritual nourishment. And, in addition, together they were demonstrating for their Hindu and Muslim neighbors what Christian community was all about. This too was part of their work.

Then there was the project to construct a Persian Wheel. The ancient Persian Wheel, used widely throughout northern India before electrification, employed a rope-pot system of lifting water from open wells. Powered either by humans or animals such as oxen, it could provide water for irrigation of their crops, which now had all the variety of a small farm: vegetables, fruit trees, and wheat. Despite Murray's years at the Agricultural College in Allahabad, he freely lamented his own ignorance: "How badly we need among us somebody who really knows farming and has not to discover each answer by trial and error!"[16]

It certainly was *not* part of their plan to demonstrate to their neighbors just how hapless these dedicated and game westerners were, learning to live an Indian village lifestyle. Only in retrospect did Murray see their frequent moments of defeat and humiliation as a gift. Trying to help build a hut of mud and straw put him in touch with his uselessness at the most basic life skills. He recalls:

> I remember those dear village men—I can see their faces now, who came there by day, and we paid them the going rate, which was diminutive. We were the coolies, we [Western] men. I mean, we *could* press our feet into water and mud. We *could* do that sort of thing. We *could* dish it out into, not buckets, but narrow things to take it to the people who were doing it. But when we tried, picking it up and then [swishing sound] against the wall, to make the wall . . . I can remember the village friends, they were always very polite, but you could see they were sort of

14. Ibid.
15. Ibid.
16. Ibid.

laughing inside themselves. Every single village boy and girl and man and woman knew how to do that. I mean, that's absolute kindergarten! And there were we, supposedly learned westerners, completely unable to make a mud of wall stand up! It was wonderfully good for us, a wonderful blessing. And that sort of thing happened again and again.[17]

Ruefully, Murray recalled another adventure. It was the story of one of their two bullocks, named Arabindo. Already he was familiar with the daily struggle many village families endured to raise their hungry children; the local cows were small and produced little milk. With high hopes for agricultural technology, he learned of a strain of cattle that not only could stand up to the heat of the area but could produce lots of milk. Excited by the potential for the village, he was thrilled to learn that a friend at the Agricultural College would send him a bull from this strain as a gift. The bull could then be offered to breed with cows in the village; the resulting offspring would be stronger, bigger, and produce plenty of milk. Murray tells the story:

> Koshi [his friend] put it on the train about three hundred miles away, and there were people on the train who gave it water and some straw, pails of corn. And it duly arrived at Kerali Station. This was a *big* moment, because we were there to bring it; it would become full-grown, it would then help the local cattle and much improve children. It would give much more milk, jolly good from a health point of view, and altogether better, obviously! A great idea!
>
> And so, I met it there. It sort of walked off the train onto the platform, and I had to sign papers for it, of course, and all that. Then I was going to walk home with it—three, three and a half miles. This bull came outside the station all right to the place where all the rickshaws stood. Of course the drivers knew me by then, they knew of this westerner who lived out in the country, crazy fellow. So, they said, 'Ah, you've got a wonderful animal!' Oh, yes, he was wonderful; you could see it. A magnificent creature! I tied a rope to him and began to walk, [trying to pull him along]. Would he move? Not an inch! He put all four feet like that, you know, and just wouldn't come with me. Not an inch. And of course, all the rickshaw haulers roared with laughter, because they probably knew exactly how to do it. And they were enjoying it enormously. I mean, it was good free entertainment without any tax!

17. Interview with Trapnell.

> Eventually, I said, well now, I can't go. I can't pull him involuntarily three and a half miles. This is impossible. By that time probably fifty or seventy-five people were gathered to see this entertainment.
>
> Now we had very dear Indian friends about three hundred yards from the station. So I went there. I explained that I was in a bit of a mess, because I couldn't move this dear creature, and I had *got* to get him home. Might I tie him up in their garden while I cycled home for help?
>
> [So I found] Fidah Hussein at home, and he came to help, looking very serious. I didn't know what he was thinking, of course; you could just discover it occasionally. He checked to see that the rope was safe. And then, do you know what he did? He just looked at the creature, patted it down round here ([pats his rump], and said, [clicking sounds], and he walked along behind him all the way. Honestly! And I came behind on my bicycle, you see, and I thought, *well*, what that teaches you!

But the teaching and the learning did not end there. Murray describes how it went deeper:

> And of course, in the end, people didn't come; none of them brought a cow to be married to our beautiful bull. They saw that if they had such a big, wonderful creature in their courtyard in the village, they'd *never* have enough money to feed it. It wouldn't be able to grow properly, just on what it could pick up around the place or in the fields, where it would be taken day by day. And the other creatures would be terrified of it, because it was altogether too big. So [the whole project] fell flat. Eventually he was turned from a bull into a bullock [castrated], and we named him Arabindo. We had another bullock given to us; and we called him Christopher.[18]

And so the two bullocks became part of the ashram. At least they could be harnessed to operate the Persian well!

Meanwhile, Mary and Heather were coping with the household—the hard work of Indian women—*and* maintaining a steady presence both in their little dispensary and in the village. Their report of June 1958 put it this way: ". . . At home Mary has been kept, if anything, too busy in the dispensary and Heather has advanced by leaps and bounds in Hindi. They have provided some three hundred children with milk each morning except in the hottest months of the year and have visited Kareli and Kargena

---

18. Interview with Trapnell.

many, many times. There is never enough time for such visiting, for Indian friendliness would urge them to sit on till long after Lamp Lighting and chapatti-making should be claiming their attention."[19]

Lamp-lighting and chapatti-making. Praying for others, and drawing water from the well. The spiritual and the physical were interwoven into each day through a sense of relationship. Growing relationships with one another, growing relationships with strangers in work and in prayer. A little anecdote offered by Murray in that same Letter was intended to shed light for friends who had not yet caught their vision: "An hour ago a village man dropped in for tea, and thereby hangs a tale." The story flowed from there:

> About a year ago Mary was called to see a man who had come from a distant village with an appallingly septic toe. For four or five weeks she and Heather went daily to dress this toe and, as much, to encourage the man himself who was worrying how his wife and their five children were going to be fed. Meanwhile we were praying for his healing along with that of others each evening at the time of the Lighting of the Lamp. The day came when, with mended toe, he was ready to go to his own village. For the first time, he came to the Ashram to say good-bye. He was obviously touched by the caring that had been shown him, and Mary and Heather were equally sorry to be losing someone who had become a good friend. "Every six or eight months I shall come back and see you," he said as he left. He has kept his word.

While Mary and Heather tended to the homely, Murray attempted to put words to their evolving vision, both at home and away. He was frustrated at times that many of their friends were confused by what they were doing. Did this promising young missionary pair really believe they could bring Indians to Christ by just living in some remote outpost of northern India? "This ordinariness of our daily life puzzles a number of our friends," he wrote. He expanded: 'How many villages are you working in?' they ask. 'What success are you having? How often are you out preaching in the villages? Do you think this 'simple living' is a more satisfactory way of doing missionary work?' It is not at all easy to persuade such visitors that we don't believe we are here for any of these reasons."

"Our calling," Murray continued in their Letter, "has nothing whatsoever to do with our living a better life than others—do we anyway?—nor with our claiming anything for ourselves or for our religion or getting certain things done. It's life on a veritable knife-edge, for the distance between believing in the Living God and believing in idols is too small to measure."

19. Letter #9.

Only a hint of their spiritual struggle peeks through, leaving the reader to wonder about the "idols" that seem to tempt. Do they include the old desire to capture Hindu souls for Jesus? Or the wish to impress friends with their spiritual accomplishments? To be successful for God? And what of the inevitable moments of self-doubt? It is easier to speak of the details of their daily life—a crop of tomatoes, the Persian Wheel, poultry-keeping. "Surely," the Letter continues, "they have some real importance, but the reason for our existence does not lie in jobs done but in worship offered and in prayer for others—what happens in the Chapel. It is almost impossible to speak or write about this side of our life—it is so thoroughly outside the realm of the measurable, but we believe we have much for which to thank God."

The work of hospitality engaged each of them. An increasingly steady stream of visitors came to the Ashram—eighty recorded in the Visitors' Book from June 1957 to June 1958. Each visitor, each relationship was welcomed; each required time and attention. Often a visitor left feeling spiritually nurtured; many were drawn to stay for extended periods: one "brother" for six months. But not all: John Watson, so eagerly anticipated to augment "the Family" with his skills and a seemingly kindred spirit, arrived in March 1958. Six weeks later he was gone. "It was apparent," they wrote, "that he was not meant for this community and we bid farewell. As we have heard," they continued, "every Christian community has such experiences; that fact makes it no more pleasant when it happens to one's own Community and an embryo community at that. No doubt it is what we all learn from this that matters most."[20]

Indeed they were learning a lot, though often not what was expected. Photographs of those early days at Jyotiniketan show Mary and Heather, two slender western women side by side, dressed in saris, slightly bent, drawing water together from the well. They too were aware of the curiosity Indian neighbors had about them, about their way of life—western women now in Indian garb. Heather recalled that "village friends" would often arrive early in the morning for some medical need. Finding their Christian neighbors still at prayer in the chapel, they would gather outside, to talk and wait. "It was just a very normal thing, that we should have our way of worship—they had theirs, the Hindus and the Muslims. I think it was a great link with them, that [our worship] was very much respected." Heather continued: "At times someone would be selling flowers. And we always had flowers by the altar, which is a place of worship for Hindus. Sometimes we'd find little flowers that had been added. So I think people did go in and out. We also had

---

20. Ibid.

a pump just nearby, so that people of the village could come and get water, which they did, for their mango groves, or for [any of their needs]."[21]

Like Murray, Heather and Mary were aware that they were objects of curiosity and that humbling experiences were to be expected. "It was very open," Heather recalled, "They knew exactly what was going on and [ultimately] that was an enormous help to us . . . Sometimes"—and she laughed—from Fidah Hussein—"we'd get little bits about what we'd been doing wrong. Sometimes we hadn't caught the light at all!" At other times, a rumor would circulate about these strange westerners. Once someone made the claim—scandalous for an Indian village: "They have a bath every day!" Of course, she explained, that was far from true; in actuality there were no baths at all, just the Indian way of bathing: pouring water over oneself with a bucket. But, in Heather's estimation, "[All this] just, in a way, brought us closer to them."[22]

It was a time when each small decision, each gesture, was intended to lead them ever more deeply into Indian village life, ever closer to God. Yet with that intention came the awareness that each step closer to Indian life, each step closer to God, drew them further from where they had begun, from their lives in Britain, the place they used to call home. For Mary and Murray, the inevitable corollary was that each step took them further, in some ways, from their children.

But Mary, whose mother's heart was tied to each one of them, no matter the distance, valiantly and faithfully battled the inevitable through her letters to them in England. Just as there was a clear division of labors in their daily lives, so, in the matter of letter writing, there was as well. Though both Mary and Murray devoted long hours to letter writing, Mary's were focused on private matters—her children and their well-being and other family and friends. In these years, Murray's letters were hardly ever addressed to his children; his role was to project the more public face of the community—to be the primary voice behind their circular Letters, in which the children were barely mentioned, and to maintain correspondence with others in the church. Cheerful and encouraging, the letters Mary penned weekly to Cheryl, Linda and Richard, were mailed with news of happenings in Kareli, and the children's return letters, more or less faithful, told them of boarding school life in England. With a sizable time lapse between the writing and the delivery, the connection could not be expected to sustain a sense of immediacy. It was, as Cheryl succinctly puts it, "family-at-a-distance." There

21. Interview with Trapnell.
22. Ibid.

was a gap—both physical and emotional—that had to be filled, at least for the children. It was the Herfords who filled that gap.

While holidays with the Martins in Scotland had proved a satisfactory stop-gap solution for the children, Mary's gift for forging strong and lasting friendships had yielded another opportunity. Now the bonds of family would be expanded in yet another direction, uniting the Rogers and the Herfords in deep and enduring ways. Again, a question emerges—a question that became familiar over the years—answered again and again with varying levels of gratitude, affection, and awkwardness: Who are the Herfords?

Their connection had begun five years earlier when Mary, traveling by ship back to India with the children, met another young British mother, Brenda Herford, who was traveling without her husband as well, but with three young daughters. Striking up a conversation, Mary learned that Brenda's husband had first gone to India as part of the Indian Army, then, after India's independence, had stayed on in the business of sugar plantations. Like Mary and Murray and so many other British families living in India in that era, Brenda and Harold Herford were managing their children's education with a series of adjustments. Their two older boys were enrolled in boarding school in England; having spent time with them, Brenda Herford was returning to India to rejoin her husband. Their younger daughters, close to the ages of the three Rogers children, were boarding students at St. Hilda's, the very school Cheryl and Linda were about to enter in south India. Immediately the children had bonded on the three and a half week voyage. Fifty years later Richard experienced a flash of a memory: their car pulling away ahead of the Herford's after they all had disembarked; he—spying the Herford girls, faces pressed against the windows, waving good-bye—asserting his four-year old self by sticking out his tongue at them![23] For Mary and Brenda too a fast friendship had been forged, maintained with letters and family visits. Thus, when Harold Herford decided to leave India for good and to purchase a farm in Herefordshire, Mary and Brenda conceived a plan. The Herford's farm, known as Hawkhurst, would serve as their home-away-from-home in England, Brenda and Harold Herford would serve *in loco parentis*, and the five Herford children would include them in their expansive family.

The Herfords were, as Linda remembered them, "all-embracing people." Their home was open not only to the Rogers children; often there were refugees of entirely different sorts in residence—deprived children from London, people displaced from the Hungarian Revolution of 1956.

---

23. Interview with author.

For Linda, who got along well with her new cohorts, it was "a wonderful home," complete with tennis court and regular assigned tasks, like carefully washing freshly laid eggs. Cheryl's memories were similarly positive, though with a lingering shadow:

> It was wonderful that we had the Herfords. From '57 on, they were completely family for us. The mother . . . was very good at coming down to school to visit us as she went to see her own children. It was sort of a big family unit, with good fun most of the time. Going to museums and Shakespeare plays—because it's not so far from Stratford-on-Avon—and parties and balls. But the father was more dominating, a tough disciplinarian for his sons and fairly hard on his wife. I was more frightened of him than anything else. He was a bit easier on us, I think, but then we never got into trouble! But all in all we were lucky to be able to go there.[24]

Although Richard did not share the good fortune of his sisters to have a Herford "sibling" of his age and gender [the three youngest Herfords were all girls], he too found his time with the Herfords "astonishingly good in most respects." Before long, the children adopted a new name that reflected the dual nature of their family loyalties: "We're the Rog-fords!" they would exclaim.

Back in India, Murray struggled with a troubling conundrum. It related not only to his children, but to the entire family and the ashram as well. It could be summed up in a single word: money. As early as 1957 he laid his concern bare in their Letter to Friends:

> Financially speaking this venture is possible because the three of us receive allowances as C.M.S. missionaries. [Our] friends in India itself are coming to see that we mean what we say in being determined to live more in accordance with India's economic conditions and more in dependence upon them [Indian friends]. The day will come . . . when such a Christian community as Jyotiniketan will exist only if members of the Indian church themselves believe God wants it to exist and will see to it that it is able to do so, even to the point of sacrifice . . . We have come to the point of knowing in our bones that this truly terrifying dependence of the . . . Indian church on western resources can only be changed when a radical re-direction is taken in the small situation.[25]

24. Ibid.
25. Lettter #8.

Certainly this conviction was not new; his aversion to what he saw as the corrosive attraction to western money and power had surfaced in the Agricultural College in Allahabad, some ten years earlier. For him, in an ideal world, he, Mary, and Heather would give up their C.M.S. allowances and take the leap cleanly out of the supportive embrace of their British benefactors. But how could they do such a thing? It would be experienced as utterly disloyal and ungrateful by their stalwart supporters in London and elsewhere—supporters like Max Warren and John Taylor, the distinguished and beloved priest who had succeeded Warren as the head of C.M.S. Through all Murray and Mary's changes, exploration, and now this unorthodox missionary life-style, rarely had C.M.S. challenged their direction or sought to rein them in. On his side, Murray faithfully kept up his Anglican assignments, serving as pastor to a small group of Anglican families in Bareilly, the city nearby, and taking services at the local churches.[26] His connection with the young people of the Student Christian Movement who had helped to construct the ashram with their work camps was another such relationship; again and again he accepted their invitations to take part in regional conferences in distant parts of India. Those responsibilities were not a burden; indeed they were a way to nurture treasured relationships and to discover new ones. It was easy to welcome this aspect of C.M.S.; wherever Murray went, C.M.S. opened doors. Yet Murray would gladly forgo whatever help they offered for what he truly longed: an authentic solidarity with their Indian neighbors. His ever-deepening awareness that their cushion of support from the West kept an invisible wall between them was a painful thorn in his side, a stumbling block and source of increasing unease.

But the most troublesome constraint to letting go of financial support was their children. If they truly believed and were to live out what they professed—that their children should be able to choose their own path in life, unlimited by their parents' choices—then C.M.S. made this possible. Life in Britain was costly; Cheryl, Linda, and Richard were enrolled in expensive public schools.[27] There was, admittedly, one mitigating factor to their financial burden. Mary's father, Frank Binford Hole, a generous and supportive man, was still living. As a strong believer in the value of the best education, he was willing to assist with their school expenses, and they accepted his help. But the maintenance of an upper class education and life in England involved further support, and the Herfords, generous as they were, could not be expected to shoulder all the incidentals of the Rogers children at Hawkhurst. Travel to and from India for family visits was a heavy financial

26. Daniel, "Remembering Charles Murray Rogers."
27. Public schools in Britain are the equivalent of private schools in the U.S.

burden as well. And despite all the accommodations Mary had made for their life in India, the emotional cost was heavy. Already the time between their visits was long. Not often, but at times Mary's stolid, stalwart façade was betrayed by maternal pain that Murray as a husband could recognize yet could not share. Giving up life in India was inconceivable; forcing their children to live like poor Indian children was unacceptable; abandoning their children completely to other caretakers in England was unthinkable. C.M.S., with its support for the children's education, made it possible to be in India, for the children to be educated in England, and to maintain at least a modicum of the connection to them they wanted. It was, as Murray later acknowledged, "an impossible contradiction." "Family-at-a-distance" was a part of that contradiction, with conventional happiness never a consideration.

Ironically, there is an exuberance that bubbles through their Letter of 1958. Their reading of Dietrich Bonhoeffer's *Ethics*, no doubt inspired by Murray's visit to his house in Germany the previous year, brought a new depth to their understanding of what it means to live the Christian life. "We have begun to taste the invigorating joy of not being tied down to principles!" Citing Bonhoeffer's inspiration, Murray writes, "Once we aim at arriving at a *state* of Christian life [such as Christian simplicity] . . . where we do not need to be forgiven because we are, we think, being Christian, precisely then we cease to be Christian at all, but legalistic, formal, self-righteous. The snag is that it is so much easier to be 'Christian' Pharisees than to be Christianly unprincipled!" This is a conundrum in which he delights, an opening of his thinking that feels refreshing and new to him. "It's fun to be free!"[28] he exclaims. He could live with the contradictions.

They were encouraged in their high spirits by their expanding network of friends who sometimes joined in their "reading parties"; but of those new friends, one stood out for the constancy and depth of his support. His name was Raimon Panikkar. A Roman Catholic priest and a professor of philosophy at the University of Madrid, he had come to India in 1954 to study Indian philosophy and religion at Banaras Hindu University in Varanasi. As he himself later said, "I was brought up in the Catholic religion by my Spanish mother, but I never stopped trying to be united with the tolerant and generous religion of my father and of my Hindu ancestors."[29] Thus seeking out western monks such as Jules Monchanin and Henri Le Saux [Abhishiktananda] who were "attempting to incarnate the Christian life in Indian

---

28. Letter #9.
29. Panikkar, "Eruption of Truth: An Interview with Raimon Panikkar."

forms,"[30] he learned too of Jyotiniketan and of the married Anglican priest who was engaged in a similar endeavor. Once the five hundred mile distance between Varanasi and Bareilly was traversed and Raimon had met Murray, Mary, and Heather, mutually enriching relationships blossomed. More than nearly anyone else, "Raymond,"[31] as he became known to his new British friends, resonated with the life they were choosing. Following one of his visits, Raymond wrote to them, "Someone asked me on the train what you were doing, [and] I said, 'I think they are doing two things, which are really one thing. They are believing in God. And, to the friends around them, they are saying, through their worship—'Believe in God.'" Then addressing them, Raymond continued, "But what an awful and wonderful thing to spend one's life believing in God."[32] Heartened and touched by Raymond's empathy, they wrote, "This friend understands our calling perhaps better than we do."[33] With Raymond's affirmations, their snatches of self-doubt and fear could fade, and the visionary light of Jyotiniketan could shine through.

Each evening then, as the sun set on another day, following their calling of believing and worshipping, Mary, Murray, and Heather, often with a visitor or two or more, would wend their way to the Chapel for lamp-lighting. There were now too many friends on their list of intercessions for them all to be mentioned at one gathering; the growing ranks of what they called "Associate Members" were mentioned in the morning; other friends in Europe and elsewhere at noontime, and still more close-by friends in the evening. The lamp they would ceremonially light was a modest one; in this poor part of the Ganges plain, only the simplest of oil lamps were available. But at the close of an S.C.M. work camp in September 1957, the students had celebrated their three year relationship with the community by presenting a wondrous gift: a beautiful large brass lamp, brought from south India. It would be reserved, they decided, for lighting on "high days and holidays."[34] And always it would remain amongst their most treasured "sacraments of unity," a symbol of Jyotiniketan—created light representing that which is beyond representation—that radiant, never-born uncreated light.

---

30. Prabu, "Raimon Panikkar, 'apostle of inter-faith dialogue,' dies."

31. Raimon Panikkar wrote under and was addressed by various linguistic versions of his first name: Raymond, Raimundo, and Raimon.

32. Letter #9.

33. Ibid.

34. Ibid.

Jyotiniketan chapel under construction

Heather and Mary at the well

9

Jyotiniketan—A Way of Life
1959–1965

> Nobody was born nonviolent. No one was born charitable.
> The first duty of the nonviolent community is helping its
> members work upon themselves and come to conversion.
> The community provides a system of rules and ways of living that oblige the individual to convert, to turnaround, to
> put the heart inside-out and up-side down.
>
> —Lanza del Vasto

JUST AS EACH DAY ended with prayer, so each day began with prayer. As their embrace of these disciplines widened, so too did their implicit acknowledgment that Jyotiniketan was their crucible for spiritual growth. Their Letter to Friends of June 1959 laid out their "time-table":

5 am rising bell.

5:20 silent worship, morning prayers and time for individual meditation.

6:45 community jobs, sweeping, cleaning out the chicken house, getting breakfast, etc.

7:15 breakfast of tea and porridge.

7:30 distribution of milk, dispensary opens, gardening and farming work.

12 noon Prayer for others in Chapel.

12:30 Lunch.

1:30–2:30 rest.

2:30–4:00 reading, writing, then tea with peanuts.

4:30 or 5:00 visiting in villages, various jobs at home.

6:00 Lighting of the Lamp in Chapel, followed by preparation of supper, making of chapattis.[1]

7:15 supper.

8:30 night prayers and bed at 9 p.m.[2]

Again in their Letter of June 1959, they repeated a comment from their friend Raimon Panikkar: "*Of course* the most important thing that ever happens here takes place before 7 in the morning." How gratifying it was for them when friends understood their priorities. "We do not think we are called to pray," they continued, "in order to get ready for the real work later in the day. Prayer *is* our real work . . . Our responsibility is to put ourselves in the place where we may be made transparent in a way that others around us may discern something of the joy and love of Christ where they do not know Him themselves."

That commitment to prayer was deepened by the withdrawal, practiced by each of them no longer monthly but "once a fortnight," to Shanti Kuti for a day of solitude and silence. Friends were offered the same opportunity; days were set aside twice a year for corporate silence and retreat as well. "We hope to discover a new form of retreat . . . suited to the life of ordinary Christian men and women who are certainly not called to be pseudo monks or nuns!"[3] Their weeklong "Reading Party" was now an annual event, along with their "Ashram Day" featuring a guest speaker and their "School of Prayer," also guided by a visiting spiritual teacher. That year, having worked their way through Bonhoeffer's intellectually challenging *Ethics*, they were visited by Hans-Ruedi Weber of the World Council of Churches. Weber, renowned for his creative approaches to Bible study, suggested they "mime the message"[4] of Bonhoeffer. Especially for Mary and Heather, loosening their British proprieties to let their bodies express their prayer was "a high dive."[5] But as Weber later wrote, "The deepest feelings of love and sorrow are often better expressed through a look in our eyes, touch, or a silent gesture than

---

1. *Chapattis*: flat Indian breads, a local diet staple.
2. Letter #10.
3. Ibid.
4. Weber, *Bible Comes Alive*, 57.
5. Letter #10.

through words."⁶ They found the practice began to open new possibilities for deeper experience—new ways to meet other human beings and God: "We may forget much of the talk and discussion [of Bonhoeffer], but we will *not* forget what entered deep into us through mime and through prayer. Normally in theological discussion it appears to be taken for granted that God created man from the neck up, his mouth and his brain! Hans-Ruedi . . . convinced us that the way to the whole man, including his mind, is . . . to be found through the action of his whole body in mime and through the action of his whole spirit in prayer."⁷

What a revelation for Murray to receive such validation for his own inner experience: that words did not have the last word; that the power of purely intellectual argument tended to be ephemeral. More and more, he accepted this invitation to mime; traditional words and liturgical movements were becoming transformed, along with their celebrant.

In the meantime, both experientially *and* intellectually, they continued to grapple with the dilemma of western support. By October 1959, they had made a decision. No longer would they accept money or allowances to be used *in* India from the Church Missionary Society. They would, however, continue to accept support for their life *outside* India and for the support of their children in England. "This decision," they wrote, "was an obvious step, something almost spontaneous, for you can't be more and more tied up to a country without its becoming unreal to continue to live by money coming from 8000 miles away."⁸ Nor would they accept any private gifts from the West for their life in India.

This decision had followed the Gift Deed from the Rev. Hearsey and his sister, the official owners of the property, signing over to Murray the plot of land on which Jyotiniketan stood. In the year following, a plan was formulated to transfer ownership to a five-person Board of Trustees, all trusted friends and, importantly, all citizens of India: Dr. Elizabeth Baker (Kuni), Marjorie Sykes, Bishop John Sadiq, Frank Thakur Das (an Anglican professor at St. Stephen's College, University of Delhi), and M.M.Thomas. "[They] enter with us into the calling of God for Jyotiniketan," their announcement declared. Then they added, "One of the most perplexing aspects of the present structure of Missions is the way . . . ethical decisions are taken thousands of miles away from the place of Christian obedience; we rather think this is an anachronism . . . in relation to our life here, which must be lived in the

---

6. Weber, *Bible Comes Alive*, 57.
7. Letter #10.
8. Letter #11.

closest relationship to our neighbours and environment if it is to have any integrity about it."⁹

There was real evidence that greater freedom from western entanglements *could* deepen their village relationships. Murray later recalled experiences that drew this connection:

> We really had begun to see how invaluable, what a gift it was, to be vulnerable. If . . . we could be quite sure that in six months' time we would have so much money, life wasn't really so good. I mean, our relationships changed . . . I'll never forget one day when a dear slightly cracked and very elderly lady came along with a grubby old handkerchief, with enough ground juwar¹⁰ for the evening meal and she offered it to Mary . . . She was dirt poor; she couldn't possibly afford it. And I remember after we thanked her and she left, we just blubbed together, because it was so overwhelming; it was such a gift, and so precious. It made us feel when we ate those chapattis, [made by Mary and Heather from the juwar], it [was] a sacrament! [We] were eating the sacrifice of that dear lady in the village, who had done it just because she loved us, poor soul . . . It was *so* precious.¹¹

Without money to give significant tangible gifts, their relationships with the poor were changed; in Murray's words, "love and compassion" flourished: "We were amazed, that we were so taken to people's hearts . . . And if something happened [that was] hard, or somebody was ill . . . they would look after us."¹²

But not everyone was happy they were there. He continued, recalling an early crisis for Jyotiniketan:

> [There was a] demonstration against Jyotiniketan by the organization that murdered Gandhi¹³—especially against 'the temple,'

---

9. Ibid.
10. *Juwar*: sorghum seed ground for flour.
11. Interview with Trapnell.
12. Ibid.
13. The organization referred to was Rashtriya Swayamsevak Sangh (RSS). It was founded by Dr. K.B. Hedgewar in 1925 to promote "the development of Indian society based on Hindutwa—the essence of Hinduism" (Kamat, "Rashtriya Swayamsevak Sangh") and in opposition to both Muslim separatism and British colonial rule. Because the assassin of Gandhi was a former member of RSS, the organization has often been accused of being involved in his killing, which it has denied. Since that time it has again been banned by the government for two separate periods: in 1975–1977, for demonstrating against the government's withdrawal of certain democratic processes, and again in 1992, for their alleged role in the destruction of a 16th c. mosque. Each

... our house of prayer. [They'd heard about us from] somebody from the town and had come up from Bareilly. A demonstration of fifty-sixty people, and they were coming out to shout: "Get rid of these Christians! Get rid of these foreign Christians! And this place of worship! It's insulting Hinduism," and all that sort of thing.

Our neighbors, Hindu and Muslim, said to us, "Now, you keep indoors. Don't try to say anything to them. We'll look after them. We'll look after them."

[But when we saw them coming, I said], "Don't you think we ought to try to tell the police?"

Mary and Heather immediately replied, "NO YOU DON'T! If we can't let God look after this without trying to get force in, then. . ."

Afterwards [when it was all over] we heard that [the villagers told the demonstrators]: "We have our *mustaphs*,[14] we who are Muslims, others of us have our temples, our *mandirs*.[15] Why in the world shouldn't these Christians, who are our neighbors and our friends, why shouldn't they have a place to say their prayers?" And they never came back.

I was so thankful [Mary and Heather said what] they did.[16]

Together they were living into their yearning to find another way. "We had tried," Murray added, the "sort of Lady Bountiful" style of helping others at the Agricultural College. "Giving people things, unless you're very sensitive about it, seemed to us to be taking away their dignity, taking away their humanity . . . We didn't want to do that." "Being vulnerable" was the essential. "It had got under our skin. We knew that we needed to do that not only to express God's love, but to be at all (*real*) friends."[17]

Yet in those early days of Jyotiniketan, little did they yet know how their desire and gift for friendship would utterly transform their lives. Visitors came and went, some staying a day or two, others for weeks or months. Each was offered hospitality, a time to share in the life of the community and in their dawn to dusk life of prayer. It was at the end of a day in the spring of 1959 when there arrived another visitor, this one unexpected. It was a particularly dark evening, and the community had just ended their evening lamp-lighting and prayers. Shirley du Boulay describes the meeting between

---

time the ban has eventually been lifted. RSS remains a powerful force in India today.
14. *Mustaph*: Arabic for mosque.
15. A Hindu temple is often called a *mandir*.
16. Interview with Trapnell.
17. Ibid.

Murray, Mary, and Heather and Swami Abhishiktananda: "The community of Jyotiniketan were ending compline as they always did, standing at the door of the chapel to give a blessing to the neighbouring villages. By the light of the kerosene lamps they saw a strange figure patiently waiting in the mango grove. He was wearing the saffron robes of the *sadhu*, a wandering monk, and the bags containing his worldly possessions were slung around his neck . . ."[18]

Murray adds, "[He was there with] a great big beard, looking just extraordinary . . . I wondered who in the world it was. Well, we gave him the kiss of peace—and that was our first glimpse of Swami Abhishiktananda! . . . We didn't have any idea just how extraordinary he was."[19]

Their friend, Raimon Panikkar, then a professor at the Hindu University of Banaras, had suggested to Abhishiktananda that he should meet them. "He had traveled over seven hundred kilometers from Indore with no apparent notice of his arrival and with little idea of whom he would be meeting," du Boulay continues in her penetrating biography of Abhishiktananda. "He had lost his way until he saw the lanterns shedding light on the little chapel."[20]

Thus began another of the most important friendships in Murray's life, as "the community took the wanderer to their hearts."[21]

Du Boulay's brief sketch provides an introduction to Abhishiktananda, born Henri Le Saux:

> Abhishiktananda was a Frenchman, an old-fashioned priest of Breton seafaring stock, who had spent . . . 19 years as a Benedictine monk in the monastery of Kergonan near Briac [France]. He was bearded and untidy, his charm lying more in his vitality, his gesticulations and his humour than in his physical appearance. His coming to India in 1948 was the fulfillment of a dream that had lingered round his consciousness since he was a novice—he wanted to bring Benedictine life to India. At the time of this meeting he was living at Shantivanam, an ashram in Tamil Nadu he had founded with another French Catholic priest, Father Monchanin . . . [22]

His intention had been to devote his life developing an Indian Christianity through a simple life of contemplation in a Christian ashram, but

18. Du Boulay, *Cave of the Heart*, 168.
19. Rogers and Barton, *Abhishiktananda*, 8.
20. Du Boulay, *Cave of the Heart*, 168.
21. Du Boulay, "The Priest and the Swami."
22. Ibid.

that was not to be. As he dipped eagerly into the spiritual life of his adopted country, he was drawn to visit its sacred mountain, Arunachala and its caves, home to many hermits and *sadhus*.[23] Soon these visits became far more than a simple introduction to Hindu experience. Though constrained by his considerable practical duties at Shantivanam, Abhishiktananda felt himself called more and more to the solitude and silence of that great mountain. He also knew he must meet Sri Ramana Maharshi, the renowned holy man who lived nearby and who was, "in some inscrutable way, 'extraordinarily ordinary.'"[24] At the heart of Ramana's teaching and of the Upanishads as well lay *advaita*: nonduality. Derived from the Sanskrit words *a-* and *dvaita*, *advaita* literally means "not two." "Its central teaching is the oneness of the individual soul with the Absolute . . ." wrote du Boulay. "Ramana taught it through the discipline of self-knowledge."[25] Moving into the domain of mysticism, words do not suffice, but Ramana Maharshi communicated to his followers the nature of the Self not only in the power of his presence, but in words. His teaching declared, "The Self is the center of centers." The Self is "the Pure Mind, free from thoughts." The way to the Self was primarily through silence, but also required "investigation." "Find out who says 'I.' Find out where from this 'I' arises. Then this 'I' will disappear and the infinite Self will remain . . . It is from within . . . Being within, you must find out yourself," he said.[26]

In Abhishiktananda's two meetings with Ramana, he was penetrated to his core. "[He] was so shaken by the Damascus Road experience of Ramana Maharshi and Arunachala, which had lifted his gaze from running an ashram to wanting to live as the purest *sannyasa*,[27] that it was almost impossible for him to give himself wholeheartedly to anything else."[28]

Following the death of Ramana Maharshi in 1950, Abhishiktananda's call to solitude and silence continued to draw him from his life at Shantivanam. In 1952 he lived for a time as a sadhu on Arunachala himself, reciting Mass in the early morning and sitting in silence until "he heard what he called 'the call to total dispossession.'" This found poetic expression in his book, *The Secret of Arunachala*:

> the call to total stripping
> which is the call to total freedom;
> since he only is free who has nothing,

---

23. A *sadhu* is a wandering monk.
24. Du Boulay, *Cave of the Heart*, 168.
25. Ibid., 69.
26. Ibid., 70.
27. *Sannyasa*: a renouncer, a Hindu monk, an ascetic.
28. Du Boulay, *Cave of the Heart*, 93.

absolutely nothing that he can call his own[29]

Yet he yearned for a living guru to guide his deepening path. Near Arunachala lived the Hindu holy man and spiritual teacher, Sri Gnanananda, and in 1955 he set off to meet him. Despite his declaration: "My *sadguru*[30] is Christ Abhishiktesvara. He is the Way, the Truth and the Life,[31] his first encounter with Gnanananda was life-changing: "[Abhishiktananda and his companion] found the guru sitting in a corner on a rickety old couch, unshaven, deeply peaceful and giving out an immense tenderness . . . He found that this first encounter with Gnanananda pierced to his heart, revealing unknown depths, 'living water of incomparable sweetness.'" He knew he had come face to face with the actual experience of realization.[32]

"Totally 'caught'" in his "overwhelming encounter[s] with Sri Gnanananda," he proclaimed that "if that man were to ask me tomorrow to set out on the roads naked and silent . . . , I would be unable to refuse." As their relationship developed, what his earthly guru asked of him was hardly less daunting: "to devote his whole time to meditation without thoughts, forgoing conversation, even reading—if he did this the full experience of *advaita*, of awakening, of realization, would surely some to him."[33] Drawn to his *guru* and the full realization of *advaita*, Abhishiktananda declared, "Is my *guru* not the very form under which Christ presents himself to my senses, to my eyes, to my ears, for my prostration, in order to help me reach himself, in the depth of my soul, where he is, which He is in truth? Christ is more truly close to me in my *guru* than in any memory I may have of his appearance on earth. The meeting with the *guru* is truly an epiphany . . ."[34]

But these experiences felt incompatible with his religious life as a Christian. It was as if he had taken a new lover—mystical Hinduism—along with his deeply committed relationship to Christ and to the Roman Catholic Church. It seemed he must choose. He agonized deeply; his journal entry on the Feast of the Epiphany 1956 laid bare his struggle:

> During these feast days, which I formerly lived so intensely as a Christian, how deep is my anguish. I can no longer appreciate anything in them. Whoever has once had the "taste" of *advaita* on his tongue, no longer enjoys the flavour of anything else.

---

29. Ibid., 74–75.
30. *Sadguru* means true master.
31. Abhishiktananda, *Ascent to the Depth of the Heart*, 31.
32. Du Boulay, *Cave of the Heart*, 125–26.
33. Ibid., 128.
34. Abhishiktananda, *Ascent to the Depth of the Heart*, 139.

> However, as regards the '*surrender*', I have not yet managed to achieve it—the '*surrender*' of my "ego" as a Christian, a monk, a priest. And yet I must do so. Perhaps it will then be given back to me, renewed. But meanwhile, I must leave it behind—totally—without any hope of its return.[35]

It was an enduringly painful path. Two years before his arrival at Jyotiniketan, he had written in his diary:

> No way out of my situation. Arunachala has taken too strong a hold on me for it to be possible for me to turn back. I am not *advaitin*[36] through reasoning or through faith. I am so because of something that is so much deeper. "You would not be seeking me if you had not already found me" [Pascal]. And at the same time [there is] my Christianity, my belonging to the church. '*You want to eat the cake and to have it,*' as someone said to me last month.
>
> I often dream of dying, for it seems there is no way out for me in this life. I cannot be at the same time both Hindu and Christian, and no more can I be either simply Hindu or simply Christian. So what is the point of living? How little heart it leaves me for living.[37]

When he arrived at Jyotiniketan that night, he was still struggling with the either/or/both/and dilemma. Still moving in traditional Christian circles, he maintained his Christian sense of identity—thoroughly Roman. Never before had Abhishiktananda met a married priest; though he and Murray immediately delighted in one another's company, he remained "chary" of them and their strange Christian practices. "At first," du Boulay reports, "when he was staying with his new friends at Jyotiniketan, Abhishiktananda would say Mass standing in his room, wearing the crumpled Roman vestments and using [his] portable Mass kit and Latin missal." In these pre-Vatican II days, he could not share their Eucharist, but Mary, Murray, or Heather always sat with him for his Mass. Yet, as du Boulay notes, "despite their different nationalities and denominations, the two men shared a vision, neither belonging completely to their own traditions and both feeling, as Murray put it, 'blessedly at home with a fellow eccentric.'"[38] Murray's immediate and "overriding impression was of a man who was deeply

---

35. Ibid., 136.
36. *Advaitin*: a seeker of *advaita*.
37. Ibid., 203.
38. Du Boulay, *Cave of the Heart*, 168–69.

authentic, open, and human. He was a solitary who loved company."[39] In Abhishikt or Swamiji, as he was lovingly and respectfully called, Murray had found a man who resonated with his own attraction to a lifestyle of poverty, his yearning to transcend his western mindset, to plunge into a more eastern sensibility, no matter the consequences. Realizing too, that Swamiji's learning and experience were far ahead of his own, he knew he had found not only a friend, but a teacher. For his part, Abhishiktananda deeply appreciated Murray's listening ear, his resonance in their seeking. Drawn together like magnets, both deeply serious, yet given to great fits of laughter, and neither intimidated by the vast distances between north and south India, Murray and Abhishiktananda found ways to meet regularly. Along with other friends, Abhishiktananda was drawn into Jyotiniketan's Bible studies, and he guided Murray in his study of the Upanishads: "Often they sat under a tree studying . . . together; Abhishiktananda would read a passage and say: 'You and I have Christian hearts. What echo is there in your Christian heart to what you've just heard?'"[40]

Mary and Heather were included, of course. For all of them it was, as Murray later acknowledged, the beginning of an intentional "inner dialogue" between the two faiths. "[We were] learning to love the Upanishads, to love the Vedas, to have them flowing through us, not as external stuff used by Indians thousands of years ago, but livingly coming through us now . . ."[41] Mary too was captivated, as she found echoes that reverberated, not only within her Christian heart, but within her poet's heart. As naturally as she had appreciated the western classics of Greece and Rome as a young Cambridge student, so now was she drawn to these ancient eastern masterpieces. While Heather's admirable mastery of the local languages was driven by pragmatism—to better understand and respond to the villagers—Mary delved into the ancient Sanskrit, the language of the Hindu scriptures—its rhythms, its cadences, its beauty—with the mind of an academic. She had found a new intellectual calling.

Running parallel to these inner explorations of Hinduism, the little community increasingly was opening to outer explorations as well. Just a few months after their first meeting with Abhishiktananda, Murray undertook a pilgrimage from Rishikesh to the Hindu Temple of Tungnath, high in the Himalayas. Walking more than sixty miles with a crowd of *Rajputana*[42] pilgrims to Kedarnath, a source of the Ganges, he was deeply moved.

39. Du Boulay, "The Priest and the Swami."
40. Ibid.
41. Interview with Trapnell.
42. *Rajputana* refers to people from the ancient land of Rājasthān, "the abode of

Questions in their Letter reflect his grappling with the great outpouring of devotion he witnessed: "It was a privilege indeed to be the one Christian amid hundreds of Hindu people, so many of them intent on the one thing that mattered, a glimpse of the Presence of the Eternal. Where does such longing, such yearning spring from? What makes the elderly and the young with small children trudge a hundred and more miles over very rough and mountainous country? From where have they caught this single-eyed desire for God?"[43]

Years later, still reflecting on that experience, his questions had become insights.

> Few words were spoken, other than the omnipresent murmur of *OM*,[44] that ineffable sound taken up by the pilgrims and echoed by stream and mountain and forest. There, high up in the Himalayas whose unattainable summits ever beckons one upwards, as also down on the broad Ganges plain where one walks amongst India's poorest people, the strongest influence of Hinduism comes not through concepts or philosophies, not through words and even less through "religion," but through life lived, through breathing a common air, sharing the working and suffering and joys of God's poorest children. The kernel of the faith of the poor comes seldom from what is said; it does not pass from mouth to mouth, from mind to mind, but rather is transmitted heart to heart, at the level of perception, in smile or tears or silence. At that level love is shared and there emerges a "way" deeper than any religious form, whether of ritual or of word.[45]

This experience prompted Murray to notice with chagrin his response to an encounter nearly ten years before with another vast crowd of Hindu pilgrims. It had been in 1950, just before he and Mary left the Agricultural School at Allahabad, when his curiosity led him to the *Kumbh Mela*.[46] Though admiring of some Hindu friends and eager to learn more of Gandhi's

---

the rajas."

43. Letter #11.

44. *OM*: the primordial sacred syllable, also, "so be it."

45. Rogers, "On the Pilgrim Path," 137.

46. Held every twelve years since ancient times, the *Kumbh Mela* is now called "the world's largest act of faith." The confluence of two sacred rivers, the Yamuna and the Ganges and a mythical third, the Saraswati in Allahabad, is one of the sites where pilgrims bathe for purification of their past sins (*karma*). It also is a place where they may gather spiritual wisdom from sadhus. In recent years the Kumbh Mela has grown to immense proportions, drawing more than thirty million pilgrims.

lifestyle at Sevagram, he distanced himself disdainfully from the immense outpouring of Hindu devotion: "I went as a spectator and mingled with the vast *Kumbh Mela* crowds, with the millions of people as they bathed in the river on the auspicious day and at the auspicious hour, led by the sages, holy men, ascetics, *nagas*,[47] and a host of simple people from the whole country. At that time it appeared to me to be a vast fair, an irrational explosion of religious fervour, a display of the human psyche when Hindu human beings in their millions jostle together within an area of six square miles to bathe amid a furor of noise. How sadly superficial and false were my impressions at the time!"[48]

Now he understood those confusing events he had witnessed with his heart, and that change had wide implications for Jyotiniketan's work. Ending their Letter of July 1960 was a statement that may have puzzled some who read it: "God has put deep within the heart of this country an unquenchable thirst for nothing less than the Source of life, the One Whom we know to be the God and Father of our Lord Jesus Christ. India has no need of another *religion*, of those who imagine they possess a superior article to sell in the religious bazaar. India needs more men and women who tremble before God in worship and love."[49]

Though Mary's and Heather's feet did not walk the pilgrim path to Kedarnath, when Murray returned and shared his experience, it became theirs as well. And all of them laid claim to that unquenchable thirst for God.

The spiritual intensity of these years was building. As Murray led the way, Mary and Heather followed, feeding the animals, keeping the *chula*[50] burning for daily chapatti-making, maintaining the clinic, and tending to the never-ending stream of guests.

They were particularly pleased when young people sought spiritual refuge with them; one such visitor was Minoru Kasai, a Japanese student at the university in Varanasi. Across the decades and cultures that separated them, they and Minoru "clicked," and he became a regular, always joining them at Christmas as well as other times of the year. Another guest, Hermien Rozemond from Holland, stayed a full two years, offering an extra pair of hands. John Cole, an American Presbyterian minister, living and working in India under the United Church of India, had also become a frequent guest and in 1961 was given permission by his church to stay with them for a year

---

47. *Nagas*: Hindu ascetics of the Himalayas.
48. Rogers, "Grounds for Mutual Growth," 3.
49. Letter #11.
50. *Chula*: a traditional Indian charcoal oven, constructed of bricks.

to discern his felt calling for a committed life of prayer as a full member of the community. This was a hopeful sign for the future of Jyotiniketan.

But for Mary the most welcome "guests" were not guests at all, but their own children: Cheryl, Linda, and Richard who, thanks to the C.M.S., had come "home" to India for their summer holidays, both in 1958 and 1960. The reunions were both joyful and awkward. Two years was a long time to be apart; both parents and children had changed. In 1958 Cheryl was just sixteen, Linda close to fourteen, and Richard eleven. Their memories contain snippets of delight, frustration, confusion and heartache. Delight in visits to the mountains with American friends and, of course, with Laurie and Kuni Baker in their lovely hideaway retreat house. "Seeing how they lived... wonderful walks in the woods... learning how to type... Bicycling into town from Jyotiniketan for church—"the church service was good," Cheryl recalled. After church there was usually an invitation to lunch at an Indian's home which was "fun and exciting." But for young English teenagers, "the toilets were horrible, the washing conditions pretty difficult." None of the children were eager to join in the daily schedule in the chapel. Silence did not come easily to any of them. Richard's memory was of being rudely "routed out of bed for silence" and of chafing at the strictness of his elders on his holiday. A startling discovery for Linda was that silence was not all that easy for her mother either. She recalls how during Mary's times in Shanti Kuti, the silent hut, she could sometimes be seen slipping out for a little unobtrusive conversation. For Cheryl and Linda, the new family dynamics could be uncomfortable. Though Heather was a well-known family friend and accepted teacher, she was now a constant third, and with other visitors coming and going, their nuclear family seemed to have evaporated. Yet they enjoyed the visitors as well; people like Raimon Panikkar took a real interest in them. Richard recalled Abhishiktananda as a bit more reserved with them than Raimon, who would sometimes kick a ball with Richard. Yet Abhishiktananda was very warm: "He was the real McCoy," Richard observed. For all of them, but especially for Mary, who normally could hold on to her children only through a thickening packet of letters, gathered and saved through the years, the visits were precious and all too short. As the holidays came to a close, they would be off on the train to the airport in Delhi for a sad good-bye. Both Cheryl and Linda remember the tears. Initially, Linda recalled, Richard would start the crying. But in later years, openly resentful of his parents' lifestyle, he resolutely refused to show emotion. Then "Cheryl would set us off... and everybody would be howling." And yet, Linda said, "Mother was, over all of her years, so extremely stoical, so uncomplaining, always uncomplaining ... It must have been frightful for her," she added. Nor was Murray impervious. Much later he confided a memory: waving good-bye to Richard on the train, then stepping behind a column to hide his weeping.[51]

Learning to take the absences more or less in stride, Mary and Murray managed occasional visits to England to their children in England, sometimes together, sometimes separately. Cheryl remembered a visit from their father to their school: "It was a very churchy school with a little service every day. But on Sundays there'd be visiting preachers, so when one's Father was invited, it was quite something! Father preached on the Sunday service, the big service. There were lots of parents who were doing good works—missionaries and all, but, being of an age to reflect, I realized Father and Mother were doing something really worthwhile. So, pretty young, I was proud of them. We were in the limelight because of the Parents!"[52]

Linda too recalled feeling "proud" of her father in his Indian cassock, but less at ease with her mother's dress. From her memories, the visits seem emotionally fraught. "I began to notice they were different," she said. "That normal parents would go shopping in London with their children, and *my* parents turned up in a cassock and a sari! Shopping was not a normal activity for them." Once when her mother had just arrived, Linda, singing in the choir for another service, suddenly passed out. "It was very odd; I'd never fainted before or since; I'm not the fainting kind!" In honor of another visit, she was asked to read the scripture in church. Standing on a box to reach the lectern, she recalled her mortification when the box suddenly caved in. "I was a little plump!" she explained. Indeed, it could be confusing for all of them. Linda recalls being so happily "settled in" with the Herfords that she began to refer to *them* as "the Parents." Letting that reference slip in the presence of her *own* parents brought a reaction: "They slightly took umbrage, and I knew it should not be repeated!" The pain had peeked out.

Richard's emotional well-being was of greater concern. On the one hand, he excelled academically at school. And his parents were proud and perhaps a little amused at his obvious attempts to emulate his father. As Murray recalled, "We had a letter from his headmaster saying 'We appreciate Richard's attitude in regards to the Suez business, but we have told him he must try very hard to be polite.'"[53] But they also noticed that the happy-go-lucky personality of his childhood was more subdued. They were startled by flashes of rebellious anger. There was the time he locked himself in his room, saying he refused to go on vacation with them. On another occasion, Murray was amazed to find his young son kicking at him in rage.

51. Interviews with author.
52. Ibid.
53. Ibid.

Yet overall there were abundant reasons to believe they had made good choices for their children, and as the months and years passed, Mary, Murray, and Heather's commitment to life together deepened. Now in their early forties, patterns emerged in their interactions, many of them reflecting traditional gender-specific patterns. It was assumed, both in the West and in the East, that men were to be leaders, women followers. And although they gave lip service to the idea of equality between them, Murray was the natural leader: the extrovert, the visionary, the patriarch, who relished his emerging role as a spiritual diplomat, a sort of roving ambassador. As the stalwart wife, Mary followed his lead.

She was the faithful mother-at-a-distance, Murray's sounding board, his literary editor, whose brilliant mind could hold names, places, and details of each visitor, each stimulating conversation. For the most part, Heather followed as well. Introverted and private, her quiet voice and gentle manner gave little hint of her steely backbone. Mary and Heather were a devoted team in the practical work of the dispensary and of keeping the community's physical wheels turning. Heather's "can-do" attitude, honed as a FANY and adapted to her life as a teacher, was a welcome addition to Mary and Murray's gifts. "[She] brought her sense of practical service to daily community life—she cut people's hair, made chapattis, dal and the evening omelette . . ."[54] Years later, Mary paid tribute to Heather in a birthday card: "We break a plate, you mend it . . . The white ants have gobbled the gate, you contrive to fix it. Outward, observable, skilful things which correspond to inner qualities of love and compassion and understanding the needs of others . . ." Though Mary's sacrifices were extraordinary, Heather also had forgone time with loved ones to be a part of Jyotiniketan; during these years her beloved father's health was failing, and she, too, spent some months in the West. Often these stalwart women were left behind while Murray travelled. They did not relish being alone for extended periods; at times, when they believed his voracious appetite for new projects was stretching them all too thin, they would join forces in trying to contain some of his boundless energy, which increasingly called him away from Jyotiniketan. Together they were his ballast—the moral weight and practical perspective to test and temper his determination and to keep the little community afloat. Together too they shared responsibility for his emotional needs, never completely met in his warm friendships with men and women outside the community. As the bonds of affection between them all grew, Heather often could provide the empathic ear or gentle touch—behaviors that did not flow so easily from Mary.

---

54. Robin, funeral tribute.

Yet, increasingly their life of prayer together seemed to generate spiritual energy that sustained them, each in their characteristic ways. For Mary and Heather, it solidified their resolve to their chosen calling, to steadfastness in the face of pain or doubt. From Murray it radiated outward, bringing yet more invitations to share himself in the world. Happily for him, these were the years when an impulse towards ecumenism was bubbling in other venues as well. Under Pope John XXIII, the Second Vatican Council had opened in 1962 in Rome, and other Christian organizations were turning their focus to greater mutual understanding and acceptance. The opportunity to contribute to Christian unity, however he could, was compelling. With verses of the Upanishads and memories of the *Kumbh Mela* touching their hearts, Murray put words to this drive, drawing a connection between the unity of Christians, their nascent ecumenical vocation, and Hinduism: "It is this promise and this vision of spiritual ecumenism which drives us forward with such eagerness to hear the Spirit speak from within the world of India. For me it is the 'crude' worship of the masses, the worship which springs from a level deeper than the cerebral, which engages the passion and heart of man, which draws me to deeper longing for the unity which Christ alone can give."

He continues,

> It is to this pleroma, this plenitude, that Christ so often points us through our neighbours and through the depths of Hinduism. How easily and often we Christians have attacked the falsity of pantheism. This country knows the equal falsity of dualism. How frequently we Christians are satisfied with intellectual formulations of the Faith, with a careful balancing of theological propositions, with a neat and tidy pigeon-holing of Christian truth, with a scrupulous respect for human wisdom and prudence. The word of the Spirit that comes to us through a deep and growing contact with Hinduism is this: that God, the Holy Trinity, and the blessed revelation of Himself in Jesus Christ, is beyond concept and idea, beyond the grasp of our minds, no matter how brilliant, beyond our greatest spiritual endeavour. In the Kena Upanishad we read:
>
> > *Other indeed than the known, above the unknown . . .*
> > *that which is unexpressed by speech,*
> > *that with which speech is expressed . . .*
> > *that which one thinks not with thought,*
> > *that with which they say thought is thought . . .*
> > *If you think 'I know well',*
> > *only very slightly, now do you know . . .*

> *It is conceived by him by whom it is not conceived of,*
> *he by whom it is conceived of, knows it not . . ."*[55]

Ineluctably Murray was drawn to carry this message wherever he could. As early as 1958, his connections with student organizations had brought him invitations, happily accepted, to international gatherings in Burma and in Sri Lanka. In their Letter of July 1960 was a report of other travels: "More than once Murray has been away to lead a retreat or speak at a conference . . . Just recently he spent five weeks in the South, one week with Swami Abhishiktananda at Shantivanam Ashram and the rest under the wing of Philipose Mar Chrysostom,[56] a Bishop of the Mar Thoma Church[57] in Kerala. We as a group feel extremely fortunate to have these links with Christians of other parts of Christ's church.[58]

It was yet another good friend and frequent Jyotiniketan visitor who facilitated a virtual explosion in their international contacts. In the same passionate article cited above, Murray paid tribute to Ilse Friedeberg of the Ecumenical Institute of the World Council of Churches in Bossey, Switzerland, though not by name: "A friend to whom we owe more thanks than can be easily expressed has joined our loving and our praying to very many people and to their 'personal worlds.' . . . By her ministry of letter writing we have a part, to our joy and gratitude, in the Little Brothers and Sisters of Jesus, in the Orthodox Churches of the Middle East, Russia, and Europe, in the Communities of Taizé and Grandchamp and in many other communities of the church most generally small and hidden . . ."[59]

The journeys, now by air as well as by land, continued to be reported in each successive letter. They were domestic—to Bangalore (1961), New Delhi (1961) and Bombay (1964)—as well as international—Bangkok (1964) and Hong Kong (1965). Happily, on a few occasions, the ripples at Jyotiniketan were more than spiritual. Here Mary describes the three day gathering at Jyotiniketan of international participants from the Assembly of the 1963 World Council of Churches in New Delhi: "After their experience of hotel

---

55. Rogers, "Jyotiniketan Ashram," 234–36.

56. Bishop Philipose Mar Chrysostom (1918–) Later to be enthroned as Metropolitan of the Mar Thoma Church in India, he is now the longest serving bishop in India. Known as the bishop with the golden tongue, he remains much revered in the Indian church, known for his "lovable-ness, humility and simplicity." http://marchrysostom.com/biography.html.

57. Mar Thoma Church: Based in the state of Karela in south India, the Mar Thoma is of the Syrian Orthodox (Eastern) tradition and traces its roots to the first century when St. Thomas was said to have visited India. It has followers throughout the world.

58. Letter #11.

59. Rogers, *Jyotiniketan Ashram*, 236.

life in New Delhi, our village meeting provided a certain contrast, as you can imagine, but everyone was immensely 'ready for anything.' The group included Père Maurice Villain from Paris, Bishop Oliver Tomkins of Bristol, Pastor Helmut Peters, Bishop Zulu, Boris Bobrinskoy, Professor Van Groot, Fr. Leo Alting von Geusau, Madeleine Barot, and from this country, Swami Abhishiktananda, Banwari Lal Choudhri (our joint family member of Sevagram days), and Sybil Bailey."[60]

Here was an opportunity for Mary and Heather to connect personally with the real people behind the names and stories Murray would bring back to them from his travels. For them this event signified much more than a list of prominent names and titles. These were people they would never forget.

Nor was Mary always left behind. In 1962, with Heather and John Cole keeping the lamps lighted and the prayers flowing for Jyotiniketan (the faithful Fidah Hussein managing the heavy work), Mary and Murray, along with Ilse Friedeberg to open doors, took off for a "pilgrimage." Their first stop was Jerusalem where they stayed with Russian Orthodox nuns in a monastery in the Garden of Gethsemane. Then they continued on to Istanbul, Athens, and Patmos. On that journey, their marvelous visit in Istanbul with the Orthodox Patriarch, Athenagoras[61] remained the most memorable for Murray. Meeting one another heart to heart, Athenagoras seemed touched by the earnest Anglican priest and his wife, clad in their threadbare Indian clothes, paying homage to some of the holy sites of Christendom before visiting their children in England. Having noticed how little baggage they carried, at the close of one conversation, he drew Murray aside. Where, he wondered, were their coats for chilly England? When Murray allowed they had none, Athenagoras, in the manner of the loving father Murray so longed for, said he would arrange for one of his staff to take them shopping for good, warm winter coats. Cost was not an object, and both Mary and Murray would now have coats that would last decades.

While Mary also treasured those moments, it may have been her reunions with Cheryl, Linda, and Richard in England that touched her the most. At the close of that "pilgrimage," Linda was completing her years at Sherborne School. Mary and Murray would be there.

But Murray's appetite to connect with people could not be slaked simply in intimate family connections or even in his warm links with village

---

60. Rogers, reflection.

61. Athenagoras: Elected Patriarch in 1948, he was known for his efforts to bring about reconciliation between the Greek Orthodox and Roman Catholic Church, to end the great schism dating from 1054. He was actively involved with the World Council of Churches and became known for his fatherly leadership and his dedication to his people.

people, where God seemed so present. His meetings with religious people around the world seemed to stoke his desire for more. Never was it easy to decline even one of the increasing number of invitations that arrived. And so the travels continued.

In 1964, Murray was invited to the Bombay Eucharistic Congress as a representative of the Anglican Communion. Afterwards he was moved to share his hopeful impressions of this large (60,000 people) Roman Catholic gathering attended by Pope Paul VI,[62] successor to Pope John XXIII, who had died in 1963. Having warmed to the new Pope's remarkable public quotations of Rabindranath Tagore and of the Upanishads, he wrote, "In years to come we may find the Christian influence of this Eucharistic Congress and of the Pope's visit to be incalculable; precisely because this Congress was *not* missionary work, was *not* witnessing to non-Christians, was *not* trying to convert anyone—[but] because . . . it was concerned with the mystery of worship, of man's being joined to God by the miracle of grace, *therefore* non-Christian friends were drawn and saw Jesus Christ, the Living Gospel."[63]

But of Murray's many journeys in their India years, perhaps those most transformative of all for him involved neither overseas travel, nor religious dignitaries, nor vast crowds of people. They were the meetings, six in total, from 1961–1966, spearheaded by Dr. Jacques-Albert Cuttat, the Swiss ambassador to India, a thirty-year student of the relation between Christianity and eastern spirituality. The year before he was introduced to Abhishiktananda, Cuttat had published *The Encounter of Religions,* with an introduction by Prime Minister Pandit[64] Jawaharlal Nehru. A deeply spiritual man, Cuttat had, in Murray's words, "an uncanny way of smelling out contemplatives and deep spiritual characters in government." He and Abhishiktananda connected effortlessly, and, as du Boulay reports, "agreed to hold a series of theological-spiritual discussions . . . bringing together a group of priests and theologians concerned with the relationship between Hindu and Christian experience." This, adds du Boulay, "for readers of the twenty-first century may seem predictable enough, but this was 1961 and

---

62. Pope Paul VI: As successor to Pope John XXIII, he continued the meetings of the Second Vatican Council. Committed to improved ecumenical relations with Orthodox, Anglicans, and Protestants, in 1964 he met with Athenogoras, the Greek Patriarch. Together they agreed upon the Catholic–Orthodox declaration of 1965, with the intention of greater reconciliation between the two church, whose unity had been broken by the schism of 1054.

63. Rogers, "An Anglican View of the Bombay Eucharistic Congress," 265.

64. The title *Pandit* indicates a Hindu of the Brahmin class who is a scholar and teacher of the Hindu scriptures.

they were pioneers in a field that had been little explored."⁶⁵ It was agreed that all the participants in the first meeting should be Christians, but of differing denominations; later meetings might include Hindus as well. Murray explains, "They were what Dr. Cuttat would describe as 'inner dialogue,'" which Murray, Mary, and Heather had tasted in their explorations with Abhishiktananda: "Unless inner dialogue happens in us Christians—*inside us*—we are in no position to have external dialogue with the Hindu or Muslim who lives down the road . . . " Years later, the passion remained: "It was so important, and I feel it still. Unless we, in our tiddly corner, have learned to love the Upanishads . . . we're not really ready to meet the Hindu [or the Buddhist or the Muslim]. When you meet on the outside, you just sort of bump up against one another . . . and it often ends up in a clash . . . [And] if you operate on the level of a comparison, say, grace in Hinduism and grace in Christianity, then each side is [going to feel they know more or have more than the other]."⁶⁶

Real dialogue, Murray insisted, could never happen that way. These talks then were preparation "centered in the heart rather than in head, in experience rather than in theory."⁶⁷ The first meeting took place in Almora in the foothills of the Himalayas at the home of the Methodist bishop of Delhi. "Their morning Eucharist," du Boulay writes, drawing from Abhishiktananda's account, "took place under an immense deodar tree, 'having as 'backdrop' for the altar the breath-taking sight of snow-clad Himalayan peaks, touched with the light of the rising sun . . . We were conscious of being in the Presence.' They were in the land of the *rishis*,⁶⁸ contemplating the mountains in which the holy men of long ago first heard 'the imperceptible murmur which sounds in the depth of the heart, like the murmur of the streams which wind along the higher slopes, but swelling continually as one descends towards the torrent, until at last it drowns every other sound in its overwhelming thunder.'"⁶⁹

Their commitment to an experiential approach was honored as they each shared how life in India had impacted their spiritual lives. In Murray's words, "We found to our surprise that we each had been personally enriched in Christ by our contact with living Hinduism. This experience of God's gift through Hinduism cut across our separateness as members of

---

65. Du Boulay, *Cave of the Heart*, 177.
66. Interview with Trapnell.
67. Du Boulay, *Cave of the Heart*, 179.
68. *Rishi*: a Vedic seer.
69. Du Boulay, *Cave of the Heart*, 179. Here she quotes from Abhishiktananda, *Hindu-Christian Meeting Point*, 1983.

different Christian confessions and became . . . an ecumenical experience entirely new to most members."[70]

"No wonder," du Boulay adds, "they found it such an exhilarating occasion: they were living with a deepening sense of the ultimate mystery, sharing their most profound beliefs in sympathetic company."[71]

At the close of the meeting at Almora, they drew a few insights. First, "that the Lord is already in India, and we need not imagine, poor feeble creatures that we are, that it is we who make him present."[72] Second, in du Boulay's words, was "a renewed awareness of the gift of interiority that is India's." This came with a profound implication that "the message of the resurrection could have no impact in India unless it is revealed in its essential interiority." The third discovery was about themselves as Christians: that they had met at a level that transcended their own denominational differences. Their experiential method had borne fruit.

More meetings of the group followed the next year in Rajpur and in Nagpur. "Cross-legged in a circle under a great tree," they entered into contemplative *lectio divina* readings of selected Hindu and Christian scriptures, coming nearer, it seemed, "to understanding some of the deepest mysteries."[73]

At that meeting in Nagpur at the beginning of 1964 the group accepted Murray's invitation to meet again later in the year; this time they would gather at Jyotiniketan. Though John Cole had accompanied Murray to Nagpur for the meeting there, this time the women could be present as well. For once, Murray could introduce his beloved spiritual friends into his life at home, allowing Mary and Heather to experience firsthand all that usually came to them mediated by Murray.

Again convened by Dr. Cuttat, it was an event to remember. The little community was stretched thin and a bit apprehensive too at this challenge of hospitality. The Chapel had been readied for worship and heads counted for community hospitality. Accustomed though they were to a steady stream of guests, sixteen for meals at their expandable tables set a new record. And somehow, everyone found a place to sleep, with the Roman Catholic Archbishop Eugene DeSouza and Bishop Mar Chrysostom of the Mar Thoma Church sharing a small, make-shift room. Mary recalled, "As the former suffered pains in his back he preferred to put a mattress on the floor and thus settled himself in the lowest place! Both seemed to survive the ordeal

---

70. Rogers, "Hindu and Christian—A Moment Breaks," 110.
71. Du Boulay, *Cave of the Heart*, 179.
72. Ibid., 180.
73. Ibid., 181.

remarkably well."[74] Describing the event to Friends, they wrote, "We were surprised by joy at the way our friends took the plunge into a life so different from their own. There cannot be many ambassadors," they continued, referring to Dr. Cuttat, the Swiss ambassador, "who have taken a turn at washing the dishes under a pump being worked by a Bengali priest!"[75]

Meanwhile, the mystery of the relation between the Christian and the Hindu experiences continued to be plumbed, and the "internal dialogue" continued to flow within each of them as the Spirit guided them through meditations on the Bible and the Upanishads.

Dr. Klaus Klostermaier, then a young Roman Catholic scholar of Hinduism and active participant, formally chronicled highlights of the event. It was Dr. Cuttat, he emphasized, who "gently but firmly steered the meetings away from being scholarly conferences about dialogue, to actual exercises in dialogue, and who impressed upon all the need to develop methods for an encounter of spiritualities rather than merely to engage in comparative religion."[76] In their internal dialogue, they should be guided, Dr. Cuttat reminded them, by basic principles. "We have to accept fully our non-Christian brother as an image of God," and to acquiesce to the other's cultural and spiritual values, "without reference to one's own Christian values."[77] It was a challenge to apply "epoché,"—to put their Christian outlook "into brackets ... to try to see with Hindu eyes." Spiritual courage was essential if they were to experience what he called "naked faith," when "God withdraws in his very presence." Klostermaier relates Cuttat's charge to them all: "There is a necessity to come to the 'point zero,' complete perplexity, and to feel our utter helplessness."[78] Though lively discussion ensued, the meeting was called back again and again to prayerful "Bible-Upanisad" meditations, reading both as sacred texts "in a spirit of reverence"[79] and surrounded in silence. The deepest sharing was to be in silence.

As their days together came to a close, Klostermaier writes, "the group became very much aware how deep a truly ecumenical spirit was created within our own hearts."[80] His notes reflect the group's gratitude to Jyotiniketan: "Next to God, we have to thank the family and the ashram of Jyotiniketan that we go back to our work with the feeling of being enriched

74. Rogers, reflection.
75. Letter #15.
76. Klostermaier, "Jacques-Albert Cuttat," 6.
77. Klostermaier, "Meeting on 'Hindu and Christian Spirituality,'" 5.
78. Ibid.
79. Ibid., 2.
80. Ibid.

and refreshed in our spirit. The regular programme of common worship of the Ashram was such a vital . . . factor for the prayer-meditation meeting that the report . . . can give only a very limited impression of what those days meant for [us]. We shall remember it with joy and gratitude."[81]

The profundity of these meetings, drawing its members together in rich community and calling them to glimpses of non-dual experience, was seen not simply as a few days of spiritual enrichment. Rather, it was noted, "'interior dialogue' is . . . the real task of their lives in India."[82]

But both for Murray as an Anglican and Abhishiktananda as a Roman Catholic priest, it was considered radical, if not heretical by their religious colleagues and lay friends alike, to read Hindu and Christian scriptures side by side. Du Boulay cites a letter Swamiji wrote to Murray: "Like you I feel a little nervous. Let us be good *advaitis,* and not mind what people may think of us, but go straight on our way, seeing only the 'atman' in everything, and being so void of everything inside that the Spirit may use us at his own free will."[83] Jyotiniketan's Letter of August 1964 gave few such details, but offered reassurance to their Christian friends:

> Such meetings are immediately related to Jyotiniketan's life, for one of the chief reasons why we believe God has put us here is for us, and Hindu friends, "to experience that pre-Christian spiritualities are 'at home' in the mystical Body of Christ." There are some Christians in Asia who are delighted and even encourage the decreasing spiritual depth of Hinduism, imagining that a 'religious vacuum' is ideal for Christian evangelism . . . On the contrary we believe that God and His church need not spiritually crippled souls . . . but strong, deep, believing Hindus who, through spiritual death and resurrection, will discover with us that all fullness, all completeness—including their own Hindu faith is to be found in Christ.[84]

As they, along with Swamiji, struggled with the ambiguous longing and dread of what was beginning to be called "double-belonging": a love of both Christianity and Hinduism, it was their good friend, Raimon Panikkar, who both set a standard for spiritual freedom and brought them to a new experiential level in the celebration of the Christian Eucharist. The first he did by unabashedly calling himself "a Christian-Hindu priest," with no

---

81. Ibid., 18.
82. Ibid., 2.
83. Du Boulay, *Cave of the Heart,* 182.
84. Letter #15.

apologies to Rome. The second came about in his 1965 Retreat at Jyotiniketan entitled "The Eucharist, the Source of our Life."

Coming on the wake of the informal Hindu-Christian dialogues and Murray's experience with the Eucharistic Conference in Bombay, Raimon's teaching, grounded in experience, touched a new depth in Jyotiniketan—despite the decades of Eucharistic celebrations that had gone before. Murray recalled, "He brought to life the Eucharist in a way we'd never begun to grasp . . . showing us that God's desire for us human beings is that we should *be* him, not *like* Jesus, or a little like him in one way or another, but to *be* him. That the body of Christ is really Christ walking down the high street. We know how inadequate we are, but when we go out after Eucharist or Mass, we are again charged with the life of Christ."[85]

Nearly forty years later, Murray still felt the spiritual impact: "When that really gets into you, it's quite overwhelming. It's more than I can really say . . . but I trust, in a deep, deep sense, that's who we are. We're called to that and we're called to live it deeply. So it changed our viewpoint. We weren't interested in being a little ethically nicer, or more charming, or more helpful. We were to be . . . (here Murray hesitates as he begins welling up) . . . it still makes me feel absolutely overwhelmed—we were called to be so empty for him to do his stuff through us."

This new inner knowing took a great weight off them, allowing a new relaxation Murray had never before experienced. "We weren't called to go down the high street or into the village to talk about Christ. We could *live* it. If we had done our inner work, which needed to go on all the time, if that was really authentic, then we didn't have to think of how to bring Christ into this conversation—or are we wrong to leave him out? All those questions that come to self-conscious, dear Christian souls were simply lifted from our shoulders."[86]

Learning from Raimon, reading Teilhard de Chardin, allowing all their work, study, and prayer to fall back into silence, they began to understand and to *feel* Holy Communion as a "cosmic act," part of a "Universal Dimension," transcending them, their "little world," whether in India, England or the entire world, and containing "the totality of everything." In other words, "The Eucharist we celebrated this morning becomes the deepest act men can ever perform."[87] Now their worship would change: "We knew God was offering us the Eucharist every day!"[88] No longer did they have to teach about

85. Interview with Trapnell.
86. Ibid.
87. Letter #16.
88. Rogers and Barton, *Abhishiktananda*, 17.

Christ or even to demonstrate to their Hindu neighbors what a Christian life looks like. "It's true," said Murray, "perhaps for years I was conscious of trying to do that. Then gradually, the trying part, the self-conscious part fell off. And I felt that's what God did. I think at a certain stage I had been very earnest," he mused. "I became less earnest. By the time I really relaxed, it wasn't that I wasn't caring, but the emphasis was more on being transparent, for God to do whatever he wanted to do."[89]

Is it any wonder that Murray found these years "the happiest time of our lives?" It was "when we were most pained by not having the children with us, when they had to go back to England," and, he continued, not missing either the irony or the profound implications of what he was saying, "when we stopped having western money and were going day to day, month to month." Of course, he admitted, "we had security [in England],[90] but for our life there day by day, we had no security at all. That," he repeated, "was really the most happy part of our lives."[91] Jyotiniketan's network of friends was expanding exponentially; soon there would be a second man making vows to the community. C.M.S. had gone along with all Murray's financial proposals and continued to be supportive; in fact, he now was regarded as one of the outstanding priests of the Anglican Church abroad, a rising star, an increasingly high profile member of C.M.S. Indeed, his stature was such that he had been a nominee to be the Anglican Bishop of Lahore.[92] No longer were they struggling to find their way, or waiting for God to give direction. Rather, with learned and spiritually deep friends like Raimon Panikkar and Swamiji and a solid group of spiritual cohorts in the Cuttat group, the mysteries of God and the universe were opening. Closer to home, Mary and Heather felt the contagion of Murray's elation—that they, and now John Cole too, were truly living a life in community. They did not feel isolated in their Indian village, but more and more in solidarity with others in the world who shared their vision. Their children were growing up, finding their way. Everything was coming together in God and from God. They longed for others to catch their experience, to catch their meaning. More and more Murray wrote about, spoke about, and lived what they were discovering together:

---

89. Interview with Trapnell.

90. As long as they remained British citizens, there were financial benefits available to them in England: health care, pension, etc.

91. Interview with Trapnell.

92. In the balloting, Murray was number two. Later, in recounting this episode in his life, his chagrin was not in his failure to be elected, but in how perilously close he had come to allowing himself to be drawn into church politics and its hierarchy.

'Le monde appartient à ceux qui brulent en silence'[93] and it is to that silence that again and again we return. Our particular vocation is not to physical withdrawal from the world; our enclosure is carried with us, the secret, inner cave, *guha*,[94] of peace where the Lord is to be met, to be loved and worshipped. This inner well of silence, so essential to love of God and love of neighbour, is fed from the Holy Eucharist, for there, most marvelous to relate, we are no longer left in our lonely weakness and spiritual poverty but are lifted up 'to share in the light, to participate in the Godhead . . .'

> 'Therefore giving thanks in mind,
> Giving thanks in heart,
> Giving thanks in the members
> Of my soul and of my body,
> I worship thee, I magnify thee,
> I glorify thee, my God
> That art blessed
> Now and evermore' (Greek Hieratikon)[95]

It was all beyond words, but gratitude was their natural response.

At prayer in Jyotiniketan's chapel

---

93. "The whole world belongs to those in whom the flame of silence burns." Murray's article lacks attribution for this quotation.

94. *Guha*: Sanskrit for cave. *Guhan*: one who lives in the cave of the heart.

95. Rogers, *Jyotiniketan Ashram*, 237–38.

10

In Love and Longing in India
1965–1967

Here is thy footstool and there rest thy feet
where live the poorest, and the lowliest, and lost.
When I try to bow to thee, my obeisance cannot reach down
to the depth where thy feet rest among the poorest, lowliest, and lost...
My heart can never find its way to where thou keepest company
with the companionless among the poorest, the lowliest, and the lost.

—Tagore

Together, Mary, Murray, and Heather were called, they said, "not to physical withdrawal from the world." It is true: they were people of the world, deeply interested, profoundly concerned, touched by world events that could stir their hope or despair. Politics and social justice issues were important, and in those tumultuous days of the sixties, there were events that could not go unmentioned in their Letters: the assassination of President Kennedy, the death of Nehru, and the passing of Civil Right legislation in the United States. Yet their greatest passion and hopes were fixed on religious reconciliation and understanding. Perhaps, they wrote hopefully, the greatest event of all these years would be remembered one day as the meeting in January 1964 between the leaders of two ancient, divided Christian worlds of Rome and Constantinople: Pope Paul and Murray's much revered friend, Athenagoras.[1] This hope, like many others, seemed destined to remain a distant aspiration.

---

1. Letter #15.

In 1965 world headlines came even closer to their life on the Ganges plain as tensions between India and Pakistan, festering since the 1947 partition of British India, erupted into a second full-scale Indo-Pakistani War. Thousands were killed in the five-week war over the disputed land of Kashmir until a United Nations mandated peace settlement ended the conflict. Jyotiniketan was rocked by news of the death and destruction, visited atop the daily struggle of poverty and mundane suffering they knew so well. How could that secret inner cave of peace and love and light withstand such depths of suffering?

Their witness to India's suffering seemed only to deepen their love, and their language grew poetic in their efforts to convey their feelings. "No one told me how beautiful India is." Thus quoting a visitor to Jyotiniketan in their latest Letter to Friends,[2] they described their adopted land—"A country full of beauty and full of suffering." Bit by bit, they had fallen deeply in love with India. In these years, a sense of intimacy, a sense of tenderness for the place and for its humble people pervades their Letters:

> For the last few days a man's singing has accompanied the last hours of our day. He is in a garden beyond the bamboos which line one side of the Ashram land, and there, while we close the day together in the Chapel and spend our last half hour before bed in reading and personal prayer, he sings away to the glory of Krishna; again and again, and still again, the same refrain, the same words. We cannot tell you when he ends his greeting of praise for we are asleep long before fatigue overcomes him.[3]

"Amid so much poverty and distress," they observed, "it is easy to fail to see the beauty and the glory. But indeed there is glory: the sunrise as we sat in Chapel this morning, the sounds of the birds greeting the new day, the nest of bulbuls in Shanti Kuti, the blue evening smoke over Kareli village, sunset by the Ramganga river, and the invincible courage of our neighbors."[4]

Decades later, the sense of loving connection was still fresh in Murray's memory:

> When we woke up in the morning at 4:30 or 4:35, before the gong was struck by one of us to wake up "the family," as we called it, it was the silence [that I remember]. Silence—though there were many sounds. The sounds of insects, sounds of frogs, and later, the sounds of the peacocks that lived around us and in our garden. But then, in the early morning darkness, the sky

2. Letter #17.
3. Letter #16.
4. Letter #17.

was very often clear, with no electric lights anywhere. And there in that little five and a half acre plot, the silence was gripping; it spoke. We didn't catch it in words—oh, sometimes we did. Sometimes words came in the silence. But generally it was— what?—a sense of belonging. A sense of belonging to silence, much as one belongs to the earth. I think of Jyotiniketan in that way, belonging to the vast open silence of the sky, and belonging on the earth, dotted with our little huts, which were made chiefly of mud, of the earth. The floors were all mud, except in the kitchen where it was cement. Everywhere else we were walking on earth, of course with bare feet, and we felt the earth when our toes twiggled a bit . . . a sort of Celtic meditation.

And of course we worked in the garden for two or three or four hours nearly every day of our lives there. Their earth is—Oh, you're wanting your vegetables to grow and your mango trees to bloom and be good. But it's more than for use. It's a very close relative; you're living from it. There isn't a chunk of leather between you and it or a cement road. We really *belonged* to the earth there; we belonged because we really *lived with* the earth. We didn't live on it; we were really *in* it. And at night we lay down on our string beds—yes, our string beds were about the only thing that raised us from the earth. But there was no separation . . .[5]

It was "a revelation," Murray said, to catch glimpses of how their "village friends" too felt such reverence to the earth. "I remember going along the road to the Ramganga—not quite as holy a river as the Ganga into which it flowed, but the Ramganga was pretty holy. We had heard there was a *yagna*[6] happening there." He described what they discovered when they arrived at the gathering place beside the Ramganga:

> . . . The holy man had arrived and made a sacrifice of wheat. There were four or five *sadhus*, and they'd received gifts of this pile of wheat, and they were burning it. Of course, like the Old Testament, it's no good giving something that you don't want. But if you give wheat, you really are giving away your life. And village friends had done that; they were coming to put their little offering to the fire.
>
> Then I inquired from one of the *sadhus*, would he explain what they were doing this for? What did it mean to them? And he explained [because the Chinese were then firing on Indian

---

5. Interview with Trapnell.
6. *Yagna*: a form of worship in which offerings are made to a deity.

troops along the border] that they were purifying the atmosphere between the heavens and the earth for the help of our leaders [Prime Minister Nehru and others], because they needed to see clearly—clarity mattered so much. And that could only be done by *yagna*, by sacrifice, to clear the atmosphere between the earth and the heavens, the blue sky, but also of course, the abode of the gods at the center.[7]

The next day, Murray continued, he related to their friend and co-worker Fidah Hussein what they had experienced. Fidah was a Muslim. "How is it with you?" Murray inquired of Fidah, continuing the little dialogue. Listening intently to the reply, Murray perceived how sharply Fidah's perspective contrasted with his own, and he dipped into his imagination to make room for Fidah's difference. He recalled the conversation:

> Fidah said, "Everything with us is close . . . the moon, the stars . . ."
> And I said, "Oh, that's very interesting. The moon, for me, is a *long* way away; it takes so many hours or it's so many miles.
> And Fidah said, "For us it isn't. It's no distance."
> As Fidah explained the feelings he had about the sky, it reminded me of those old, old pictures that have no depth in them. You know, it's all there, whatever the painter was putting there, but it didn't look as if anything was further away from anything else. It was all like that, it was all immediate, it was all pressing on you.
> And Fidah observed,"Of course, that's what it is, isn't it?"[8]

Thus the family of Jyotiniketan deepened its understanding also of the Indian sensibility and its essential difference from that of the West. Their view of the heavens seemed to extend to the earth and to human relationships as well. Hindu and Muslim friends, he noticed—at least the simple, unsophisticated ones—"took us in with a remarkable ease . . . They were so incredibly welcoming, and it seemed as if they took us as being united with them; only afterwards did they discover the things in which we differed." Not only were the heavens and the earth seen as one, Murray explained, but "they start off with unity; they see *everything* as one. It's a presupposition they never question. I mean they wouldn't think everything is completely the same, oh, no! But it's what you start off with. Whereas in the West, you see, my first intuition, when I hear you're coming and I've never met you before, [I think to myself]: 'It'll be very interesting to meet that man.' But

---

7. Interview with Trapnell.
8. Ibid.

[you're] separate—an *other*. We'll find we have many things in common, but it's always the separation first."

Continuing, he said, "With Indian friends, it's all close. We are all made together; we belong together. Our religions [are different], yes, but that comes along later. And unless there's some sort of shock of division, they just say, "Well, of course you do this, and we do that. Why not?"[9]

They found this eastern attitude simply wonderful. Within it seemed to lie the possibility of finding even deeper belonging, deeper connection to these poor neighbors. It was, they acknowledged, the "growing intensity of our longing to *be* and to *live* for unity" that led them to a step they had not anticipated.

Being so in love with India and with their life in Jyotiniketan, it now seemed only right to consecrate their love in formal vows of commitment. Thus in 1965 they wrote, "We had until now decided that definite promises were too formal an engagement to God and to the Ashram but we have changed our minds. We trust we have followed the leading of the Spirit in the decision."[10]

Continuing in their Letter to Friends, they repeated the vows they had made before a small crowd of witnesses: "In this solemn promise we each, in the presence of God and of his church, bind ourselves 'anew to a life of service to our Lord Jesus Christ in this Ashram for six years, believing that this is a call from God for the rest of [our] lives.'"[11] Swami Abhishiktananda, who had become a spiritual mentor to Murray first received Murray's declaration. "I desire to be consecrated to a life of service to our Lord in Jyotiniketan Ashram, to a life of worship and disciplined work, of simplicity and submission, and for the unity of all men in Christ." Then Murray, "as *acharya*,"[12] received the vows of the other three: Mary, Heather, and John Cole. These four components: worship, disciplined work, simplicity, and submission, lived day by day for the unity of people in the love of Christ, were the heart of Jyotiniketan.

And why this change of heart in taking formal vows, pledging faithfulness to their Ashram family? One factor, perhaps, was their children, who, it appeared, were making a good transition into young adulthood. Though young Richard remained a student at Monkton Combe School in Bath, in only two years he would be ready for university. "He finds the classics

9. Ibid.
10. Letter #16.
11. Ibid.
12. *Acharya*: an Indian term for a religious leader.

and rowing a whole time job,"[13] Mary and Murray reported reassuringly. Cheryl had finished her schooling at the Sherborne School in 1961. With Hawkhurst and the Herford family still a reliable touchstone in England, Cheryl had grown comfortable with travel and increasingly at ease with herself and with her parents as well. Having decided to follow her mother's footsteps into teaching, she took "a gap year," and headed off to India. In this first stay at Jyotiniketan without Linda and Richard, she still found the daily regimen of prayer and silence "pretty difficult." Though a religious sensibility stirred within her, then and there she determined that she was not intended for the sort of religious life her parents had chosen. Happily, for a part of her time in India, she was in Delhi, assisting a teacher in a school and confirming, as well, her desire to teach. From India, following her father's suggestion, she headed for the Ecumenical Center of the World Council of Churches in Bossey, Switzerland where their good friend Ilse Friedeberg was based. It was for Cheryl "a wonderful experience" in which she lived and worked for several months in the home of one of the Directors of the World Council, a black African family, the Makulus. As the *au pair* for the fifth Makulu child, a small boy, she was dubbed "A Blue Angel," along with other girls who were at the Center to help with cleaning and childcare, but also to be immersed in the lives of the international community of Christians who were, as she recalled, "fantastically involved in their church life." There was even the added spice of a girlish romantic crush—unrequited, yet warmly memorable—on a married American priest. The next year, settled at Homerton College, Cambridge for a teacher-training program, Cheryl joined the Student Christian Movement and began attending church regularly, just as her parents had done before her.[14]

Two years later, Linda too had completed her schooling at Sherborne and followed suit with a similar gap year. Flying to India with her mother, she spent some months there before heading off to Bossey, also to serve as a "Blue Angel" at the Ecumenical Center, following Cheryl as an *au pair* for the Makulu family. At the close of the year, she returned to England to begin a nurses' training program in London.

Somehow they all seemed to be weathering their "family-at-a-distance." Looking back on the experience, Cheryl wryly observed, "Indeed I think our Parents were extremely lucky none of us did go off the rails. I

---

13. Letter #14.
14. Interview with author.

didn't in any way go wild, as a teenager. I didn't 'kick against the pricks,'[15] as it were and react badly. We could have gone wild!"[16]

In fact, many of these happenings were formally recorded by their parents in the main body of their Letters to Friends in this period—in distinct contrast to earlier years when personal family matters were mentioned briefly in a postscript or not at all. With family relationships continuing to evolve, in 1963 Mary and Murray acknowledged their time with their children: "It was a great happiness to experience again the personal family life with which this joint Ashram family is so closely linked."[17]

Perhaps Mary and Murray were also feeling some relief that their children were progressing in their lives, leaving them nearer their goal of providing a good British education for their children with doors open to choose their own life paths. Now, they may have felt more at ease devoting themselves to Jyotiniketan, to fulfill their belief, despite their limited vows of six years, [perhaps in deference to John Cole] that their call was to "a lifelong commitment . . . only taken under the impulse of God's will, for as with marriage is it 'for better and for worse.'"[18] With their children more settled, they could continue the process of stripping down materially, *not*, as they wrote, "simply to essentials, but to the abandonment of essentials."[19] Their practice of what Henri Nouwen later called "downward mobility" had often created distance between them and their children; now they could deepen their embrace of what Nouwen would preach some twenty years later: "The story of our salvation stands radically over and against the philosophy of upward mobility. The great paradox which Scripture reveals to us is that real and total freedom is found through downward mobility. The Word of God came down to us and lived among us as a slave. The divine way is indeed the downward way."[20]

More strange to western sensibilities than to eastern ways of thinking, this "downward mobility" is, in fact, a time-honored path in India, often called the way of renunciation. Pankaj Mishra, a contemporary Indian writer, born in Uttar Pradesh, the Indian state where Jyotiniketan was located, comments on this very ancient tradition: "It included the thinkers of the *Upanishads*, who had retreated to forests, and the wandering *sramanas*,[21]

15. 'Kick against the pricks': a British expression meaning to fight authority.
16. Interview with author.
17. Letter #14.
18. Ibid.
19. Letter #16.
20. Nouwen, *Selfless Way of Christ*, 29.
21. *Sramana*: A wandering monk in several ancient religious traditions of India,

of whom the Buddha himself was one . . . Their rejection of the sensual life and voluntarily chosen hardship inspired respect among the ordinary people they approached for food, clothing and shelter. The renouncer continues to be revered in India today, sometimes for no more than his act of renunciation . . . As the Buddha saw it, the *bhikshus*,[22] who had reduced their personal desires and lived interdependently with like-minded human beings, had much to teach a society that was involved increasingly and fractiously in the pursuit of wealth and pleasure."[23]

As Murray, Mary, and Heather identified more and more with Indian life and spirituality, their words and actions echoed these beliefs. Their friend Abhishiktananda's example of renunciation piqued their spiritual aspirations and tugged at their sense of spiritual inadequacy as well. In 1968, Swamiji had left Shantivanam, the Christian Ashram he had founded with Father Monchanin, and was spending good portions of his time living as a *sadhu* in a cave on Mt. Arunachala, deepening his life of prayer and his quest for *advaita*. Despite the vast geographical distance and the solitary life he had embraced, Swamiji's visits became more frequent. For Swamiji, Jyotiniketan provided a place of welcome for his spiritual intensity and for his irrepressible extroversion as well. Murray recalls, "When he came down to stay with us—and we had one silent day each week—I would say to him, 'Tell me if you would like a quiet day . . . there is a hut you can use.' Swamiji would then say, 'Why do you think I come here? I come here to talk!' I don't think anyone who wasn't a pretty deep hermit could have said that! He knew himself so well. He just loved to gas away, more than any other visitor we had. Yet . . . when he wrote to us he would say he had had a wonderful month with no visitors, and I know it *was* wonderful for him. He was utterly human."[24]

Though *both* men were utterly human, their circumstances were very different. Abhishiktananda was a celibate Roman Catholic priest, with few constraints to his spiritual seeking, while Murray and Mary were married, with family responsibilities to their biological family and to Jyotiniketan as well. Yet their friendship with Abhishiktananda was a constant reminder, especially to Murray, of how far he had yet to go in his spiritual life. The tendency to compare himself with Swamiji was difficult to contain. "When we first met," Murray said,

---

known for their renunciation of material goods to attain spiritual goals.

22. *Bhikshu*: A Buddhist monk who lives in community and has renounced all property, living as a beggar on alms given by others.

23. Mishra, *An End to Suffering*, 211–12.

24. Rogers and Barton, *Abhishiktananda*, 16.

... all the dualities were very much with us—between the spiritual and the material, the supernatural and the natural and what not. Swamiji, though not at the very beginning ... was coming to see that all the separations and distinctions he had drawn in his mind ... all the lines—right and wrong, true and false—they just didn't fit any more. Something was happening to him in India which was taking him beyond dualities ... This was our pathway too, in a way. Very soon we saw that Swamiji believed more and more in the Incarnation. Anything to do with faith that was just sitting on the side of the swimming pool and not plunging in—he knew it wasn't genuine. And therefore dear old Swamiji always travelled third class ... And if you saw him, as I often did, going off to his next place, well ... it was frightfully crowded and to get onto a train at all was difficult. It was desperate. Sometimes he got in and out through a window! ... And he could only with difficulty be made to eat properly. He just knew he had got to be poor with the poor. *Sannyasa,* as you know, means radical renunciation, and he was discovering that you can't be half re-nunciated! You've simply got to go the whole way.[25]

For them as a family, *sannyasa* remained out of reach. But pressing on, embracing life in community as *their* spiritual crucible, they translated that tradition of renunciation into their own vernacular. For them the operative words were neither "downward mobility" nor "renunciation" but rather simplicity. "Simplicity tells us," they wrote, "to rejoice in having less rather than more, to be more content with privations and sufferings, with every diminishment and loss, than with pleasure and success and achievement ... knowing that God is all and we are nothing."[26] For them this was also the Christian way. Aware of the radical implications of their path, they continued, "Can it be that God is preparing us to follow Christ in that moment of 'failure' and 'powerlessness' when He simply stood, saying nothing, nothing? We tremble as we think these things, and then we remember the words of Paul Claudel that 'if man does not suffer, it is because life has suspended its work on him.'"[27]

Life had not suspended its work on any of them. Much as they admired the sense of "unity" in their Indian neighbors and longed to emulate them, as westerners their hope for transformation was in their life in God

---

25. Ibid., 12–13.
26. Letter #16.
27. Ibid.

and in community. "Unity begins at home," they wrote to their Friends, "but its ripples spread until they touch the whole universe."[28]

Writing for a Christian publication, Murray expanded on the goal of unity. "Each year the universal thirst for unity seems to be growing; you can see this in economic life, in human relations, in political affairs, and you can see it in the increasing longing and prayer for unity among Christians."[29] With Pope John XXIII's call for *aggiornamento*,[30] an unspoken echo in Murray's words, he articulated their vision of this renewed sense of Christian unity within their little ashram:

> To love God in community; community for us means that by God's decision and by ours we accept responsibility fully for one another as in marriage, and this applies as much to material as to spiritual responsibility. Full members belong to one another in Christ and for an unlimited period, that is, until we die. We share such money as comes to the Ashram for our common life [always from India and never from abroad] and share the decisions as to what we think is the will of God for our life together. One of our members is chosen and accepted as leader, or *acharya*, and while all of us would learn what it means to live in submission to one another in the love of Christ, so the members willingly take upon themselves the freedom which comes from being obedient to the leader, or, more truly expressed, to Christ through the leader.[31]

On a practical daily level, they struggled with how to live this out. In keeping with the model of Indian ashrams, there was little formal structure to the community, no rule or constitutions as one would find in western Christian communities. The Spirit was there to guide, but the discernment left to the leader of the community was, Murray admitted, "an awful responsibility." Yet, in other ways, the responsibility was shared. "We shared everything," he said. "We shared our money; we shared what we did about our money; we shared what we ate, we shared our timetable, we shared everything, really . . ." So in spite of his recognized leadership role—his designation as *acharya* or even occasionally as *guru*—in spite of his natural, even charismatic leadership skills, Murray and thus the others as well, clung

---

28. Letter #15.

29. Rogers, "Jyotiniketan: A Community of the Church."

30. *Aggiornamento*: The term used by Pope John XXXIII to refer to the task of the church in the meetings of Vatican II to bring the church [literally] "up to date." It implied open-mindedness to other religious experience and to changes within the church.

31. Rogers, "Jyotiniketan: A Community of the Church," 4.

to the vision of shared decision-making. "I don't think we organized it . . ." Murray reflected, "that we all shared our decisions because we ought to; we just did it naturally. We belonged together," he mused, "so who was I to say things?"[32]

Wisely, they counted on the presence of "Father Confessors" from outside the community to give them spiritual assistance. "Each of us knew enough about ourselves that we needed other people to help us see what the will of God was,"[33] he explained. At first, their Board of Trustees could lend its spiritual wisdom to decisions concerning the community as a whole. Then in the smaller, more intimate decisions they encountered as individuals, they began to call upon Abhishiktananda, whose profound spiritual depth and deep connection with Jyotiniketan made him a friend trusted by them all. In addition, their close friend Raimon Panikkar, also deeply admired not only for the brilliance of his mind, but for his spiritual wisdom, by mutual agreement gradually took on the role of "Visitor"[34] and spiritual director. When assuming this role, Swamiji or Raimon would meet with them in the Chapel following evening prayers. Taking as their model a practice of the Little Brothers and Little Sisters of Jesus, monastic communities who had houses in Banaras,[35] and to whom they had become connected through Raimon, they would try to share any hurts or concerns experienced during the day, asking forgiveness of one another before they went to bed.

Yet in practice, there was no denying the power of Murray's persuasiveness and of his extroverted drive that seemed nearly unstoppable. Murray's own recollections belie the purity of their mutuality and shared decisions. Speaking of his travels and his now frequent invitations to be present at faraway meetings, he asserted that his decision to go would always be by consensus. "It was part of the obedience," he explained. "We wanted to live in obedience to one another in every direction. So I would never go away without us together considering whether we thought it was the will of God." He continued, "But, of course, I loved it; it was frightfully stimulating . . . and the invitations took me to places I'd never have been otherwise. But it's so difficult to discern one's original motives. Yes, I felt I had something to share . . . Yet I've sometimes wondered whether I wasn't escaping things

32. Interview with Trapnell.

33. Ibid.

34. Visitor: In western monastic life, the person charged with the responsibility both of observing the community at large to see that it is living up to its agreed upon purpose and to serve as well as one who listens to its individual members and discerns whether their life is being supported and nurtured in life of the community. Walmsley, "A Legacy of Leadership," 7.

35. Banaras is now known as Varanasi.

that were hard at home." Continuing his reflections, he said, "It was plainly obvious to me that Mary and Heather carried a tremendous amount [in my absence] . . . I mean, I never went without the permission of the others. In a way, I could always get Mary's permission easier, because she wanted to agree with me, perhaps. But Heather's quite tough when she digs her heels in! [Murray laughs.] You know where you are, and she was quite difficult. And then I wouldn't go, of course. I would only go if they really felt that they wanted to say yes."[36]

But more often than not, Murray did go. Believing they belonged together, yet also believing he must go, he went with their blessings, however reluctantly they were given. And always he went believing that their prayers and his contacts might bring an Indian brother or sister to Jyotiniketan, to share their life, to ease their burden, and to be an outward and visible sign of their unity with the Indian people, their ongoing life and belonging there.

While he was gone, Mary and Heather maintained not only the daily round of tasks, but the discipline of worship as well. Though the Eucharist had become a daily, rather than weekly, celebration, when Murray was away, there were evolving forms of Morning Prayer [not requiring a priest] that began to diverge from the traditional Anglican service. As Mary explained, "We have a simplified morning prayer of the Anglican Church, having made linguistic changes and adaptations . . . producing, we hope, something contemporary in spirit and language but which. . .maintains rhythm of worship and prayer day by day. . .We have [also] adapted some of the Syrian Orthodox services of the South that answer, we feel, to the needs of the Indian spirit . . . and we interpose quite a lot of silence."[37] Midday was a time for intercession, and a weekly program organized their wide-ranging concerns: Mondays, prayers were offered for the spread of the Gospel, Tuesdays for children and young people, Wednesdays for unity among Christians, Thursdays for justice and peace, Fridays for "those who suffer in the name of Christ," Saturdays for Christians in their everyday jobs, and Sundays for the universal Church. All were offered in specificity along with prayers for neighbors, friends, and any other concern prompted by the news of the family or of the world. The work of intercessory prayer was particularly hard, though a touch of humor could lighten the load. Occasionally, when the list of prayers was just *too* long to bear, one of them, in a burst of spontaneous irreverence would call out: "Pray for ick-a-poo!" and the group would collapse into giggles. It was an inside joke, taken from a sign on a local church exhorting the faithful to "Pray for the sick and poor," but with sev-

---

36. Interview with Trapnell.
37. Rogers, reflection.

eral key letters missing. As Mary said, "It is to be admitted that all of us feel dissatisfied with our noon prayers from time to time. It is difficult not to be discursive, repetitive, trite, too detailed, too long, and a host of other minor sins! Sometimes we are very nearly asleep because of weariness or the heat, but we persevere . . ."[38] This was Mary, sharing a glimpse of her struggles. In Murray's absence, and perhaps at times in his presence, she and Heather simply carried on, day by day, week by week, month by month, morning, noon and evening, in their life of prayer. Perhaps they quietly mentioned their own loved ones in the prayers, but their sufferings never spilled forth into public view. Thus, when Mary's revered father, Frank Hole, who had contributed so generously to their children's education and to their vacations in Europe, died in January 1964, Mary was present only in spirit for the large funeral service in Sutton, England, that honored his life's work. She remained in Bareilly with Heather, keeping the prayers flowing and the lamps burning. That month, Murray was off to Bangkok to serve as a member of a consultation on Asian missionaries, which preceded an East Asia Christian Conference where he served as chaplain. His travels took priority.

In 1965 he spent five weeks in Hong Kong, again to serve as chaplain to a regional Christian meeting—this time the Theological Study Institute, charged with exploring Christian worship and music in southeast Asia. As in Bangkok and Bombay, it was the friendships and spiritual contacts that were the highlights—especially the chance to get acquainted with two more communities of the Little Sisters of Jesus [founded by Charles de Foucauld], one of them living on a Chinese junk in Hong Kong's Aberdeen Harbor. There were other visits as well in Hong Kong—time spent in a Trappist community and a weekend in the Buddhist monastery of Po Lin. Other travels inevitably followed, more meetings, some entirely Christian, some interreligious. With the Roman Catholic Church now more open to dialogue with other religions as a result of Vatican II, the World Council of Churches had stepped up its efforts to create opportunities for interfaith exchanges. Thus, there were more conferences and meetings in Thailand, Switzerland, Vietnam, Laos, Japan, and many others in India. Murray was present at most of them. Though his continuing travels were too many to recount, in 1967 there was a visit to Jerusalem that carried special emotional valence. By happenstance, Murray's arrival in mid June was just days after the end of the pivotal Six Day War.

During those six days, reacting to threats from the Arab states, Israeli forces had struck preemptively and decisively against combined forces of Egypt, Jordan, and Syria. In a campaign of air and ground forces, they

---

38. Ibid.

wrested control of Sinai and Gaza from Egypt, East Jerusalem and the West Bank from Jordan, and the Golan Heights from Syria. Entering the Old City, they had captured the so called Western Wall, sacred to Jews. It was a war of enormous import as Israel established itself as the preeminent military power in the region, and began its occupation of the territories seized.

Though Murray grieved the loss of life on all sides, it seemed natural to interpret Israel's victory as a breaking forth of the Spirit in the season of Pentecost. Caught up in prayer at the Western Wall with the throngs in the Old City, he shared a sense of fulfillment for the Jews—at last Israel had reclaimed more of its ancient and sacred heritage. Given his sensitivity to the plight of refugees he had encountered in his unforgettable overland trip to India back in 1951, perhaps he was not aware of news reports that more than a million new refugees were fleeing from the West Bank and East Jerusalem across the border into Jordan. But in those heady days of celebration, his primary view was from Israel and his heart, like those of his Israeli hosts, was filled with hope. Little could he have imagined how his life and that of Mary and Heather one day would be tied up with that holy and conflicted land.

11

A Deepening Journey of Light and Darkness
1966–1971

> The heart itself is but a small vessel,
> yet dragons are there, and there are also lions;
> there are poisonous beasts and all the treasures of evil.
> But there too is God, the angels, the life and the kingdom,
> the light and the apostles, the heavenly cities
> and the treasuries of grace—all things are there.
>
> —St. Macarius

THE PREVIOUS YEAR, 1966, was a pivotal year for Jyotiniketan, a year of completions and new beginnings. That year was the sixth meeting of the Cuttat Circle. Though they had dearly hoped there would be another, Dr. Cuttat was back in Switzerland, and future meetings were uncertain. Also that year, Richard completed his school at Monkton Combe. The event, to be celebrated with him in England, prompted plans for another European journey for Mary and Murray, with the opportunity to weave together their various families—small f, capital F, and an ever broader spiritual Family as well. For Murray a week or more of the Easter season was spent in Italy—Rome and Assisi—and Cheryl, who was teaching in England, was able to join him. While they never ceased being under the spell of India, now the little family duo was under the spell of Italy as well. Again, love was in the air. For Murray it was the love of St. Francis and the amazement of discovering he was considered part of a wider family there. "I'm such a lucky guy, I can't tell you!" he recalled. "They invited me to Assisi for a conference of

Anglican religious and Roman Catholic religious ... They invited me and they called me 'a semi-religious.' And I had a wife! I was the one lucky one!"[1] At the time they shared a more subdued version of their Assisi experience in their Letter to Friends: "We remember with joy some days spent in the Eremo Francescano near Assisi, so strangely reminiscent of an India ashram, and discovered for ourselves how wonderfully alive and present St. Francis, the Little Poor man of Assisi, still is."[2]

For Cheryl, it was a different sort of spell. Having arrived in Assisi without plans for transportation Cheryl and Murray encountered a small group of young men from Paris—Roman Catholic seminarians—led by a priest. Their tour of Assisi was just beginning as well, and they had a van with two extra seats, which they hospitably offered to them. The days in Assisi were a spiritual whirlwind, but for Cheryl it was the companionship of the seminarian André Poutier that cast a heavenly glow over the ancient town. When, some months later, Mary and Murray learned that Cheryl had plans to visit her new friend André in Paris, they knew all too well what heartache could lie ahead for the young pair. In July, just a few months hence, he would be ordained a priest.

Heather, meanwhile, was in Britain with her biological family. Her beloved father was seriously ill; it was agreed she should spend time with him before finding renewal through Jyotiniketan's spiritual family as well. Heather, of all of them, most loved the silence of their life. Whenever possible, she nourished her own "deep listening stillness"[3] in spiritual retreats. This trip was a veritable feast of well-deserved renewal for her with three different retreat experiences. At the same time she was a roving ambassador for Jyotiniketan, creating new relationship links. In Oxford, England, she stayed for a time with the cloistered Sisters of the Love of God [also known as Fairacres], in France, at the Priory of the Epiphany in Eygalières, and in Es Abiodh, Algeria, with the Little Sisters of Jesus. Now the tables were turned, and it was through Heather that all of them shared *her* gifts of spiritual friendship and renewed strength.

When their time in Europe was done and Richard had celebrated the completion of his education at Monkton Combe, he joined his parents in India for a time before heading off to Greece for the rest of the summer. Richard agreed to Indian trips reluctantly. For his alternate year visits, he recalled the miserable hours spent on "a bone-rattling version of a plane,"

---

1. Interview with Trapnell.
2. Letter #17.
3. Robin, funeral tribute.

arriving to spend six weeks with a family where he did not feel he belonged.[4] Certainly, when he was there, they were eager to spend time with him, but for Richard, "It didn't feel natural." Expected to join the life of the community, Richard resisted: "I really didn't want to plunge in." The dilemma was that he did not experience a real sense of belonging with the Herfords either, kind and generous as they were.

By then both Mary and Murray were aware of Richard's anger, never far from the surface. Yet if they had somehow fallen short with Richard, the die had been cast, and they reassured themselves that Richard's alienation would fade as he matured.

For them and for Heather the return to Jyotiniketan brought them back to where they truly belonged, to India and to one another. When they could overlook the fault lines in their relationship with Richard, they were flooded with gratitude: "What an immense Family we belong to in Christ and how deeply grateful we are to God and to the members of the Family who were so wonderfully good to us."[5]

Yet there was no time for complacency. Their time in the West with loving friends had done nothing to soften Murray's resentment towards its institutions. Now, more than ever, Murray chafed at his continued association with C.M.S., which, despite his warm personal relationships with many of its members, had come to symbolize for him all that was wrong with the western missionary movement. He and Mary knew they were complicit in depending upon its financial support; they had lived this "impossible contradiction" for so long, tending to avoid speaking of their own inability to fully practice what they preached. But with Richard ready to begin Queens' College, Cambridge, the financial burden of their children's education was complete. And now, with prayers that an Indian man or woman would join Jyotiniketan still unanswered, they could not help wondering if their association with C.M.S. was an impediment.

A small volume by Paul Gauthier, a Roman Catholic priest, provided validation for their profound dis-ease with their situation. Titled *Christ, the Church and the Poor*, the book lifted up the Gospel teaching on the poverty of Christ, as expressed in the Beatitudes, and highlighted the blindness of the Church to the suffering of the poor. "Geographically," Gauthier wrote, "we can see a dividing line drawn between the Church, which is well established in the more prosperous countries and the poor peoples of this world, who see the Church only from the outside." Referring to Mary and Murray's friend, Father Maurice Villain [who had visited Jyotiniketan following the

---

4. Interview with author.
5. Letter #17.

New Delhi conference], Gauthier continued, "On returning from . . . the conference, Fr. Villain expressed his sorrow at having to admit that in those countries of famine the churches appeared as rich tourists representing only a very small minority."[6] Jyotiniketan's Letter underscores the weight of his argument for them: "Paul Gauthier points to the sad scandal in the separation between the church and the poor, a separation which, if the Gospel be taken seriously, is at the same moment a tragic separation between Christians and their Lord."[7] As Gauthier writes, "Possessing no material wealth and having no bank account, the poor man, like the child, reminds the world of the primacy of being over having. Perhaps that is a reason why Jesus desired to identify himself with the child and the poor man: 'What doth it profit a man if he gain the whole world and suffer the loss of his own soul?'" Affirming their identification with Gauthier, their citation of him continues: "'I have no silver or gold, but what I have I give you,' said St. Peter." Then, in their own words, they complete his thought: "and what he had to give was life and strength and healing. We modern Christians and our agencies of Mission do our utmost to avoid being in the position of saying with St. Peter 'I have no silver or gold,' and our consequent spiritual impotence is sadly apparent."

If Gauthier's book mirrored their sense of frustration, it was a more concrete event that tipped the balance and gave them the justification they needed to take action.

1966 was a time of severe economic crisis in India. The Indo-Pakistani War of the previous year had depleted national resources, and a devastating drought was leading to widespread hunger and even famine. With a large trade deficit, India was forced to devalue its currency. In June of that year, the value of the rupee fell by 57 percent against the British pound. High inflation compounded the pain. Then towards the end of 1966, in the midst of—and perhaps in reaction to—the crisis, the Church Missionary Society decided to increase the personal allowances of its missionaries in North India, the area hardest hit by famine, by 25 percent.

They were outraged. "For this to be done at such a time . . . of acute economic stringency . . . of no hope of similar increases for workers except those paid in foreign currencies . . . is, we feel, a profound mistake and an affront to social justice." Recalling that eight years earlier in 1958, they had given up their missionary allowances and accepted support only for their children's expenses and their expenses in Europe, they added, "True, this 25 percent rise did not affect us financially, but by remaining members of the Society we would have subscribed to a policy of 'looking after one's

6. Gauthier, *Christ, the Church and the Poor,* 58.
7. Letter #17.

own people' which is contrary to social justice and the Spirit of Christ, as we understand them."[8] Now they believed they *must* completely sever their relationship with C.M.S.

Few details are readily available regarding the reaction of C.M.S. to their resignation. But it is fair to say that the impact was keenly felt in England, particularly by the Rev. John V. Taylor. Having succeeded Max Warren as General Secretary of C.M.S., John Taylor was a man of vast experience within the African and Indian missionary field and stature within the wider church. Earlier in his life as a priest, Murray had been deeply influenced by John Taylor's book, *The Primal Vision*. Essentially it was a vision that Murray shared of "a world of presences, of face-to-face meeting . . . a universe of I and Thou." In his work in Africa, Taylor had been drawn in his own way to simplicity, wishing to be known not as a "Prince Bishop," but as a "working shepherd."[9] He and Murray had much in common, and, over the years, they had become friends. Murray knew him as others did: as a liberal man, a shy and prophetic thinker, whose God was cosmic and in whom gentleness, humility and artistic gifts were fused. Also known as a "startlingly decisiveman,"[10] it was he who most felt the heat of Murray's angry departure, and John Taylor would not soon forget its sting. It was painful not only because C.M.S. had been unfailingly supportive of Murray and Mary's meandering journey and unorthodox work as missionaries. But from Murray, whose wide international connections and reputation had made him a high-profile member of C.M.S., the resignation came as harsh judgment. Though for many years, Murray's views on the missionary movement had been no secret, yet always he had constrained his anger, hoping and believing that his powers of persuasion could lead to a change in the system. Was the 25 percent increase in missionary allowances the proverbial straw that broke the camel's back? Or was the last bill paid to Richard's school the key to their declaration of independence? Somehow the convergence of the two made the perfect storm, and Murray's pent-up frustration was unleashed, leaving John Taylor not only dismayed, but with a deep sense of betrayal. Efforts were made by Max Warren to patch things up; late in the year, the retired General Secretary of C.M.S. went to Delhi where he and Murray met together. But regardless of Murray's affection and respect for these two distinguished Anglican leaders, he refused to soften his criticism of their missionary organization.

---

8. Ibid.

9. Simon Barrington-Ward, "The Right Rev John Taylor," *Independent*, Feb. 7, 2001.

10. Alan Webster, "The Rt Rev John Taylor: Bishop whose Christian view of the world embraced all faiths," *Guardian*, Feb. 6, 2001.

The outspoken message of his resignation reverberated in a long letter written early in 1970 to John Taylor.[11] The letter begins by acknowledging the personal impact of Murray's actions on their relationship. Taylor, it seems, had declined an invitation to visit them in Kareli as he had visited in the past. It reads: "How much I wish you could have visited us again last month here in the Ashram. We could have sat together to discuss, and the twinkles in our respective eyes would have softened the harshness of words on paper! Seeing that we have both put ourselves—our actual lives—behind what seems to us to be the will of God about Mission makes our difference of opinion about as radical and deep as it could be, but I am convinced that our belonging to one another in Christ can stand it."[12]

Murray surely knew that he was taking a risk in speaking so plainly. Perhaps "their belonging to one another in Christ" could not withstand his words, but he was undeterred:

> My growing conviction [is that] the best thing you Mission Board Executives in the West could do would be to go out of business and stop sending foreign missionaries to India. I'm serious. To supporters of Missions in the West, who have been for years caught up in a sentimental mystique of Mission which is so often marvelously out of touch with historical realities . . . such a suggestion may be outrageous . . .
>
> Don't get me wrong. Missions and countless missionaries have done a marvelous job in their day: men and women, worth double most of us modern editions, have shown courage and brilliance and immense love for God and for their fellow men. I thank God for them and still find myself inspired and challenged by them—but that is the past.

The letter continues:

> In much of this country the Church came in with the historical age of imperialism and colonialism . . . thank God those historical forces were softened to a small extent by Love for God and Man through the Christian mission . . . but with those come to an end . . . , the Missions remain tied to the same bit of past history.
>
> You are still tied; that's the truth of the matter. Foreign missionaries who come from the West are tied spiritually, economically, socially, far more firmly to New York and Paris and London

---

11. The published edition of the letter is actually addressed to "Dr. Taylor-Jones," presumably to disguise the identity of the recipient of such harsh judgment.

12. Rogers, "Missionary, Go Home?" 48.

than they are to Delhi or Madras or to the Christian Church in this country. People have said for years now that the foreign strand in the life of the Church here prevents the Church from "incarnating Christ—its real vocation—and without this it will be held back from deep spiritual experience, the spontaneity of its living and proclaiming the Gospel will disappear, and men of other faiths will be blocked from knowing who Christ is.[13]

For several more pages, Murray continues his jeremiad, adding a quotation (unattributed) from his scholarly friend, Raymond Panikkar:

"We have 'equated the dominant form of Christianity today—a particular sociological form—with Christianity itself' and this has involved us in a 'particularism incompatible with catholicity and an anachronistic theological colonialism that is absolutely unacceptable.'"

Murray then reaches the crux of his personal frustration:

Some would say we need more patience. For 20 years of life in India I myself believed the Mission "world" could change. Fundamentally, far from changing, it remains cussedly and determinedly the same—led by you friends, the Mission Executive officers in the West. Meanwhile the church in this country cannot step into life in the modern world, which means it cannot discover in reality what it means deeply to believe in God, to love Christ, to witness to him and to serve our neighbors in this time of upheaval in Asian society.

Could he have imagined John Taylor, as Secretary General of C.M.S., would withstand such a direct verbal assault and still not take it personally? Murray seemed to hope so, as he closed the letter:

Are you really surprised that I long for the death of Missions—for Christ's sake, to free Him from an institution which years ago served Him wonderfully but is more than ripe for euthanasia in the second half of the 20th century? . . .
Of course it is hardly the first time we Christians and Christian institutions have tried to hold up the course of history, but it never has worked and it never will—thank God.
We would love to see you again when you are next in India.

Yours very sincerely,
C. Murray Rogers

---

13. Ibid. 48–49.

P.S. Don't forget that some of my best friends are missionaries and Mission Executives! It is not them I am firing at, but at the system.[14]

Murray's pain and frustration, so long contained, had erupted in an angry barrage. It is hardly surprising that John Taylor did not choose to visit them again in India. It was to be a long-lasting break in a valued relationship—yet another source of pain.

It was true: anti-missionary feeling had been on the rise in India since independence from Britain in 1948. In 1956, in an attempt to limit the flow of missionaries from the West, the so-called Foreigners' Act had been passed requiring missionaries to obtain a special visa for travel to India. Since British citizens were still not technically considered "foreigners," British missionaries were exempt from the required registration. A British passport was all that was required to enter and to stay in the country. By the mid-sixties, however, this exemption was ended, and British missionaries, too, were required to register and to get a special visa. A deadline was set by which time registration must be complete in the local city. From this circumstance arose a more light-hearted story in their movement away from the missionary movement. Murray delighted in its telling:

> Of course, we were pretty convinced by then, that we were not missionaries . . . We didn't intend to be missionaries, so we didn't register in Bareilly . . . About a fortnight after the date had gone by, the chief police officer in Bareilly came out on his cycle, saw us, and asked if he could have a word with me? I said "By all means," and we sat down outside the ashram.
>
> He said, "I've come because I've got to report to Lucknow, our provincial capital, and then send it on to Delhi, how many British missionaries there are in this area. Could you kindly tell me why you have not registered, because you are missionaries."
>
> So I said, "I don't think we are missionaries. But if you could tell me what a missionary is, I can tell you here and now, face to face, whether we are or not."
>
> And he said, "Yes, right. A missionary is a man, or a woman, doing religious work, and . . . belonging to a foreign institution."
>
> So I said, "Well, in that sense, we are not missionaries, because we have nobody abroad who controls us in any sense. Now, I work under a bishop here in India, in Allahabad, and I'm under him spiritually—that is where I fit in. But every decision we take, we hope we are taking it as God wants us to do, but that's a decision of us here."

14. Ibid., 51–53.

So he said, "Right, in that sense, then you're not missionaries."

I said, "Is there some other definition about it?"

And he says, "Yes, missionaries are people who receive money from abroad."

So I said, "Well, in that sense, we are not missionaries. We *were* missionaries for well over a decade. But we are not now, because not one penny of money comes from England or anywhere else, to help us live here in this ashram." Then I said, "Is there something else?

He said, "Yes, missionaries try to change other people's religion. We can appreciate much that they do—he echoed old Thakkar Bapa[15]—that's of great service to India, but in general, they try to change people's religion."

So I said, "Well, it so happens that again, I came to India with that intention, but for years now we haven't had it. I'm not interested in trying to convert, because I don't think it's our job. I feel God needs to convert us all, you, a Hindu bugger, and me, a Christian bugger, [laughs] and everybody else. We need to be converted in ourselves, not to something we aren't, something different, but to ourselves!

He said, "I agree!"

So I said, "Well, then we're not missionaries."

He said, "Yes, you are not missionaries."

The story might have ended there, but Murray had not yet reached the climax. He continued:

Then the policeman said, "May I see around the place?"

And I said, "By all means."

And he inquired about a day's program; we showed him the two silent huts where we and our visitors would go to have a little retreat. We went all around, then we went to the chapel. We took our shoes off outside, of course.

When we stepped inside, he suddenly turned to me and said, "Father Rogers, have you experience in prayer?" And you know, I think for about thirty-five, forty minutes, we talked about prayer together.

In the middle of this very happy discussion about prayer ... his sort of prayer, my sort of prayer—he suddenly said, "OH! I must remember why I came here!" And I laughed, of course, and so did he. So, we went back, had our little pot of tea, and he

---

15. Thakkar Bapa: the friend of Gandhi who first introduced Murray to the Gandhian movement and provided an invitation to Sevagram.

said, "May I see your passports?" So I got the passports, and he looked at them, Mary's first. The occupation [listed] was "wife," and he said, "That's still true, isn't it? She *is* your wife?"

And I said, "Yes, indeed, she is my wife."

"All right," he said. He put it down, then said, "Now, Miss Sandeman, she's down as teacher, but you've told me that she hasn't been teaching since she left her school in South India. So, that isn't strictly true, is it?"

So I said, "No, not strictly true." And then he opened mine, and he read my occupation: "Clerk in Holy Orders."

And he said, "Well, this is very remarkable. Clerks—we have our clerks, sir, and generally they don't go very much with holiness. And what are Clerks in Holy Orders?"

I explained that this is a way of describing an Anglican priest in England.

So he then said to me, "Would you please send Miss Sandeman's passport, and your passport, to the High Commission in New Delhi, and ask them officially to take out teacher, and Clerk in Holy Orders, and put in "religious devotee? Then it will be transparently clear that you are not missionaries."

And we did. We became "religious devotees," and we went in and out of India after that and nobody ever asked us a question. The only thing that happened was once when Heather was coming back to London, a youngish man opened [her passport], looked at her, and said, "Ooh! I've never met one of them!" [Murray laughs uproariously.][16]

Truly, this was the sort of encounter that gave Murray the most joy—a surprise meeting with a down-to-earth Indian man, in which the conversation turned to God and prayer, and, without noticing, all sense of time was suspended. A conversation, too, of unexpected commonalities and hearty belly laughs. Along with their stimulating meetings with Swamiji and other dear friends, conversations such as these brought a keen sense of God's loving presence.

Yet the joy and merriment stood in stark relief to darkness and pain as well. For as their prayers continued that others be drawn to join the community, there was another parting-of-the-ways. In 1967 their Letter contained this brief note: "We are sorry to say that John Cole has not been well and has had an operation in the U.S.A. from which he is now recuperating. Please pray for him."[17] John Cole's name no longer was among the signatories as it

---

16. Interview with Trapnell.
17. Letter #17.

had been for the past five years. The Letter was signed only by Mary, Murray, and Heather. Now they were three.

And what had happened? It remains unclear. Even years later, Murray spoke reluctantly of what had come between them. Though John had accompanied him to several meetings, he recalled how John would sometimes be left behind with Mary and Heather when he was away from Jyotiniketan. "Dear old John, the American Presbyterian, was there, but . . ." Murray hesitated before continuing. "He was a very quiet man. Frightfully good with the language, much better than we were. *Much* better. But he wasn't in any sense a leader. Very dear. He was plainly a homosexual friend who was so uncertain of himself that it was difficult. He couldn't help much in taking the leadership role in any way."[18] As a clergyman and perhaps as a man as well, it seemed to be assumed that John would fill Murray's leadership sandals when he was gone. Murray continued, "Things always went on [when I was away]. Mary and Heather saw to that—the worship and the children coming for milk, and the dispensary, and the visiting of the women and children in the villages. And John would do things, seeing the men and . . . " Again Murray trailed off. "I don't know what to say about that,"[19] he said, before changing the subject.

Pain and joy—life shared and life hidden—in these "happiest years" in India. With their liberation from missionary ties, they felt more free to follow where the Spirit led. But beneath the freedom lurked a sense of unease. Mary and Murray were now in their early fifties; for nearly fifteen years they had been praying for Indian members for their community, that Jyotiniketan could begin its transition to an Indian Christian ashram. As western people, they had changed their dress, learned something of the languages, and adopted, as far as they could, an Indian lifestyle. How long, they wondered, could they keep up the hard labor of working the land and keeping everything going without help? Recruiting members for their community was out of the question: "We can't have people sent here as a job, because that isn't what it is. It's for people who feel that God can send them or love can send them."[20] Their uncertainty seemed only to deepen their spiritual quest. Now, little by little, as they continued to absorb the scriptures and wisdom of Hinduism, their own prayers and worship were also undergoing transformation.

While affirming, as had Abhishiktananda before them, their "fundamental loyalty to Christ," yet yearning to go "beyond the *dvandva*, the

18. Interview with Trapnell.
19. Ibid.
20. Ibid.

dualities" of Hinduism and Christianity and to seek what Abhishiktananda called 'the meeting point,'[21] they cast aside well-intentioned fears of some of their Christian friends: that they might "lose [their] Christian faith and bearings and become, if not outwardly then inwardly, Hindu."[22] Nearly ten years before, they had casually mentioned a key phrase to their Friends as they began their Letter: "The other day we came across these words: 'He who knows Him who is hidden in the cave and set in highest heaven, he obtains all desires.'"[23] Then, in 1959, they were not yet ready to fully share this spiritual stirring, the longing for union with God beyond all thoughts, beyond all dualities, which they came to call by its Hindu name: *advaita*. It was more important to translate the news into Christian language, Christian experience. "That little phrase 'hidden in the cave,'" they continued, "often crops up in the Upanisads; it is an exciting jumping off point for the Christian once he begins to know that the Lord Christ is to be found indeed everywhere, in the cave of the human heart, in the cave of the Hindu scriptures, in the cave of Bethlehem, in the cave of the Empty Tomb."[24] But now, throwing caution to the winds, they were ready to bring their contemplative readings of Christian and Hindu scriptures from outside, or more literally out-of-doors, where they sat cross-legged on their mats under a shady tree, directly into the Chapel, into their daily worship, into the very heart of Jyotiniketan. It was, as Murray later wrote, "a matter of throwing oneself into the stream, entrusting oneself to it, allowing it to do what it would . . . Whether it was that extraordinary mystical document, the *Katha*, or some other *Upanishad*, or the *Bhagavad Gita*, the resonances within our own 'Christian' souls made it impossible any longer to judge this deep Hindu source as being 'outside,' another source than ours." Thus began the practice of reading a passage from the Hindu scriptures, followed by the Epistle and Gospel from the New Testament, and "the converging streams flowed together . . . as part of our daily spiritual nutrition."[25] There were *Vedic* hymns, too, voiced as "psalms" of praise and gratitude:

> Homage to him who presides over all things,
> that which was and that which shall be;
> to whom alone belongs the heaven,
> to that all-powerful Brahman be homage! —*Atharva Veda* X, 8

21. Murray cites Abhishiktananda's *La Montée au fond du coeur* (*le journal intime du moine chrétian-sanyassi hindou*), O.E.I.L., Paris, 1986.
22. Rogers, "Hindu Influence on Christian Spiritual Practice," 139.
23. Letter #10.
24. Ibid.
25. Rogers, "Hindu Influence on Christian Spiritual Practice," 139.

And there were prayers:

> O God, Scatterer of ignorance and darkness,
> grant me your strength.
> May all beings regard me with the eye of a friend,
> and I all beings!
> With the eye of a friend may each single being
> regard all others! —*Sukla Yajur Veda* XXXVI.18[26]

But words were not all. As Murray wrote, "Words, however deep and appealing . . . can so easily remain on the conceptual level . . . It is as pointers, icons beckoning to us to dare to go beyond, that these Hindu scriptures and prayers are an invaluable gift for us Christians in our spiritual practice." Drawing on their experience with Hans-Ruedi Weber who had encouraged them to discover "the marvelous medium of their bodies,"[27] they adopted gestures and symbols of their Hindu friends. There was, for example, the *arati*, the waving of fire, one of Hinduism's most sacred rituals. Mary, writing during that time, told of how it became woven into their evening service: "We [had] discovered how sacred . . . in a traditional Hindu home is that moment at twilight when the sun sets and the first lamp of evening is lit—the task of the mother of the family who greets the light with a reverent gesture of folded hands as she puts it in the puja corner. A hush lies over the village courtyard at that moment when the divine and human seem very close and intimate. This moment seemed to us to have a particular significance and beauty and demanded to be assumed into our Christian worship . . ."[28]

Mary describes their use of their beautiful oil lamp brought as a gift from South India by students in their first work camp for this evening ritual. For worship particularly centered around the theme of light, the lamp was lit either by her or by Heather from the small altar lamp. Differing prayers would then be offered according to the seasons of the Church's year beginning with Advent, Christmas, and Epiphany and continuing "right through All Saints tide." Included as well was *Divali*, the great Indian Festival of Light with readings from the Upanishads. "And," she adds, "we have now added an '*arati*' at the end with the utterance of a three-fold acclamation of praise to Christ, the Light of the World. This *arati* is concluded by all those who so desire coming forward to participate in this light of Christ by holding their outstretched palms for an instant over the camphor flame, next touching

---

26. Ibid., 140.
27. Weber, *Bible Comes Alive*, 59.
28. Rogers, reflection.

hands to forehead in a gesture which symbolizes a desire to convey this light to their mind and heart."[29]

Mary and Murray's voices blend as Murray describes other *mudras* or hand gestures: "the *anjali* or joining of the hands in greeting, or the offering of flowers in worship with a sentence of praise—*OM namah*—sung as each of eight flowers[30] are offered. Never," Murray continues, were these gestures or symbols considered "ends in themselves, but ways the person may 'pass over' to the experience of the [Divine] Mystery." With retrospective clarity, Murray describes how this had happened for them: "I now see that the Hindu reality began to merge with my Christian reality before ever I realized it was happening, through friendship, the sharing of faith experiences, the bearing together of suffering and joys . . . It was in those times of sitting at the feet of the *rsi*, the vedic seers, and also in times of silence and solitude which must accompany any serious listening to that call, that the need to go beyond the *dvandva* [pair of opposites, like heat and cold, pleasure and pain], the dualities, became clear . . . we were slowly becoming aware that these were our spiritual sustenance as well as theirs."[31]

But at the time, they remained circumspect in describing this development to 'Friends': "Each morning we join, with great gratitude, in the Eucharist: that is the centre of life—ours and, we believe, the life of our neighbours in Kareli and Kargena, the 'moment' of deepest solidarity with Christ and with the world. With increasing use of Indian symbols and ways of worship, including hymns and readings from the Cosmic Covenant of Hinduism, we are finding our way to what one day may be called an Indian liturgy."[32]

Quoting their friend Archbishop Anthony Bloom of the Russian Orthodox Church, they wrote: "'If we want to learn to pray we must first make ourselves deeply one with the total reality of man, his destiny and the whole world; we must take it to ourselves. . . Intercession consists in taking a step which carries us to the heart of a tragic situation . . .' That is exactly our job here," they added; "You can see why we need your prayers."[33]

---

29. Ibid.

30. The eight flowers, arranged as on points of a compass, carry symbolic meaning from Hindu tradition, found in the ancient Vishnu Purana: "There are flowers of eight kinds which are dear to the Lord. / The first, the flower of harmlessness. / Then the flowers of self-forgiveness./mastery and compassion, and the lovely flower of forgiveness. / The flowers of peace, of steadfast endurance, of contemplation, and with them the flower of truth" (Sykes, 3).

31. Rogers, "Hindu Influence on Christian Spiritual Practice," 139.

32. Letter #18.

33. Ibid.

While many friends were concerned for their physical well being, most could not have imagined the spiritual suffering they experienced. Few could comprehend how very painful it could be to take steps to the heart of a tragic situation, or even what it might mean. Being drawn empathically into the lives of others, whether in the village or around the world, required great spiritual endurance, for the more they were drawn into solidarity with "this world of immense suffering and poverty and frustration,"[34] the more that suffering and frustration became their own. Why did God so often seem silent? Surely the spiritual transformation they continued to undergo with Raimon Panikkar and Abhishiktananda as their guides brought great joy, but there was also self-doubt. How could they reconcile their great love for India and their commitment to Jyotiniketan with God's seeming reluctance to respond to their prayers that it become an Indian-Christian ashram? Love and suffering seemed to go hand-in-hand.

The pain of the world penetrated ever more sharply within their souls. The more deeply they pushed into new spiritual frontiers, the more distant was any sense of comfortable faith. Violence in India itself had shaken them. Murray's frustration with the institutional church had boiled over. Needing to share their belief that this tragic situation was deeply unstable, that the Church was living in "a world of mutation," a sense of urgency exploded from their Letter: "Whether or not it is to our liking, business as usual in any realm of life will not continue for long . . . At such a moment of new conditions of existence . . . it is faith itself, our ultimate convictions, that are questioned. Can we not welcome precisely this upheaval as an occasion for a far deeper commitment to Reality and a deepening of our life in God? What we need so badly is an unshakable fidelity and the imagination not to maintain the old ways but to overhaul and, if necessary, to scrap and start anew. We Christians cannot afford to be 'elderly' in the new world!"[35]

Were *they* being called to "scrap and start anew?" Perhaps, they pondered, they themselves were the impediment. Perhaps there was something about them that was too "elderly." After all, Mary and Murray—more than Heather, who had been born in the East—knew they could not cast off their western roots. Though India felt like home, they were British; their children were British. Perhaps they would need to leave Jyotiniketan for some other place in their beloved adopted country to make room for Indian Christians to take over. It was nearly unthinkable because, with their vows to Jyotniketan, they had affirmed their intention to be there "forever and ever, until we

---

34. Ibid.
35. Ibid.

died."[36] But while continuing their process of discernment, they determined they must explore every option. They needed help.

For certain spiritual and practical discernment, they could still count on Bishop Christopher Robinson and other trusted Trustees of Jyotiniketan for advice. But Abhishiktananda and Raimon Panikkar remained their most intimate spiritual guides. With "Swamiji," the discernment process was complex. Murray summed it up in a letter to Raimon early in 1967: "[Soon I'll be having] a week with Swamiji when I hope we may share a lot about his *rêve*, to begin to see whether it's God's *rêve* too, for us included!"[37] Could they embrace Swamiji's dream? As Christians more and more steeped in Hinduism, they were deep spiritual companions. Yet many of Swamiji's choices had differed from theirs. Since his departure from France as a young man, despite devoted family relationships there, he had never returned to visit. Indeed, he had embraced India completely, becoming an Indian citizen. As a celibate priest who now had left his ashram, could he understand their family dilemmas? Could his dream be theirs as well? Despite their mutual devotion, there were areas beyond his ken.

Raimon's guidance, on the other hand, and his role as spiritual director had grown in a more intimate area of instability—to the very intersection of spiritual and family tensions. Late in 1966, another letter to Raimon read as follows: "We need you very badly . . . to minister to our needs, personally, and as a community . . . to help Mary . . . and Me and Heather too. If you could spare two full days for us we would be most grateful and at the earliest moment if at all possible for we need your ministry perhaps more seriously than you think . . . Forgive us for troubling you like this but I cannot help thinking that maybe God has given you to us for such moments as these, moments when difficulties and possibilities seem equally big."

A few months later, writing again to him, Murray's gratitude for his response was overflowing, "We remain thankful, very, Raymond, for your visit. They were days I will not forget, not because I exactly want them again, but because I believe they were a way on and through to growth. I need deeper and deeper love and, just as needful, I think, is a fearless courage to plunge in again and again even when one can't swim!"

These were days, it seems, when longing and pain, usually unspoken, had been laid at the feet of their confessor. And Raimon had shared guidelines, both spiritual and emotional, for life ahead together that touched areas of deep intimacy.

---

36. Interview with Trapnell.

37. This citation and those following in letters to Raimon Panikkar were entrusted to Andrea Andriotti and made available to the author.

Only later had they gained perspective on what they came to call their "special situation." Focused as they were on spiritual goals, some of their deepest emotional needs had been allowed to fall by the wayside. In a letter to Raimon, Mary reflects on her blind spot: "It took a long time." she writes, "for it to bear in on me just how difficult it is to live a sort of monastic life, cherishing and loving values that are most often cherished in monastic circles, and at the same time be fully a married couple." Almost imperceptibly, she now realized, Heather's emotional sensitivity had filled the gaps between husband and wife. Though this shift may have been evident to observant friends such as Raimon, Mary admits she was not prepared for it. She recalls Raimon's ever so direct comment to her some years earlier: "You've got to recapture him sexually," and the way his advice had rolled off her back.

But now she had become aware that Heather and Murray were spending more time together, that there were emotional and spiritual confidences between them that she did not share. Though it was difficult for Mary to articulate her feelings in person, she was able to put on paper to Raimon what she was experiencing: "I do, of course get attacked sometimes by thoughts and pains and succumb pretty badly . . . because it is, after all, an *affaire du coeur* and one has to live with one's heart, does one not?" Day by day, the reality was before her and she was faced with the daily task of continuing life with a breaking heart. Within Jyotiniketan's covenant "to live in obedience to one another in every direction," Mary's pain was compounded. "I find it strange and painful not to be able to share that heart with the two people nearest to me—husband and friend—but experience seems to show that it is much happier for all when we get on with living and caring for each other and the needs and people of the day and make no reference to our 'special situation.'" Mary's conviction that continued stoicism was called for carried the day. "It is both detrimental to happiness and clumsy," she continues, "to try and fix my pair of spectacles on to either of their noses and this is what I would be tempted to do." Yet she also saw that her silence might be working against her as she writes about herself, "It is a bit ironic that though wisdom and charity seem to impose silence, this may well increase the idea that 'Mary is unable to share spiritually . . .'"

Five years down the road, she had gained clarity. Again she writes to Raimon: "Just about exactly then I was happily looking forward to what you might call the third stage of a marriage relationship—child-bearing over—consequent freedom not to think of that aspect of the relationship either positively or negatively—a freedom therefore to go forward, except in so far as our manner of life tended to preclude it, but nevertheless didn't entirely, and I remember some particularly happy moments." She had believed them to be living "on a sort of happy hang-over, even a happier 'harbour reached' sort of feeling on my part" a life free of sexual necessity. But this, Mary says, "was not true to . . . the relationship as it really was . . . We were really weathering a fair number of strains and stresses, what with Heather having grown into the community so much that she'd grown also into Murray's life in a very inextricable manner and John Cole being so wound up in his own problems of relationship (or non-relationship, rather) that he provided more than enough problems for everyone else!" Mary's analysis continues, "M. had to suppress pretty vigorously his instincts toward the first and a few negative reactions towards the second, which must have meant for him far too much suppression all round—and as I see it and as he also sees it, the net result of this was a sudden cessation of urges in my direction." In retrospect she sees how she could have missed the cues that Murray and Heather were becoming emotionally connected in a way that threatened their marriage and indeed the community as a whole. "One attempts to treat the demands and commitments of community life with generosity," she wrote, "and it is fatefully easy not to see or to ask somebody's counsel too late." Mary faults herself for not being more aware. "I didn't really think that there was anything particularly to be on my guard against—and that was a very big mistake." She continues, "I could write a little book now on things to be careful about, quite simple obvious things such as not, out of consideration for a third person (or persons), failing to retain one's own identity and one's own little bit of home together, etc."

Heather and Murray too were caught up in the painful tensions of the relationship triangle, of their vows to one another and to Mary, and to the life and future of Jyotiniketan. Following Raimon's intervention, Murray searched for words to convey their struggle in another letter to him:

> We have begun to discover again . . . that hope of which you speak, in this strange situation in which we find ourselves. Heather relayed to us something of your talks with her. Although in many ways your words were similar to what you had said to me, the reality of them struck us and I think we began to accept them. Without being able, on paper, to explain, (no need anyway, for you understand) we gave each other up (knowing more deeply than ever that in Christ there is no such thing) and from then another "thing" has come in. I think, I hope and believe that by God's strength we are ready to give each other, and ourselves, and Jyotiniketan, for any changes God may bring about in our lives. True, we don't see clearly at all any immediate changes—doors don't seem to be opening up in front of us—but I think we are ready for moving, for changes—painful and joyful

too, when the way forward becomes clear. All is not "solved" once for all, I know very well, but the eyes through which we see each other and ourselves are somehow different. Hope has returned and we are grateful, very, to God, and to you. I know, thankfully, that you will not stop praying for us . . .

Years later, Murray concurred with much of Mary's assessment. Sadly, he confirmed that since Richard's birth, Mary had grown disinclined toward any physical relationship and seemed loath to share her spiritual self as well. Murray missed both the sexual and spiritual connection they once shared. It was puzzling, for in their physical absences from one another, Mary's expressiveness and her love for him emerged in her letters. As Murray read her fastidious accounts of daily events, scrawled in her fine hand on parchment thin paper, he caught hints of her deeper self. But in person she was all practicality, passions fully contained. He, on the other hand, had grown more and more expressive. "I'm full of emotions of every sort!" he exclaimed, describing his frustration. "I could hardly have a spiritual conversation with Mary." But with Heather spiritual intimacy could be shared. "I reached an explosion point," Murray recalled, adding, "What a salvation it was for me to have Heather!" But with their spiritual intimacy "all mixed up with sexuality,"[38] the situation had become a crisis.

Perhaps the oblique "giving each other up" with the other "thing" coming in, as Murray wrote to Raimon, signified Heather and Murray's acceptance that their relationship would never be physically consummated, that their love for one another must remain chaste. They had gone to the edge of the precipice but resisted the leap. Years later Murray stated simply, "We never had sex. It wasn't I who saved us from that; it was God."[39] Undoubtedly, Heather deserved some credit as well.

As Murray had written, all was "not solved." The longing and love between Murray and Heather remained; the loneliness, loyalty and love, too, between Murray and Mary remained; the devoted friendship between Mary and Heather remained. Life in Jyotiniketan went on.

Mary's letter of January 1969 to Raimon continued:

> Murray has been away in Bombay . . . and in Vietnam . . . So Heather and I have been here on our own hoping for a little of the quiet and *shanti*[40] that ashrams are meant to afford and which seem so difficult in practice to have when one needs to eat and keep clean (moderately at least!) and to attend to one's

---

38. Interview with author.
39. Ibid.
40. *Shanti*: peace.

neighbours' needs . . . However we have had a happy and united time. Now I eagerly await Murray's return on Feb 5th. As for being beset by thoughts and pains I can report that, on the whole, I am not. A few quiet changes here and there and one finds one has a different situation. May it be so, do you think?

Mary's plaintive question echoes Murray's sense of hope returned. Hope and continued prayer would be their sustenance. In one of their Letters to Friends they had quipped, "This is no Garden of Eden as is occasionally implied!"[41] Indeed, it was not.

Nor was life for the Rogers children, now young adults in England, a Garden of Eden. Cheryl, pursuing her calling as a teacher, had found that her attraction to André, the young seminarian had not faded, nor had his to her. Though he had been ordained a Roman Catholic priest in France, they were deeply in love and facing their own impossible and painful contradiction.

At the same time, Linda was completing her nurses' training in London and finding life as a nurse did not at all suit her. What suited her much better was a young man named March whom she had met at a friend's wedding in London. Both Linda and March Hancock had grown up far east of Eden, but, coming together in, and perhaps through their less than perfect worlds, love had bloomed, and happiness had broken through. March was, as Linda notes, "blessed with a strong personality," and coping well for a young man with a difficult childhood.[42] Indeed they had much in common:

41. Letter #14.

42. March Hancock was born in 1944, the first child of a Cambridge educated Army enlistee and his wife. Following a long recovery from wounds suffered in the second wave of D-Day, his father was posted with his regiment to the Indian Army Staff College in Quetta [now Pakistan]. It was late 1945, and his wife and young March joined him there. March writes, "I have some photos of him and my Mother but unhappily no memories, of what was a pleasant colonial life after the rigours of war and separated families." His continuing narrative follows:

"Partition and independence for India and Pakistan took place in 1947. The civilian and military Brits left in a mostly orderly manner. However, Muslims and Hindus started to slaughter each other as Muslims fled mostly north to Pakistan and Hindus fled south to India. Over a million died after centuries of living in relative harmony with each other. The Regiment, including wives and children, entrained for a four day trip to Bombay to catch a troop ship back to England. Unfortunately the train was attacked by Hindus and the Muslim drivers fled, leaving some British soldiers to drive the trains. This became a six or seven day trip with little or no food or water and some children died en route. My little sister Grizelda, about ten months old, died on arrival at Bombay. To add to this misery, polio broke out on the ship going home and more died. Those still fit nursed those that weren't, and my Mother was amongst those that unknowingly [contracted the disease] en route. [She was] struck down just a week after arriving back in London and died within three days of being admitted to hospital. She was twenty-eight. I was not quite four. My poor Father, who was thirty, went 'awol' and disappeared

Cambridge-educated fathers, early lives in India, and families, other than their own, who raised them. Thus, on July 7, 1967, the family converged in Cambridge to gather at St. Ben'et's Church, where Linda and March were married, standing before the same altar where Mary and Murray had exchanged their wedding vows. Though Mary and Cheryl were on hand for some pre-wedding festivities, it was Murray's sister Olive who had made the local arrangements for the young couple. Murray arrived a bit later, but in plenty of time to officiate at the service, sharing a joyful reunion with Evered Lunt, now Bishop of Stepney, the friend and mentor whose priesthood had awakened Murray's own priestly call so many years before in his university days. Linda recalls their big reception at a local hotel with its notes of cultural dissonance: "Mother was in her sari and Heather was too. March's Father was on to his third wife, and she was dazzling in a multi-coloured dress with gigantic peacock hat!!! *Honestly*. But we remember it as a happy moment and I left the reception in the shortest pink dress with a big-brimmed pink hat bought for some reason with Muriel, Father's other sister."[43]

To this day Linda wonders who may have footed the bill for that big party. She hopes she was properly grateful.

But for Cheryl and André it would be nearly another three years of untold anguish before they too could claim such happiness. At last by 1970, having resolved to choose marriage to one another over André's priestly vows to the Roman Catholic church, they needed Rome's permission for André's re-laicization. Paperwork completed, the prospective bride and groom happily made their wedding plans. There were to be three ceremonies—one civil at the *Mairie*[44] in Paris, one religious in Paris, and another in England in Coventry Cathedral; all were scheduled in good time for the official dispensations to be complete. But in a letter to Raimon, dated March 4, 1970 and posted in India, Mary fretted: "Cheryl and André's wedding is hoped most fervently to be on March 30. The *Mairie* marriage ceremony has to be booked 3 weeks in advance and also all is prepared with Stephen Verney[45] in Coventry for what we hope will be a very happy service of Unity and Blessing in the Cathedral Chapel of Unity on April 11 so that friends

---

for weeks. I stayed with my Godmother and her family, then in quarantine. I was then brought in part by her family, and later on by a Great Aunt, who had brought up my Father, since both his parents had died by the time he was twelve."

43. Interview with author.

44. *Mairie*: City Hall

45. The Rev. Stephen Verney was canon of Coventry Cathedral from 1958–1970, known and respected for his creativity and progressive thinking in establishing the athedral as a center for reconciliation and renewal. He was later elected Bishop of Repton.

on the English side of the Channel can come and meet Cheryl and André afterwards . . . it worries me to think there might be a question of excommunication if the *Mairie* goes on before the papers are received from Rome."

Nor was that her only worry. Murray had already left for another trip, and they would be meeting in Paris for the wedding. She ended her letter on a pleading note: "Please remember us from time to time, Raymond, during this time in Paris—especially when it's both Murray and myself with the family. Murray does not always find it easy to adjust to family life after the sort of life he'll have been living in Israel, Beirut, Istanbul and we want it so much to be inwardly as well as outwardly harmonious. I'm sure you understand—and afterwards, also in April . . . With love, Mary . . ."

Her worry regarding the papers from Rome was for naught. Cheryl, who had moved to France the previous year to continue her teaching career, with André's help, had the arrangements well in hand. Uncertainty and anguish had dissolved into joy. André recalls that the dispensation from Rome came through with little difficulty—not surprising since, as Cheryl notes, as a promising young priest with leadership capabilities, he was much-loved by his fellow priests and supported by superiors. They understood. Many of them who had been present in Assisi when Cheryl and André had first met were on hand for the ceremonies, civil and religious, which took place on March 28th. With snow falling from the Paris sky, they were married by a Roman Catholic Archbishop, Monseigneur Pezeril at the Bishop's Palace Chapel. A small party followed the ceremonies, and the following day André's family hosted a gathering at their home.

"Of course it had been a disagreeable surprise for his parents to learn of my existence," Cheryl acknowledged. Not only were they initially displeased that he would forego his priestly vows, but also that she came from England, a land despised by the Poutier family since André's uncle had been killed by the English in the Battle of Mers-el-Kébir[46] in 1940. But, like the church authorities, they had been cajoled into acquiescence, and that day whatever reluctance remained was transcended with good food and wine. To this day Cheryl and André chuckle at the memory of André's father gamely and repeatedly trying to ease the tension and bridge the cultural gap between him and Murray with a quintessentially French invitation: "*Encore une petite goutte?*"[47]

---

46. The Battle of Mers-el-Kébir took place on July 3, 1940. By then the French had signed an armistice with Germany, and England feared that the French fleet would fall into German hands. Thus, to prevent such an occurrence they attacked the French off the coast of French Algeria, destroying the fleet and inflicting heavy casualties.

47. Loosely translated: "A little more to drink?"

But it was not only the warm French hospitality that touched Mary's heart. Another letter to Raimon from Mary just a month later found her nearly over the moon with joy:

> Murray and I were both deeply impressed by the Marriage Office. The readings were chosen by André and read in French by the priest assisting the Archbishop and by Murray in English. We thought that the question and answer part was beautifully and simply phrased, and the whole thing was a joy."

She continued on a more personal note of deep happiness:

> I cannot tell you how much I feel we have to be thankful for and rejoice in when I see Cheryl so happy with André, Linda with March and, last but not least, Richard with Alice. Yes, but I'm wrong to say "last but not least" because I think we are the last to be mentioned, Murray and myself. And there too I feel very thankful because I feel we are together again, two people who belong, even recapturing certain areas of life together. Though I know I mustn't bank on it or be depressed and pained if we have a few regressions, when our circumstances revert once more or I hit the wrong chord. Yet I rejoice in the here and now and hope to build on it.

Then off they went to Coventry for the ceremony and greeting of English friends, just as Mary had hoped. When it all was over, Cheryl and André settled into "a mini-flat" in Paris, and André began the transition from a life of priestly poverty to one requiring at least a modicum of financial security. Raimon Panikkar, Cheryl recalls, was one of their first visitors.

As Mary's letter had noted, love was blooming in England as well. Only a few months later, Richard followed suit with his own wedding to Alice Monroe. They had met as students at Cambridge. Richard was taken not only with her gentle charm and intellectual acuity; he was impressed with her family as well. The Monroes had met at Bletchley Park during the war, and, according to Richard, Alice's father was "celebrated" for the "enormous role" he played in bringing the war to an earlier ending through his top secret work of de-coding enemy messages. Thus, on August 8th, 1970, Richard and Alice were married in Burgess Hill, W. Sussex. It was, as they both wanted, "a smart English-style wedding,"[48] followed by a honeymoon in France. Richard, who had no desire to follow his parents' footsteps in any way, looked forward to a solid career in government administration. At last he had found a place where he could truly belong.

48. Cheryl Poutier, telephone interview from Elancourt, France by author, 2007.

Following the two weddings, Mary, Murray, and Heather returned to Jyotiniketan, with a collective sigh of relief. Fraught though their life was with uncertainties there, they were back to their beloved India. For Mary that return offered special solace, for she was finding new life in a milieu that suited her best—that of the intellect. Wonder of wonders, her gifts had been called into service by the person she most trusted in the world, her spiritual director, the seemingly peripatetic Raimon Panikkar.

As early as 1967, Mary had begun collaborating with Murray and Raimon, serving as translator for articles written by Raimon relating to Hindu spirituality and interfaith dialogue. Murray, by then well known in interfaith circles, had moved into a pivotal role within the East Asia Christian Conference and the World Council of Churches. In 1969 he was charged with the task of seeing that "a comprehensive policy statement of the [World] Council's relationships with men of other faiths and ideologies" be prepared for consideration by the World Council in Addis Ababa following year. Their memo read, "It is obvious that, in the living context of dialogue with men of other faiths in Asia, the East Asia Christian Conference is in a significant position to make an effective contribution to the theological stance which the W.C.C. might like to take towards men of other faiths."[49] In this "crucial moment" Murray, the point man, called upon Raimon for consultation and articulation of the key theological issues.

Thus it was that Mary and Murray found new partnership in these intellectual challenges, with Raimon serving as a resource for both. Aware of Mary's remarkable linguistic gifts, Raimon turned the tables and drafted her to be a resource for him. By 1969 her work had gone well beyond translation of individual articles, as she agreed to join a small team of scholars, collaborating to assist him in the creation of a vast English anthology of the ancient Hindu Vedas. Bettina Bäumer, an highly respected Indologist of Austrian origin who had made her home in the ancient city of Varanasi, was one of the team and would become a lifelong friend of Jyotiniketan. Periodically they would gather at Raimon's home, also in Varanasi, to share the work he assigned. Mary would grapple with the Sanskrit texts, adapting them fastidiously and tenderly to preserve both their meaning and their beauty in English. Early in the process she wrote to him, "I am now most happily embarking on Section VII of the Cosmic Prayers. I've taken a long time getting back to it but now hope to let myself go on it, and then on anything else that comes my way."[50] She could hardly have imagined just *how much* was to come her way. It would be a nine year commitment to Raimon's

---

49. Rogers, letter to Raimon Panikkar, 1969.
50. Ibid.

ambitious work. Just as surely as Heather had been emotional salvation for Murray, this meaty intellectual task would be salvation for Mary.

At the same time, Heather's linguistic talents were being put to use as well. Fluent in French, she was translating many of Abhishiktananda's writings into English. The work tapped into her deep spiritual resources, her own dedicated life of prayer and silence. But seldom were her considerable accomplishments acknowledged, save by their closest friends. Neither she nor Mary sought the limelight.

In the meantime, Mary, Murray, and Heather were searching for ways to remain in their beloved India, to join their lives with Indian people. Though their clear intention was, as Murray put it, to live in India "forever and ever until we died," the writing was beginning to appear on the wall. He offered another rationale for their failure:

> We'd been praying for ages that God would send somebody. By the time we got to '68, '69, it was rather plain that it was unlikely to happen, partly because we'd been thinking of North Indians, not South Indians. North Indians . . . being much poorer, and much more dependent on status . . . Very understandable, I could see it. If one's been frightfully poor all one's life, to really live as poorly as we were living looked a bit barmy. And they were being told by missionaries that God wanted us to have an abundant life, and an abundant life meant rupees, dollars, and pounds! . . . Therefore, in a way we weren't surprised, but we couldn't see how Jyotiniketan could go on [with us there].[51]

But if they were to get out of the way so that Jyotiniketan could become fully Indian, where would they go? For as Murray later recalled, "Of course, we expected to be in India . . . [But if] God doesn't mean us to be *here* (in Kareli), (still) we think he means us to be in India."[52]

There were options. One was for Murray to become a parish priest in Nainital, high in the Himalayas. But the thought of settling back into the Anglican hierarchy seemed "totally illogical." There was another proposal as well—this one seriously considered—from a group of Roman Catholic sisters in Poona—that they join in the creation of an ecumenical retreat center. Bishop Robinson was part of the negotiations, and with an architect ready with drawings to renovate a lovely old Anglican ashram [*Christa Prema Seva Sangha*],[53] they were strongly attracted to the idea. Yet there

---

51. Interview with Trapnell.
52. Ibid.
53. *Christa Prema Seva Sangha* was founded in 1922 as *Christa Seva Sangha* by an Anglican missionary, Father Jack Winslow, who led a group of men in a simple ashram

were doubts as well. How likely would it be that Indian men would feel called to join a community of mostly women? And if they truly believed that Christian communities in India were disadvantaged by western influence, wouldn't their presence in this new endeavor tip the balance in exactly the wrong direction? Murray, seeking support from Raimon and Swamiji, wrote to Raimon: "If real Hindu cooperation isn't forthcoming then will it not be the old way again, Christians, and largely westerners, launching something with the hope that one day others will join? My other doubt is whether any of you friends in Varanasi are ready to be fully committed, not only to the idea but also to its working out? I do think such a commitment is very important and it is a little difficult to see how any of you can really give it at the moment."

He continues, lightheartedly, but with earnest intent, "I'm hoping perhaps Swamiji and I may be able to go there in January. It's time now for me to work on Swamiji's conscience! He's been at work on mine for long enough!"

The urgency of his entreaties for "commitment" to a joint project were driven by another consideration. For God, it seemed, was answering their prayers for Jyotiniketan to become a truly Indian Christian ashram.

The breakthrough had come in May 1969. Murray was at a large Roman Catholic meeting in Bangalore. Between sessions, he found himself chatting over a cup of tea with an Indian Franciscan priest. Having shared a bit of their lives, they were preparing to bid farewell when Murray said, "Now do, Father Augustine, pray for us. Pray for Jyotiniketan. God knows we long for it to continue, but we don't know how unless somebody comes who really believes God has called them there in a complete way."[54] Father Augustine had told Murray how he served in a large seminary, teaching theology. He had often longed, he said, to live more like St. Francis amongst the poor. Twice he had requested of his superiors to be allowed to leave the seminary to live more simply. On both occasions they had refused: he could not be spared from his teaching of theology. Reluctantly, he had obeyed. Now in his fifties, he had reconciled himself to living out his life there.

And so they parted company. But a few weeks later, a letter arrived from Father Augustine saying, "I've thought about our conversation at tea, and I think I'm the man to come to Jyotiniketan." But, of course, he warned,

---

lifestyle. Their first rule set out a way of life for single men and married couples to live together as equals. Later versions of the Rule (1928, 1929) separated the community into three orders: single men, single women, and married couples. It is now an ecumenical community, commonly known as Christa Prema Seva Ashram.

54. Interview with Trapnell.

he would need permission from his superiors; he could not come without their blessing. Thus began a long process.

This time his superiors were willing to consider Father Augustine's request, but they needed to visit Jyotiniketan. They were, after all, responsible for his well-being. It was nearly a thousand mile journey from Augustine's seminary to Jyotiniketan. But eventually the Franciscan Provincial[55] and his assistant arrived and settled in for a stay of several days. Reassured that Jyotiniketan was not motivated by financial aspirations, they left with abundant pleasantries, but no indication what their response to Augustine would be.

Arriving back at the seminary, they gave Augustine their answer. No, he could not go. Yes, they could understand why he would want to go, but they simply could not accept the responsibility of his being there, living so poorly. It could be a threat to his health. Augustine, Murray recalls, was outraged, saying to his superiors, "Now this is ridiculous! Those people are foreigners. We are all Indians, and we say that *they're* living too poorly? And we call ourselves Franciscans?" His dander up, he added, "This confirms to me that I must go there."[56]

Still they refused. And so Augustine, faithful to his vow of obedience, told them he would not go without their blessing. But if they would not give it, he would appeal to Rome.

Thus it was that they relented and granted their permission. Augustine could come to begin his own Indian community at Jyotiniketan. Mary, Murray, and Heather would leave. Lacking concrete support from Swamiji, there seemed no viable alternative.

For the time remaining, they would drink as deeply as possible of what they loved most in India. For Heather, that would be her homely work in the villages, saying good-bye and around Jyotiniktan itself, making sure everything was ready for Fr. Augustine. For Mary it would be honing her translations and staying in touch with Raimon, who now had left India for a semester at Harvard. And for Murray, it would be time with Swamiji and a pilgrimage to the Indian sites holiest to him.

On one level, the bond between Murray and Swamiji had been strained by their decision. Murray had fervently hoped that Swamiji would lend his support to their efforts to create a new community in Poona, but as a dedicated *sannyasa*, living mostly in his *kutiya*,[57] he was unwilling. And

---

55. Provincial: An official in the Roman Catholic Church in charge of an ecclesiastical province.

56. Interview with Trapnell.

57. *Kutiya*: hut.

ultimately, no matter how Swamiji had leaned on Murray's conscience, they had not been able to live his *"rêve"* that they continue in India. "Swamiji," Murray later said, "was so sad, and sort of angry . . . and felt that we'd let everybody down."[58] Yet their deeper connection remained intact. As before, Murray found his way to Swamiji's abode in Gyansu, high in the Himalayas by the banks of the Ganges, the place where he had gone from Shantivanam, and where his "longing for 'Being there, simply,'"[59] was fulfilled.

As was their custom and their delight, they celebrated the Eucharist together, but this time the celebration was one of reconciliation, if not full forgiveness. Their ritual was as it always had been. Before beginning they would sing together—joining their voices in songs from the Upanishads that Swamiji had sung in his cave at Arunachala. Then they would strip down to only a *dhoti*[60] to celebrate, Indian-style. Murray recalled:

> [We] would carefully select an altar stone from the river and clamber up the ladder to the attic chapel, for all its roughness and lack of Anglo-Saxon order more perfect, perhaps than any cathedral I have been privileged to experience. We sat side by side on our mats on the floor—no man could have stood in that cathedral. The altar was a rough box . . . under which Swamiji kept many treasures, little brass dishes for the *arati*, camphor and water, a sandalwood rosary from Haridwar, papers on which he had typed many Sanskrit verses from the Vedas and Upanishads without which no Great Thanksgiving would be complete . . . Everything served, the sound of the river which sometimes almost drowned the words, the little vessels and papers and saffron cloths, the stone chalice and paten discovered with joy in the bazaar in Haridwar . . . There followed an unmeasured time of silence, a silence from the depth of which one could almost audibly, tangibly sense the emerging *OM*.[61]

"The Mass," du Boulay adds, "would sometimes go on for hours, but to Murray it always seemed too short."

Murray and Abhishiktananda were deeply connected in the Eucharist, to one another, and to God. Their ten year relationship had had a profound effect, not only on Murray, but on Swamiji as well. "I was astonished,"

58. Interview with Trapnell.
59. Rogers, quoted in du Boulay, *Cave of the Heart*, 206.
60. *Dhoti*: a long loincloth, traditionally worn by Indian men. Murray later reflected: "It's fascinating that when Indians celebrate sacrament, they take off clothes, and we western people put on clothes. There's quite a lot in that, I think, what we put on and take off. We, so to speak, dress up. They dress down." (Interview with author.)
61. Rogers, quoted in du Boulay, *Cave of the Heart*, 208–9.

Murray said, "that within a year or two he could be so marvelously at home with us, and we could feel so at home with him."[62] Left far behind were the early days of their acquaintance when Abhishiktananda, skeptical that any priest who was not Roman and not celibate could be legitimate, kept to his room to celebrate the traditional Roman mass. Gradually, along with the multiple layers of his liturgical vestments, he had shed his preconceptions and opened his mind and heart to new understandings of God's relationship with the human family. Soon he had grown to "appreciate the value of a married priesthood, even referring to 'the sacerdotal value of the couple.[63]'" and rejoicing in concelebrations[64] of the Eucharist with his married Anglican friend. Of course, this transformation, so sensitively chronicled by Shirley du Boulay in her biography, sprang in large part from Swamiji's encounter with Ramana Maharshi and the years of dedicated asceticism that followed. Yet Jyotiniketan also played a role. Murray recalled an early visit by Swamiji when, having fallen ill, he was taken to the hospital run by Jyotiniketan's Quaker friends, Kuni and Laurie Baker. Following his recovery he exclaimed to Murray, "Mooray,[65] I am amazed! I am amazed! They believe hardly anything they are supposed to, but they are among the deepest Christians I have ever met!"[66] Murray told too of a later conversation Swamiji shared with the community about the Benedictine Order. "He was very sure they were the 'real boys!'" he laughed. "We caught him . . . at this élitism and pulled his leg unmercifully when he referred to St. Francis and his followers as 'one of the newer communities!'"[67]

From Murray's side, more than anyone else, Abhishiktananda was the teacher who guided his spiritual evolution, yet Raimon Panikkar's spirit was reflected as well in Jyotiniketan's evolving liturgies and in the new ways Murray experienced his priesthood. In Abhishiktananda's *Guru and Disciple*, translated by Heather, was an essay entitled *The Mountain of the Lord*. It told of the pilgrimage, shared by Raimon[68] and Swamiji to Gangotri, the very source of the holy river Ganges. In a Preface, Murray wrote: "We heard it from the lips of those who made this pilgrimage and are happy to share

---

62. Rogers and Barton, *Abhishiktananda*, 9.

63. Du Boulay, *Cave of the Heart*, 169.

64. In deference to the Roman Church, their con-celebrations never occurred in public.

65. Murray's name as pronounced with Abhishiktananda's strong French accent.

66. Rogers and Barton, *Abhishiktananda*, 10.

67. Interview with Trapnell.

68. Though not identified by name in the text, Raimon Panikkar's identity is apparent.

with others the joy which we experienced on hearing it."[69] In that moving story from high in the Himalayas is found a clear articulation of Raimon's Eucharistic theology, shaped by his own experience with Hinduism. It is there that we hear of the "cosmic Covenant" and of his identification with the old priest Melchizedek, known for his blessing of Abraham [Abram]. This was the mystical vision that Jyotiniketan had embraced, recounted by Swamiji:

> One day my friend said to me, "I am a priest of the Lord, with him and in him after the order of Melchisedech. I owe it to myself, to God and to the Church to celebrate the Eucharist here. Look at those priests of the temple of Mother Ganges, the ones of Kedar, Badr, and of all the sanctuaries of the mountains and plain; are they not the very brothers of the biblical Melchisedech? It was he who blessed Abraham and whom the priest of the Roman rite commemorates each day at the most sacred moment of the liturgy. Melchisedech is truly the type of the priest of the cosmic Covenant, and it is according to his order, not according to the order of Aaron, the priest of the special Covenant with Israel, that Christ wished to be a priest, and in him I also have my priesthood.
>
> The offering of Melchisedech, priest of the Most High, as it says in the Bible, foretold Christ's offering. And at the same time Christ's offering is foretold, and will be for ever 'till he comes' by the offerings of these Melchisedechs of India, whose brother I am, both by my blood and by my sacred ordination in Christ. Priests make their offerings in the temples, sadhus meditate and fast in their caves, pilgrims strive and pray and chant on their way to the source. All this is the mystery of Christ who is still hidden, of Christ who is already present although still invisible. The Spirit himself is already present in all this, bringing everything that happens in time and is done by men, into the mystery of Christ.
>
> The role of the Christian priest is to bring all this to its eschatological completion under the sign of the sacrament . . .[70]

The passage continues with a mystical integration of Hinduism into a Christian vision:

> . . . The bread and the wine which I shall offer here in my Mass will be the calling towards God of all these pilgrims at the sacred sources of rivers in the Himalayas, of all the priests, all ascetics,

---

69. Abhishiktananda, *Guru and Disciple*, 135.
70. Ibid., 168.

those of our time, of days gone by, and of the future, for the Eucharist transcends all time.

The ascent of Israel to Jerusalem had to find its fulfillment in Jesus ascending the cross. Likewise the ascent of India to her very source must culminate in the Eucharist, the return to her origins on coming to the end. The return to the source is the final act of bringing together in its primordial unity the whole multiplicity of being . . . Believe me, the Eucharist is the highest sign of the *advaita* of being, on which our *rishis* and wise men are so constantly meditating. That is why the Eucharist must be celebrated here at the source of the river by both of us, you who are the monk and I who am a priest of the Holy Church . . . Our Upanishads speak of the deepest depth of the mystic cave which conceals the final interior mystery, and which is never reached as long as any glimmer of light from outside can penetrate within and attempt to light it up. And such is the mystery of Being, of the bosom of the father . . .[71]

Little wonder that Mary, Murray, and Heather had experienced a sort of spiritual explosion when in 1965 Raimon had led them in the retreat, "The Eucharist, the Source of our Life." For Raimon, there was no agonizing inner battle between Christianity and Hinduism as there had been for Swamiji; he could claim his identity as a Christian-Hindu priest. And, as a gifted teacher, melding intellect with experience of the heart, he had pointed the way to a lasting transformation in the life and worship of Jyotiniketan.

In 1970, Murray, Mary, and Heather wrote to their Friends, "Looking back over a year or two there have sizable changes in our Liturgy of the Holy Eucharist and in our worship at evening *sadhana*.[72] The Indian spiritual "world" has crept in—rather, been welcomed in and has enriched our life in Christ more than we can yet measure. Reading the Upanishads day by day, pondering the spiritual experience expressed in them, is no longer a foreign intrusion into Christian worship; it belongs there. We know it now to be God's gift to us too and we are deeply grateful."[73]

In 1971 the Liturgical Commission of the newly formed Church of North India was ready to receive their offering. Distributed under its aegis, it was a hand-typed [by Murray] booklet: The Jyotiniketan Ashram's

---

71. Ibid., 169, 171–72.

72. *Sadhana*: influenced, perhaps, by their friend Anthony de Mello, the Indian Jesuit priest and writer, they began to use this term to refer to their evening worship or spiritual practice.

73. Letter #19.

"The Holy Eucharist."[74] It truly was a labor of love. In the meantime, the last precious months in India were slipping away. Grieving his own impending loss, Swamiji returned Murray's visits with more frequent sojourns at Jyotiniketan. Early in 1971, as their departure loomed, they embarked with him—Mary, Heather, and Murray, along with Father Shigeto Oshida, a Dominican priest visiting from Japan, on a profoundly moving spiritual pilgrimage along the ancient pilgrim path to Haridwar and Rishikesh.

They had told their Friends of their decision and shared how their love for India had matured. "Don't imagine please," they wrote, "that we are 'starry-eyed' about India. The mystery and the wonder remain, the conviction that the Spirit has given human beings in this part of the world great and precious spiritual gifts (that are all too rapidly being lost), but the "mystique" that afflicts some western friends has melted away . . . And now, with less self-righteousness and more clear vision, we are left with the real drama . . . of a vast part of the human family struggling, sometimes with success, often with failure, to reach a fuller humanity, to be what almost instinctively we know we were created to be, free and responsible human beings."[75] Love and anguish flowed through their words as they watched the days disappear: "The sun is setting on another day of work and joy and suffering in the villages of Kareli and Kargaina. For those who carry a corner of Asia in their hearts, this is bound to be a special moment: the dust over the village, caught in the rays of the setting sun, the smoke from the fires where the women are beginning to cook the evening meal, the cries of the farmer as he encourages the bullocks to do a few more rounds at the Persian wheel before they too turn in for the night . . . The body and blood of this day's life is only a hair's breadth away from that other Body and Blood of Christ whose Presence carries forward this little universe of the Indian village."[76] Already they were seeing their India through the eyes of loss, as if from a distance.

"Very mercifully," they wrote, "we do not have to judge our years here. They have meant more joy and more suffering than we could have ever foreseen away back when we first heard the name Kareli. They have been a wonderful gift of God and we are deeply grateful." They could not help noticing a spiritual lesson: "It is not without significance," they observed, "that it was precisely when we were ready to 'die out' that the Indian friends for whom we have prayed for the last fifteen years appeared on the horizon."[77]

---

74. See Appendix 2 for the full text.
75. Letter #19.
76. Letter #20.
77. Ibid.

When it was nearly time to go, Father Augustine arrived to spend about ten days with them, to be introduced to the faithful Fidah Hussein and village friends and to learn the ropes. Everything—their beloved Chapel, the small buildings where they had lived, the thatched huts where they had sat in silence, even the bullocks, Aurobindo and Christopher, the newer animals, right down to the string beds were being left to Augustine. But since relinquishing their support from C.M.S., Mary, Murray, and Heather had come closer to their desire to be poorer than ever before. Ever so briefly, Murray squirmed: "I think we only had nineteen rupees, which was about two pounds. So, I remember I felt frightfully embarrassed ... And I remember, saying to dear Augustine, 'You know, I feel awfully badly, because we have hardly anything at all to leave behind.'"

And Augustine said, "Oh, Murray, don't worry about that. This is just what I've been wanting for years!" [Murray laughs.][78] And now Augustine could assume a new name embracing his poverty: "Swami Deenabandu," friend of the poor.

And so, as Murray reported, they "slipped away."[79] Never to be forgotten, he wrote, were the crowds of "village friends with whom we had shared so much, especially Mary and Heather with the women and children, accompanying us down the village road and over the fields."[80] As they pulled away and out of sight, turning back, they could see their neighbors waving and strewing flowers in a fond and sad farewell to their Christian friends. Overcome with grief, could they remember the consoling words of Rabindranath Tagore on which they had meditated for the past months?

> I know that whatever lags behind in this life
> laden with slowness is not altogether lost.
> I know that my dreams that are still unfulfilled,
> and my melodies still unstruck,
> are clinging to some lute-strings of thine,
> and they are not altogether lost.[81]

---

78. Interview with Trapnell.
79. Ibid.
80. Letter #21.
81. Letter #20.

12

Jerusalem: Seeking Peace, Meeting Conflict

1971–1973

> Jerusalem, Jerusalem, the city that kills the prophets and stones those who are sent to it! How often have I desired to gather your children together as a hen gathers her brood under her wings, and you were not willing!
>
> —Luke 13:34

AT THE TIME, IT had seemed barely worth a mention. Yes, their visit to Jerusalem in 1962 had been a warmly memorable part of their pilgrimage with their friend Ilse Friedeberg. Through her they had stayed in a monastery in the Garden of Gethsemane with a group of hospitable Russian Orthodox sisters. Their mutual commitment to prayer and friendship had been bolstered by the connection made between Mother Mary, the monastery's Abbess, and Mary Rogers. Yet on that trip, it was the visit with Athenagoras in Istanbul that had most touched Murray's heart, resonating as it did to the Patriarch's expansive generosity of spirit. Mostly eclipsed was a brief exchange between Mary and Murray and Mother Mary that had occurred one evening after supper, just before they left for Istanbul. Mother Mary set forth a surprising suggestion, recalled here by Murray:

> Would we pray in India [to discern] whether we weren't meant by God to come and be a little center of friendship and prayer in Jerusalem? She said there were many people doing admirable and good and lovely things in Jerusalem working with other people, but she sensed very much the need for some little group to be there just to do nothing. Just for friendship. For worship

and silence. I remember so clearly: this suggestion was a bit of a shock because we were completely in India.

I said, "That's very sweet of you, Mother Mary, but we're going to go on living in India. Thank you very much. We hope to die there too."[1]

For nearly ten years, the memory of that conversation had "gone completely underground."[2] The invitation was lovely but not very relevant.

But, Murray added, "when all the doors seemed to close in India, we said to one another, 'Do you remember old Mother Mary once asked us to go to Jerusalem? Do you think it may be what God wants us to do now?' And that's when I wrote to Mother Mary,"[3] asking if she still thought it might be God's will that Jyotiniketan come to Jerusalem.

When the response came it was from Mother Barbara, with the news that Mother Mary had just died and she was to succeed her as Abbess. But her response was affirmative: "We do indeed think it may be God's will." Only then did Murray write to the Anglican Bishop in Jerusalem to see if he, too, thought that ancient city might become their home. Bishop George Appleton had also responded positively and offered them temporary housing within the close of St. George's Cathedral. While accepting the bishop's invitation, Murray remained circumspect: "I didn't want to go there and be too tied up with the Anglican Church, because our experience in India made us want to belong to *everybody* . . . All these separations and little huddles of different denominations . . . we just don't feel that they are real."[4]

Though Murray, Mary, and Heather had come to believe that separations are unreal on the level of the heart, they were all too familiar with the harsh reality of denominational and inter-religious strife. And they saw if they were to have any hope of bridging the separations endemic to Jerusalem with its age-old rivalries between denominations, religions, and political allegiances, they would have to choose their place of residence carefully. "Very quickly," Murray explained, "we realized that it was essential for us to live in the Old City, the very heart of it, because that's the only place where people don't decide because of [where] you're living that you're pro-this or pro-that. Every other place, outside, you'd be pro-Palestinian, pro-Israeli, pro-Zionism, pro-this, pro-that."[5]

1. Interview with Nelson.
2. Ibid.
3. Interview with Trapnell.
4. Ibid.
5. Ibid.

Their new home was in the Muslim Quarter of the Old City, just inside the Damascus Gate. The big old house where they found lodging was steeped in colonial history. It was the house where the retired British General Gordon[6] had stayed in 1882–83. There, gazing from a window, he had perceived the shape of a skull in a nearby rock formation, and, filled with Christian fervor, concluded it must be the site of the crucifixion and tomb of Jesus.[7] During the First World War, when disease and hunger ravaged the city, the house had been owned by an American named Horatio Spafford, who made it available to the so-called "American Colony"[8] for a soup kitchen. Later, in 1925, Spafford's daughter, living in the house she had inherited, offered shelter to a motherless Arab baby. Thus began the Spafford Children's Center, which eventually became the only children's hospital in the Old City and the West Bank. Just before the arrival of Mary, Murray, and Heather, it had transitioned to become a day clinic for children and their families, and extra rooms were made into living quarters. It was, by all accounts, a picturesque place, located high on the wall of the Old City and approached by 160 steps from the Damascus Gate. Their space within the house was simple but comfortable, with plenty of room for the three of them. Within Heather's bedroom was a curtained-off area for their Chapel. Below the family quarters was a spacious room for larger gatherings. And with the help of a friend, Jean-Paul Mahieu, who, they wrote, "combines wonderful carpentry with a priest's vocation,"[9] two smaller rooms for guests were carved out of the large room with rough but serviceable plywood.

Settling into this new home, their community routine of prayer and worship, so firmly established in India, continued. Each day commenced

---

6. General Charles Gordon (1833–1885): The renowned British General, known for his military exploits in the Crimean War, in China, and in North Africa. He was later killed in the Battle of Khartoum.

7. In 1883–1884, between military assignments, General Gordon, who some years earlier had embraced evangelical Christianity, lived in Palestine. This idea was put forth in Gordon's book: *Reflections on Palestine*, written during his stay. Today many evangelical Christians continue to honor this site as the true place of Christ's crucifixion.

8. The American Colony: Founded by Horatio and Anna Spafford, who arrived from Chicago in 1881, the group began with their family and a small number of others from their church. Though not missionaries, they intended to work to alleviate suffering in the Holy Land, whether the need was with Jews or local Bedouins.

They were eventually joined by others in their simple life of sharing goods in common. As the larger group could no longer be accommodated in the house in the Old City, they acquired a former pasha's palace nearby which became their primary residence. The American Colony became well-known for their neutrality and for their acts of benevolence, and the building where they lived now remains in East Jerusalem as the American Colony Hotel.

9. Letter #22.

with a celebration of "the Great Thanksgiving," the Jyotiniketan Liturgy. As before, there were two other times of worship, silence liberally scattered through them all. Cushions on the floor allowed for sitting, cross-legged. Life in India flowed into their family meals as well. Out of the shipping boxes came the metal *thalis* for serving their curried vegetables; rice and dal remained their daily sustenance.

Having left India, India had not left them. John Landgraf, an American archeologist living in Jerusalem, who would become their devoted friend, recalled his first impression. "I had seen them around before I met them," he said. "Mary and Heather in their saris, Murray in his Indian cassock." Aware of the myriad eccentric little groups, religious and otherwise, drawn to live in that city, he thought to himself, "Ah, some more crazies have arrived!"[10] Though still carrying their British passports, deep within they were Indian. Looking through the eyes of strangers looking at them, they understood the confusion they provoked: "No doubt we are strange types . . . people from Britain originally, [but] who feel themselves to be as much, if not more, tied up to the Orient, both in their spirits and ways of feeling and in outer ways of living and dress." Thus, it was especially sustaining when some of those strangers became friends: "Just because we are rather difficult people to place in a tidy and easily comprehended 'box,'" they wrote in their Letter to Friends, "we have appreciated all the more friends of all communities (and Jerusalem abounds in communities!) who have borne with us long enough to understand who we are and what we carry in our minds and hearts."[11]

Day by day, their lives reflected who they had become and their longing to share what they carried in their hearts. Long gone was any missionary ardor to carry the Gospel to the unchurched with an eye to conversion; their message had been transformed. "From the world of further east, of Hinduism and Buddhism, we [are] plunged into the world of the three monotheisms: Judaism, Islam and Christianity," they wrote. "We are *not* impressed with the supposed superiority of the one "world" over the other; we *are* impressed with the increasing sense that the one approach to the Divine Mystery without the other will never discern the fulness which we believe God desires for us his children in both east and west."[12] What they now longed to live out and to impart to others was how their Christianity had been deepened by its engagement with the mystical traditions of the East. Thus it was that they began occasional Saturday night gatherings called "Evenings Facing East," to share the contemplative dimension of Hindu and Buddhist

10. Landgraf, telephone interview with author, 2011.
11. Letter #21.
12. Ibid.

scriptures—and of Christian readings as well with new friends. Though they had left India, never could they turn away from its spiritual gifts. John Landgraf was often amongst them, finding spiritual nourishment. And if he had initially pegged them as "crazies," he soon learned he also shared their preference for the simple life and their vegetarianism.

As they plunged into life in their new surroundings, their daily rounds took on a familiar rhythm. Heather, true to her lifelong desire to connect with local people, was determined to learn Arabic. Taken under the wing of a kind Palestinian neighbor woman who guided her around the Old City, she traversed its narrow stone passageways and befriended vendors with suitable goods and fair prices. Though the local language had changed, their diet would not. And though the sign on the little nearby "Afhghan Bakery" was misspelled, Heather, whose happy days in Afghanistan were still dear to her heart, would not consider buying a loaf of bread anywhere else. Just as in India it was she who cheerfully bore the primary burden of stocking the pantry with fruits and vegetables, lentils and rice, tea and biscuits, and eggs for the evening omelettes and who, with Mary's assistance, would be sure the meals were cooked and served on time, with plenty to share with the steady stream of guests. Happily for all, it was Murray's tradition to step into the role of clean-up when the meal ended. As in India, their community meals and times of worship formed the backbone of their common life.

Fleshing out their days were other activities, sometimes together, sometimes as individuals. Heather's energies were focused on visits with Palestinian mothers and children who came to the Spafford Clinic. On an occasional day off, she would steal away for some quiet time, often in nature, returning hours later spiritually refreshed bearing freshly painted watercolors. In quiet moments at home, she was putting the finishing touches on her latest translation for Abhishiktananda, soon to be published in England as *Guru and Disciple*. In that work, her heart and mind could fly to India. Swamiji's words that she lovingly translated beckoned her within: "As long as a man does not allow the Spirit to plunge him into his own depths and does not lose himself in that 'ray of darkness', he remains utterly incapable of understanding anything of the depths of the One who is born of the Father. Herein lies the real significance of the call of India: that it invites men to enter those inner depths which are beyond all that human reflection can attain to, or human thought or words can express."[13] Swamiji's words in French became hers in English and spoke her longing, not only for India but for God. Whether amongst the women and their babies in the Spafford Hospital, blending into the landscape she lovingly painted, or back in her

13. Abhishiktananda, *Guru and Disciple*, xii.

spare little bedroom on the Old City wall, Heather's work became her prayer and her comfort.

For Mary's part, her initial commitment to study Hebrew along with Murray was soon overshadowed by truer passions. The first, of course, was her children, who were never far from her thoughts, and weekly letters to each of them continued to flow in her fine hand. Knowing they were happy was a blessing, but how she longed to share firsthand some of that happiness, to see her daughters as they assumed their new roles as mothers. In 1970, Linda and March Hancock had become parents to little Oliver, Mary and Murray's first grandchild. Now Oliver had been joined by a little French cousin, Marie-Hélène Poutier, as well as a little sister, Victoria Hancock. Most summers, her wish to spend time with her grandchildren was granted in marvelous extended visits to England and France.

Another great love was her translation work for Raimon's Vedic anthology, moving slowly towards publication. Her painstaking efforts to preserve the stylistic beauty of the ancient texts were now stretching into their fifth year. It was a monumental undertaking for all involved. Referring to its exceedingly long gestation period, they had affectionately dubbed it "The Elephant." Despite its light-hearted nickname, never was the importance—the sacredness even—of the task questioned. In fact, when in the winter of 1973 Raimon's "team" was gathering for some intensive collaborative in Varanasi, India, despite the distance, it went without saying that Mary would be there. Together with Murray, who had been invited to lead meditations in an eastern mode at a World Council of Churches conference in Bangkok, she happily boarded a plane and headed east, leaving Heather to keep the home fires burning in the Old City. When their respective tasks were complete, Mary and Murray came together for a nostalgic visit to beloved people and places in India. Visits with Abhishiktananda and with Swami Deenabandu (formerly Father Augustine) at their old ashram in Kareli were arranged and joyful reunions celebrated with old friends and neighbors. As they wrote, "The web of friendship and joy in which we are so gratefully caught amazes us—a marvelous gift of God."[14]

As Mary quietly worked on her manuscripts, she was settling into life in Jerusalem, ostensibly curious and eager to meet new people. Though Heather's gifts for hands-on care were more natural than Mary's, when an urgent need arose, Mary could be pressed into service. Writing to Raimon, she reported, "Heather and I are going to work temporarily just three mornings a week in an Old Peoples' Home in Bethany." Alluding to her recent visit with her new granddaughter, she continued gamely: "In the early summer I

---

14. Letter #22.

bathed and spoon-fed Marie-Hélène who is at the début of life, while in the early autumn I do the same to dear old decrepit ladies."

It was, of course, Mary's love for her husband and her devotion to Jyotiniketan that took her to the Old Peoples' Home. It was that love and devotion that limited the time and attention she could lavish either on her children or on her scholarly work. Her attention and her energy were demanded in a myriad of ways, not necessarily of her choosing. With Murray in the lead, she trekked Nablus Road to St. George's Cathedral, where she and Heather would join the worship he led there. At other times, she would allow herself, despite the discomfort, to be locked into the Church of the Holy Sepulcher for the night. Murray described their "silent nights" in the Christian heart of the city, using the name they, along with Eastern Christians, preferred: The Church of the Resurrection. "During the day," he explained, "it's like [Grand] Central [Station] at rush hour, it's just so noisy and impossible . . . to pray or to be in silence." He continued, "But at nighttime you let yourself be locked in at 7:30 or so. Somebody comes round, some priest, and says, 'Go out, go out! Don't be locked in, don't be locked in!' And we simply said to them, 'Thank you very much. [We're] here to be locked in.' Then [we were] allowed to stay. We had marvelous times. We used to take ecumenical groups there, and we always invited somebody to lead four or five meditations. There are loos of a rather primitive nature. So . . . you throw a rug, or you sleep on a bench."[15] The three would find a spot to settle until the new day broke—perhaps in the Armenian Chapel where St. Helena was said to have found the cross, or perhaps higher up in the Calvary, a Greek Orthodox chapel where Jesus is traditionally said to have been crucified. For Murray, "It was beautiful. Beautiful to be in Jerusalem, because of what God had done for us through Jesus."[16]

As the time neared for the final version for Raimon's anthology to arrive for proofing, Mary was determined to see it through to publication and, to that end, shared her concerns with him. It was not only her deteriorating eyesight and impending cataract surgery that concerned her:

> I hope I can manage anything that comes my way, but the operation will probably knock me out for a month or so as regards reading . . . Strangely, perhaps, the Elephant is for me remarkably non-tiring. I have always found it so, probably because I love those old texts so much. So I'm sure there'll be no problem. I'm encouraging myself just now not to read too long at a stretch. I virtually never have the opportunity anyway and

---

15. Interview with Trapnell.
16. Ibid.

always find that the stretch of time to which I look forward with joyous anticipation invariably recedes to the future. I try to regard my present position as, on the one hand, an invitation to 'live within' and, on the other, an indication that my life will be made up *pro tem.* of a few rather simple and external 'home' occupations."

The "external 'home' occupations," never her passion, were more distracting than ever in Jerusalem. Neither she nor Heather ever gave full voice to the spiritual and emotional upheaval that had occurred in their leaving India, with its familiar routine and culture. For Mary, it had not been anticipated. Perhaps, they once had thought, they would settle peaceably in Bethlehem, near a group of Benedictine sisters and Grandchamp sisters. In a letter to Raimon Panikkar before their arrival from India she had written sanguinely of their future life: "We have not forgotten your forebodings, Raymond, about such a change of habitat being too difficult at our time of life. But somehow we do not feel that in the Bethlehem possibility the change from Kareli would be all that great and that in a situation of such complexity and intensity, we wonder if a more unaligned contribution might not be quite helpful."

Yet, years later, when asked to describe the change from India to Jerusalem, the first word that sprang to Murray's lips was "devastating;" Mary and Heather would likely have concurred. None of them could fail to notice that "everybody was divided from everybody else," and they now knew that remaining "unaligned" would be extremely difficult. There was fear and "incredible tension you felt emotionally in the air." Much of the intensity of feelings was between Christian denominations. As he crisply put it, "Everybody wants a foot there because Jesus lived and rose from the dead."[17]

Of course, deadly serious rivalries had been in play for hundreds of years, first between the Greeks [Orthodox] and the Roman Catholics, known there as "Latins", and later the Armenians and Copts. Later still arrived the Lutherans, Presbyterians, and Anglicans, all attempting to convert one another and to claim as large a piece as possible of the Holy Land and its sacred sites. Under the long domination of the Ottoman Empire which began in 1516, the long-standing conflict between the Latins and the Greeks grew increasingly intense and bloody. Finally, in 1852, Sultan Abdul Mejid, fearing a war, issued a *firman* or decree directing that the *status quo* be maintained in all the places considered sacred by the Christian factions. It laid out in exacting detail each piece of land or property considered sacred and when each denomination should have control over it. The placement

---

17. Interview with Trapnell.

of each candlestick and icon, each religious gesture, even the sweeping of shared steps was a matter of grave import, as each could imply a claim to the place. Officially called the *Declaration of the Status Quo in the Holy Places*, the document became the law of the land. Disputes would be mediated not by Christians, who were deemed untrustworthy for the task, but by neutral "Moslim Guardians." An illustrious Muslim family literally held the keys to the Church of the Holy Sepulcher. Though that is no longer the case, to this day, the *Status Quo* governs whatever quarrels continue to arise amongst Christian denominations, and now amongst Christians, Muslims, and Jews as well. Now, as then, it is the land and property and control over it that drives the ongoing tension and rivalries of which Murray spoke.

It was, as he related, "a place where every square inch matters, institutionally." The dominant attitude amongst rival denominations, he said, boiled down to this: "'This is *my* bit, and you're jolly well not going to do anything there, and that's *your* bit over there.'" As an "arch example," he told of the meeting that had occurred in 1964 between Pope Paul VI and Athenagoras, the Ecumenical [Greek] Patriarch he so loved. It was a meeting that, from afar in India, had filled his heart with hope—hope that one of the great religious schisms of all time soon might be healed. Since coming to Jerusalem, he had heard the story of what was indeed a warm and productive encounter, but tinged with the harsh reactivity of the religious ambiance of Jerusalem. The meeting was on Calvary, within the Church of the Holy Sepulcher. Murray told the story this way:

> On Calvary you've got some very old steps. Marvelous place in so many ways, and marvelous to think that God's immense love for mankind was shown there. On the right hand side [of the steps] that commemorates Christ being nailed to the cross: that is Latin. On the left side, there's a hole in the rock where traditionally the Lord's cross was put—you can put your hand down into the hole: that's Greek Orthodox.
>
> Now, when these two very prayerful and godly gentlemen met each other on Calvary, of course the Ecumenical Patriarch was on the side of Calvary itself, the cross place, because that's the Greek side. The Pope was on the other side, the Latin side. And really, you can't help laughing, because when they met, old Athenagoros was there all togged up, and obviously they were both very keen to meet one another. And [when] the younger man, the Pope, stepped forward to put his arms round Athenagoros, he stepped over that little, almost nonexistent line. And, you know, a Franciscan Father got him round the tummy, and pulled him back onto his side of the line. Because you see, *there*

was the danger, felt all around, as the *Status Quo* had described. Everybody knew that if somebody got over to that side, and did anything religious, they would have got the land, you see. They would have got the number of feet. Somebody could have said: "Well, the Pope came here. He embraced, and he got over onto the Orthodox bit. Nobody stopped him." So that would have been a real cause for friction.[18]

To learn of this intrusion of ancient religious suspicion and mistrust on a moment so replete with the promise of reconciliation was a stark reminder of the gap between their vision and the reality in which they now lived. Yet they were determined not to lose hope in the human evolution toward "universal man," as articulated by the Indian poet Tagore.[19] In their first Letter to Friends from Jerusalem, they wrote, "We remain still all too circumscribed by the littleness of our spiritual sensitivity but we rejoice again and again in being alive at a moment in history when man's consciousness of the universal, of the cosmic, of the unlimited, begins to erode and break our narrow domestic walls of religion and culture."[20]

Daily life, however, brought ever-increasing awareness of the depth of the conflict. They would shake their heads sadly when they heard of yet another altercation amongst the Christian denominations within the very walls where they spent their "silent nights," when yet again, Israeli police were called in to separate brawling Christians, wielding huge brass candle stands as weapons.

Of course the conflict in Jerusalem did not end there. Beyond the walls of the Church of the Resurrection lay Jewish and Muslim holy sites, all laden with the weight of centuries of devotion and conflict. The Temple Mount, revered as the holiest site in Judaism, is known as the place where Abraham's binding of Isaac occurred and where two Jewish temples had been built and then destroyed, first by the Babylonians in 586 BCE and then by the Romans in 70 CE. Traditionally it is seen as the place where the third [and final] Jewish temple will one day be built. Yet from the Muslim perspective, that site is known as the Noble Sanctuary. On it stands the Dome of the Rock, completed in 692 CE, which stands over the place where the Prophet Muhammed is said to have ascended to heaven. Nearby the al-Aqsa Mosque is considered the second holiest mosque in Islam [after the Masjid al-Haram in Mecca]. Thus the Temple Mount has been bitterly contested by Arabs and Jews for centuries. All of these holy places—Jewish, Christian,

---

18. Interview with Trapnell.
19. In 1961, Tagore published a series of essays entitled *Towards Universal Man*.
20. Letter #21.

and Muslim—are within easy walking distance of one another. As Murray declared, "It's as if God is saying, 'Dear children, you've simply *got* to live together in 'peace!'" Yet, he continued, "each of our groups, speaking generally, doesn't want the others there, because each of us believes that *we've* got the revelation of God, thank you very much. We Christians can't get away from Jerusalem. The Jews can't get away, and the Muslims can't. It's a tragic dilemma."[21] To this day, it remains a tragic dilemma and sticking point to peace between the Palestinians and the Jews.

Beyond Jerusalem lay the West Bank, where animosities were similarly intense. Following World War II, the United Nations General Assembly passed Resolution 181 [Future Government of Palestine] which sought to establish a two-state solution to disputed lands. But in the Arab-Israeli War of 1948, the land was captured by Jordan and boundaries were established in an armistice agreement. In 1967, however, when Israel emerged victorious over the Arab states, control of the West Bank was lost by Jordan and came under military occupation by Israel. It was that Israeli victory that Murray had so joyfully celebrated at the Western Wall on his visit, but living in the Old City, he, Heather, and Mary as well, began to see that injustice and suffering were rife on every side. "Never," they wrote in their Letter, "have we lived in a human situation where forgiveness is more needed and where we all, with no exceptions, need more urgently to ask for the forgiveness of others."[22]

Their drive to be instruments of forgiveness and reconciliation magnetically drew them to other little communities involved in ecumenical or interfaith work. Thus the time they spent with Mother Barbara and the sisters in the Garden of Gethsemane was limited. Though it was she who had urged them to come to Jerusalem, she was, Murray fondly recalled, "a marvelous old aristocrat, brought up in the Kremlin. The most loving, dear lady. Totally unecumenical!"[23]

But other opportunities abounded. Early on, by dint of his considerable experience and writing on interfaith dialogue, Murray was invited by the Anglican bishop to attend a meeting of the Rainbow Group, an intellectually prestigious and elite Jewish-Christian society comprised of Israelis and Palestinians, Jews and Christians. He was voted a member and joined their monthly discussions. He also became a member of the Ecumenical Theological Fraternity, an interdenominational Christian group devoted to deepening relationships between Christians and Jews and the Jewish state.

21. Interview with Trapnell.
22. Letter #21.
23. Interview with Trapnell.

The Tantur Ecumenical Institute on the southern edge of Jerusalem, recently founded with "scholar-monks" in residence from various parts of the world, drew Christians of many denominations together for study and interreligious understanding and became another focal point of Murray's interests. There, warm friendships were formed, and before long, Tantur was a venue where he could offer retreats and even extended courses on topics such as "The Experience of Salvation in Hinduism."

On earlier trips to Jerusalem, Murray had met people like Father Bruno Hussar, an Egyptian Catholic priest, Jewish by birth. Following the Six Day War, Father Bruno had founded a little ecumenical center in the city where Jews and Christians could study together. Inspired by the vision of Isaiah: "My people shall dwell in an oasis of peace . . . ,"[24] he called it the House of Isaiah. When Mary, Murray, and Heather arrived, he was deeply committed to a new project—a center where Jewish and Arab families might live together. It would be called *Neve Shalom/Wahat al-Salam*, literally Oasis of Peace in Hebrew and Arabic. He had been given land in Latrun, halfway between Jerusalem and Tel Aviv in a demilitarized no-man's land separating Israel from the West Bank and was living a primitive existence there, praying, much as Jyotiniketan had prayed for new members, that families would come. Not until 1978 did the first family arrive at *Neve Shalom* and the community take root. Between Father Bruno and the little Jyotiniketan family, there was much in common: a yearning for interreligious understanding, a passion for peace. A bond developed between them.

In the service of religious cross-fertilization, and at Murray's urging, they frequented the neighboring Zen Buddhist Centre. For Murray, interest in Buddhism was not new. Through his years of interfaith dialogue, he had met many Buddhists and formed lasting friendships with some. Familiar, of course, with Buddhism's Hindu lineage, his personal connection had been sparked back in 1969 when, visiting Japan, he had been touched by a profound spiritual experience. It happened at a Zen Temple in Takamatsu, where he had been invited to be a zen novice for a short period. On his arrival, he had been gently guided by the Master around the temple, introduced to the little *tatami* room where he would sleep, shown the cooking quarters where he would prepare vegetables and the garden where, for three hours each day, he would pull weeds. He was then taken to the *zendo* where he would sit on his cushion, *zazen*, in meditation, for six or seven hours daily, as well as to the chanting hall, where at 3:00 each morning, he, along with the other novices and monks, would chant the Buddhist scriptures. He recalled how lovely and quiet the temple was, how soft-spoken his guide.

---

24. Isaiah 31:18.

As they ended their introductory tour, he related how the Master turned to him and said, gently and in broken English, "I understand, Father Rogers, that you want to share a little our experience." The Master continued: "If you want to share our experience . . ." and coming closer until he was but an inch from Murray's ear, he shouted at the top of his voice, "*First you must die!*" Murray was shaken to his core; his knees quaked, and he retreated to his cell where he lay stunned on his *tatami* wondering if he had been mad to come to Takamatsu. Would he survive? What could this mean? Gradually the impact of the message began to penetrate, deeper and deeper, to a depth he had not known before. In the hours of meditation and weeding, chanting and sleeping, he explored the parts of himself that needed to die, parts that kept him from the true fullness of life and joy. He began to see too that the Zen master's message was in complete alignment with that of his own Master, Jesus Christ: namely, that "only through dying to the unreal self—discovering illusions about yourself—would one truly live . . . Meditation, silence, prayer is the way."[25] It was the message of Buddhism, but also the message of the self-emptying servant, who chose death on a cross. For Murray it was an unforgettable experience.

His connection with Zen Buddhism continued to deepen through his friendship with Father Shigeto Oshida, the Japanese Dominican priest, who described himself as a "Buddhist who had met Christ." Already a deep spiritual friend who had accompanied them and Swamiji on their farewell pilgrimage in the Himalayas, he became a regular visitor to Jyotiniketan in Jerusalem as well. During his weeks there, he led the community and others who cared to join in times of *zazen*.[26] While Murray and Heather joyfully welcomed these opportunities, Mary was a more reluctant meditator. A highlight of Fr. Oshida's visit in 1972 was a weeklong *sesshin*[27] in Bethlehem; both Murray and Heather hoped the extended retreat would be an opportunity for Mary to deepen her practice. On the last day of the retreat, Mary, having withdrawn early back to Jerusalem, wrote to Raimon Panikkar of her experience. "I wanted to be in on it a bit but guessed rightly that three days would be long enough for me and various things claimed my attention here, so back I came. *This*, really, is my retreat," she added, referring to her time alone to write and tend to her work on "The Elephant." Then, looking to Raimon for spiritual direction, she continued: "I hope the Lord looks on a spot of willingness and a spot of effort as amounting to something and

---

25. Rogers, "Who am I?," 232.

26. *Zazen*: sitting meditation, zen-style.

27. *Sesshin*: an extended group silent meditation practice, often accompanied by instruction.

forgives the ... inability to enter into Zen sitting. I really don't think it's my way, even if I sat for a hundred years. On the other hand, preserving community solidarity, I'm happy to sit on occasions here, for the silence is something I value and there are many sorts of silence. Do you agree?"

Perpetually feeling that she was not as spiritually adept as Heather and Murray must have been frustrating and discouraging, compounding the confusion and pain she felt at their emotional resonance with one another. How could it be that over the years she had patiently molded herself to the needs and challenges of her husband, sacrificing so much, yet still she found herself marginalized spiritually and emotionally? Her question to Raimon pleads for validation, that her way—the way of intellect and action—might also be acceptable to God.

For her, this Zen way of seeking "emptiness" seemed elusive. As did the Hindu way that pointed to God through the dissolution of all dualisms in the mystical experience of *advaita*. It must have been comforting that Raimon Panikkar, a man of brilliant scholarship who appreciated her fine mind, could offer her spiritual sustenance and reassurance. What a challenge it was that many of their closest friends were brilliant scholars and professors, yet drawn, like Murray, to a spirituality of inner experience in which traditional intellectual debates were dismissed as "third leg of chicken."

It was Fr. Oshida who first brought that odd phrase to Jyotiniketan, and soon it became one of Murray's favorite retorts to what he believed was the excess of intellectual hot air encountered at many interreligious dialogue meetings. "Third leg of chicken!" he would exclaim dismissively, as he encountered a strong opinion clothed in intellectual certainty. At a Jyotiniketan gathering for the wider community in their big downstairs room, Oshida-san[28] spoke about the perils of discussion on the word level alone. "Third leg of chicken," he explained, relates to abstract ideas:

> The right leg of the chicken is not the left, and vice-versa. This is true not only logically but also as a fact. One cannot fit the right and left legs together completely. When a farmer talks about the leg of a chicken he is referring to a specific leg, the right one or the left one or both. In this frame of reference there is no problem. However, if one speaks about the leg of a chicken merely in one's mind, a problem arises. This leg, conceived intellectually, can be the right leg or the left leg or both legs. Conceived in an intellectual way, this leg, which can be the right leg or the left or both, is not by this fact either the right leg itself or the left leg itself, nor is it both legs. Such a word conceived only in

---

28. *San*: a Japanese title of respect.

one's mind, I will call "the third leg of the chicken." Here it is a general, abstract, or logical concept.[29]

The use of abstractions can be fruitful, he continued, "as long as it intertwines with reality as a whole, which contains many contradictory features." But pitfalls lurk when a deeper reality of nuance and of spiritual experience is overlooked and words take on a black and white certainty, when, as Oshida says, "the third leg of the chicken begins to walk by itself."[30]

The pitfalls were those Murray had encountered in his ecumenical meetings where progress seemed so elusive. But more immediately they were the tragic religious conflicts bubbling ominously in the Holy Land. On October 6, 1973, two years after their arrival from India, conflict erupted into renewed war, as the Egyptians, seeking restitution for their bitter defeat in the Six Day War in 1967, invaded the Sinai Peninsula and the Syrians forcibly reclaimed the Golan Heights. Variously known as the Yom Kippur War, the Ramadan War, or the October War, depending on one's point of view, the nearly three week engagement claimed thousands of lives on both sides and precipitated a confrontation between the United States and the Soviet Union, who were supplying arms respectively to the Israeli and Arab sides. After an initial rout of unprepared Israeli forces, Egypt and Syria's gains were reversed in engagements on land, sea, and air. Bitter fighting continued as the United Nations tried to negotiate between the combatants. Though Israel resisted a ceasefire until it had regained the upper hand and taken back much of the territory lost, it remained deeply chastened by effectiveness of the surprise attack. On October 25th, both sides agreed to a ceasefire.

Though Jerusalem itself was never threatened, the uneasy peace that had prevailed in the region was shattered. Only a week earlier, Raimon Panikkar had ended a visit. Together he and the community had enjoyed a picnic in Galilee and a moving celebration of the Eucharist on Mount Tabor, often said to be the place of Jesus's transfiguration. Now that site was littered with the detritus of war. "It seems amazing," Mary wrote to him, "that it is less than three weeks since we were enjoying the quietness of hill and lakeside in Galilee. There's an English hymn," she mused, "'Oh, Sabbath rest of Galilee, Oh, calm of hills above.' It seems little hopeful," she continued wryly, "when some of the hills in question are the Golan Heights." Recalling Mary's resilience during the bombings of their home in Plymouth during the Blitz, it's not surprising she responded with equanimity, simply reporting and reflecting: "Here in Jerusalem there is quietness, calm, but of course

---

29. Oshida, "Zen: The Mystery of the Word and Reality."
30. Ibid.

much anguish and tenseness, but apart from an alert or two and a blackout, nothing. The *suq*[31] is more or less normal. Only there is such quietness at night one might think one was back in Kareli minus the peacocks."

But if her ground was not shaken by bombs in the distance, her inner world was still unsettled. During Raimon's recent visit, she had found time to talk with him, but her heart was not fully unburdened. "It was a help and relief," she wrote in a long, emotionally transparent letter, "to have some time with you. Things shared lose much of their heaviness and darkness. Otherwise one would feel very stupid to make mention of one's little sadnesses and inadequacies when there is so much real anguish around, more now than ever." It was her longing for "a real husband-wife relationship" with Murray that continued to slip through her fingers. Raimon had counseled either of two "courses": if possible, a courageous effort on her part to rekindle their physical relationship or, if not, an acceptance of things as they were, living her own life as fully as possible. Mary was not ready to accede to a life of celibacy. The second option, which she dubbed "oriental acceptance" she wrote, could mean "consent to the idea of no-change-or-growth-for-the-better and to . . . further fading of love, outwardly, at least . . . That is something I want to avoid," she continued. "I want to recover more warmth rather than less." But something held her back. How could she "recapture him" as Raimon had suggested? "I am not exactly young and not exactly beautiful or alluring." Her self-doubt entwined with an extraordinary protectiveness, not just of herself, but of Murray, she continued, "For this reason, you see, I have felt that it's a very sensitive point for him and I just don't want him to feel humiliated, with the bitterness and/or self-reproach that it might entail. I don't know whether I'm sensible there because if I were very clever and courageous, then perhaps I should succeed in rekindling things. But I'm not very clever and courageous . . ." She was fearful, she admitted, of interrupting Murray's time of reading at night "when I have flopped on my bed and pretend that I'm going to sleep, though in fact I seldom do . . . Perhaps," she mused, "these are excuses . . . Anyway, all this I hold in my mind and shall hope to be not without courage—to discover how to love better than I have done in the past."[32] If only Mary had known how pained Murray was by her seeming reluctance to touch him, how he longed for physical warmth. It had been nearly thirty years since Richard had been born; it was then that she had seemed to retreat from him. For all those years it had puzzled him that she stayed so physically distant, seeming to have no needs of her own. Had her mother's shocked revulsion at the subject of sex taken

---

31. *Suq*: an open-air market in the Middle East.
32. Ibid.

such deep root in her? Could it be that she was a lesbian? Now he himself had moved to Raimon's second course of acceptance, remaining a loyal husband, filling the gaps of emotional and spiritual fulfillment elsewhere. And still he depended on her deeply for her companionship, her intellect, her loyalty, and courage.

Mary's warmth and emotional depth often found fuller expression on paper than in immediate physical presence. In this time of turmoil, her heart had been moved to reach out quietly to a young woman. Some months earlier she had met Verena Tschudin, a nurse in her late twenties, Swiss in origin, but trained in England. Verena was closely linked with Neve Shalom, the community of Fr. Bruno Hussar. She was living with a friend just outside the Damascus Gate in "No Man's Land."[33] Mary had been drawn both to her gentleness and strength and had invited her to visit Jyotiniketan where Heather and Murray quickly warmed to her as well. Then Verena returned to London, this time for more extensive oncology training. On completion of that training, she had secured a job at Hadassah Hospital and arrived back in Jerusalem just days before the October War began. Now she needed lodging where she could feel more secure, and it was quickly agreed to offer her one of the guest rooms on the lower level. Mary and Heather were eager to make her feel comfortable. As Mary wrote to Raimon, "We want to provide a calm and supportive base for her as she has now resumed her nursing, not as expected in the oncology department, but as circumstances demand in the intensive care unit—a very intense and often harrowing place to be." Referring to the Israeli war casualties being brought into the hospital for treatment, she added, "She is a very courageous person." And so, without much ado, it was agreed that Verena would join them in their home in the Old City.

In the aftermath of the war, while Mary and Heather kept up their daily rounds and Verena commuted to her nursing work in West Jerusalem, Murray found his Rainbow Group colleagues and others within the Christian community distraught and divided. Some, eager to support wholeheartedly the Israeli cause, began circulating letters to gather signatures, and others joined them. "But," as Mary wrote, "for those friends who felt acutely the dilemma of both sides and the terrible injustice suffered by both, it was not possible to sign." They, of course, were among those "friends," Christians all, unable to sign on unequivocally with the Israeli cause. Murray's response was rooted in his belief that heart to heart dialogue was the way forward.

33. No Man's Land was a disputed area between East and West Jerusalem that originated in 1948. Its governance was meant to be decided in the near future, but the small area in which Verena lived had remained to that date beyond official designation as belonging to either section of the city.

As Mary explained, "Being unable to identify wholly [with the Jewish side], he found it more important to spend time visiting as many Israeli friends as he could to stand with them and listen and understand as much as possible. This he found opened up far deeper levels of really knowing each other than he had got to before—far, far deeper than what happens at all these Rainbow Club Meetings..."[34]

"My best friend amongst Jews," Murray recalled, "was Dr. Wiener.[35] A beautiful man, and so is his book about Elijah." Though Orthodox, Dr. Wiener was drawn to Buddhism; he heard of Jyotiniketan's "Evenings Facing East" and began to attend. One day, after an evening together he said, "Murray, do you think we could meet on the Shabbat? I go to the synagogue, and then I come home. Come round, let us just sit together."

"Now *that* was real heavenly interfaith dialogue," exclaimed Murray, "though we never called it that." Thus began their times not only of sitting in silence, but of sharing their lives in a spirit of concern and respect. Out of the silence came trust to share joy and heartache. And over time the spiritual began to meld into the political, a meeting of the hearts flowing into a meeting of the minds. Dr. Wiener told Murray of his deep distress over the positions his government was taking—leading Israel and Zionism in a direction so contrary to what he believed was the heart of the Jewish religion: the requirement of justice for all, including the Palestinians. And Murray recalled the moment several years later when Dr. Wiener reflected on their relationship: "Isn't it strange? You're a Christian, I'm a Jew. I love my faith; you love your faith. I have no intention of becoming a Christian; you have no intention of becoming a Jew. And yet I'm so thankful for these

---

34. Ibid.

35. Aharon Wiener, author of *The Prophet Elijah in the Development of Judaism*, had emigrated to Jerusalem in the 30s. He was closely associated with men such as Judah Leib Magnes, the first president of the Hebrew University, Hugo Bergman, professor and dean of the Hebrew University, and Martin Buber, the renowned scholar and Jewish mystic, who also taught at the University. Together they promoted the idea of a dual-national area where Jews and Arabs would live peaceably together. In the late 30's they also founded an organization, Ichud, dedicated to peace and justice between Arabs and Jews. The following is quoted from a brochure printed in 1956 by a group called American Friends of Ichud for Arab-Israeli Understanding and Peace: "We believe that the Arab-Israeli problem is fundamentally a moral one... Jews in the Holy Land must live in cooperation with the Arabs and not merely next to them. Unless both peoples realize they have a common destiny in the area and come to mutual understanding, the whole Middle East may erupt into conflict which could produce a military clash between East and West." (Cort, Howard. "Martin Buber's Israel/Palestine Unity Movement," 1956. http://www.spiritualprogressives.org/article.php/20090810084113685.)

times we've had together. You know why? Because you make me want to be a deeper Jew."

"As we sat in silence," Murray added, "I marveled." Then came his reply to Wiener: "[Yes], isn't it a strange business? Because people think of me as a missionary; I'm supposed to be turning you into a Christian! Of course, I don't really agree with doing so; I don't want to. I don't think it's just copying what you said, but I think it's [true for me too]. I want to be a deeper Christian because meeting you and respecting you so deeply for the way God has led *you* makes me want to be a deeper person than I am."[36] This was a shift for Murray, perhaps an inevitable outcome of the time and place—that spiritual depth should lead not just to God, but back to the concerns of the world.

There were other Jewish friends as well. Dr. Israel Shahak,[37] another professor at Hebrew University, controversial for his strong advocacy of human rights for Palestinians, and exceedingly popular with his students, became a frequent visitor at Jyotiniketan. Shahak reminded Murray of the Old Testament prophet Amos. "For me," Murray recalled, "he was Amos all over again, but a very intellectual Amos."[38] More and more, whether with Jews or with other Christians, Murray found himself drawn to those who could see the dilemma of Palestinians. Ironically, it often seemed to be fellow Christians who were least able to see the Arab perspective. Within the Jewish-Christian dialogue groups, especially the Rainbow Group, the strain between Christians whose sympathies tipped in favor of the Palestinians versus those whose sympathies were unequivocally supportive of the state of Israel intensified. Feeling pressured by some fellow Christians to abandon their sympathies for the suffering of Palestinians as well as of suffering Jews, Murray, and thus Mary and Heather too, held their ground. In conversations at home, Verena, who saw the agony of Jewish patients and their families, and who spent most days speaking Hebrew, could offer more of the Israeli perspective. Writing to Friends, they poured out their anguish:

---

36. Interview with Trapnell.

37. Dr. Israel Shahak (1933–2001) was born in Poland to a pro-Zionist Ashkenazi family. After his father's death in a Polish concentration camp, Shahak was imprisoned at Bergen-Belsen along with his mother. Following his release he emigrated to the British Mandate of Palestine where he was educated, receiving a doctorate in chemistry, and serving in the Israeli military. Following the 1967 War, he became a leader for civil rights for Arab citizens of Israel and for residents of the Occupied Territories. His writings were extensive, including *Jewish History; Jewish Religion: The Weight of Three Thousand Years; Open Secrets: Israel's Nuclear and Foreign Policies*; and, with Norton Mezvinsky, *Jewish Fundamentalism in Israel*. (Network of Spiritual Progressives).

38. Interview with Trapnell.

> We live and—can one say it?—die this human tragedy more and more deeply. Less than ever can we be pro one group of humanity and anti the other, pro one nationalism and anti the other . . . We remain determined to try to live the saying of Staretz Silouan:[39] "my brother is my life." Unless we human beings find new eyes, new ways of seeing both ourselves and one another across all our particularities of race, religion and culture, and until we find joy and strength in, precisely, the varieties of human and spiritual experience, instead of regarding them as grounds for enmity and superiority, this city and land will continue to suffer violence and bloodshed instead of finding peace.[40]

Day by day as the hostilities continued, they followed the news with rapt attention, speculating how peace might come and what it might bring. While the Jerusalem *Post* was confident Jerusalem would stay united, the *Guardian*, England's liberal voice ran the headline: "Feisal[41] Jihad for Jerusalem." Their unofficial sources were diverse as well: Verena—reporting daily from Hadassah Hospital; Arab clergy associated with St. George's and the Anglican Diocese; and of course the Jewish and Christian members of the Rainbow Group. The stories were riveting; each day was fraught with uncertainty. Mary speculated: "Shall we be living in an international city and visiting St. George's in some other sovereign state? Will Verena be living in one country and working in another?"[42] It was now clear just how impossible had been their dream of being serenely unaligned in this land of conflict. Committed as they were to their home in Jerusalem, their ties elsewhere in the world could be a welcome distraction.

Travel was on their minds. Mary's hope was to fly to Santa Barbara, California, where Raimon was now teaching, to continue their collaborative work on "The Elephant." But that hope would be postponed in deference to Heather, who had been left behind when she and Murray had visited India the previous year. Plans for Heather to visit her beloved India gladdened Mary's heart: "I personally shall be happy to think of Heather having such a trip, both because she would love to see the village friends . . . and because after my expedition last year, it is most certainly her turn . . . I don't want to [travel] again, even to see my children, until she's done *her* bit of traveling." Noting how single-mindedly generous her impulse might seem, Mary

---

39. Staretz Silouan, who lived from 1866–1938, was a highly venerated Greek Orthodox monk and teacher.
40. Letter #22.
41. King Feisal of Saudi Arabia had withdrawn his country's oil from world markets in protest of western support of Israel.
42. Rogers, letter to Raimon Panikkar.

added, "The latter motive, as you can see, is a bit mixed."[43] With the oblique confession to Raimon that she would welcome a respite from the relationship triangle with Heather and Murray, Mary may have thought she was baring a human flaw. But what truly comes into the light is deep integrity in her painful life dilemma.

Murray too was looking to Asia, where he had been invited to participate in a "Multilateral Dialogue" meeting of the World Council of Churches in Sri Lanka the following spring. Happily, as Mary noted, that trip would take him "within possible range of Abhishikt. for wherever Abhishikt. is, there Murray would like to be for a few days." Compelling as the conflict was between Israel and its neighbors, Murray's attention never strayed far from the spiritual drama, then being played out with Abhishiktananda in north India. That summer, in the temple at Ranagal with Marc Chaduc, his spiritual disciple, Swamiji had been caught up into a state of spiritual ecstasy. As Chaduc wrote, "The inbreaking of the [Holy] Spirit snatched him away from himself, and shone through every inch of his being, an inner apocalypse which at times blazed forth outwardly in a glorious transfiguration."[44] Only days later Swamiji had suffered a serious heart attack, falling stricken on a street of Rishikesh, as he ran to catch a bus. Taken to a nursing home at Indore, he was expected to recover. As he rested there he wrote to his friends "astonishing letters," as Shirley du Boulay observed, "not the letters of a sick man; [but] by someone who had had the most important experience of this life and who was rejoicing in it."[45] "Like anyone who has broken barriers, Abhishiktananda was ahead of his time, and few were ready to receive such insights."[46] But Murray *was* ready, absorbing Swamiji's words penned to him directly into his soul: "The discovery of Christ's 'I AM' is the ruin of any Christian theology, for all notions are burnt up within the fire of experience . . . I feel too much, more and more, the blazing fire of his I AM, in which all notions about Christ's personality, ontology, history, etc., have disappeared. And I find his real mystery shining in every awakening man, in every mythos."[47] While Swamiji's spiritual encounters might have shaken some orthodox Christians, his letter to Murray served only to strengthen Murray's faith. The joy of it all for Swamiji was palpable: "Really a door opened in heaven when I was lying on the pavement. But a heaven which

43. Ibid.
44. Rogers and Barton, *Abhishiktananda*, 34. For fascinating detail on this time in Abhishiktananda's life, the reader may refer to Shirley du Boulay's account in the chapter titled "The Final Explosion," in *Cave of the Heart*.
45. Du Boulay, *Cave of the Heart*, 236.
46. Ibid., 238.
47. Ibid., 238–39.

was not the opposite of earth, something which was neither life nor death, but simply 'being,' 'awakening' . . . beyond all myths and symbols . . . If we meet someday, I shall tell you the whole wonderful story; til then 'magnificate Dominum mecum.'"⁴⁸ It was signed, "Dans la joie de Dieu toujours.⁴⁹"⁵⁰ Murray longed to hear Swamiji's story; he yearned to share his experience of life in Jerusalem as well. Late in November, Murray wrote to him, closing with these words, "The longer we live here, Jerusalem, the more I know the vital importance of living—being—'beyond the level of name.'⁵¹ So many of our troubles here—fightings and fear—understandably, considering history, are because of this importance given to the 'name.' It is in fact a tremendous battle for people bound by so-called monotheism to go 'beyond.' Meanwhile, very many around us are terribly insecure, almost on the point of despair. The external for them seems to be all-important.

Love from the three of us, in the joy of the Lord, Murray."

Little wonder that Murray longed to be wherever Swamiji was, to share Eucharist and life beyond the level of name, if only for a few days.

But in December came the news that jolted them all from their daily preoccupations: Swamiji had died. In their Letter to Friends, it was news that eclipsed any mention of the recent war. Leaning heavily on their faith, they tried to share Swamiji's joy: "Died hardly describes what happened! He went to the Father. Dear Swamiji thus had his desire of many years fulfilled, he at last has become truly a-cosmic, thus realizing to the full the vocation which the Spirit through Hindu *sannyasa* had put deep inside him."⁵² The day after the news arrived, the little community proceeded with their customary weekly Eucharist in the Chapel of St. Abraham in the Church of the Resurrection. There, where their common patron saint, the pagan priest Melchizedek who had blessed Abraham, seemed mystically present, they struggled grief-stricken through the Jyotiniketan liturgy. Their Letter told the story: With "so much of it [Swamiji's] inspiration, lived so often by him and us together in that open-air chapel in Kareli—[it] evoked such powerful memories that we could only go forward in silence." With them, sharing their loss, was Fr. Shigeto Oshida: "The Lord," they wrote, "surely knew that Swamiji's passing would affect us deeply and He made a lovely arrangement to comfort us [with Oshida-san's presence] . . . Strange that the whole world

---

48. *Magnificate Dominum mecum,* from Psalm 34:3 may be translated as "O magnify the Lord with me."

49. *Dans la joie de Dieu toujours*: In the joy of God always.

50. Abhishiktananda, *Swami Abhishiktananda: Essential Writings,* 198.

51. "Level of name" for Murray referred to the labels, categories, and divisions—religious included—with which people identify themselves.

52. Letter #22.

can be an emptier place when a dear friend departs from it, and yet he has not departed . . . In the Eucharist . . . it seemed as if old Swamiji, as we used to call him affectionately, were very close, telling all his friends . . . not to mourn but to wake up to what we are, to live deeply, truly, the Real Mystery of God's Presence everywhere and always."[53]

Though they could pay lip service to life without mourning, for Murray in particular the void left by the loss of his dearest friend and treasured spiritual guide would never be filled. For him Swamiji's death would forever demarcate the end of what he would later see as the "best years" of his life.

53. Ibid.

13

A Community of Resistance
1974–1980

Everything begins in mysticism and ends in politics.

—Charles Péguy

Yet life did go on, and the travels resumed. True to Mary's word, she stayed at home that autumn of 1974 with Verena, while Heather departed for India. There, finding the respite she needed, she enjoyed a month of silence in an ashram in Varanasi. There were several weeks of visits with friends as well, including Sisters at the ashram in Poona where, perhaps, Heather had once prayed she might live out her life with Mary and Murray. How might she have weathered the agonizing months of discernment before that last option to stay in India was rejected and the final decision was taken to move to Jerusalem? Would she have voiced such desires, or would she have demurred, bending to Murray's discernment and leadership? The latter seems likely; like Mary, self-sacrifice was in her nature. But now, going even to the places she loved most in the world was not easy for Heather; she was not the intrepid traveler that Mary and Murray were. More and more, anxious parts of her needed reassurance.

Murray, on the other hand, seemed only to grow more emboldened in his convictions. Though his heart ached as he flew off to Asia, knowing the visit with Swamiji he had so longed for in India could never come to pass, his grief was channeled into a passion to live the insight Swamiji had shared—that ultimately "all notions are burnt up within the fire of experience." His destination was Colombo, Sri Lanka, to participate in a meeting entitled "Towards World Community," sponsored by the World Council of Churches. With its ongoing series of interfaith meetings to address what it saw as the emerging historic context, the Council's concerns and goals now seem prescient. They were articulated by the chairman of the gathering, S. J. Samartha, the Indian Christian scholar who wrote: "There is, on the one hand, the terrifying anxiety created by the relentless march of science and technology. Many people feel that this is leading mankind into a maze from which there seems to be 'no exit'. Can the resources of religion, they ask, properly understood and critically interpreted, provide a basis for hope in this predicament? On the other hand, in spite of the tensions within nations and conflicts between classes, there is a sense of growing interdependence among people for better or worse which demands at least a critical look at tentative gropings towards 'world community.'"[1]

It was an elite gathering of about fifty representatives of five religions: Hindu, Buddhist, Jewish, Christian, and Muslim, many of them ready to present a scholarly paper on the subject at hand. Murray recalled the parade of intellectuals, drawing on their different faith traditions to present their thoughts. As the days passed, it became clear that difficulties with terminologies, tensions between theistic and non-theistic members, and confusions that Murray might have attributed to a "third leg of chicken" focus were threatening to derail any forward movement. Samartha was concerned. "Murray," he said, "this is becoming much too academic. We must somehow bring it down." He asked that Murray take a morning's session to "really give us something different." It would be an 'experiment.' Murray should invite anyone he chose to help him. Delighted with the opportunity, he chose Swami Chidananda, a Hindu *sannyasi*, ["a beautiful man"] and Thich Nhat Hanh, the Vietnamese Buddhist monk, with whom he was already acquainted. "We sat together; we were silent together; we talked together," Murray recalled. "How, we wondered, could we express the depth of life that our learned talk wasn't touching at all?"[2]

He credited Thich Nhat Hanh for the initial idea that became "The Pebble, the Flower, and the Encounter." Universal symbols would be invitations to explore the depths of human consciousness, the connection with nature, and the experience of human suffering. Before beginning the process, the accustomed tables had been removed from the room, and chairs were placed in a circle. Participants, asked to divest themselves of books and papers, were put off-kilter, wondering what was about to happen.

First, Thich Nhat Hanh distributed to each a small pebble, with the instructions to sit quietly for about twenty minutes, imagining that just as a pebble sinks into water and settles, they were to allow their consciousness to sink deeply into inwardness and tranquility. Thich Nhat Hanh closed

1. Samartha, "Reflections on a Multilateral Dialogue," 637.
2. Interview with Trapnell.

that portion of the experience with a few words. Then it was Murray's turn. Quietly he handed a flower to each person. Suggesting they might walk with their flower in the garden, he instructed them to stay with their flower, listening for what the flower might have to say to them. No analysis, he cautioned; just allow the flower to speak. Finally, as the group returned, Swami Chitananda led the group a few hundred yards down the road from the hotel where they were meeting for 'the encounter.' It took place in a home for severely handicapped children, where Murray had previously visited, where he knew the children were lovingly tended. Chitananda's instructions were that each person should walk through the rooms silently, not judging, but allowing the experience to touch their hearts. At the end, they were invited to come outside onto a verandah where they could sit amongst some of the less disabled children. There Swami Chitananda led a brief meditation, and the experience drew to a close.

Then came the reaction. No sooner did the group return to the hotel than Murray could see that people were "absolutely wild." Well over half of the group were furious, claiming they had been manipulated. There followed a heated plenary session with many delegates voicing their outrage and demanding that steps be taken to prevent anything like this from ever happening again. The force of the anger seemed aimed at Murray, the convener of the 'experiment,' and Murray was feeling somewhat responsible.

"Poor old Swamiji Chidananda," Murray recalled. He too was taken aback and could hardly believe what had happened.

Shortly after this explosion, he and Thich Nhat Hanh saw each other in the hotel. Thich Nhat Hanh observed, "Murray, you're looking a little anxious."

Murray continued: "Well, to tell you the truth, Thây, I am. I can't understand what's hit us. What have we done!?"

And he said, "Don't you worry. Don't you worry. I think I can tell you that after three years, the part of this conference that will be remembered is 'The Pebble, the Flower, and the Encounter.'"

As the rumpus and finger-pointing continued into the evening, the chairman, a German professor, declared that until they knew better how to deal with interfaith dialogue, they simply could not allow this sort of thing to take place. And though he was "a dear man, a friend of mine," Murray reacted: "I jumped to my feet and responded, probably stupidly and too quickly: 'If you want to *deal* with things that are to do with God, you'll never get anywhere. He's dealing with us, or the Spirit is dealing with us, and it seems to me it's happening, whatever spiritual family we belong to.'"

The debate wore on, some defending what had happened, others continuing their angry tirades, when suddenly at the back of the room there was a slight movement. It was Thich Nhat Hanh, who, with a small gesture, signaled that he was going to bed and slowly walked out of the room. "He's so mild, so quiet," said Murray, but added, laughing, "He's a tartar,[3] really!" Shortly thereafter the meeting came to an end. "He completely disorganized us," Murray noted, admiringly.

Later, Murray assessed the negative reactions. "All of the things that they knew they could do—" he said, "—to be learned, or to judge, or analyze—all those things were taken away from them. They just had to *be*, you see. And they didn't like it. They were furious!"[4]

The conference chairman, S. J. Samartha, while suggesting that better preparation of the group for such a new experience might have been advisable, supported Murray's assessment. Participants, he wrote, wanted "conceptual clarification." And, he added, "even those who on other occasions talk about the need for harmony between man and Nature felt strangely uneasy when flowers were actually before them in a different setting than in a vase in a chapel."[5] He concluded his assessment of the conference: "People are afraid that the dimension of the 'spiritual' in human life might be either corroded through secularization or diluted through syncretism. But they are afraid to 'experiment' or find new ways of experiencing and understanding it. That is why the debate will go on."[6]

And that is why, little by little, Murray's view of formal interfaith dialogue was becoming jaded. Since the halcyon days in the early sixties of the small gatherings in India with the Cuttat Circle and its experiential approach, since his cross-legged explorations of the Upanishads with Swamiji under the sky, he had grown increasingly impatient with experiences of dialogue that were purely discursive, exclusively intellectual. Believing, as Raimon Panikkar did, that "religions meet in the heart, rather than the mind,"[7] he also shared with his now estranged friend and mentor, John Taylor, the view that "real dialogue in its radical or Buberian form involves a venturesome unfolding to each other in authenticity."[8] It was what Dr. Cuttat had called "inner dialogue" that mattered most to Murray.

Ironically, before another World Council of Churches in Ajaltoun, Lebanon, some four years earlier (1970), Murray and Swamiji had themselves

---

3. Murray's usage of "tartar" seems to mean trenchant, or able to cut to the core.
4. Interview with Trapnell.
5. Samartha, "Reflections on a Multilateral Dialogue," 664.
6. Ibid., 645.
7. Robinson, *Christians Meeting Hindus*, 71, quoting from a later version of Panikkar's *Unknown Christ of Hinduism*.
8. Ibid.

conspired to write a paper—a sort of anti-paper—to be presented to that assembly. Entitled "Hindu-Christian Dialogue Postponed," it was written tongue-in-cheek, yet laden with their deepest beliefs, from the perspective of a Hindu who has been asked to participate in dialogue by a Christian. Excerpts follow:

> Now you want to have a dialogue with us. You tell us very nicely that you have to learn from us. You begin to speak . . . about our scriptures, our traditions, the religious experience of our mystics . . . Some wonder, however, at your intentions. Is it not true that all Semitic religions, be they Judaism, Islam, or Christianity, are founded on the notion of a chosen people which has received from God directly the mission to convert the whole world to their particular tenets? Do you not realize then that such an approach to the religious sphere affects immediately all attempts at a real dialogue? . . . But let us come back to our initial point. To allure us to dialogue you keep telling us that we have to learn from each other. Excellent! Without any false pride I confess that we Hindus have already learned a lot from you Christians, on the external level. But do you think sincerely that formal and academic dialogue is the best way to learn? Why all this fuss about well planned and prepared official dialogue? If you really want to learn from us the best we can give you—why not take the traditional Indian attitude of the disciple? Go with humility and sincerity to the feet of some real guru, a knower of the scriptures and at the same time a man of personal experience, as the *Mundaka*[9] says . . . Do not forget that spiritual experience cannot be the object of courses or lectures. Words are necessary of course to prepare the mind, but they can convey the truth only indirectly, for no word can express adequately the Mystery. The Mystery is the object of personal and direct experience only . . .
>
> I am afraid really that when you call us to dialogue you do not understand spiritual knowledge in the way we do. You want information; you want learned discussions on the phenomenal aspects of religions . . . ranging from rituals and sociological aspects of it up to mythology and doctrinal formulations. All are things of human interest, I do not deny it, but all remain short of the ultimate—the *parama pada*—which alone really interests the man who has got even a glimpse of the inner Mystery.[10]

---

9. The *Mundaka*: One of the earlier *Upanishads*.
10. Du Boulay, *Swami Abhishiktananda: Essential Writings*, 127–28.

Sure enough, what Murray most recalled years later from that meeting in Ajaltoun was that after all the papers were read and formal discussions completed, it was an experience of unscripted spontaneity that touched his heart. He described a tiny glimpse of the Mystery:

> One evening after supper Kenneth Cragg, the Suffragan Bishop in Jerusalem, suddenly felt moved to say, "May I have five minutes of your time?" [A group of us] were sitting around the drawing room. He said, "I would love to try to share with you very simply why I'm so thankful to have come into touch with Islam." And seeing that he's an Anglican who knows more about Islam than anybody else, we all listened. And of course, there were Muslims there. What he said was very lovely, very simple. Anybody could have understood what he was saying.
>
> When Kenneth had finished, there was silence. We had nothing to say. It was a very special moment.
>
> Then a dear man, a professor of Islam from Hyderabad said, "I don't think I can be silent any longer. I want to tell you why I, a convinced Muslim, am so thankful to have been allowed to know Christian people."
>
> And I'll never forget it, because you know, we disagreed utterly about what the cross means.
>
> And this man said, "I think I can put it this way. We Muslims, we know how to win, with strength. You Christians, you know how to lose."
>
> We were totally surprised, but we could see he was talking about the cross, that he understood.[11]

For Murray, that was a moment of real connection, a simple expression of "inner dialogue." Those were the moments that kept him always coming back for more, despite his skepticism. But, he wondered, was it really worth the "enormous business of moving fifteen, twenty people around the world, to come and spend a fortnight together?" Was there value in the formal scholarly discussion? Murray's response, years later was simply, "Very little."[12] People, he admitted, became friends, and it was always good to see them. But it was not simply the people, but the opportunities for unexpected "sparks," like those he felt at Ajaltoun, moments of synchronicity in which the Spirit was at work that touched him. To Murray, those sparks were intimations of the blazing fire in which he longed to be consumed. So of course he would go.

11. Interview with Trapnell.
12. Ibid.

Just a year after the "rumpus" in Colombo, Murray was off again to "Nairobi 1975," the World Council's vast gathering (664 delegates from 286 churches and other attendees totaling nearly 2500 people). There the contention around interfaith dialogue continued, with the western delegates inveighing against a sense of "spiritual compromise" or syncretism and those who, like Murray, represented Asian perspectives, insisting that dialogue "in no way diminishes full commitment to one's own faith," and "far from leading to syncretism, safeguards against it."[13] Grateful as he was for the "wider outlook such opportunities give to our small community," Murray particularly relished a moment in Nairobi when one of the delegates approached him warmly, asking where they might have met before. Then suddenly, the man remembered. "Ah," he said, "It was in Colombo. 'The Pebble, the Flower and the Encounter!' Thank you for that; I'll never forget it."[14]

Back in Jerusalem, Jyotiniketan was still "perched on the city wall," still the community to which they each would return, where their spiritual grounding lay. While their Letters of this period seemed to intensify in passion, there were reassurances of their commitment to their vows of worship and prayer, disciplined work, simplicity of life, and submission to one another and to God. The Eucharist, they said, remained central to each day's life, "the real reason we are here."[15] With a steady stream of visitors of all ages flowing through Jyotiniketan, Murray would often lead retreats and meditation-walks, sometimes in the desert, other times in the countryside. One such visitor, the Rev. Michael David, an Anglican priest and close friend, who enjoyed two extended sabbatical visits with Jyotiniketan, described not only the hospitality, but the spiritual challenge. There were trips into Galilee and down to the Dead Sea, exploring historical sites. And, Michael David recalled, "an inner exploration into contemplative prayer under Murray's guidance." He continued, "Every week we were joined in the Meditation room by some thirty people of all ages, some sitting on stools but most sitting cross-legged on the floor. By invitation we were led by people who had explored the beauty of the Sufis of Islam." Decades later, he shared another facet of Murray's spiritual instruction and its lasting imprint: "Murray sent me out once a week into the Judean wilderness. I left at 3.00 am and returned at 4.00 pm. It was an exercise in learning to *be* rather than always doing. As these expeditions involved passing by an Arab village, [villagers] gave me a crucifix made by the sisters of the Fifth Station of the Cross, later

---

13. World Counsel of Churches archive.
14. Interview with Trapnell.
15. Letter #23.

blessed by Murray at the Eucharist. It remains a constant reminder of God's love and their love and concern for me. Thanks be to God!"[16]

For all of them, the more this inward focus stayed steady, the more clarity they found on issues that called for their action. Not, as Michael David said, "doing" or busy-ness, but meaningful action. And ever more boldly, Murray led the way.

Thus it was, perhaps unwittingly, at least at first, that their Eucharists became a political flash-point. They would find their way to Mount Tabor, as they had done with Raimon Panikkar, or to a quiet place on the banks of the Jordan River, or to the Garden of Gethsemane. Wherever they were: looking over the Galilee countryside, beside the stream, or beneath the ancient olive trees, they would sit on the ground and assemble the elements on some rocks. Those celebrations were highlights of their life: "heavenly times,"[17] as Murray recalled.

But amongst the Anglican powers that be at St. George's Cathedral, there was consternation. It was insisted that Murray, one of their own priests, simply could not celebrate the Eucharist in those places, as any religious act clearly violated the *Status Quo*. Anglicans could be accused of trying to claim the land where Jyotiniketan had celebrated, perhaps to grab a bit of the Garden of Gethsemane, and that could certainly disturb the fragile peace! He was told to discontinue the practice.

Murray found it all utterly preposterous and let the authorities know he simply was not prepared to comply. Years later, his view was unchanged. "It's scarcely credible that we grown-up and deeply religious human beings can be so utterly 'kindergarten!'" he said with a rueful laugh.[18]

Then there was the matter of a Palestinian bishop for Jerusalem. While most foreign bishops around the world had retired and been replaced by local bishops, Palestinians had not yet been allowed to choose a bishop from their own people. For Murray and many others as well, that restriction seemed yet one more indignity suffered by the Palestinian people who, since the establishment of the State of Israel in 1948, had suffered so many losses. Just as in India, where they naturally identified with the poor and the marginalized, their sensitivity to people being treated as inferior strengthened their bonds with the Palestinians. And they were elated when, for several years, church authorities assured Palestinians that the next bishop would indeed be one of their own. In India, of course, that had long since happened.

---

16. Michael David, letter to author, 2010.
17. Interview with Trapnell.
18. Ibid.

Then as the time grew near for Archbishop Appleton to retire, Murray began to hear whisperings that a different decision had been made—that there was no one deemed "ready" to be a bishop among the Palestinians; that the retired Bishop of London would be appointed to the post.

Murray was outraged. He had experienced this process in India, with westerners insisting that the Indians "weren't ready" to govern themselves. He had heard his fill of such admonitions: "Oh, they're not ready, You can't go too fast, Murray. You must go slowly . . . I didn't believe it," he said, "because I maintain that nobody's ready to be a bishop! It's by the grace of God they can be bishops, and even if somebody has six doctorates, it doesn't make him ready to be a bishop. He'll still need to go there with some of the poor to receive the riches of God: that's my perspective. So when this happened in Jerusalem, I said, 'People need to know that Murray feels this is very dreadful. We can't go back. It's not honest. We can't tell people one thing for five years, or ten . . . and then somebody says, "Awfully sorry, not going to happen. We're going to have another Englishman."'[19]

But Murray, wise to church politics, knew it would be fruitless to protest in Jerusalem. It was in England that the decisions were made, so it was right to the top of the hierarchy—the Archbishop of Canterbury—that he lodged his vociferous grievance by letter. When the Archbishop replied, obviously nettled, it was with denials and a strong admonition that Murray not mention to anyone else what he had written to him. But by then the letter Murray also had written to the London *Times* on the situation had already been published,[20] and an international spotlight had been thrown on the controversy. Just a few weeks later came the official announcement that in fact the gossip had been correct and the retired Bishop of London, the Rt. Rev. Robert Stopford, would be appointed Vicar General of the diocese.

Murray recalled Bishop Stopford's arrival in Jerusalem: "Of course, I was one of his clergy, and he knew all about it. I'll never forget it; it was a Saturday morning. I went into his study. I'd never met him before. We were both, I think, a bit awkward. I said, 'Bishop, as a human being I want to welcome you. You've got a terribly difficult job. Really, I don't think you ought to be here at all.'"

"The Bishop, awfully nicely, said, 'How do you do, Murray? Good to meet you. Yes, I know you don't think I ought to be here, but I don't think that should make too much difference.'"[21]

---

19. Ibid.
20. See Appendix 3 for complete text of letter published Dec. 24, 1973.
21. Interview with Trapnell.

Thus it was, more and more, that Murray's reputation as an iconoclastic priest, ready to cause embarrassment to his superiors if his sense of justice required it, often preceded him. "All this," Mary observed, "has brought Murray much nearer the Arab clergy . . . though he is probably anathema to the Archbishop!"[22] Certainly, it was neither Mary nor Heather's style to be so outspoken. Yet, as his boldness increased, so too did their quiet embrace and defence of his views. Writing to Friends, Jyotiniketan retained its unified voice—three individuals braided into a single strand. "It may sometimes appear we would be stronger if we were firmly within the Anglican 'Establishment,' a recognized institution, however small, of the churches. Yet our experience since 1954 when we began the little ashram in India, is that precisely that 'weakness' is our strength, that the wind of the Spirit, within and outside the boundaries of the churches, has less to blow down when our structures are of mud and straw rather than of concrete!"[23]

Clearly, these were not Murray's first challenges to authority, nor would they be the last. But in the religious-political crucible that was Jerusalem, the passionate flame that had burned within him, perhaps since hearing the call of Isaiah in that adolescent conversion experience, was fanned to a new intensity.

It was an intensity that revealed itself within the little Jyotiniketan family as well.

Verena Tschudin, brought into the community in the midst of the October War of 1973, was startled by its unexpectedly sharp edge. She had been welcomed, she recalled, in a little service as a novice to a spiritual community, without expectation of a life commitment, but as an integral part of the community nonetheless. In their Letter to Friends of February 1974, they acknowledged their happiness that she had "begun to be a part of our small 'family.' She . . . brings to us a new angle of vision."[24] Verena spent her days at Hadassah primarily among Israelis, speaking Hebrew. Never before had Jyotiniketan included a person with a full-time professional position. Little thought seems to have been given to how Verena was to live out the vows of worship, disciplined work, simplicity, and submission. But as she groped her way towards inclusion, she soon became aware of the strong bond between her three companions. They were truly a unit, finely tuned to one another's needs, with their various strengths working in harmony to maintain the lifestyle established through their years in India. Each knew their roles; little verbal communication was necessary for the daily round

22. Letter to Raimon Panikkar.
23. Letter #23.
24. Letter #22.

to be accomplished. Verena, unsure of expectations, struggled to blend into their routine while maintaining her own sense of identity. Her nursing schedule required her to board a bus at 6:00 a.m., too early to join the morning Eucharist and quiet time. Though she tried to be present for the evening meal, she did not revel in their vegetarianism. Nor did she find it easy to join them each evening for their conversations; after intense days with patients, she needed time alone. But she joined them both in private and in public as she could. Yet in their public outings, she sometimes felt embarrassed to be perceived as yet another "hen"—and a very young one at that—to Murray's rooster. Murray, had grown accustomed to teasing comments about the appearance of having two or three wives, had adopted a phraseology, apt for the Middle East: "Murray and his *har-eem*." He *did* deserve the ribbing, he ruefully admitted. Despite the propriety of their relationship, this was uncomfortable for Verena, not a joking matter.

Nominally part of the community, yet not fully integrated, she contributed as she could and as she was asked. A gifted seamstress who made all her own clothes, she tended to the sewing needs of the community. New cassocks were beautifully stitched for Murray. And she brought in revenue from her nursing. But her ability to contribute financially seemed a mixed blessing, triggering their complicated relationship with money. Verena recalled that while much of her pay went to the needs of the community, "Murray always thought I was earning far too much money," and he pressured her to give away substantial sums to the Homes of Mercy in Bethany. Sensing the growing tensions between their lifestyles, she found that Heather, who, said Verena, "seemed to hold the whole thing together" with her cooking and cleaning, was the one to whom she could turn. Heather, who always seemed to be happily smiling in the background, was more approachable for Verena than either Mary or Murray. Warm and friendly, she would try to "smooth things over" when the need arose.[25] Undoubtedly, Verena's ambivalence was readily apparent, her reluctance a shadow over their sense of unity.

The day came when Heather's efforts were not enough. Verena, stressed not only by her sense of being "an outsider" within Jyotiniketan, but by professional tensions at the hospital, was beginning to contemplate leaving. Nonetheless it came as a rude shock when Murray simply announced, "We need your room." While anticipating the possibility that she would be requested to leave, she had expected there at least would be a conversation. But there was none, or, if there had been, it had taken place without her.

In retrospect, speaking of her nearly two years with Jyotiniketan, Verena concludes: "The good things dominate in the end." She particularly

---

25. Interview with author.

recalls her fond relationship with Heather, her admiration for the open-mindedness of the community as a whole, and her exposure to the fascinating and diverse parade of friends who would come to visit, occupying the room next to hers. "It was a time," she said, "when I grew up."[26]

In the weeks following, as she prepared to return to London, Verena's relationship with them was cordial, but tense. And it became apparent that her place would be taken by another woman, perhaps better suited for the role, Rosmarie Schönholzer.

While Verena's sense was that she could never penetrate the inner workings of Jyotiniketan, Rosmarie's experience would be very different: she would become what Murray later called "a lynchpin."[27] Like Verena, Rosmarie was Swiss, having come to Jerusalem as a member of the Swiss-based Christian Movement for Peace. In the years she had already lived there, she had become immersed in the segregated world of the West Bank—working for relief agencies, becoming fluent in Arabic and developing a network of colleagues. When they met she was a highly respected member of the staff at the Orthodox Homes of Mercy in Bethany, caring for handicapped boys. Her entry into the community would be a very different process, more gradual, more thoughtful. Though in 1975 she moved into the room Verena had left, not until two years later was she first introduced via their Letter to Friends. There, without fanfare, they acknowledged her presence in the "family" and the way she had enriched the community by her "many friends."[28] It was true: among others, Pfarrer (Pastor) Veronica Thurneysen, Rosmarie's close friend and colleague from the Christian Movement for Peace, had become an important friend of the entire community. And now Rosmarie was the fourth signatory of the Letter.

It was happenstance, of course, that their decision to say farewell to Verena (and to her income) came only months before news that precipitated a small crisis in the community. For their wider family of Friends who may have been wondering how they were surviving financially, here was a fairly transparent bulletin. Devoted as they were to a life of insecurity, they were concerned, they wrote, about their "bread and butter situation." The grant that had been provided by the Episcopal Church of the United States to cover their rent and "simple vegetarian food" would no longer be available: "Our new bishop, Bishop Faik Haddad,[29] has many commitments which he feels have a prior claim to the money; we sympathise with this decision and

26. Ibid.
27. Interview with Trapnell.
28. Letter #24.
29. Bishop Faik Haddad: in 1976, a local Palestinian bishop had been appointed.

are happy that as a token of his desire that we should continue here, he has promised us a contribution which will cover our rent for three months or so of the coming year."

Before asking their Friends for help, they continued: "As if to assure us of His love God let this news . . . reach us on the very day when Murray was giving a lecture in Jerusalem on 'The Joy of St. Francis' in connection with the 750th anniversary of the death of the saint! That 'poor little man' of Assisi believed that poverty and joy go together and taught his brothers that begging, though humiliating and embarrassing, could also be a blessing, both for those who have to do it, and for those who respond! That gives us courage!"[30]

With their request came the reassurance that "whatever you may give us will *not* go to jet travel." Mary's expenses to visit their children and grandchildren were covered by funds left to her by her father for that purpose; Heather's travel was similarly covered by an inheritance from her father. As for Murray's travels to various conferences: they are "always looked after by those who invite him."[31]

They hoped they would not have to leave their flat for a cheaper one; they loved their location in the Old City with its room for their frequent visitors and meditation room. But perhaps IL.980 a month (roughly U.S. $98) would be more than they could afford. They wondered, should Heather or Mary take paid work?

Despite the reliable generosity of Friends, the need to move to smaller quarters did become apparent. Local friends, John Landgraf in the lead, stepped in to make it happen. Their new home was in the Armenian Quarter of the Old City. It was, in Murray's words, "a lovely little tiny flat with two of those wonderful domes over our chapel room and Heather's bedroom (a curtain in between) and over our sitting room. It was beautiful there—a sort of little rabbit warren. Downstairs there were two Palestinian families living. Upstairs a Palestinian lady [on one side], another [on the other side] in her little room. A Mennonite American friend, a delightful young man living next door to us, one room, and then ours. We had two rooms, another sort of passage way which became our dining room, and a bathroom."[32]

Tiny though the flat was, the flow of visitors from all over the world did not diminish. And though silence was often the deepest meeting point for the four of them, their openness to conversation—heartfelt sharing of life's sufferings, challenges, and joys—drew a steady stream through their old courtyard. On one Advent Sunday in 1977, it included a pair of Africans from Lesotho, an Italian monk in the company of four German students,

---

30. Letter #23.
31. Ibid.
32. Interview with Trapnell.

and three new acquaintances from India, who, like the Africans, had been studying at Tantur. To top off the afternoon, there arrived an American Jesuit for a brief visit. "All days," they wrote, "are not quite as intense and special as that, but the spectrum of callers and friends is not unusual and indicates, we feel, that width of variety which God so clearly loves and which is to be found in this old [city]."[33]

Other friends' visits could be for more prosaic, albeit still important reasons. Friday afternoons, they learned to expect John Landgraf on his trusty bicycle, laden with vegetables. John had discovered that when, on Friday afternoons at 2:00, the Machane Yehuda Market up the hill in West Jerusalem closed for Shabbat, lots of leftover food was thrown into dumpsters. Quickly and unceremoniously John would retrieve a selection of fruits and vegetables in a small act of defiance to human profligacy. Then, with his bicycle baskets overflowing with beans, mangoes, and melons, he would coast back down the hill, straight through the Jaffa Gate and round the corner into the Armenian Quarter to delightedly share his haul with Jyotiniketan. Often there was enough for all of them and a surfeit for the Homes of Mercy in Bethany as well.

Friendship in their new neighborhood led to other, more significant acts of defiance. In 1976 they learned that Arabs living nearby were "in great trouble." They had been notified by the Israeli authorities that, because their old houses were unstable, they were no longer safe to live in; the families were to vacate. Along with that news came the sickening information from Palestinian friends that large mechanical excavators had previously come down the road, presumably for routine underground work, but digging, intentionally, or so it seemed, to destabilize the houses. That they were located nearby the Jewish Quarter which, since the war in 1967, had been rapidly expanded through a variety of means from confiscation to bulldozing, only added to the suspicion. And though the residents had first been told they could return when the houses were repaired, the information soon changed: they would not be allowed back. The houses would be reserved for Israelis. Helpless outrage swept the local community. Murray delineated the tragedy they saw unfolding for these Arab families who had lived in their houses for hundreds of years: "Very often the great great grandfather, the [patriarch], the sort of Abraham of that family, had been buried in the courtyard. So when they were asked to leave, it wasn't like us leaving. It was a complete upheaval, because people in the Mideast find that the land really is very, very precious to them."[34]

This news was in the local papers. There were protests, but nothing was done. "It became clear to me," Murray explained, "that if we were going

33. Letter #24.
34. Interview with Trapnell.

to . . . really make the authorities sit up, we'd got to write letters abroad." It was a familiar strategy: a letter to the London *Times*. Three others from St. George's Cathedral joined him in signing. The text follows:

Human rights in Jerusalem

From The Dean of St. George's Anglican Cathedral, Jerusalem, and others

Sir, Let's play a game.

On December 28, three days after Christmas, three Jewish families living in adjacent houses in Bethnal Green were evicted from their homes in order to make room for recently arrived immigrants from the erstwhile British colonies. On that Tuesday morning a detachment of British troops surrounded the area as bulldozers completely demolished the houses. Thirty-one Jews were involved, chiefly school children. When the authorities in Whitehall were questioned about such apparent injustice, they assured the complainants that very adequate flat accommodations had been offered in Croydon for the evicted families at a price beyond their means.

Stop one minute before phoning your MP. For Bethnal Green read Jerusalem Old City and for Jewish families read Arab families.

Are you surprised that Christmas has been a heavy time of year here in the Middle East, what with the irony of a pile of arms being placed immediately outside the door of the Church of the Holy Nativity (of the Prince of Peace!) in Bethlehem on the morning of December 24, and yet another tramping upon human rights as reported above . . . ?

Who, we wonder, are the anti-Semites? We who think it is important for the world to know such facts, or the Israeli authorities who order such action? There are, to our personal knowledge, many Jewish people, Israeli friends of ours, who deeply regret such actions, but tragically they remain a small minority in Israel. Not for the first time, very much depends on a brave and unpopular remnant.

Yours faithfully,
C. CLIVE HANDFORD
EDWARD EVERY
C. MURRAY ROGERS
ADELA M. EVERY

St. George's Close
PO Box 19018
Jerusalem
December 31

When on January 7, 1977 the letter was published, the reaction was swift and furious. Soon there was another letter in the *Times* from the Chairman of the Rainbow Club, Professor Zvi Werblowsky, denouncing what had been written. The Israeli ambassador in London sent off his own missive to the paper. There were others—"Oh! I had some stinkers!" Murray recalled—from people he knew, and from people he did not. And though there was steady but muted support within the Palestinian community, the intensity of the storm within both the Jewish and Christian communities supportive of the Zionist movement was focused on Murray rather than on any of his co-signers, for the others were already known to be in sympathy with the Palestinian cause. But Murray, as a member of the Rainbow Club, suddenly found himself the *enfant terrible* for a good portion of the Jerusalem interfaith community.

Until that time, Murray had been a steady but ambivalent participant in the group. Though he had found good friends there in both the Christian and Jewish communities, and though discussions were interesting, they were, he said, "highly third leg [of chicken] . . . very academic." And he had harbored a suspicion that the gatherings were undergirded by an unspoken political purpose: "I felt there was something more at stake than interfaith dialogue, especially when quite a few of the Jewish members didn't believe in the faith part at all. It was a cultural dialogue; it was very learned. It was very, very gentlemanly, with all frightfully polite. But we had some extremely powerful Zionists there, you see, including a Dominican." A Greek Catholic priest colleague, the Palestinian Elias Chacour[35] shared Murray's sense that "if they could get the leading Christian people there, then when any trouble blew up, they could sort of quieten it down before it got out into the open."[36]

As the weeks and months wore on, the controversy did not fade. It was said in letters and in the press, both in Jerusalem and in London, that what he had written was beyond the pale, that he should never have been allowed to be a part of the Rainbow Club. But precisely *what* he had said that made him such a *persona non grata* was elusive. The truth of the statements

---

35. Elias Chacour: b. 1939, is now Archbishop of the Melkite Greek Catholic Church. He is the author of *Blood Brothers,* and co-author of *We Belong to the Land,* and most recently, *Faith Beyond Despair.* He has been a three-time nominee for the Nobel Peace Prize for his work in the Middle East.

36. Interview with Trapnell.

about the displacement of the Arab families was undisputed. Then, in an unguarded moment, one of the Rainbow Club members let an unspoken premise slip in public—no one should be allowed to engage in interfaith dialogue with the group unless they fully accepted the ideology of the Israeli state. That was all Murray needed to hear; for him "the cat was out of the bag." At the next meeting, he picked up the gauntlet. Indeed, he stated, he did *not* accept the ideology of the Israeli state or, for that matter, of the British government or the Indian government. For him interfaith dialogue was interfaith dialogue, no ideology, no strings attached. And if interfaith dialogue were sullied with politics, it would be nothing more than "humbug." Professor Werblowsky and others responded: their disapproval had nothing whatsoever to do with politics or government. Murray simply had behaved in a manner thoroughly unbecoming for the gentlemanly group. By then, Murray later acknowledged, with his back against the wall, his attempts at diplomacy fell away. "No doubt I spoke more and more clearly in those days . . . Nothing [could] stop me now, so I went to town."[37]

While pressure mounted within the Rainbow Group for him to resign, behind the scene, there was keen interest in his perspective. He was invited—secretly—to confer with the Archbishop of the Greek Orthodox Church, and with the Jerusalem representative of the Vatican as well. Both urged him—privately—to stay the course and not to resign. There was support from other sources as well. Murray recalled how the Jerusalem correspondant from the London *Times*, straying from his objectivity, offered encouragement that was appreciated, though hardly necessary: "'Murray,'" he advised, 'simply say what you believe. Don't try to play politics. You may be wrong; that won't matter. But you must say what you believe, otherwise'—and I always remember this—'they'll get you.'"[38] Then there was a letter from his devoted Jewish friend, Israel Shahak, with words to this effect: "I hear that you're having some trouble with my people. I only hope and pray that you will stand firm." Years later the letter remained one of Murray's treasured keepsakes.

But amongst members of the Rainbow Group, there was a mixture of hostility and emotional distancing. Murray recalled an American Baptist, previously a close friend, who said to him, "Murray, I don't agree with everything you say, but I agree with a great deal of it. I simply cannot say so: I would lose my visa." Others connected to the university seemed to fear reprisals as well, and it became, in Murray's words, "pretty lonely" as old friends, Christians in particular, recoiled from his outstretched hand,

37. Ibid.
38. Ibid.

falling in line with Werblowsky's stance. The shunning was for him "quite a new experience." Only one member, the Provincial of the Jesuits, offered his support. Any time Murray needed advice or strength—and that was not infrequent—the elderly priest was there. "He was a great anchor for me,"[39] Murray recalled.

When all was said and done, four months after the publication of his letter in the *Times,* Murray was expelled from the Rainbow Club with only one vote dissenting—that of his Jesuit friend. Officially the grounds were for the "tone and style" of his letter; unofficially there were accusations of "anti-semitism." Jewish friends rushed to his defense, but the Israeli government had taken notice. The period of Murray, Mary, and Heather's visas, which had been routinely renewed annually, was now reduced to five months. And the dominoes continued to fall, in Britain as well. The *Times,* which had actively followed the affair, ran another article reporting on Murray's visa situation. Whereupon the Chief Rabbi of Britain, active in the British version of the Rainbow, raised the issue, triggering an intervention from Sir John Lawrence,[40] who said, "What's all this going on? I happen to know that man, Murray!"[41] Challenged by Sir John, the British Jewish community became so concerned about the publicity that before long the Archbishop of Canterbury had been called to calm the storm. Years later, Murray still marveled at it all, that the whole rumpus had begun in their little corner of the Armenian Quarter, when six Arab families were displaced from their homes.

It is hard to imagine the intensity of the prayer that was lifted up from Jyotiniketan in those months of tension and strife. Though never neglecting their intercessions for others, they implored God for their own spirits, living the words they espoused: "Pray not for Arab or Jew, for Palestinian or Israeli, but pray rather for ourselves, that we may not divide them in our prayers, but keep them both together in our hearts."[42] Could they manage to do that? Where was God in all of this, and what were they called to do?

Surely the experience must have been especially agonizing for the contemplative Heather who weathered the days serving faithfully at the Spafford Children's Centre. Mary would have been deeply pained as well at the turn of events. Accustomed as she may have been to her husband making waves, this level of misunderstanding and vituperation was unparalleled.

39. Ibid.
40. Sir John Lawrence, a prominent writer, diplomat, and churchman. According to his obituary in the *Guardian* on February 2, 2000, he was the nearest to a professional layman that the Church of England has ever had—and a good deal more influential than many bishops."
41. Interview with Trapnell.
42. These words were attributed by Murray to an unnamed Palestinian friend.

Rosmarie, new to the community but hardly naive of the harsh political climate in which they lived, may well have taken it more in stride. Perhaps she was a good sounding board for them, with some independent thinking of her own to offer.

In their Letter to Friends at the end of 1977, they offered reflections on their ordeal:

> We experienced just how contemporary the Gospels are; it seems that the human situation remains astonishingly much the same, as does God's way of coping with us all. Life still comes by way of death; the truth is still as intolerable . . . Positively, we learnt what real friendship means when people stand by one even when it does not pay; we learnt that silence means consent; we learnt not to put people into religious boxes—the line doesn't run there. For example, of the only two who refused either to speak or to shake hands with Murray, one was Christian and the other was Jewish. It was a Jewish friend who was the first to deny, publicly, that Murray is anti-semitic . . . We learnt—this above all—that God carries us along when times are hard, not unscathed but certainly strengthened.[43]

In that pivotal time, the little Community's prayer and soul-searching had yielded an evolving sense of identity as well. While their commitment to Eucharist and prayer, disciplined work, simplicity of life, and mutual submission to one another and to God remained steadfast, they now needed to articulate a new dimension of their spiritual life. Using a phrase inspired by Thich Nhat Hanh and Daniel Berrigan,[44] they wrote:

> We want to be a '*community of resistance*' against the insidious idea that some people matter more than others, that God loves some, looks after some, more than others. Put positively, this means that God loves every man, woman and child of every religion and of none . . .
>
> We see ourselves called to resist the widespread acceptance of violence as the only way of dealing with opponents . . . But does faith run deep enough in ourselves to generate the hope and courage it takes to act non-violently in the hardest situation?
>
> Here (and elsewhere in the world) there is a dangerous idolatry of absolutised ideologies, our local version being Zionism and anti-Zionism; these are our two local "gods," seen either as absolute good or as absolute evil and therefore requiring total

---

43. Letter #24.

44. The phrase "Community of Resistance" came from *The Raft is not the Shore*, Orbis, 1975.

submission or total enmity. This is made infinitely more dangerous and powerful by the use of religious emotion to build up the mystical-chauvinist element potentially present in any national consciousness.

Each of the above points of resistance are points of struggle within ourselves first, before they become points of struggle outside. This is preeminently so in the demand to love rather than to hate . . . to love our enemies and those who despise and reject us. Unless this inner battle for love and forgiveness is fought again and again, and, by God's grace, sometimes won, what is the point of Jyotiniketan, here or in India? Friends, pray for us, for otherwise there is not a hope of really living out this life of resistance against . . . and resistance for love.[45]

Where might the small community focus this resistance against the idea that God loves some more than others? One frontier seemed to be fundamentalist interpretations of the Bible. Having left far behind the "fundamentals" of their own religious backgrounds, they now noticed how in certain scriptures Christians share with Jews, God seems to command and even bless the slaughter of one group to preserve another. Did not the naming of the Jews as God's chosen people give permission and justification for the violence that continued to plague the land thousands of years later? Murray had seen the dilemma in the Jewish-Christian dialogue groups. For if Jews believed in their hearts that God had given them the land to worship God, then it would follow that they must take possession of it, no matter the means or the sacrifices they had to endure.

He had witnessed suffering from the Jewish perspective as well as from the Palestinian side. In those years, there was a surge of suicides amongst young men serving in the Israeli military. Seen by Jewish friends as a man with strong pastoral gifts, he was asked to visit a few of their families, and he never forgot the desperation of a bereaved mother who cried out, "Tell me, Mr. Rogers, am I to have children simply to see them killed in this struggle?" The cycle of violence was all too clear. "As the wrongs against Arabs increase," they wrote, "so do the sufferings of the Jewish people. They quoted one of Murray's Jewish professor friends who had remarked, "'The demoralisation of my people increases, especially among the young, every year that military occupation of the West Bank and Gaza is maintained.'"[46]

And so Jyotiniketan focused on the interpretation of certain scriptures—writings which, if understood literally, they believed were used, consciously or unconsciously, to justify violence. From the biblical conflict

45. Letter #24.
46. Interview with Trapnell.

between Jacob and Esau, down through the generations to the slaughter of the Christian Crusades to the death camps of Nazi Germany, God's supposed preference for one group over another had justified horrendous violence. Now, right under their noses, they seemed to be witnessing another iteration of that tragic human propensity. They spoke plainly in their Letter to Friends:

> If we continue to believe, and, more terrible, teach children to believe, that God commanded to be "utterly destroyed all that breathed,"[47] are we not adding yet another example of the sad, sad things done in this "holy land," supposedly for God and at His command? This religious fanaticism—by no means the preserve of one religion—shows its head again if we understand God's choosing of Jewish people in an exclusive sense, thus insulting intolerably His universal love; "chosen-ness" is indeed true, blessedly true, but for every single soul, every single people. The Jews were "chosen;" they still are, and now in the Light of the Gospel we know that *all* people are chosen, so staggeringly all-inclusive in the Love of God![48]

By 1980, Murray's preaching and teaching, indeed his world view, had been changed, even radicalized. As they wrote, "Nine years' life in Jerusalem has taught us this, that there is no escaping the cross, no cheap grace; superficial smiles at ecumenical gatherings and impressive liturgies unrelated to life are utterly useless in furthering the Kingdom."[49]

Yet satisfactions and even joys remained. There was nothing superficial about the smiles that broke out on all the faces of Jyotiniketan when at last the news arrived of the safe delivery to the world of "The Elephant": Raimon Panikkar's *The Vedic Experience, Mantramanjari*, published at last after its nine year gestation and weighing in at nearly a thousand pages. Mary's quiet, mostly unsung labor was finally to see the light of day. Though it was Raimon's name that would grace the cover, he paid tribute to the indispensability of his four-person team of collaborators in the Preface to his *magnum opus*: "One could hardly have found a more unselfish and devoted group of helpers than the one that has made this anthology possible. One does not fly alone . . . M. Rogers has revised the style, especially allowing the texts to reflect the beauty of the original through the genius of the English language . . ."[50] For Mary the work had been a labor of love; at home or in the world, she was accustomed to playing a self-effacing, yet indispensable role,

---

47. Joshua 10:40
48. Letter #25.
49. Letter #26.
50. Panikkar, *The Vedic Experience, Mantramanjari*, xxxvi.

allowing others to stand in the spotlight. Often it was Mary's poetic sensibilities that shimmered unacknowledged beneath the surface of Murray's passion in their Letters to Friends. But now those who knew her work and her contribution, both on The Elephant and in Jyotiniketan, stood, briefly at least, in awe.

And for Murray not all seemed useless. With his official interfaith dialogue ended, he welcomed unofficial dialogue, like the invitation from a Jewish rabbinical school in the Old City to participate in a conference on peace. In his talk he shared a Gandhian-inspired, experience-infused message: "To dare to go the way of Truth and Non-violence—the one way I know of to peace—demands of each of us self-purification and a great inner discipline; it needs as much attention, as much training, as much dedication, as is applied by men and women in their waging of war." Never had one of their favorite Vedic prayers, cited earlier, felt more compelling. As reported in their Letter, he ended his speech with its timeless four thousand year old words:

> O God, scatterer of ignorance and darkness,
>
> grant me your strength.
>
> May all beings regard me with the eye of a friend,
>
> and I all beings!
>
> With the eye of a friend may each single being
>
> regard all others![51]

More than ever, their deeply held beliefs were translated into action. "Without hiding . . . the misery . . . of this human situation and our own failure again and again to respond to it with humility and love, we still can bear witness to the extraordinary liveliness of God's presence and action."[52] Now they relaxed into the impossibility of neatly segregating the political from the spiritual. And they were heartened when a sense of synchronicity arose, as it did as they led an ecumenical group for nightlong silent vigil in the Church of the Resurrection. The unplanned convergence of auspicious events—the Muslim Feast of *Eid al-Adha*,[53] the Christian feast of Christ the King, and the arrival that very day of President Anwar Sadat of Egypt to Jerusalem—the first Arab leader to visit Israel to advance the cause of peace—seemed to offer a flicker of hope, a touch of the Spirit.

---

51. Letter #25.

52. Ibid.

53. *Eid al-Adha*: The worldwide celebration commemorating the willingness of Abraham to obey God to the point of sacrificing his son Isaac.

At other times the opportunity to bear witness presented itself in political events—as in the controversy regarding Nablus Mayor Bassam Al Shak'a. An outspoken critic of the military occupation of the West Bank, he had been detained by government authorities and threatened with expulsion. In response, Jyotiniketan joined a number of others—Jews, Christians, and Muslims—for a time of "prayer, fasting and solidarity."[54] In allying themselves with prominent dissidents like Bassam Al Shaka'a[55] and Professor Israel Shahak, (who lived at times with threats of a grenade being planted in his garden), they had a sense of commitment to an important work in alignment with the oppressed. They found hope in their bravery, in their willingness to speak their truth in the face of physical danger.

To Friends they further explained the apparent discontinuity of their calling:

> We have discovered very vividly . . . that the inner logic of Christian discipleship presses us to be both contemplative and actively involved, or, to put it another way, that our striving for inner awareness and serenity—qualities that the East values so highly—includes an involvement in struggles for justice and peace. We see now, it's in our bones through personal experience, that we are not called to weld together the contemplative and active poles of our vocation; they are together from the start. We can no more truly choose one or the other than we can choose between the Lord Jesus Christ who prayed to His Father and the revolutionary Christ who lived for the poor and oppressed. We, along with a multitude of other Christians, were brought up on that dichotomy between the active and the contemplative; events here and elsewhere in the world have shown us that it does not exist![56]

As the intensity of Jyotiniketan's commitment to resistance deepened, so too did their grounding in their spiritual disciplines and their mutual commitment to one another in community. More and more, this included Rosmarie. "Rejoice with us please," they wrote, "that Rosmarie, after our years of growing together, now well and truly belongs to this little 'family.'" Partaking in their daily vegetarian meals, she was present as they assuaged their spiritual hunger as well, in their prayer and worship and regular days of retreat. Those days, when "largely in silence . . . they pondered together a

---

54. Letter #25.

55. Two years later, Mayor Al Shaka'a was the victim of a car-bombing in which he lost both of his legs.

56. Letter #24.

quotation from some spiritual master of east or west," were "very essential nutrition for such a life."⁵⁷ Their friend Vroni Thurneysen, pastor of a parish in Switzerland, often managed to join them for those quiet days and, along with others, for their rich diet of Eucharists in the Chapel of St. Abraham just above Calvary.

Along with their inner work, they tended their deep spiritual roots beyond Jerusalem. Returning to places and people they loved brought blessèd relief and respite. Travel was a way of life. For Murray in particular, what could appear as restlessness or wanderlust, he now described as a call from the beyond. In 1975 he wrote to Raimon, "Life beckons, doesn't *It*, from over the next hilltop. Abhishikt makes me long to keep moving as he did." Mary, too, was always ready to go, beckoned by her love and curiosity for the world, but most of all by her family.

From Jerusalem in the 70's with Europe easily accessible, annual visits to their children and grandchildren became the norm. Cheryl recalled their times together in France: the ten-day visits, "occasionally with Heather in tow." Unaccustomed as Mary and Murray were to modern parenting styles, there were "sometimes tense moments, as in any family," but they did attempt to act as real grandparents on these occasions," and the children were "fond" of their unusual grandparents. Cheryl recalled too: "lots of good conversation and laughs at table" over the hearty vegetarian meals she prepared. For Murray there was a special rapport with André, his fellow priest-at-heart: "Father particularly loved watching sports with André on the T.V. and had great laughs watching Benny Hill and Mr. Bean!" Harkening back to their Cambridge days as a young couple when movies were a "forbidden fruit," they happily indulged in the cinema on their European visits along with visits with friends, both theirs and Cheryl and André's in Paris. "Naturally," Cheryl said, "we all went to church together and Father was sometimes asked to participate [in the Roman Catholic service]. On one memorable occasion—First Communion for young James Poutier—the officiating priest, a widower and father of six, invited Father to celebrate Mass with him." Beginning the service he introduced himself and Murray as "two grandfathers," raising eyebrows in the congregation who were unused to anything but celibate priests, and delighting Murray who never shied away from shaking the assumptions of people in the pews.⁵⁸ Family visits such as these, whether to France or England, always generated new stories, recalled with merriment at future reunions.

57. Letter #25.
58. Interview with author.

In 1978, at the invitation of the Archbishop of Perth, Murray traveled to Australia to offer a series of spiritual workshops for Anglican clergy. It was an opportunity he welcomed, not only for the fellowship and sharing, but, going to and fro, for the chance to spend precious days in India, to be with his most treasured mentors, whether in the flesh or in the Spirit. Begging off a request to attend an interfaith dialogue meeting, he wrote to Raimon: "I would be happy, very, to meet the friends . . . [but] really you do not *need* me at the official meeting. There are many others much better at these things than I am. I am rather clear that I mustn't allow my mere five days in Swamiji's country to be diminished . . . My little corner in trying to continue Swamiji's work is not really in a committee."

In 1977 in another letter to Raimon, he shared his thirst for time with him—a kindred spirit: "Hardly a day goes by without my knowing, gratefully, that you are traveling with us and that time and space do not have the last word! I think that old Swamiji has been teaching us since he 'departed' that external unrealities are to be known for what they are . . . and we try to learn. And still . . . sometimes we long to see you again and to experience externally and internally (the same thing really) our unity . . . Would there be a chance of our meeting? More, would you consider our spending five or six days together in and around Rishikesh, in silence, speech, or just being there, linked with Swamiji?"

Swamiji's mysterious words about his marvelous beyond-life-and death adventure alone were enough to draw Murray, not just over the next hill, but across the world. Comparing his awakening to an atomic explosion, Swamiji had written to him, trying to express the inexpressible: "The 'Word of God' comes from/to *my* own 'present;' it is that very awakening which is my self-awareness. What I discover above all in Christ is his 'I AM . . .' And a few weeks later, he wrote, "The Christ I might present would be simply the 'I AM' of [every] deep heart, who can show himself in the dancing Siva or the amorous Krisna!"[59]

His words echoed what he had written to Murray in a letter cited earlier: "The discovery of Christ's I AM is the ruin of any Christian theology, for all notions are burned within the fire of experience . . . I feel too much . . . the blazing fire of his I AM in which all notions about Christ's personality, ontology, history, etc. have disappeared. And I find his real mystery shining in every awakening man . . ."[60] Here was Swamiji, just weeks before his death, sharing a transformation of which they had so often talked together. In Swamiji's death, as in his life, Murray wanted to be near, to learn from

---

59. Du Boulay, *Cave of the Heart*, 238.
60. Ibid., 238–39.

him. Thus he and Raimon returned to the Kumeon Hills with the Himalayas beckoning beyond. Following the pilgrim path to the temple at Ranagal where Abhishiktananda had experienced his awakening, they could share a rich communion and Murray could plumb his own depths, contemplating this *advaitic* mystery, still elusive for him, in silence.

Beyond the sacred silence of India came an infusion of energy from well-loved places and friends. First was their old home in Kareli. "There was great cause for thankfulness," their Letter reported, "to find how doubly alive the ashram has become since we left in 1971—maybe precisely because we left! . . . Swami Deenabandhu and the Sisters are living a life full of love, simplicity, and service that rejoices our hearts more that we can say."[61] Nor were other old Jyotiniketan friends forgotten: on the return trip Murray visited South India, spending time with Laurie and Kuni Baker and M.M. Thomas. It was an extended journey that slaked the thirst of his parched spirit.

The following year brought more invitations. Mary and Heather flew off for three weeks of "beautiful holiday" at the home of their generous friend, Hugh Pilkington,[62] in Nairobi, Kenya. Pilkington's energy and fortune were dedicated to relief and education of young Africans. He fashioned a time of renewal for the two steadfast companions that met their needs, not only for the soothing balm of nature, but for the intellectual and emotional stimulation of the lively African culture. Resting amidst gardens and distant hills, they shared his "very open house" with Ethiopian refugees who had fled the genocidal "Red Terror" of Col. Mengistu. Then, knowing they were ready to partake of the "real" Africa, he arranged a stay with a local family "in surroundings very similar to Jyotiniketan, Kareli," Mary wrote, where they joined in "5¼ solid hours of an African Independent Church with drums, dancing and much love and joy." Familiar though they were with Indian poverty, the slum they visited with a group of Taizé Brothers seemed "the worst of all possible slums." The diminutive, soft-spoken western ladies in eastern garb may well have seemed a curiosity to the Africans they met; no casual observer could apprehend their vast spiritual resources.

For cultural contrast to a Nairobi slum, the invitation Murray accepted that Lent was vast. As the Rev. Bradford Hastings, an Episcopal priest on sabbatical in Jerusalem, had met the members of Jyotiniketan at St. George's, shared their Eucharists in the Old City, and joined in their contemplative

61. Letter #25.
62. Dr. Hugh Pilkington, PhD, dedicated much of his life and fortune (from the family glass business in England) to the cause of peace in East and Central Africa through the education and training of refugees. Though he died in a car aceident in 1986, the Windle Charitable Trust, which he established, continues to support his vision.

prayer, he knew that his traditional and well-to-do Episcopal parish in Greenwich, Conn., would be enriched by Murray's teachings and presence. He announced the arrival to parishioners in a parish bulletin: "You have heard me talking about Murray Rogers, and you will hear me keep on talking because I don't want you to miss out on what he is going to bring us during Holy Week... A resident of Jerusalem, he will be with us... for eight days as a spiritual guide who will lead us along the road to Calvary which he knows so well. But more, as a man of visible spiritual depth, he will help us draw ever closer to the Risen Lord who LIVES and in whose power we come alive..."

Murray's well-meaning friends challenged his choice; why, they asked, would he, who felt called to be with the poor, waste his time in a community where people seemed to "have it all?" What *are* you doing? they asked. But having made up his mind, he was not to be deterred.

Across the Atlantic, word went out and traveled quickly through the staid community of the heralded visitor, who, amazingly, had arrived carrying only a small cloth bag holding little more than a single change of clothing and a small stack of books and papers. He seemed a warm, outgoing yet contained man, curious and eager to meet anyone who wanted to meet him. When Murray joined the Palm Sunday procession, the church was crowded with the eager and the merely curious. There he was, with his shock of wavy white hair, his ruggedly handsome face, and his tall, slightly bent frame. His sense of presence was palpable, his movements and pace, his gestures seemed to convey meaning and import often lost in the habituated ritual of the liturgy. His words, when they came, were resonant, measured, even sparse. Was it, some wondered, the resonance of Cambridge that brought old words to life? Or was he simply a charismatic speaker, with a well-practiced and choreographed presentation? There was, it seemed, a confusing cognitive dissonance of a man who, in background and education, was one of them, but who had rejected all they had worked so hard to attain for something else—what was it? A deeper knowing? Was it God? Whatever it was, for many a deep intuitive sense that touched unknown wellsprings in themselves was tapped. For some the response was silence, for others it was tears. A photographer discreetly snapped a photo focused on the hem of his cassock and his unshod feet; the next day it appeared in the local paper, and in the following days, more and more came to his early morning silent meditations, to his teachings, to the daily services, to whatever event was on his schedule. For Murray, usually far beyond concern or surprise at any reaction to him, years later still remembered the photograph of his stockinged feet in the Greenwich paper. "Extraordinary!!" he laughingly recalled. "Just extraordinary!" Indeed it was an extraordinary start to an unlikely relationship between a conventionally wealthy suburban American parish and a non-conformist Gandhian-Anglican priest. Lives were to be changed in small ways and large. Jyotiniketan's ever-expanding family network would continue to grow.

"There is," they wrote in 1979, "a whole network of people who belong closely together in the Spirit across so many of the barriers and divisions that tear society apart. On the conceptual level, the level of 'third leg of chicken,' these barriers seem insurmountable, while on the level of the Spirit, of the heart, where little people meet little people, there is a quite extraordinary consciousness of unity and love. This awareness is a sort of limitless ocean of belonging and love where what we are on the label level is gloriously irrelevant."[63]

For them this "network" with whom they stayed connected, whether by visits, letters, or in prayer and recollection, included significant personages and communities like Raimon Panikkar and Thich Nhat Hanh, the Taizé Community, and the Little Sisters of Jesus. But their address book bulged with other names from throughout the world, people with whom their paths had crossed, connections made, and for whom they continued to pray. For them the "label level" of religious categories, academic degrees, personal wealth or poverty, race or nationality was not what mattered. What was relevant was a willingness to connect through the heart and an awareness of a common humanity.

Each summer, visits within this network were intertwined with family time. "Although our links with friends and communities is wonderfully enriching we never stop rejoicing in our personal families,"[64] they wrote in 1980. But there was one family member in whom they had never rejoiced and only reluctantly had included in occasional strained visits, who now was gone. Murray's father, Edgar Rogers, had died in 1979 at the age of 96. Though no perceptible softening towards his son had occurred, the year before his death, Murray had received a startling letter. Edgar Rogers was writing to him, not as a father to his son, but as a penitent to a priest, to share his concern about "the state of his soul." And so Murray had responded, sharing the Gospel story that for him carried a message of unqualified love and forgiveness: the Prodigal Son. As a priest, but only as a priest, he told his father that he was forgiven. Murray wondered: Had his father come to believe that his being a priest was worth *something*?

Summers were spiced with family events, many highlighting the turning of the generations, the passage of time. There was the wedding

63. Letter #25.
64. Letter #26.

of Heather's niece Alison, celebrated by Murray. Visits with children and grandchildren and holiday gatherings in Switzerland were punctuated with quiet days in their friend Vroni Thurneysen's Swiss chalet. With the birth of Richard and Alice's second child in 1980, a grandson named Murray, the grandchildren numbered eight. Eager though they always were to greet a new arrival, from Cheryl, Linda and Richard's perspective, "The Parents," as they called them, were still "family-at-a distance." Visits passed quickly; intervening months made them relative strangers to their growing grandchildren, who found them curious. Not knowing or understanding them too well made it hard to feel close. These were among the clouds that shadowed their hopeful existence, their determination to accept God's will and live into the future. Again, Mary shared her feelings privately with Raimon by letter, responding to a greeting he had sent that seemed "meant specially for me." She repeated his words, "May the *Alleluia* fill our hearts in the same measure that we say *Amen* to our lives," before confiding: "Sometimes I still find it hard to say that *Amen* . . . and I guess it is so true that we are only able to receive the *Alleluia* in our hearts to the extent to which we are saying the *Amen*. Have I got it right? It's perhaps a question of saying the Amen in the *un*conscious rather than the conscious. So please, dear Raymond, pray for me . . . that both the *Amen* and the *Alleluia* may be there—and thank you for that word." Though her loyalty to Murray never allowed her to share so directly to him, he could not help but be aware of her multi-faceted pain. It was an unspoken reality between them.

Mary stayed on her pilgrim path. And life continued in Jerusalem, as the Israeli government renewed their visas month by month, keeping them on a tight leash. Friends, worship, and prayer remained their sustenance. "When one is battered by events and by the struggles of one's own heart and mind, the Spirit's gift of inner quietness and the ability to accept both oneself and one's neighbours needs to be renewed constantly," they wrote. "This city of Jerusalem has a knack of confronting one daily with one's own poverty and God's extraordinary riches, and one of his special gifts to each of us is the others in this still small Community."[65]

In that respect, in the midst of a weeklong silent retreat at the small monastery they had grown to love in Bethlehem, April 30, 1980 became "a red-letter day." Murray shared the announcement. After months, indeed years of earnest prayer and discernment, Rosmarie had decided to formalize her relationship with the community; she would be welcomed "as a sister" into Jyotiniketan. The "Act of Commitment,"[66] embedded into the Holy

---

65. Letter #26.

66. For the complete text of the Act of Commitment, see Appendix 4.

Eucharist that day in April, was laden with grave and noble aspirations. Having affirmed her belief that "Christ calls [her] for love of Him to belong to Him with no limits and no reserve, to the end of [her] life and hereafter," she affirmed her intention "to live out this resolve in this Community of Jyotiniketan, for as many years as God may give us, in simplicity of life and in mutual obedience." The rite concluded with her vows:

> I, Rosmarie Schönholzer, thankfully believing and trusting that God calls me to belong solely to Him, promise to Him, in freedom and joy, my self, my whole being, to be His for ever, for richer, for poorer, in sickness and in health, for this life and the next, in the name of the Father and of the Son and of the Holy Spirit. Amen.[67]

With a ring blessed and placed on her finger by Murray "as the outward sign of your inward belonging to Christ Jesus your Lord in joy and fidelity until your life's end," and a blessing prayer that she be "filled with all the fulness of God," the Holy Eucharist continued.

Her good friend, Vroni Thurneysen, remembers the poignancy of the day. Vows complete, it became a joyous celebration—a feast day for the four. But for Vroni, understanding the gravity of the commitment, it was bittersweet; a part of her also longed to join them; and while they were gaining a sister, it felt as if she were losing one.[68]

The decision had not been easy for Rosmarie. While she loved community life and longed to make a final commitment, she found it hard to imagine leaving her work with the Palestinian people, whom she had grown to love. The choice then had been entirely hers; Murray, Mary, and Heather were united in their belief that no one could be pressured, or even asked, to join Jyotiniketan; the call must come from within.

And though she knew that bravery was required of them all, Rosmarie's first test arrived on the very heels of that joyous day.

Nearly a year before, a letter had arrived from Peter Lee, a Chinese Methodist friend from Murray's ecumenical conference days, who was spearheading a small, independent ecumenical group based at the Christian Tao Fong Shan Centre in Shatin in the New Territories of Hong Kong. The Center had deep ecumenical roots; its founder, Karl Ludvig Reichelt[69] was

67. Text shared by Veronica Thurneysen.
68. Interview with author.
69. Karl Ludvig Reichelt (1887–1952) was the author of several books on Chinese Buddhism, including *Religion in Chinese Garments*, published in 1951. Biographies of his life include at least one in English: *Karl Ludvig Reichelt: Missionary, Scholar and Pilgrim*; Eric Sharpe, 1984. Tao Fong Shan Ecumenical Centre.

a Norwegian missionary with deep experience of Chinese Buddhism. The letter offered the startling suggestion that Jyotiniketan relocate there from Jerusalem to become a spiritual anchor for the group. Though the idea of freedom from relentless religious and political tensions of the Middle East and the fresh air of an entirely new perspective was appealing, the invitation seemed impractical. With Mary and Murray both past sixty, were they not too old to plunge into a new culture? To learn a new language? The idea was quickly dismissed as "outlandish." Then a year later, another letter from Peter Lee arrived: Wouldn't they reconsider? "Slowly, slowly," they wrote, "our minds were changed." After times spent apart from one another in various parts of the world, they each noticed a sense of dread in their return to Jerusalem and a new openness to the idea of complete change. The invitation to bolster a small ecumenical group within the Tao Fong Shan Centre was all the more compelling, Murray later reflected, as they realized it "had nothing to do with institutions"; each member of the little group was acting individually and from "different spiritual sources."[70] That spring when Murray went to Hong Kong for nearly a month to explore the possibilities, the warm welcome of its members and the serendipitous arrival there of their dear old friend Father Shigeto Oshida ("joy, oh, joy!" exclaimed Mary, when she heard of his presence and encouragement), the invitation seemed no longer outlandish but providential. Back in Jerusalem, as Murray returned from Hong Kong, Vroni was again visiting. She recalled how they gathered 'round, waiting with bated breath: "I'll never forget his words: 'I think God wants us to go to Hong Kong!' he said, as they all listened, astonished."[71] To their Friends, they explained, "Meeting friends and discovering 'coincidences' . . . seem to us to be God's way of nudging us to dare, and when we found that we were being welcomed by people from various denominations, not least by the Anglican bishop, our hearts were brought to say 'yes'—with joy and trembling."[72]

For Rosmarie the trembling outweighed the joy. But her commitment was made; for better or for worse, she had cast her lot with them, and she would go. The move would tear her away from Palestine and from the handicapped friends of the Homes of Mercy. For all of them there were countless others who had shared their joys and their sufferings, partaken day after day with them in their worship—neighbors, colleagues, so many, they said, "whose names [are] written on our hearts . . . However eager we are to begin to breathe this new "air" of Chinese sensitivity and life, it is not easy to say

70. Interview with Trapnell.
71. Interview with author.
72. Letter #26.

goodbye to Bethany and the Old City and to this dearly-loved little house of Mr. Dickranian who has been the best and most considerate of landlords."[73]

Yes, they would be leaving, but Murray's fighting spirit was far from quelled. Living in Jerusalem had brought all of them to a conversion experience, quite different from Murray's youthful inner response to the call of Isaiah, the joyous, "Send me!" This conversion had taken more time; it was a turning of heads and hearts, a *metanoia* that had led Jyotiniketan on an unexpected path. They had been disillusioned and radicalized. Just before their departure, they wrote to Friends, in words reflective and descriptive of the change:

> Thirteen years ago this week Murray went with crowds of Jewish people to the Western Wall . . . after the end of the Six Day War; he shared the exhilaration, the hopes of Zionism. At that time he was oblivious to the bulldozed Arab homes that made that pilgrimage possible. Now, however, it seems that the positive potential in Zionism is almost lost and the slim chances of it being turned to success become less month by month. When a movement of liberation such as Zionism proceeds to crush opposition by collective punishment and the deportation of citizens, by the seizure of land and the appropriation and control of water (a drastic means of coercion in a dry and thirsty land), then, unless lessons are learnt and unless change and repentance happen, we human beings, whether Jews of Gentiles, are on a terribly dangerous course. In days of long ago it was a perilous thing to make and worship a golden calf; it is obviously no less dangerous to worship as ultimate either land, nationhood or security. It is this single-eyed devotion to force, whether organised or not, and to "security" that makes us tremble for the peoples of this land, for fanaticism, religious or a-religious, so clearly growing year by year, could easily bring, here and elsewhere, the end of western civilisation as we know it.[74]

Deliberately, and with prophetic words that rang out, they spoke the change they felt called to live. But for the community as a whole, life in Jerusalem had become wearing. Its joy was muted. "It became apparent to us that our little life, which had set out to be just a tiny little cell, hidden away in a lump, 'for friendship, for worship and silence . . .' without any of our choosing, had become a real nuisance . . . We just couldn't play the game according to the powers that be . . . the church . . . the government . . . We

73. Ibid.
74. Ibid.

were never thrown out, but we were certainly unwanted."[75] They had done what they set out to do: their friendships were legion, their nine years there had been imbued with worship and the silence. But despite the countless moments of wonder and beauty, life in Jerusalem had become too painful. "This all could be so beautiful," Murray later reflected, "and we [human beings] have made it nearly hell. *Dominus flevit*.[76] *Dominus flevit*. We just don't see."[77]

Their departure reaffirmed their conviction—"So many of the *real* things that matter are the unseen, hidden things . . ."[78] Hidden things—like the three hundred and more early morning celebrations of the Jyotiniketan liturgy with its Upanishad readings and its Sanskrit songs in the Chapel of St. Abraham of Melchizedek in the Church of the Holy Sepulcher. The little core group for those Eucharists was usually four or five, squeezed into the tiny chapel; often additional visitors who had come to share the "Cosmic Sacrament" would appear. "We even wonder," they mused, "whether that almost unknown 'work' was one of the chief reasons why we came here—to be allowed that tiny part in the universal redemption of mankind!"[79]

Despite their dire warnings, hope remained their wellspring as they looked to the future: "We wish to follow the Light that has been given us, and, by listening and waiting, by silence and joyful worship, by service and simple friendship, to discern more clearly the new horizons of God's purpose in His love for all humanity, a purpose which remains to be realised in all its cosmic splendor and glory . . ." They signed off their last letter from Jerusalem with a greeting of St. Paul: "May the God of hope fill you with all joy and peace by your faith in him, until, by the power of the Holy Spirit, you overflow with hope." And, they added, "May the hope of which [Paul] speaks hold us firm in whatever the future (yours and ours) may hold."[80]

75. Interview with Trapnell.
76. *Dominus flevit*: Jesus wept.
77. Interview with Trapnell.
78. Ibid.
79. Letter #26.
80. Ibid.

— 14 —

Hong Kong: Growing into Weakness
1980–1986

The downward way is God's way, not ours.

—Henri Nouwen

Despite their oft-repeated assertion that "the *real* things that matter" are "unseen" and "hidden,"[1] Mary, Murray, Heather, and Rosmarie were hardly prepared for the rocky transition of their first year in Hong Kong. Whereas in the past, they had freely chosen their ways of being unseen and little, now the experience had not been of their choosing. Not until a year and a half after their arrival were they at last prepared to put words on paper, sharing their new perspectives in a Letter to Friends. A few lines, hiding in plain sight amidst their ever fascinating news and observations, alluded to something important. Cryptically and without irony, they wrote: "We believe God took seriously our prayers to be little and unimportant, to be more like Jesus in His poverty of spirit and, yes, ineffectiveness."[2]

No sooner had the four touched down from their various family visits in Europe, were they greeted with the news that they had arrived earlier than expected, and their anticipated abode on Tao Fong Shan ("The Hill of the Wind of Tao") would be unavailable for a month. Surprised and disappointed, they welcomed a night's shelter they were offered at the rather grand Bishop's House by the Anglican Bishop Gilbert Baker. By the next day they had gratefully accepted the hospitality of five Chinese Roman Catholic Sisters, who were closely linked to Anthony de Mello, the Jesuit priest and writer, their old friend from India. Their community on Lamma Island, a forty-five minute ferry ride from Hong Kong, welcomed them.

1. Interview with Trapnell.
2. Letter #27.

But communications gone awry yielded an unexpected blessing. As Mary recalled in a letter to Raimon,

> What a grace that proved! . . . It was the best possible introduction to our new setting. These sisters are living . . . like the Little Sisters [of Jesus]—doing their own work, growing their vegetables, teaching part-time, but wanting to be more and more present to God in prayer and in silence. We somehow fused our lives during those four weeks, joining their times of prayer, offices, and Mass of course—they (the two who spoke English, at least) joining our Bible-Meditation and also a bit of *Tao Te Ching*[3] meditation . . . It was an initiation into Chinese culture and ways and on such a beautiful island where hitherto there have been no motor roads—yes, positively no cars—just paths. Low mountains, grasses, flowering bushes, bamboos . . . Also it gave us time to be with one another again after a couple of months of separation, not to mention starting to get at least a few rudiments of Cantonese, that very difficult seven-tone language.

Sister Louisa and her four companions, they all agreed, "welcomed us . . . so generously and sensitively, in a spirit of such joy and unity, that we are still marveling at God's goodness! Our life here on the edge of China was given an altogether special ray of light by that first experience of God's Chinese children."[4] Unsought and unexpected, their friendships assured them that God's abiding presence would carry them through challenging days ahead.

Their living quarters, made available by the Anglican Bishop, were a half hour's walk up the hill from Tai Wai. En route, about half way, was the Tao Fong Shan Centre, which, with its ecumenical group, was to be at the core of their new life. To their delight, their little dwelling had been named St. Francis House, for their beloved patron saint.

Its history was reflective of the Anglican wartime experience in Hong Kong when Bishop Ronald Hall,[5] serving under the difficult Japanese occupation, had acquired a comfortable country house to which he could retreat from the city proper. Because leaving Hong Kong was forbidden during those years, he had added a second story of three small rooms over

---

3. *Tao Te Ching*: A foundational text of Taoism.

4. Letter #27.

5. Bishop Hall was the first bishop in the Anglican Communion to ordain a woman to the priesthood. Under the Japanese occupation, priests were unable to leave Hong Kong to serve Anglicans in nearby Macau, and resident Anglicans were left without a priest. Believing conditions warranted the action unauthorized by the church, in 1944 he ordained Li Tim-Oi to serve that population.

the adjoining garage to accommodate his priests for short holidays or even for their honeymoons. In the ensuing years, the main house and most of the property had been sold to a rich Hong Kong family who surrounded it with a high fence guarded by a pack of large, menacing dogs. Just slightly removed, in earshot of the often growling, barking dogs, the garage, a chicken house, and an overgrown garden remained, still owned by the church. That adapted garage was to be home for Murray, Mary, Heather, and Rosmarie for the next eight and a half years.

Though in a state of general disrepair and neglect, with the application of enterprise and elbow grease, the property responded to their efforts. The downstairs room where Mary and Murray slept could double as a sitting room when their guests numbered more than two or three. Upstairs, accessible by a separate outside stairway, was the little wartime flat with three small rooms. Rosmarie's room served as a small sitting room, while early each morning Heather's bedroom became the chapel. Alongside was "a slip of a kitchen."[6] Downstairs was, as Mary said, "a bathroom of sorts," adding brightly: "all very tiny, but we find it just right."

Nearly thirty years before, Mary and Murray had tamed an unkempt mango grove in the heat of north India and made it their home. Now, both past sixty, they were again starting anew, taming a jungly, runaway garden and transforming a ramshackle garage into livable space. Happily, Heather and Rosmarie, their especially creative sisters, were blessed with green thumbs; ingenuity and adaptability had become second nature to them all. Soon the chicken house was transformed to a Meditation Room; it served also as sleeping quarters for guests. In addition, a toolshed was constructed by a carpenter friend from a pile of discarded doors they discovered in a dumping ground down the hill, enthusiastically retrieved and lugged up the hillside. Indeed, as their letter impishly explained, "[In] Hong Kong's very unique rubbish dumps... you can find almost anything if you keep in touch with them!"[7] Familiar with dumpster-diving in the Holy Land, scavenging in Hong Kong was a natural step.

Their scavenging, of course, was less reflective of desperate need than a witness to the profligacy of Hong Kong's waste; before recycling became a byword in mainstream society, it was a way of life for Jyotinketan. New friends, like those at Holy Trinity Anglican Church in Kowloon, soon learned they welcomed gifts of basic household necessities, but only if the supplies they offered—pots, plates, and chopsticks—had been already used and set aside by others. Shopping trips were necessary, of course, to stock

6. Letter #27.
7. Ibid.

the larder; Rita and John England, old friends from India days now living nearby, arrived weekly with their car to help. And though the nourishment of their bodies with generous servings of curried vegetables, lentils, and rice remained a priority, it was friends—new and old——who fed their souls. As in Jerusalem and India before that, their circle continued to expand, and their needs were met. "Yes, friendship. . ." they wrote, "is it not what we all need and live by? God's friendship, which we usually call His Love and Compassion, and people's friendship too."[8] Just as it had been for Bishop Hall, their out-of-the-way spot on the hill above "New Town" [*Sha Tin*] was a place of refuge for Jyotiniketan. Though in Jerusalem they had been determined to live in the heart of the Old City, now their needs were different. They could manage the long walk up the hill, though sometimes a lift was offered. Rising from sea level, despite the often intense heat and humidity, the situation was a lovely one, wooded with graceful bamboos and rambling bougainvillea. Just adjacent on the clay hills were acres of nature preserve for quiet meditative walks. As Mary wrote to Raimon, "Happily, we have a good many contacts but are also sufficiently far removed from the vast hurly-burly of Hong Kong, Kowloon and even Shatin to have peace and quiet. Thus friends can find their way here to visit if they really want to and, more particularly, to have Quiet Days either singly or in little groups." As Murray later added, "Sometimes we've been considered . . . sort of zoo pieces . . . people [want] to come and see these strange creatures. We didn't want to be that. We really only wanted the people for whom it was a bit of a nuisance to come . . . And many did."[9] The location allowed them to separate friends from the merely curious.

But even friends could disappoint, and the lack of readiness for their arrival by the ecumenical group at Tao Fong Shan whose invitation had drawn them across the world was a harbinger of deeper disappointment. The four had believed that Jyotiniketan's life of prayer and worship would be shared with them. Thus they prepared their space, extended invitations to join in their liturgies, and opened their doors as they had already opened their hearts. But, more often than not, no one came. Occasionally a Swedish couple from the Center joined in, but within a year they had returned to Sweden. Language seemed a barrier to many of the Chinese Christians. Peter Lee himself did not partake. Day by day, puzzled by the absence of Tao Fong Shan friends, they watched their dream of a richly collaborative relationship dissolve, the spiritual gifts they offered mostly left unopened.

8. Ibid.
9. Interview with Trapnell.

This unforeseen denouement to a relationship of such promise was a bitter pill. Had they misunderstood God's call? Both in community prayers and discussion they must have shared the hurt and confusion, groping to understand what had gone awry. "We guess," they wrote, "there have been many times when Chinese friends have been very patient with us new people, overlooking our boorish ways!"[10] Undoubtedly, responsibility lay on both sides. But if there was blame from Jyotiniketan, it never was uttered. Having endured, they simply acknowledged the spiritual struggle and suffering: "Our first months here, in a new world, made us experience more than we ever have before our inadequacy and uselessness, our inner poverty and 'nothingness', and this was hard to live with and to accept happily and thankfully. Your prayer helped us greatly in those hard times. To be beginners even at 25 isn't easy, let alone at over 40 or even 60!"[11]

Why then had they come to Hong Kong? More than a year later, with the "hard times" behind them and unfettered by anger or cynicism, their answer came in a reaffirmation of their life in community and in the wider human family. Perhaps more than ever before, they felt themselves in a "stream of friendship with a marvelous variety of tributaries all adding their particular gift to the stream as it makes its way to the ocean . . ." Recalling with joyful amazement the numbers who have felt 'at home,' with them, they declared, "That is what Jyotiniketan is really all about." They then added, "Of course none of this is what we 'provide' or 'bring about.' It is a gift of God to us through so many, nearby or afar, whose pilgrimage way has crossed ours." Intimations of chastening experiences peeked from their further comments: "It isn't a bit by chance, we reckon, that the coming of the Spirit, long ago or today, always beckons to a new style of life, a deeper relationship of belonging to people of all sorts, and thus toward community. On a very small scale whether in India or in the Middle East or here in China, our little 'family' has discovered this and we long to live it more deeply, with greater integrity."[12]

Only in retrospect could they name the presence of the Spirit in their difficulties.

But to the extent that they had felt called to something new on their pilgrimage way, Hong Kong did not disappoint. Jyotiniketan had settled in a very different world, where monuments to religion were overshadowed by monuments to financial achievement. When they arrived in 1980, Hong Kong was a city in transition, its future as a British colony in doubt. That

10. Letter #27.
11. Ibid.
12. Letter #28.

status had stood since the end of the Opium War in 1842 when Hong Kong Island, then little more than a collection of fishing villages, was ceded to Britain by China. It had remained an outpost of the British Empire, growing in significance as a center of trade and manufacturing until 1941, when it fell to the Japanese military. Under Japanese occupation conditions were harsh: Chinese citizens were massacred; many westerners were imprisoned at the notorious Stanley Prison; food was scarce. With the surrender of the Japanese in 1945, Hong Kong reverted to its former status under Britain, but change was swift. Following the war, the population swelled as Chinese refugees fled the fighting between Nationalists and Communists; in 1949 when the Communists took over China, fears that Hong Kong would simply be overrun were rampant. But the Chinese government, recognizing the economic importance of a stable Hong Kong as a gateway to the mainland, allowed the status quo to continue. The fifties and sixties were decades of foment: strikes protested the lack of labor standards and inhumane working conditions; riots reflected the social upheaval of Mao Zedong's Cultural Revolution in mainland China. But the local police stood with the colonial authorities to maintain order; improvements in working conditions were made, and Hong Kong resumed its economic climb. Until 1973, most of Hong Kong's population was contained on Kowloon and Hong Kong; only then, as Hong Kong's infrastructure was improved, was the first 'New Town' built with its vast public housing projects for the burgeoning population. Deng Xiaoping, who had taken control in China after the death of Mao Zedong, had allowed Hong Kong access to and from the mainland; thus, Hong Kong boomed. But in the air remained an ominous uncertainty of what would happen next as he forced Britain to the bargaining table to plan an end to British rule. How long would communist China allow Hong Kong to develop freely under its capitalistic system? Without the orderly British rule, what would happen? Would China attempt to absorb Hong Kong into the Peoples' Republic? Within the business community, a sense of living on borrowed time was pervasive, and the boom was fueled by a drive to make as much profit as possible, while it was still possible.

It was against that backdrop that Mary, Murray, Heather and Rosmarie arrived, and though their "littleness" was now fully acknowledged, the clarion voice of their identity as a "Community of Resistance" continued to ring forth: "The background for our life is . . . the 'world' of Hong Kong, a fascinating yet terrifying 'crown of capitalism,' where God's children are experiencing what happens when people come to see themselves as lords of the universe and when the idol of money demands human sacrifice as surely and as cruelly as did any ancient idolatry. The story of Babel takes on a new significance. We admire the hard work involved, but the underlying competition and strife and the emphasis on external 'success' and achievement makes us tremble..." In their view neither capitalism nor communism held the answer. Both shared "many features in common [resulting in] the suffering of the poor and oppressed in either system."[13]

As in Jerusalem, their lives, intentionally set apart from the frenzy of their adopted city, fell into a daily rhythm. With the original focus of their life there dissolved, they refocused on just being available; as Murray phrased it, "We put the brake on, so as not to be busy."[14]

Writing to Friends, they explained: "Inside this small house *and* inside our small selves, there is much life to live each day, the domestic work and the work of worship, prayer, silent meditation, together and individually. It seems to us clearer than ever before that this life within, the life received rather than the life organized or consciously planned, is of prime importance in a human situation where the making of money and the acquisition of possessions and status and success are so often accepted as the goal of life."[15] As part of their spiritual discipline, one of them was always at home to welcome unexpected visitors.

Living in St. Francis House, perhaps it was inevitable that two of those unexpected ones who came, not only to visit but to stay, were not human visitors. "Two amiable black dogs... have adopted us!" they announced. "They are owned by the neighbours of the big house just above us, whose band of Alsatian dogs expelled them from their company and consigned them to the lower level (that's us!). As a throw-back to our Gandhian days ... we call these two Hari (short for *Harijan*) and Ambie! They represent God's four-footed creatures in our community!"[16]

Other visitors were much anticipated. Happily, in that first challenging year, those included beloved family members, easing, particularly for Mary, the sense of dislocation in this new part of the world. She delightedly reported the holiday visit of Cheryl and André along with their three active children, aged ten, eight and four: "A very kind and generous family of friends offered us the loan of their house (with swimming pool and air-conditioning laid-on!) down the hillside ten minutes walk."[17] The family provided more boisterous companionship than their typical guests, and the swimming pool was a welcome diversion for children unaccustomed to the more sedate ways of their grandparents.

13. Letter #27.
14. Interview with author.
15. Letter #28.
16. Letter #27.
17. Rogers letter to Raimon Panikkar, 1981.

But most who found their way up the hill were those seeking conversation or a more extended quiet time and often arrived unannounced, since there was no telephone. Mary and Heather were most likely to be found at home. They, and perhaps Murray too, might be tending the house and garden. "Our life of any one day is distinctly earthbound—literally in the garden with the dogs, the plants, the birds, the rocks..." Earthbound also, in another sense, they added, "because we are no family of spiritual giants!"[18] The garden was where Heather lavished much of her love, and it responded with abundant blooms. She was their "resident artist, handy woman and maintenance person." Constantly summoned to the latest domestic emergency: "Oh, Heather, the white ants are at it again in the toolshed!"—, they affectionately noted that she divided her time between "prayer and repair."[19] At times Mary could be found working alongside Heather or, more often, happily focusing on her latest translation or letter-writing project.

Rosmarie was less likely to be at home. As in Jerusalem, she served as Jyotiniketan's personal link to local people. Energetic and game, she threw herself into the difficult study of Cantonese at Chung Chi College at Hong Kong University. Their first letter acknowledged her progress: "We rejoice that after much hard work the seven tones begin to flow [while] the others of us do our elderly best with a book and tapes!"[20] Gradually her fluency sufficed for work with local people; again she was drawn to the elderly and handicapped, the deaf, and the blind. A skilled and creative musician, she combined her athleticism and musical ability to bring movement to music to a group of over sixties in the nearby Caritas Centre. At home, her music and original melodies brought a new dimension to their worship. Through her, contacts were made; Chinese friends, often handicapped, would visit. She was, as Murray had acknowledged, a lynchpin in their new situation. Yet as the newest member of the community, inwardly she struggled to believe she was worthy of her vows; wherever she went, she carried the words of her formal commitment close to her heart on thin and increasingly worn sheets of paper.

As for Murray, he too joined in the domestic chores, claiming for himself "a Ph.D in washing up!"[21] Or he could be found writing letters or preparing for increasingly frequent speaking engagements. Longing for those local contacts, yet more constrained by language, his enthusiasm for friendship and real spiritual connection remained undimmed.

18. Letter #28.
19. Letter #32.
20. Letter #27.
21. Letter #29.

Very early on, a taste of the spiritual unity for which they longed did appear where they least expected it. The first Sunday they had arrived on Tao Fong Shan, they had looked for a place to worship. At the foot of their hill was St. Alfred's Roman Catholic Church, a big Chinese congregation, so they wandered in, Murray in his old brown Indian priest's cassock. They joined the Chinese worship, and received the sacrament. After the service they were warmly greeted by Don Carlo, an Italian missionary priest who said to Murray, "What were you doing sitting in the congregation?"

Murray recalled his explanation: "Well, Father, I'm not the same sort of Catholic priest you are. I'm an Anglican Catholic priest; you're a Roman Catholic priest."

Don Carlo's reply, again recalled by Murray, was as heart-warming as it was unexpected. Surely, he had said, in that part of the world, where there were so few Christians, such distinctions were of little consequence. "Next Sunday," he had exclaimed, "don't you dare come without your cassock... We'll provide robes, and you will concelebrate with us."

Murray continued, "I was astounded! I was thrilled! It happened for a year, and that was such a glorious gift."[22]

But, alas, the ecumenical love fest was short-lived. A scrupulous Roman sister had lodged a complaint about the unauthorized practice, and the local Roman Catholic bishop felt obliged to intervene. For the sake of Don Carlo, who took the rap, they took care to be discrete about the interdenominational bond. Their presence with one another continued, but the concelebration ceased. Only to Friends abroad did they mention St. Alfred's Parish, "where the Spirit has given us gifts of deep spiritual unity, even when on the institutional level the outward expression of such inward unity is not yet countenanced. The Spirit often goes ahead, it seems, of institutional hesitations,"[23] they added, with wry understatement.

Anticipating life in Hong Kong, they had imagined rich conversations and perhaps some inward unity too with new Chinese friends around the spiritual jewels they had already discovered in Chuang Tzu, the Chinese spiritual Taoist[24] master. Back in India, Thomas Merton's small volume *The Way of Chuang Tzu* had opened this spiritual path to them; now in China, they deepened their study, using Taoist readings along with the Gospel for their Eucharists and dedicating Wednesday afternoons to meditative study of Chuang Tzu with a group of friends. They were eager to absorb the local culture and spirituality. But as Mary wrote to Raimon, "It's rather sad how Chinese

---

22. Interview with Trapnell.
23. Letter #27.
24. Taoism: the School of Chinese philosophy that flourished 550–250 BCE.

nearly all connect Lao Tsu and Chuang Tsu with labouring through rather unintelligible material in antique language at school. Several have found it quite a revelation when Murray has read a bit of Chuang Tsu to them as mediated by Thomas Merton. In this respect we find Hong Kong far behind India; Murray has come across just one P.I.M.E.[25] Father who is keenly interested and delights in it all and one Chinese priest—otherwise no signs that anything much is happening, or none that we have discovered..."

The P.I.M.E. Father to whom Mary referred was Fr. Sergio Ticozzi, another Italian priest. Under his tutelage, "pondering" Taoist wisdom, they moved beyond their initial disappointment and encountered "a thrilling pilgrimage of discovery." Through Taoism they found a deepening awareness of "the Presence of God, of the Real, expanding in ever widening circles from His sacramental presence in our chapel," becoming "more transparently the Source and Centre of our life." To Friends, they wrote, "The unique spiritual treasures that God over the millennia has given to this Chinese part of His human family" through Chuang Tzu and Lao Tzu, "fascinating purveyors of this treasure [are] surely not unrelated to the One we Christians call the Blessed Trinity."[26]

Central to Taoist philosophy is *wu wei*, or life in accord with the Tao, sometimes described as "non-action" or "non-ado."[27] It made an impression on them. Did *wu wei* then reveal itself in their quieter life? Or were moments of *wu wei* easier to embrace as non-striving acceptance in light of their disappointments? Was their quieter life tied to the diminishing energy of their aging bodies? Or reinforced in revulsion to Hong Kong's striving culture? Perhaps it is not necessary or possible to choose. But their choice of a "taste of Chuang Tzu"[28] to share with Friends suggests they had been led to see aspects of their own spiritual striving in a clearer light. Taken from Merton's book, it is entitled "The Need to Win."

> When an archer is shooting for nothing
> He has all his skill.
> If he shoots for a brass buckle
> He is already nervous.
> If he shoots for a prize of gold
> He goes blind
> Or sees two targets—
> He is out of his mind!

25. Pontifical Institute for Foreign Missions.
26. Letter #27.
27. Merton, *The Way of Chuang Tzu*, 101.
28. Letter #27.

His skill has not changed. But the prize
Divides him. He cares.
He thinks more of winning
Than of shooting—
And the need to win
Drains him of power.²⁹

Father Sergio recalled their grappling with the implications of Taoism for their life together in those years. He wrote, "I often smiled at Murray's strong efforts to overcome his past education based upon a strict sense of duty and responsibility. When we were reflecting and sharing on the spontaneity and sense of freedom of Chuang Tsu . . . I could see him appreciating this attitude and struggling for it, but at times admitting almost failure. Then we laughed together."³⁰

They had concluded, along with Chuang Tzu and Merton that "our material riches . . . imply a spiritual, cultural, and moral poverty far greater than we see"³¹ and had adapted their lifestyle to reflect this insight. They were drawn to the quintessential spiritual master, described, again by Merton, as "one who knows the unknown not by intellectual penetration, or by a science that wrests for itself the secrets of heaven, but by 'littleness' and silence. . .the existential mystery of life itself."³² Following Abhishiktananda, they had lived a bit of that, had strived for it. But, as they had said, they were not "spiritual giants," and if "reaching" the Tao meant "a spiritual change of one's whole being," and a virtuousness that "does not strive"³³ then, much as they tried, they were far from that way of being. Each of them, in their own way, were strivers. And as such, Father Sergio observed, "they positively accepted the limits of their 'inculturation.'" Despite their love for the East and their disdain for western influences, they remained deeply western. In the moments they could recognize those limitations and move beyond the chagrin, ego fell away and laughter burst forth. Indeed, laughter was one of the hallmarks of their life together, at times a saving grace.

Still they were searching, always searching for God. Murray spoke of the quest: "We knew, really, in our bones, that God had done wonderful things in China before we ever turned up, before there was a single Christian, before anyone had heard of Jesus Christ . . . That there's never been a

29. Merton, *Mystics and Zen Masters*, 107.
30. Ticozzi letter to author, 2011.
31. Merton, *Mystics and Zen Masters*, 69–70.
32. Ibid., 73.
33. Ibid., 74.

moment when the reality behind Jesus wasn't drawing people to the Father. (That's in our Christian phraseology.) And we were very much hunting, not academically exactly, but we were always on the look out, trying to catch the smell of what God had been doing there."[34]

But the smell, while not absent, was elusive. The Chinese people they met primarily were educated western-style. Fluent in English and mostly Christian, their minds were trained in western ways. Other Chinese, the ones they longed to understand, who frequented the back alleys of Hong Kong and hued to traditional ways, did not speak English. Thus, more than anyone else, it was Father Sergio, who had come to know those people and could speak their language, who became their bridge into the spirit of China. From Father Sergio they discovered that there is no Cantonese word for God, but that traditional Chinese people were intent upon what they called "chance." Chance, they learned, was more than a random happening, perhaps not quite equivalent to God, yet imbued with a sense of mystery and meaning, evoking the western idea of synchronicity.[35] Thus, dependent on chance, traditional Chinese lacked the sense of control that western people may believe they have through prayer or a particular lifestyle. Nor did non-westernized Chinese experience the unfolding of time as westerners do. As Rosmarie discovered in her work with local people, because they were unable to see the future, they experienced that the future lay behind them while the past, which they could see, could be found in front of them. Even names were assigned differently than in the West. Local Chinese tended to eschew given names and relied instead on personal characteristics: thus, Father Sergio was not Sergio Ticozzi; he was "The Smiling Priest." In short, Murray acknowledged, it was "95 percent a totally different world of perception,"[36] very opaque, and not a world they could penetrate much at all.

But, undeterred, they embraced what they could, including a new descriptive Chinese name for themselves. It came about by chance—or by the grace of God—inspired by their acquaintance with a former Buddhist monk who had taken up solitary residence in a little abandoned house in the hills nearby. With Taoism and Chinese Buddhism so entwined, their friendship with him allowed further explorations of Chinese symbolism. When he arrived one day with a gift of bamboo, their awareness of the relevance of that quintessential Chinese plant to their life began to take shape. Thus, it was

---

34. Interview with Trapnell.

35. Synchronicity: a word coined by Carl Jung briefly defined as a meaningful coincidence.

36. Interview with Trapnell.

decided: while not relinquishing the name Jyotiniketan, as long as they lived in China, they would be called "One Bamboo Hermitage."

Atop a Letter to Friends appeared a seal with the name in Chinese calligraphy. Beginning with the caveat that no English translation could ever fully convey its meaning, they attempted an explanation. The "One," depicted by a single line across the top, was freighted with import: "the Centre and Source of our life, of all life," as well as "a call to unity . . . between all human beings, a working to transform differences and variety into gift and richness rather than tension, struggle and competition . . . as well as unity between people and creation . . ." The next word, "Bamboo," they wrote, "never depicted singly . . ., is a symbol of peace. It beckons us by its straightness and simplicity, its flexibility, emptiness and usefulness . . . Would that we humans beings could learn our lessons from the bamboo!" Finally, the seal contained a more complex character that could, they said, "require a whole meditation!" It showed a small house, "where people on a human/spiritual path live and work . . .; thunder and lightning of Reality are there;" some small fields are there too, denoting their outdoor work, and cups and saucers for shared food and drink. "And all in one character that we translate 'Hermitage!'" they exclaimed before adding, "You will know from a pondering on our name that we should not be unemployed!"[37]

Surely, despite *wu wei*, unemployment was not in their nature. Murray lived with the weighty urgency and responsibility to share his spiritual message in this secular, driven city. The painful gap left by the Tao Fong Shan Centre's seeming indifference was soon filled, not only by the Roman Catholics down the hill, but by invitations to preach, lead retreats, and attend conferences that flowed in a steady stream. Each message was tailored to his audience.

In 1981 he spoke at St. Stephen's College to a group of secondary school principals, sharing much of his distilled wisdom of his years in a deeply personal credo:

> If you reverence your self, your body, your spirit, giving yourself time and space for the image of God to become clear in you—and that involves real care and attention—then you will reverence

37. Letter #29.

the bodies, the spirits of your pupils and they will catch from you—much as we catch measles from one another!—the secret of cultivating their own being-in-God's image. That reverence or deep respect for the other person, so much more necessary for real life than passing examinations and filling one's mind with a mass of information, is a crying need in a world where people are being turned into numbers, digits on a computer, mere human-animals trained to fit into slots that will serve the economic ends of society, whether capitalist or communist.

A Christian teacher's life of worship and prayer will again and again show itself, in how she or he relates both to herself or himself and also to all around. Most generally this will happen with no verbal reference to God or to Christ or to the Christian Gospel, for it will be so bound up in ordinary meeting with people and with day to day events that it would be unreal, an introduction of something from the outside—that who is *never* outside—to talk about Jesus Christ. By means of this intangible, spontaneous 'thing', the look in the eye, the gentleness of speech, the respect for the other, your students will recognise that you live from 'beyond' yourself, from beyond the label level which is far too often the level on which society lives . . .

Murray's belief statement continued:

For long enough the West—in these (almost) passed centuries of colonialism—has taken it for granted that the western way is superior, the way to be copied, and that the culture of the East is of little value except as a museum piece, destined to fade away in the face of the power and prestige and vitality of the West. As a Christian man of the West who has spent the greater part of my life in the East I question these assumptions most vigorously, and, having received wonderful gifts of God through the cultures and spiritual paths of the East, I believe very deeply that God indeed created us, from east and west, to receive from one another, to be enriched by one another, to live more deeply through one another. Pluralism, cultural and religious, is a gift of God, for He so clearly loves variety, and I believe we Christians have as a gift from Him the exciting possibility of sharing in this enriching variety.

And finally, with a personal challenge that was becoming a hallmark of his preaching, he asked: "How far are you, friends, in your schools and colleges enabling your students to drink deeply from their own Chinese inheritance, as well as having their hands wide open to receive the best and deepest that God has given to other parts of the one human family?"[38]

In 1982, speaking to a very different audience, this time a gathering of clergy, he drew his message from Jesus's stunning words to his bickering disciples: "Whoever wants to be first must be last of all and servant of all."[39] Murray did not mince words:

> Looking at myself and at my fellow priests and ministers, and looking at us Christian people as a whole, I'm struck that the vast majority of our fellow human beings take so little notice of us and of our Christian Faith. They wouldn't be seen dead inside a church at worship time; the whole thing bores them stiff. Why? Why? I ask myself; more and more this is a question I cannot dodge and forget.
>
> It seems to me, from the Gospels, that people could very reasonably hate Jesus; He was abominably upsetting! Others could love Him, follow Him and be what their friends might think madly in support, but what you never, never meet in the Gospels is people who were bored with Him. That's the one thing nobody was when Jesus was in the vicinity, bored, uninterested . . . Passionately in favour or passionately against, but never bored, and that is what a majority of people are today, in the so-called Christian west . . . That makes me feel we've got Him wrong, that we Christians have—unconsciously, no doubt—twisted Him, misheard what He asks of us, for otherwise people meeting us would catch a bit the Presence of Jesus and just wouldn't react with this awful boredom . . .
>
> Instead of listening to His more outrageous sayings and demands, instead of hearing Him, *really* hearing him, we've watered Him down so that instead of feeling embarrassed or frankly speechless, we can still pretend that we are Christians, while in practice we turn a blind eye to what we don't want to see and hear. To twist the Way of Jesus Christ simply to suit ourselves is humbug—however much we may dress it up as being learned and reasonable—and we need, I think, to say a prayer for each other so that we'll resist going that dishonest way. We remain free to agree and to go the way Jesus calls us to go, and we are equally free to say, "No thanks; I think that's a crazy way; I'm going a more reasonable way." What we cannot say and do, at least with any integrity, is to say "yes" and then tame Him

---

38. Rogers, *'No More Humbug!' Says the Fool: Sermons, Talks and Articles by Charles Murray Rogers*, 108–109.

39. Matthew 20:26–27.

and His words so as to leave us comfortably unchanged in our present attitudes and habits . . .

Then came the challenge from Murray:

> Doesn't this saying of Jesus make us ask how far you and I go out of our way to protect other peoples' interests rather than our own? After all, a servant's business is to do just that. What is our attitude to getting alongside the person who is unable to protect himself or herself? What is our attitude to oppressed people in society? Are we simply thankful we're not among them, or do we struggle to find a way of supporting and serving them? . . . So there's the Lord's question for us this week: "If anyone wants to be first, he must make himself last of all and servant of all"—do you agree with Him? What then are you, what am I, going to *do* about this estimate of Jesus on qualifications or the lack of them? Don't let yourself off the hook too quickly! In His opinion it was a crucial issue in the Kingdom.[40]

Murray, striving never to let himself off the hook, had recently spent some nights with a particular local subculture, Hong Kong's own illegal immigrants from mainland China. It was an eye-opening experience. Living on ramshackle junks in a typhoon shelter in the harbor in the shadow of towering skyscrapers, they risked arrest if they came ashore. This, for Murray, was the essence of the idolatry of Babel. In their Newsletter they had recently written: "Does not the Gospel call us to a life vastly different from an 'improved Babel?'. . . Here and there, generally among the poor and underprivileged, we find glimpses of another way . . . We want to believe it more and more deeply. Please pray that we may have the courage to live it also."[41]

Indeed it was about living it all. In 1984 in an article in the *Diocesan Echo,* an Anglican Church publication, addressing the topic "Spirituality and Action," Murray mustered his most straightforward language:

> You cannot have one without the other. 'Sunday spirituality' is pseudo. If being human involves what we eat, how we earn our money and how we spend it, how we are related to other people and how we are related to our own selves, how we treat things, nature and matter, then surely all life, every bit of it, is of interest to Christ, our Master. He had a marvelous way of doing away with so-called "opposites": spiritual/material, heaven/earth, natural/supernatural, religious/secular, chosen/not chosen,

---

40. Rogers, *'No More Humbug!' Says the Fool: Sermons, Talks and Articles by Charles Murray Rogers,* 112–113.

41. Letter #27.

inner/outer, divine/human, transcendent/immanent. Therefore, any thinking or theology that presupposes these distinctions, is, it seems to me, bound to be phoney, un-real, that is, against the way things are. We'll probably need a whole lifetime to wake up fully to this Totality, Completeness . . . and joyfully dive into It/Her/Him . . .[42]

Nor did he back away preaching to the congregation of St. John's Anglican Cathedral, even knowing that in its pews was a good representation of the power elite of Hong Kong. Echoing the words of the Anglican liturgy and Gospel reading, he threw down a verbal gauntlet: "'Praise to Christ our Lord.' Were you really thinking when you said that? Do you know what you were praising Him for? 'Love your enemies'—'Do good to those who hate you'—'Be kind to the wicked'—'Don't judge; don't condemn'—'Give to everyone who asks you' . . . The impossible sayings of Jesus—many more! What are you and I doing with them?" He continued, ironically citing options that would make the Gospel more palatable:

> 1. Pretend—not for us! For the spiritual giants, for St. Francis and his like. And then hurry on to other more harmless parts of the Gospel, especially the parts that comfort us.
>
> 2. Tame Him! Theological books trying to make the Lord rational, reasonable. Trying to prove that Jesus didn't mean what he said about violence, hatred, riches, not judging, pride.
>
> 3. Put such sayings, put Him, into quarantine! Shut these impossible requests up in church! Read them piously, say 'Alleluia' or 'Praise to Christ our Lord' and then go out and do the opposite in society, in the family, in business, in politics, in international affairs. Needs a bit of juggling with one's conscience but there are church officials who will help you with that . . .

His indictment of the church continued:

> For the first 250 years of the church's life Christians *knew* that demand of Jesus applied to them—they knew the Lord asked them to believe and to act out the fact that love, compassion, non-violence is stronger than violence (no Christian during those years would belong to the army). Then the Church got power, prestige, property, possessions—it became an elite—and discovered that to keep these—security, we call it—needed violence and arms. All our official churches still believe that.

42. Rogers, *'No More Humbug!' Says the Fool: Sermons, Talks and Articles by Charles Murray Rogers*, 124–125.

This was August 5, 1984, the Feast of the Transfiguration. Asking his listeners to "ponder the fact that on that very same feast day in 1945, so-called 'Christian nations' dropped the first atomic bomb on Hiroshima,"[43] he offered deeper insights, and again the challenge:

> And still the Lord says, "Love your enemies," "Pray for those who hate you." Wouldn't it be more honest frankly to say, "That's nonsense"? If we aren't prepared to say "nonsense," to Jesus, then for God's sake, let us consider with some seriousness what we are going to do about it . . . Mind you, any man or woman who takes these sayings of Jesus seriously will find themselves out of step with the majority in the Church and in society . . .
>
> *"By God's grace I will never allow anybody to be my enemy."* It was Gandhi, a Hindu, who in various ways dared to follow Christ rather more seriously than many, many of us Christians, who said that. *"By God's grace I will never allow anybody to be my enemy."*
>
> . . . We can only live out these sayings of Jesus when in a mystical way beyond our control we discover that we carry in us, in our little ordinary persons, our own unfathomable secret: the Life of Christ. Only when you and I begin to experience, in the depth of ourselves, in our bones, in our thinking and acting, that Christ is not outside little me and little you but is quite literally the source of our life, every minute, every day, that we'll find it happening—God will be doing the impossible—love will be in fact, in action . . . stronger than hate—soul force, love, will be stronger than all violence. Friends, dare we let Him do that in us, through us?[44]

Murray's voice was heard regularly too over the airwaves of Hong Kong Radio. Just before Christmas 1984, in a program called "Morning Magazine," he shared his reaction to his interviewer's request that he talk about "Love."[45] Though not unprepared for the question, the spontaneity of his response is telling:

"I began by feeling as if you'd taken me to Repulse Bay and told me to swim the Pacific!" he said. "A bit too much."

---

43. For another more complete sermon preached three years later at St. John's Cathedral on the Transfiguration, see Appendix 5.

44. Rogers, *'No More Humbug!' Says the Fool: Sermons, Talks and Articles by Charles Murray Rogers*, 127–129.

45. Murray Rogers, interview by Maggie Britton "Morning Magazine," Radio Television Hong Kong, December 21, 1984.

"But," undeterred, he continued, "somehow love IS an ocean, and though you can't swallow an ocean, you can swim in it, you can taste it a bit, but there's always more. You can never, never come to the end of this thing. It's unlimited, without boundaries, all-embracing."

This was, after all, a subject close to his heart in every respect. He had been reading Ernesto Cardenal, the Latin American poet and liberation theologian. Reflecting on Cardenal's assertion that "All things love one another,"[46] Murray shared his skepticism: "I thought to myself, 'The man must be crazy.' Because look at the world. Just *look* at it! *Love?!* Oh, bits and pieces we run into every now and then and that's lovely, but there's an appalling amount of what looks uncommonly not like love . . . [But] I came to the point of seeing that conflict is not . . . an absence of love, but a love that's not being recognized, but a love that's gone crooked . . . Hate is misdirected love." His reflections then grew more personal: "I thought about little me of course, and I could see the truth of what he's talking about."

"What is it in us," his interviewer, Maggie Britton asked, "that turns us so vicious when things go wrong?"

Murray's unrehearsed reply, intended to speak for all humans, flowed with passionate intensity:

> I think a vast hunger for love. A vast hunger to be embraced. Hugging and kissing and caressing is not reserved for human beings. It runs right through the whole of creation. We are made to be linked, and if I can't be linked with people in a way that's lovely, good, beautiful, then I'm going to be linked to them in some way. I can't help it. I was created with this terrific craving to be related to other people. And if I'm alienated, as perhaps all of us are in some way . . . from people at home, from one's children, from neighbors, then this fire of love isn't going to go out inside us. Love isn't something outside that affects us from outside. Love, I reckon, is . . . this great burning energy inside you and me.

He then put love in the context of Christmas: "See," he continued, "we celebrate at this time each year a bit of human history that says love isn't a dream. It's a basic law of creatures, of human beings, of everything, created free to give ourselves to others. It's an invitation to open our eyes and look at the world around us, and see—it's all festival . . . A festival meal right in front of us."

---

46. Cardenal, *Abide in Love*, 3.

And how do we partake of the feast? For Murray, that unspoken question led him on to the essence of life's journey. Validating his interviewer's comment about the struggle to love, he said:

> Of course you're dead right, Maggie. The experience of every one of us shows that love is often full of contradictions, full of conflict, full of bitterness. Which one of us doesn't know that? Love and hate, love and greed, love and fear, love and lust, love and envy. And a whole lifetime isn't long enough to get rid of the mixture. To discover that the essence of everything is simply love. To discover the ways by which we can leave behind the mixture. That we find we can cope with that hate and greed and fear and envy and lust that we all have. It's in all of us. And [to know], like Julian of Norwich . . . that God wants to be experienced as our lover. I think she put her finger on something. *Yeah.*

As that deeply exhaled "yeah" ended the interview, it seemed that the nearly six decades that had passed since he first fell in love with God at that boys' camp were flashing before him. Years of seeking love and intimacy. Years of relationship with God, with human beings, with creation. Years too of struggle. A longing always for that oceanic feeling of union, of *advaita*, of, as Swamiji put it, Christ's 'I AM' experience.

With life and the world a festival feast, despite advancing years, Murray's appetite—his vast hunger for love—both human and divine—remained undiminished. And though they spoke of their dwelling as "a hermitage" where simplicity was the byword, never did any of them feel the need or desire to remain sequestered there.

They noted the irony in another Letter to Friends: "Strange that this very local, ordinary life that God gives is so palpably linked with *everywhere*.[47] After more than twenty-five years in community, both their Visitor's Book and their stream of intercessory prayers bore witness to their human connections. And day by day, those ties were lived out with unique particularity. With each new or strengthened relationship, with each extraordinary—or ordinary—individual, came deepened conviction of the "everywhereness" of God.

As the world continued to call to them, they responded with travel across the continents, sometimes as individuals, sometimes as a community. But their first priority as a community had been to go "home" to India. Two years after their arrival in Hong Kong and with more than a year of planning, they had embarked on a soulful *yatra*[48] to many of their old

---

47. Letter #30.
48. *Yatra*: (Sanskrit) In Hinduism, a pilgrimage to a sacred site.

haunts in India. The logistics were a *tour-de-force* of balancing competing needs—community and personal family, reflecting, perhaps, a growing awareness on Murray's part that over the years his needs had too often taken priority over the others'. Mary and Murray would embark together and share three weeks alone as wife and husband with friends like Laurie and Kuni Baker in south India, while Heather would be sharing a holiday in Kashmir with her sister and brother-in-law. Rosmarie, who had been in Switzerland with her aging mother, would join them along with Heather in Delhi. The four then would be together for the next five weeks.

It was a many-faceted journey—a return for three of them, and, for Rosmarie, an introduction to the land and the people that had so deeply shaped her sisters and brother in Christ. It would, they all hoped, fill some of the gaps of community history Rosmarie had not shared, thus deepening her sense of belonging. Writing to their friend Raimon Panikkar on the eve of their departure, Murray brimmed with the joyful anticipation of a child awaiting Santa on Christmas Eve: "In a few hours we are due to leave our home here to return to India, that blessed and crazy country that remains very near indeed to our hearts. I can hardly imagine it yet—that by this time tomorrow, all being well, we will be feeling and seeing and smelling India and with all that something deeper still will be bubbling up. How eagerly we are looking forward to it!" Anticipating familiar stops along the pilgrim path: Badrinath and the "eternal snows," the Source itself, where the Ganges sprang from rocks high in the Himalayas; Haridwar and Rishikesh, all places they had walked with Abhishiktananda, Murray continued, "As you can imagine, 'our' dear Swamiji will be close, and so will you, and we pray that as much may happen *inside* us as outside us—a call to the further shore." Then on they would go to Almora, where, in the halcyon days of interfaith dialogue with the Cuttat group, Murray had basked in the warmth of spiritual discovery of the Hindu scriptures with like-minded Christians.

It was as they had hoped. Everywhere old friends awaited them. There was Bettina Bäumer in Phulchatti and Varanasi. Then, descending to the Ganges Plain and Kareli, they were "nearly overwhelmed by [the] welcome and love," of village friends and the brothers and sisters of the Indian Jyotiniketan Ashram, still led by their devoted successor, Swami Deenabandu. Best of all, just as they had prayed, and as Murray exclaimed, it had become *Indian*, "utterly Indian!" The joy of that reunion was tempered with the news that Deenabandu had been told by his Franciscan superiors he was too old for life in the ashram. But despite the uncertain future, not just for the original Jyotiniketan, but for all of them, India was what it always had been for Mary, Murray, and Heather—a place where, in their words, they could feel "almost palpably the finger of God beckoning us on to the Kingdom's outer horizon,"[49] the "further shore." It was their spiritual home on earth.

Yet they could not dwell in the past; the finger of God beckoned them beyond India. From Hong Kong, their proximity to Japan allowed other spiritual families to inspire their experience—Murray's in particular. Speaking later of Japan, he observed, "So much happened to me there: a tremendous strength in God's wisening the old heart, [allowing me] to see where Christ is, [while] in those far-off days [of early ministry], I wouldn't have believed he [could be]."[50] In the familiar pattern, God's finger gestured to them in human relationships and then pointed back, as it always did, to the Source, which was Jesus Christ.

Their very deep friendships with Minoru Kasai and Fr. Shigeto Oshida, both forged first in India, infused their lives not only with the deep humanity of these two men, but with their Japanese spirituality as well. Their ties to Minoru dated from the sixties when, as a university student in Varanasi, he had been a regular visitor to Jyotiniketan. Nearly always present for Christmas, Minoru gradually and unassumingly became an informal part of the family. Not a traditional Christian, he was aligned with Japan's Christian Nonchurch movement,[51] espousing its ideals of social justice and pacifism. He was, Murray recalled, "deeply into silent meditation [as] his spiritual way, . . . more intellectual, by far, than me . . . Beautifully integrated." With a doctorate from Hindu University in culture and religion, Minoru had returned to Japan where he served on the faculty of the International Christian University in Tokyo. Speaking of Minoru, Murray said, "He was a close companion on the way with us for years and years, and still is . . . It was chiefly he who . . . called the old heart of me to be in Japan for a very good many weeks altogether."[52]

Fr. Shigeto Oshida, the Zen Buddhist/Dominican priest, claimed a central role in their lives as well. It was he who had shared their friendship and dialogue[53] with Swamiji, trekked the pilgrim path in India with them, and, following Swamiji's death, had been present in Jerusalem to share their grief. And it was the extraordinary confluence of events that brought

---

49. Letter #28.

50. Interview with Trapnell.

51. Japanese Nonchurch movement: Founded in 1901 by Uchimuro Kanzo, its members met in small groups for study and reflection but eschewed creeds, liturgies and ordained clergy. Dedicating themselves to Bible study and a moral Christian life, they remain known for their learnedness and their pacifist beliefs.

52. Interview with Trapnell.

53. Fr. Oshida himself disliked the term "dialogue," finding it placed too much emphasis on words. He preferred to call those times "meetings at the depth."

Murray, Minoru, and "Oshida-san" together in Hong Kong that had tipped the discernment balance and convinced Murray they were meant to leave Jerusalem and come to China. Fr. Oshida's birth into Zen Buddhism and conversion to Christianity as a young man meant that, like Swamiji, and like Raimon Panikkar, he understood "double-belonging," a full embrace of the "both/and." Reading Fr. Oshida's words about that experience, one can imagine his spiritual resonance with Murray and the rest of the community: "I have never tried to integrate Zen in my Christianity," he said. "Zen is a constituent part of my soul and my body since my birth. If there has been integration in me, it is Christ himself who did it, without warning me."[54] Thus it was that his own Christian-Zen experience had led him to establish a spiritual community at Takamori, where the Christian life was lived out in accordance with Zen principles. And thus it was through those two friendships in Christ, with Minoru and "Oshida-san," that Murray was drawn, again and again, to Japan.

Since that first unforgettable visit to the Zen Monastery in Japan back in 1969 (*"First you must die!"*) had awakened Murray to the spiritual challenge of Zen, he had welcomed any opportunity to return. When, just a year after their arrival in Hong Kong, an invitation arrived from Fr. Oshida to participate in a weeklong interfaith meeting at Takamori, Murray eagerly accepted. The meeting was called in response to the "extreme predicament of mankind" in the face of nuclear proliferation. By design the gathering included no learned papers, no committees, no action plans. Instead, much of its time was devoted to shared silence, reflecting Jyotiniketan's conviction that deep connection to the mystery of life through contemplative silence could transform the politics of mutual fear and destruction to peaceful understanding. It brought together a small group of Christians, Buddhists and Hindus, and even the grandson of the Sioux Chieftan, Black Elk.[55] There too was the wonderful old Korean Quaker, Ham Sok-Hon, known by then as the Gandhi of Korea. Together, listening in silence for "the Voice" without the "unlimited talk" of most ecumenical conferences, it proved, they wrote, "vastly more fruitful."[56]

Emerging from the bond of shared silence were words that reverberated down through the years for Murray, words that strengthened his resolve. They came from Ham Sok-Hon, shared towards the end of their days together. Already those gathered had learned of his remarkable history—his

54. Almadas, "The Breath of God."

55. Black Elk, the grandfather, was an Ogala Sioux leader and shaman who became known through the account of his life, *Black Elk Speaks*, written in 1932 by John Neihardt. It remains a spiritual classic.

56. Letter #27.

birth to a privileged family in North Korea and his lifelong struggle against oppression, primarily the colonial occupation of the Japanese. They knew he had been imprisoned multiple times for his outspoken writing and teaching and beaten, imprisoned again and nearly executed by Soviet authorities whose rule followed that of the Japanese. They knew that his family—a wife and seven children—had suffered profoundly too through the years of his imprisonments, and that he was the first Korean to be nominated for a Nobel Peace prize. Sharing his gentle, unassuming presence, Murray and three or four of his fellow Christians one day had turned to him in wonder, seeking his wisdom. Murray recalled: "As we met that afternoon in one of the huts, we said to old Ham Sok-Hon, 'Would you help us please? We know a bit about your life—you have shared it with different ones of us—and that you've been so brave. Now could you tell us—because . . . if we are really going to stand for Christ in these coming years, we'll be asked for tremendous courage to speak what we believe is true, like you have. *How* do you do it? *Where* does it come from? *How* have you been able to have machine guns pointing at you, and not lose your balance, Christianly, peacefully?'"[57]

The essence of Ham Sok-Hon's reply remained etched in Murray's memory. His recollection follows:

> He said, "I have an [uncomfortable] feeling you think I'm special. I'm not special at all, you know. I'm as frightened as anybody. But when these things happen to me, I simply pause, perhaps for a split second, and I say to God, 'God, I can't do it, you must. I don't know what to say, and I don't know what to do. All I know is that you're inside me.'
>
> "You know, it's extraordinary. Sometimes I've been hearing myself say things, and I've said [to myself], 'Who is saying that!?'
>
> "So, don't feel that you have to be special. To have courage, you just have to know that God takes you over, and then go ahead. Don't think of anything that's going to happen. You don't have to think about the future or the past; you're just there, God's there. God's in you."[58]

"Such a beautiful man he was!" Murray exclaimed as he finished the story. Here indeed was further validation of the "everywhereness" of God and indeed of Murray's own vision and experience. Steeped in the teachings of Lao-Tzu, Chuang Tzu, and other eastern philosophies, Ham Sok-Hon, a devout Quaker, had held fast to his Christian beliefs while affirming that

---

57. Interview with Trapnell.
58. Interview with Trapnell.

all religions shared common ground and deserved respect. Little wonder that Murray made sure this marvelous new connection would continue; the delight of the little community in Hong Kong when Ham Sok-Hon later came to stay with them there was unbounded.

In 1985 their friendships with Minoru and Oshida-san led to a five-week stay in Japan for all four of them—Mary and Murray, Heather and Rosmarie. With the teahouse at Minoru's university as a home base, they explored the country with home visits arranged for them, tasting both the joy and agony of this ancient land. There was contemplative time and rest and sociability, of course, at Fr. Oshida's community at Takamori. Beyond Takamori a heart-searing highlight was their visit with the artists Iri and Toshi Maruki, creators of a monumental series of panels depicting the horror of Hiroshima, reinforcing their commitment to speak out against threat of nuclear war. "Can we human beings dare do this again?" they implored. Five days in a remote island hermitage drew a response of hope: "There is another way than that of power and violence..."[59] Then, for sheer delight, little could top their Mount Fuji experience. On their way up the narrow mountain road, Shigeto Oshida suddenly stopped the car and pulled cushions from the trunk. Out they all came, bundled up, gathered in a little circle and meditated together in the snow. "So much laughter!"[60] Murray recalled. Writing effusively of their experience in their Letter to Friends, they exclaimed, "The openhearted friendliness with which we were welcomed into Japanese homes amazed and humbled us, not least when we found ourselves, to our surprise, the guests of a parish of the Tenrikyo Church, one of the larger of the "new religions" of Japan. Here was interfaith dialogue—the real thing—life together, worship together, meals in common, and much sharing. It was as if we said to one another: 'Welcome to my home! Come and see where I belong.' What a bonus!"[61]

Following that sojourn, Murray wrote an article entitled "The Far Away Look: Reflections on the Tao of Interfaith Dialogue." It described a spiritual exercise, as taught by Shigeto Oshida and its transformational potential:

> Oshida-san took us out into the garden to look across the sea to an island. "Look at that island," he said. We did; we focused our attention on the island. "Now look a little above the island until your sight takes in the whole area; see the island as a part of the totality. Practice that look. Make it a part of your personal

---

59. Letter #30.
60. Interview with Trapnell.
61. Letter #30.

experience of silence, and see how it will change your whole perspective."

... I have done just this and I have discovered that this "look" takes in the small in its intimacy and the large in its totality, that this way of looking at people and situations and subjects of study and experience of God gradually softens borders and separations and differences. Dualities begin to shade off, a new consciousness begins to emerge, a stretching out towards a Oneness in everything. Over the last centuries we have been trained to look at one thing after another, to distinguish one person from another, to assess one doctrine or ideology over against another, and all of them in separation from life. With this, too often, has gone an almost compulsive need to compare and judge and then to swallow up "the other." Duality has become second nature to us of the West and, thanks to our tragic proficiency in this type of analysis, is now almost universally so. It takes a lot of practice to see things whole, to see people and historical happenings and religions and denominations in relationship as a part of one another—which in truth they are. Take anything you like; unless you see it in terms of countless linkages with everything else, your astigmatism will distort what you see. The "thusness" of anything, or anybody, consists in innumerable connections; wholeness and unity is written into all things. Oshida-san's phrase "the far away look" has more in it than at first met my eye.[62]

In this exercise Murray had received the invitation of the East to practice what is sometimes called "big mind" or a sort of panoramic perspective. Taoism too, he said, called them beyond dependence on the rational mind. He offered a "sample for the tasting":

> The man of Tao (the Way, the Spirit)
>
> Remains unknown
>
> Perfect virtue
>
> Produces nothing
>
> "No-Self."
>
> And the greatest man
>
> Is Nobody [63]

---

62. Rogers, "The Far Away Look: Reflections on the Tao of Interfaith Dialogue," 430.

63. Ibid., 434. Rendering by Thomas Merton.

These experiences remained, of course, not invitations to become Buddhist or Taoist, but to a deeper conversion to Christ, "'the Beginning and the End', Alpha and Omega."[64] At times, Murray wrote, they were tempted to "fall back into dualism, to say: 'No, this cannot be; this contradicts the Christian experience of Reality.'" But, even with "great demands on patience," they persevered. "We are determined to listen and listen, to probe within ourselves to hear whether, deep within our own awareness of God and God's love, there are not echoes of this great stream of Chinese consciousness." Could they move into closer alignment with the mind of Christ, with "faith and courage [to] *bear a* Christ who is cosmic, who encompasses every particularity"? Their longings to become "cosmic" along with a Cosmic Lord, "daring to fall into the ocean joyfully, knowing that they are the Ocean!" . . . and "for the doors of the church [to be] thrown so widely open that the Cosmic Lord may in fact be God, Alpha and Omega, in and for every creature"[65]—such were their visions.

Glimpses of the unity behind the dualism of everyday life were but glimpses; the spiritual treasures revealed in the East could provide no final resolution to their ongoing challenge—to balance the need for constancy in community with individual calls and yearnings. Yet their spiritual experience gave them the ongoing strength to live with the contradictions. In the reality of day-to-day life, there were few "either/ors" but many "both/ands."

Thus was the call of the East maintained in tension with the call of the West. While for Mary and Rosmarie visits to the West were primarily times to renew their family bonds and tend to family needs, for Heather and for Murray, those visits were multi-faceted. Heather, while devoted to her biological family, found herself needing deeper silence and sought ways to connect with western spiritual communities, where a sense of spiritual family surrounded her. As for Murray, the most gregarious of them all, he found family everywhere, and the West was no exception. With any he met on his path, he would share, sometimes in words, and sometimes only in his way of being, those glimpses of the East that he fervently hoped would open eyes and hearts to the spiritual unity beneath dualistic assumptions.

Of all Murray's and ultimately their destinations in this decade, family visits apart, the American parish of Christ Church in Greenwich, Connecticut was the most frequent. But visits to Greenwich usually meant family visits would be part of the journey across the world as well. Following his first visit from Jerusalem in 1980, the invitations, now issued by a new rector, the Rev. Jack Bishop, continued to arrive, and Murray was eager to return.

64. Ibid., 436.
65. Ibid.

Those biennial sojourns were, surprisingly to some, to a place where, in their words, Murray had become "extraordinarily much 'at home,'"[66] and where he found warm receptivity for the "great burning energy" within that he experienced as love. As his sense of spiritual family there grew, he knew he must include Mary and Heather. From 1984, they often joined him. For friends from previous visits, their presence—slender, elderly ladies dressed demurely in their Indian saris—added to the curiosity of Murray's communal life style, but also bore witness to its embodied reality. Staying in the background, they too found receptivity and friendship.

During each two or three week visit, he again filled the role of "theologian-in-residence," preaching, teaching, and socializing, all with his infectious enthusiasm and warmth. Its demanding schedule began at Murray's request at 6:30 a.m. with an open invitation to their usual silent meditation. There were Lenten retreats for church staff, parishioners, and friends; small discussion groups and, as the season's climax arrived in Holy Week, an intense discipline of Eucharists and teachings mornings and evenings in the Christ Church Chapel. In Greenwich, response was warm; each day it seemed that the word of his presence had spread; the congregations grew until by Good Friday's ecumenical three hour service, the church's parking lots were filled to overflowing. And though many faithful churchgoers were accustomed to dropping in for a half hour or so on that day, friends found themselves sharing a different experience: "I didn't plan to stay for three hours, but I simply couldn't leave!"

Welcomed into family homes, now with Mary and Heather as well, just as in Japan, relationships deepened, spanning the generations. One perennial host, Eleanor Parker, a deeply revered dowager of the parish known for her generosity, intelligence, and the twinkle in her eye, was a favorite. "Dear old Ellie!" Murray would exclaim with pleasure. There, at her comfortable home, there would be afternoon tea served up with homemade lemon squares and rollicking, laughter-filled conversation to break the intensity of the day. There too would be understanding of the need for afternoon rest time. But he could be equally comfortable at the simpler home of Barbara and Chuck Goldschmid, whose youngest son William Duncan at fourteen found a sounding board for his nascent spirituality. Now a spiritual teacher himself, William recalled those times: "He would come down to my room and we would discuss scripture. The first thing he taught me was the *Bhagavad Gita*. I really loved those times with him."[67]

---

66. Letter #29.
67. Email reflection to author.

Trips to Greenwich allowed for visits with other American friends. Bo and Sita Lozoff,[68] located in Durham, N.C. where they ran their Prison-Ashram Project, were always included. The unlikely spiritual connection had begun when, in far-off Hong Kong, Murray was given a copy of Bo's book, *We're All Doing Time*. The book, inspired and funded by Bo and Sita's spiritual mentor Ram Dass and distributed free of charge to imprisoned convicts, offered encouragement and tools to use their incarceration as a time of spiritual discipline and practice, as if they were living in an ashram. Meditation and yoga practices were described and illustrated. In response, letters from prisoners had poured into their little North Carolina office, and, in turn, each was answered with a combination of compassion and tough love.

From Murray's first visit to Bo and Sita, there was a spiritual ignition. For the next visit, Mary came as well, and, as Sita recalled, "we became life-long friends." Murray agreed to take a place on their Board of Directors, later assuming the role of "Visitor," serving as the sort of spiritual mentor Raimon was for them. Their eyes had now been opened to the world of prisons.

On the lighter side, the West provided the respite and refreshment of family. For Mary, it might be what she called "a grandmotherly month" with Linda and Richard and their families. Or in 1985 for Heather it was the wedding of her niece Jane, celebrated by Murray, that brought her family and the Jyotiniketan family together for a joyous reunion. With or without special events, summer holiday visits were part of their life's routine; Mary in particular, could sustain the life of "family-at-a-distance" only with regular letters and the promise of visits to come. Accustomed as she was to setting her own needs aside, the perennial ache to be with her children and grandchildren never seemed to abate. Bearing allegiance to two family groups on opposite sides of the world was her own painful "double-belonging." But she could manage.

There was more reason for concern about Rosmarie. When her spiritual brother and sisters traveled beyond Europe, Rosmarie devoted her time to her mother in Switzerland. On her return to Hong Kong her mood sometimes seemed low. Though still convinced that "Jyotiniketan was her way," and deeply devoted to Murray as her spiritual teacher, she seemed haunted with doubt that she was worthy of her call and guilt that she was absent from her ailing mother. Vroni Thurneysen recalls Rosmarie's mother as "a woman of simple faith" who liked Mary, Murray, and Heather but simply could not

---

68. Bo Lozoff died in 2012. Sita Lozoff continues their work through the Human Kindness Foundation. http://www.humankindness.org/

understand the nature of the vows her daughter had taken to the community. She begged her to come home to Switzerland. But for Rosmarie, her promises were as binding as marriage vows; when her mother told her that an angel had appeared to her in a dream, promising Rosmarie would return to care for her, Rosmarie felt herself at a spiritual impasse.

With annual visits to Switzerland, she soldiered on. To Mary, Murray, and Heather, she was a treasure, deeply missed when she was gone.[69] Her musical gifts had embued their worship with a new dimension: to a community of undistinguished voices, she brought her own lovely voice, her lyrical flute-playing, and repertoire of songs. From friends in the Chinese community she passed along the gift of *Tai Gik*, a version of *Tai Chi* they practiced daily and shared with others simply as "Chinese exercises." Aware of her role as a "lynchpin" in the community, knowing that her connections with the local people were a door for the rest of them to enter as well, she worked creatively and tirelessly—or perhaps not as tirelessly as it seemed. In addition to her work with the elderly and handicapped young people, she had offered her services to the Missionary Sisters of Charity, organizing activities for big groups of pre-school children of Vietnamese refugees, who, with the end of the Vietnam War, had poured into Hong Kong. Her work with the Prisoners' Friends Association had earned her a visitor's pass, which she used to offer support and forge connections. Mary and Heather joined her effort, writing weekly letters to prisoners. Her work in the world, her love for her community seemed exemplary. Even her friend Vroni, who corresponded regularly with her and experienced their harmonious relationships herself in extended visits, could not fully plumb the depths of a malaise that Rosmarie most often kept at bay. Did Rosmarie believe her inner doubts made her unworthy? Her vows, after all, had included these words: "I can know whether or not I am a companion of the Risen Jesus by whether I dare to live to the uttermost, in relationship with each of my fellows." Was the stark black-and-whiteness of this affirmation becoming overwhelming to her gentle, conscientious soul? Like Mary, she too found ways to manage.

As they closed another Letter to Friends they wrote, "We are so thankful that you accompany us with your thoughts and prayers as we try to live this life which is simple enough and yet asks more of us that we can easily give."[70] Indeed the path of diminishment, marginalization, and self-doubt was painful.

---

69. See Appendix 7 for a birthday card, dated January 4, 1984, for Rosmarie who was then staying for a time with her mother in Switzerland. Composed by Mary of sentimental doggerel, it offers a snapshot of Rosmarie's central role in their lives.

70. Letter #31.

15

Septuagenarians Looking Ahead
1986–1989

> The old ship is not in a state to make many voyages,
> but the flag is still at the mast and I am still at the wheel.
>
> —WALT WHITMAN AT SEVENTY

CHANGE WAS AFOOT IN Hong Kong. In 1984 the Sino-British Joint Declaration had been signed by Deng Xiaoping and Margaret Thatcher on behalf of their respective countries, agreeing that Britain would hand its sovereignty over Hong Kong to China on July 1, 1997. Uncertainty was in the air.

In 1988, in a letter to their friend Raimon Panikkar, Mary acknowledged the uncertainty in their own lives. They could not ignore their own advancing age. Nor could they ignore the reality that Murray's outspoken views had made his position with the local Anglican authorities somewhat tenuous. She wrote:

> Hong Kong is proceeding on its way towards 1997 (by which time we ourselves will be 80 and 81, and I really don't see us among the bamboos footing it up and down our hill by that time!) . . . It is certainly an interesting time to be here, but disquieting too. There appears to be increasingly a polarisation between those who are conservative, very careful to do nothing to 'rock the boat' vis-à-vis China, wanting to preserve the structures of 'stability and prosperity' (the watchwords used) in Church and State . . . Meanwhile there are others who see the running-up period as very important from the point of view of getting a more participatory society: hitherto there has been scarcely any democratic representation . . . Our Bishop belongs

to the first group and exhorts all the clergy to be good boys and stick to their 'spiritual ministry' church services, etc., whereas we would tend to be, even hope to be, in the second group. Hence Murray—and we—are in a sort of a way 'banned' as regards much of the Anglican Church. Mercifully, the divide goes through the churches and there are many good friends . . . on the same wave-length . . . We shall see how it all turns out. We are waiting for the green-lights and red-lights that may indicate the way.

There was much to consider with those red and green lights of discernment. Death and a sense of their own mortality seemed to occupy their minds, as well as the violence of life around them. Death and violence had even touched their little hermitage. As they reported to Friends, "After a three-week illness, our dear adopted dog Hari, who found it impossible to be anything but a friend to all, quietly died. [And] on Holy Saturday night, Ambie, Hari's companion and one of God's gentlest and dearest creatures, was slaughtered by two guard dogs—a violent reminder of where riches and violence lead when both men and animals are "blown out of shape" (*cf.* Chuang Tzu xi-i) by our craving for 'security' and possessions . . . The passing on of these two animal-friends was hard to bear; they taught us so much in ways of being and perceiving that extended our imagination."[1]

The successive losses of other close human friends caught their attention. When in 1987, their friend Anthony de Mello, who had often visited with them in Hong Kong, died suddenly, they were moved to share his story of "The Salt Doll," a reflection on death:

> A salt doll journeyed for thousands of miles over land, until it finally came to the sea.
> It was fascinated by this strange moving mass, quite unlike anything it had ever seen before.
> "Who are you?" said the salt doll to the sea.
> The sea smilingly replied, "Come in and see."
> So the doll waded into the sea. The further it walked into the sea, the more it dissolved until there was only very little of it left.
> Before that last bit dissolved, the doll exclaimed in wonder, "Now I know who I am!"[2]

---

1. Letter #29.
2. Letter #31.

They had loved Tony de Mello for his irreverent humor, his willingness to be outrageously unorthodox.[3] He would come to visit with their old friends, the Lamma Island sisters, and they would share retreat time together. Murray, in his own story-telling mode, described one such occasion:

> Tony would just sit on a table and tell us stories. And one religious sister got a little nervous about his not being orthodox and said to him, "Father, I'm a little worried about one thing. Would you tell me, do you believe in hell?"
>
> And good old Tony said, "Well, thank you, Sister, for asking that question. Instead of answering you now, I would like to think on it overnight, and I will answer it in the morning."
>
> The morning came, and he quite forgot about it. At midday, the poor sister was almost bursting a blood vessel, because she [imagined] he hoped she'd forget, and was fairly well guilty, because he couldn't honestly give a reply. So at lunch time the sister said, "Father, you told me you were going to tell me this morning the answer to my question."
>
> And Tony said, "Oh, Sister, how dreadful. Yes, I entirely forgot. Tell me, what was your question again?"
>
> She said, "Do you believe in hell, Father?"
>
> And he said, "Yes, sister, I do—And there's nobody in it!"
>
> We all roared with laughter.[4]

"Tony," Murray added, was "a free man . . . free because of what God had done for him." As he quoted de Mello further, surely he was reflecting on his own life so far and the distance he had still to go. "When I was younger," de Mello had said, "I wanted to be known as a saint. As I got older, I wanted to be known as someone who loved a lot. Now, I want to be known as a free man."

Death and freedom had become topics for much pondering. Though their dear friend Abhishiktananda had found his full awakening in this life, it seemed likely that for them complete freedom would be found only in

---

3. More than ten years after his death, writing on behalf of the Congregation for the Doctrine of the Faith, then Cardinal Ratzinger [later Pope Benedict] composed "A Notification Concerning the writings of Father Anthony de Mello, S.J." which stated: "In order to protect the good of the Christian faithful, this Congregation declares that the above-mentioned positions (cited in the text) are incompatible with the Catholic faith and can cause grave harm." (Vatican website) Today there is a de Mello Spirituality Center at Fordham, the Jesuit University in the Bronx, NY. The Sadhana Institute, founded in Pune, India, by de Mello has been relocated to Lonavla where it continues its work of integrating spirituality and psychology in an experiential way (sadhanainstitute.org).

4. Interview with Trapnell.

death. Perhaps only then would they, like the Salt Doll, be entirely dissolved into God, knowing fully who they were.

From those ponderings flowed a series of radio talks by Murray on the theme of death, simple reflections, perhaps intended to soften a taboo subject, perhaps to reassure himself. These words, spoken in 1988, are excerpts from those talks:

> Friends ... I'd like to talk with you about something that will happen to each single one of us. I've just turned seventy and so naturally I'm thinking about my death more than I did when I was younger. Obviously, as none of us lasts for ever on this plane of existence, it will be my time before many years go by to die, to lay aside this body of mine that on the whole has served me very well, and to go on to what lies ahead.
>
> Of course I could pretend that death isn't for me ... I could avoid mentioning dying, either because I'm frightened or because I think it is bad luck to talk about death. But I don't think pretending does any good, either about death or anything else. We just drive the fears inside us and make ourselves and other people miserable, and, anyway, I am convinced that dying isn't a happening to fear. We accepted our birth—the moment when our soul and our body came together—as a gift of God and of our parents; not many of us are sorry to have tasted life. I want to accept my death also—that moment when this body of mine will be laid aside, with thanks for all the service it has given me—as the gift of God, and to go on, the deepest 'me', into new and fuller Being, into fuller Life.

The challenge, he acknowledged, was our tendency to identify ourselves as our body, as our mind:

> When we think that is all we are, time passing becomes a huge burden—it feels as if we are running down, as if life is draining out of us, and we have no control over this process.
>
> But—and it is a big But—you and I are much more than our body; God has linked each of us with His Life and that means that death is like a marvelous window facing the future. Far from death being a disaster, it becomes a blessing—something we can celebrate!
>
> ... You are quite right; it takes quite a lot of practice to know that we don't die when our bodies die ... They are put quietly and reverently into a grave or are cremated, but the heart of you and the heart of me—what is often called the soul—continues on into Light and peace and greater Life. That is why I'm hoping

that my funeral may be an occasion of praise and thankfulness to God, not because of me—a little perhaps—but much, much more because God in His Love has lent me this body for seventy or so years and is now going to introduce me into more secrets of Life with Him, Life in Him . . .

When we have [this] attitude, then this thing death can't frighten us any longer.[5]

Embedded in these meditations on death was a short sentence that spoke volumes about his approach to life, repeated here: "I don't think pretending does any good, either about death or anything else." For Murray, speaking openly and freely had been important from his young manhood, though, more than once, his words had landed him in trouble with the authorities. Growing older, as the moral imperative grew even more insistent, he was moved to share a text he had taken as his own: "I cannot be quiet; no, I cannot pass by indifferently before the pain of so many persons. No, I am not able to be quiet. My friends will have to forgive me, but I have a commitment and I have to sing the reality."[6]

Now again he was finding himself at odds with the authorities; quiet compliance and "being a good boy" had never been his strong suit. In 1988 a more public statement on the radio made his position clear. After quickly reviewing his life in different parts of the world, he continued:

This bit of personal history has led me to be more and more disenchanted with religion and religious institutions; they may be administered well, but, forgive me, they often seem irrelevant; they seem to make people frightened of freedom, or, to put it another way, like sheep who just follow the leader and accept the world as they find it.

Jesus wasn't one bit like that. Mind you, he got into trouble, and too often religious people take care not to get into trouble. He was disturbingly free—he didn't say what the religious authorities thought he ought to say; he didn't fit in with the state authorities either. He was just himself, a unique sort of character, though to his followers a not infrequent embarrassment. He intended them—he still does—to follow in his steps.

Of course "following in his steps" doesn't mean going to live in Jerusalem or Galilee, but it does mean sharing his way of seeing people and things; it means letting God work on us—work in us—that we may "catch" his way of thinking, his way

---

5. Rogers, *'No More Humbug!' Says the Fool: Sermons, Talks and Articles by Charles Murray Rogers*, 201–202.

6. Letter #31.

of approaching problems. It means—or so it seems to me—discovering that following Jesus is much more about life and love, about suffering and laughter, than about religion and belonging to religious organizations. So today, this week, would you join me in asking yourself often, in the actual situation where you are: "What would Jesus do?" Try to decide what Jesus would do, and then, taking your courage in both hands, go and do it . . .[7]

Though he could make it sound simple: "What would Jesus do?", the reality of the little community's discernment was more complex. Beyond prayer, they often found indications of God's direction in books. Thus, when they came upon a slim volume by the American Roman Catholic James Douglass entitled *Lightning East to West: Jesus, Gandhi and the Nuclear Age*, they were thunderstruck. Here was a man who had taken his "courage in both hands" and done it, a man whose actions were informed by contemplation, and who, along with his wife Shelley, was repeatedly willing to risk arrest and imprisonment for his beliefs. His message—that human spiritual energy had the potential to disarm, non-violently, the ferociously destructive energy of nuclear militarism—found resonance in their own hearts. The message was not new: their friend Shigeto Oshida had embodied the connection between contemplative awareness and peace, as had their Quaker friend and mentor, Marjorie Sykes, those many years ago in India. And certainly the Korean Quaker Ham Sok-Han had embodied the courage. But Douglass articulated the unity between mystical experience and engagement with the world in a way they found "remarkable,"[8] dissolving the dualism Murray was experiencing in the church and decrying in the world about him. The book's citations stirred old memories and validated their life experiences. There was Ramana Maharshi, Abhishiktananda's guru, teaching again: "As you are, so is the world."[9] There too was Gandhi's speaking of non-violence through truth-grasping [*satyagraha*] as "the ultimate transforming power" and affirming the "fundamental oneness of reality." Douglass quoted Gandhi's words: "I believe in the absolute oneness of God and, therefore, of humanity. What though we have many beliefs? We have but one soul. The rays of the sun are many through refraction. But they have the same source. I cannot, therefore, detach myself from the wickedest soul nor may I be denied identity with the most virtuous."[10] The hearts

---

7. Rogers, *'No More Humbug!' Says the Fool: Sermons, Talks and Articles by Charles Murray Rogers*, 189–190.

8. Letter #30.

9. Douglass, *Lightning East to West*, 48.

10. Ibid., 43.

of Jyotiniketan's family reverberated with Douglass' conviction: "Once we begin to see this profound interpenetration of inner and outer worlds in a oneness of reality, the insoluble enigma of the world of evil gives way to the edge of the unifying mystery of Oneness, or of Love, a mystery which we cannot fully understand but which we can in fact move into with our lives and participate in to the extent of experiencing an ever-more-united world in Reality."[11]

This vision of transformation as lived out by Jesus and Gandhi, was, as Douglass noted, rarely practiced because it is so costly and so difficult, because poverty is at the heart of the work of self-emptying love. Nor can it be dualistic: the public cannot be split off from the private. Citing Gandhi's "constructive program" in which self-emptying love must be practiced daily with one's sisters and brothers in "very concrete, personal ways,"[12] Douglass explored an important sub-text: his own "hardness of heart"[13] towards his wife and their relationship as he took public actions they had not agreed upon. He acknowledged that it took some years to experience *metanoia*—a change of heart and soul—to acknowledge his culpability. But only in that "way of metanoia," with its opening to the concern of another without regard for the consequences to oneself, could there be a way, he wrote, to "fullness of freedom." Little wonder, as they "centred [their] attention on [their] own small part in the universal work for peace," *Lightning East to West* merited "a serious pondering."[14]

Within Jyotiniketan, Mary and Murray found agreement on actions they could each take in their work for peace. Together they shared training for peace activism with Hildegard and Jean Goss,[15] whom they counted as friends and who inspired them in their commitment. When in Europe, each connected with different peace communities: Mary visited with women activists at Greenham Common Women's Peace Camp,[16] while Murray lent

11. Ibid., 51.
12. Ibid., 15.
13. Ibid., 12.
14. Letter #30.

15. Hildegard (1930-)and Jean Goss Mayr (1912–1991): Roman Catholic and European-born, as wife and husband, they worked both within the Church and around the world from South America to the Philippines for the recognition and practice of active non-violence. Together they were recipients of several international peace prizes. Of Hildegard Goss-Mayr, Thomas Merton said, "[She] is my candidate for sainthood." She remains the honorary president of the International Fellowship of Reconciliation.

16. Greenham Common Women's Peace Camp: A protest movement outside Royal Air Force Base Greenham Common in Berkshire, England. Begun in 1981 in response to a decision to locate cruise nuclear missiles there, the group gained international attention with their non-violent protests and were ultimately instrumental in having the

his presence and support at Molesworth Peoples' Peace Camp.[17] Locally the 1986 Chernobyl nuclear disaster galvanized them to take action, and together they joined thousands of others in demonstrating and writing letters of protest against government plans to build a mammoth nuclear power plant at Daya Bay, just north of Hong Kong. It was these actions, in fact, that had drawn the disapproving attention of Anglican Church authorities described in Mary's letter. Their bishop, the Rt. Rev. Peter Kwong, whose consecration as the first Chinese bishop for the Anglican Church they had celebrated in 1981, and by whose leave they continued to occupy their little abode on Tao Fong Shan, had informed them their actions were unacceptable. The Church, it seemed, did not want to "rock the boat" as the time approached for Britain to turn over its power to the Chinese. They were informed that Murray's standing in the Anglican community in Hong Kong was at stake.

But true to his word, Murray would not keep silent. On Palm Sunday 1987 at St. Matthew's Church, preaching on the entry of Jesus into Jerusalem, he said:

> . . . We have sometimes been told that our Lord Jesus did not take political action; that is not true. Here in this demonstration of advancing into the capital city of his country as a King, mounted on a donkey, with ordinary people, many of them children, cheering Him, He was saying something. He was saying: "Yes, I am a King, but my power is not the power of the police force nor of armaments and guns; it is the power of non-violence, the power that comes from ordinary people demonstrating for Love, for the King Jesus who has no army, no prisons, no physical force. Jesus that day invited His followers to demonstrate; He invited them to say by walking in the streets of Jerusalem with Him that real power, God's power, does not lie in the Government and does not lie in those with much money or with much status. Real power lies with those who trust in God and in His Love.

Murray then arrived at the crux of the parallel he was drawing between the situation Jesus faced in Jerusalem and the situation he saw in Hong Kong, boldly proceeding to his point:

---

missiles removed.

17. Molesworth Peoples' Peace Camp: A protest group inspired by Greenham Common Women that set up camp outside Moleworth, a Royal Air Force base near Cambridge. The group organized non-violent anti-nuclear protests beginning in 1981 when nuclear missiles were located there and remained for nearly ten years.

> What Jesus ... did that day was a great challenge to the Roman colonial power of his day, and it was a great challenge to the religious authorities of His day who owed their position to that worldly power of Rome. Where Church and the power of the State co-operate against Love and Respect of people, then once again the followers of Jesus need to demonstrate where real love and power are to be found ...
>
> ... All Jesus did that day of the procession and Royal Entrance into Jerusalem was non-violent. If he had been a King of the World, He would certainly have ridden on a horse and not on a donkey; if He represented worldly power there would have been police and soldiers and guns, as were laid on when Queen Elizabeth came to Hong Kong a few months ago. With Jesus ... it was quite different—He needs no police; He needs no army. He has palm leaves instead of guns ...

He closed his sermon with his emblematic challenge:

> Those first disciples asked themselves whether they dared to follow their Master Jesus on His journey to Jerusalem. Are you and I ready to follow our Master Jesus into our city of Hong Kong? It's easy and comfortable to be a Christian by label, by name; it is very costly to follow Christ truly and sincerely.[18]

And how did Mary, Heather, and Rosmarie react to Murray's outspoken messages, knowing that further marginalization would surely be the outcome? We cannot know how many conversations were shared, how many sleepless nights endured, how many prayers offered. All of them knew from experience that following Murray was unpredictable and costly; it went without saying that he was the leader, they, the women, the followers. As a community they maintained their solidarity, their dependence, perhaps, upon him.

Their modest daily life continued, as they wrote, "in the Chapel and out from there in many ways."[19] There were visits with friends, work in the now beautifully blooming garden, and meditative walks in the hills. Rosmarie stayed constant with her volunteer work for the handicapped, refugees, and prisoners, while Heather maintained the household and made sure meals were on the table. For her, leisure meant time to bring out the watercolors once again, and her work graced the walls of their little Bamboo Hermitage. Mary might be found contentedly at work on her latest literary project,

---

18. Rogers, *'No More Humbug!' Says the Fool: Sermons, Talks and Articles by Charles Murray Rogers*, 159–160.

19. Letter #32.

translating from the French a book on women ascetics of Jainism written by N. Shanta, her good friend and colleague from Raimon Panikkar's monumental book project. Or it might be her day to volunteer for Friends of the Earth, supporting their environmental work.

As they conscientiously worked to deepen their littleness, they bridled at the displays of wealth around them and the gap between rich and poor. How could it be that the city with the most Rolls Royces per capita in the world could also resort to locking up the homeless at night in cage-like structures along Waterloo Road? Later on, Murray would observe: "It was in that place I learned you can be very rich and miserable at the same time."[20] Perhaps more accurately he might have said he learned—again—that truth first learned as a small boy in his home outside London.

Their own riches were often counted in small keepsakes and symbols gathered on Murray's desk and in their chapel, reminders all of their friendships and life in God. All were treasures to them. "Millionaires without a salary, with no fixed income!"[21] they exclaimed. But there was little self-congratulation as they expressed their gratitude to friends, year after year:

> We never cease to marvel at the generosity, the gratuité of God expressed through so many of you friends, near and far. It is that love and caring that keeps us fed and housed and (generally) well in health month after month, and we are indeed grateful to Him and to you. Sometimes we bow our heads in shame, especially when we remember the vast numbers of poverty-stricken children of God who are dying because we wealthy insist on keeping our riches, for our standard of life is distinctly up since our days in Kareli, India (yes, with fans and refrigeration . . .). Yet we still struggle to "live simply that others may simply live," to ring the changes on a somewhat basic yet healthy diet and to wear what we have until it falls to pieces (more or less!).[22]

With that help of family and friends, their travels could continue. In 1987 Heather enjoyed a "marvelously enriching return" to India, along with her niece Elizabeth. The same year Murray set off for two more interfaith dialogue meetings. For the first in Kyoto, Japan, at the behest of the World Council of Churches, Murray wrote and presented a paper entitled "On the Pilgrim Path,"[23] that shared in a deeply personal way his own spiritual evolution through more than forty years of life in Asia. The second took

---

20. Interview with Trapnell.
21. Letter #30.
22. Letter #29.
23. See Appendix 12 for complete text of this paper.

place at the University of Manitoba, Canada, at the invitation of Professor Klaus Klostermaier, Murray's old friend from India days. While such meetings were no longer as controversial as twenty-five years earlier when the Cuttat Group was breaking new ground, the lure of old friends and new perspectives to share had not diminished. Nor did the Canadian Rockies fail to impress. There was also a trip to India for Murray, made financially possible by a Hindu friend whose "immense generosity" connected him with two Hindu ashrams including that of Dada Vaswani, the Hindu spiritual leader born in 1918, just a year after Murray. Viewing the visits through more elderly eyes, they reported them "extraordinarily enriching for us who are on our way to the Eternal through Jesus Christ." Continuing, they reiterated one of their favorite themes: "Surely God has no favourites! We suspect He hardly notices religious labels and the discovery of His Spirit operating everywhere is a cause for wonder and gratitude."[24]

Of course, there were times spent with families in Europe as well: "How much kindness we receive from them and what a rare joy to watch the younger members growing and flowering," they exclaimed.

Increasingly, their returns to Hong Kong carried a sense of dis-ease. As Murray wrote to Raimond Panikkar in 1988, "Hong Kong is very conscious of 1997; in fact, the important happenings are taking place years earlier—now. The institutional churches are unaware, largely, I fear, of what really matters. Buildings and money continue to be all-important and doubly so in H.K." To his deep dismay, Murray saw his own Anglican Church, as he later explained, ". . . keeping a very careful and fearful eye on the wishes of the powers-that-be in mainland China, very dependent on the power and prestige of property and educational institutions."[25] Unlike the Diocese of Jerusalem, where the appointment of a local Palestinian bishop had enhanced the responsiveness of the office to the local people, in Hong Kong's Anglican Diocese, the Chinese bishop seemed to carry deep resonance of centuries of Chinese emperors, adopting as well the tradition of old-fashioned English bishops living in their palaces. Murray elaborated: "That mixture was very powerful. Complete control from top to bottom, the clergy powerless to voice any opinion contrary to the bishop. Certainly the most hierarchical of any bishop in whose diocese I've worked. A sad and wonderful recipe for a formal, largely uninspired church." He continued: "Of course, there were glorious personal exceptions, people who had tasted Christ Jesus alive—alive and living in them. Oh, those can't be stopped! But the organized church was utterly British in its worship. If you went to the cathedral now in

---

24. Letter #32.
25. Interview with Trapnell.

Hong Kong Island, if you sadly were blind and couldn't see, and you listened to that service, the prayers, the music, the anthem, the clothes everybody was wearing, you might be in Sheffield! And that is a recipe for disaster."[26]

Murray could not be silent. In 1987 there was an intensely destructive typhoon that hit Melanesia, killing hundreds and inflicting vast damage. In response to an appeal for help, the new dean of the Cathedral, recently arrived from England, noted large reserves of money and saw to it that a generous contribution was sent. Then suddenly the new dean was gone, edged out quickly and quietly, it seemed, by the Bishop. There were whispers of what had happened.

For Murray, that was the *coup de grâce*. Resorting to familiar if devastating tactics, he wrote a letter to the newspaper in Hong Kong, speaking the truth as he knew it. The bishop responded angrily. Refusing to retreat, Murray wrote to him, telling him that if there was any untruth in his letter, he would apologize and ask the paper to publish his apology. Murray reported that the bishop responded through his administrator: "Oh, the Bishop's complaint and antagonism to what you wrote has nothing to do with truth, Murray." It was a reply reminiscent of the one he had received in Jerusalem when he was expelled from the Rainbow Club for his "tone and style." As he noted wryly, "Truth there wasn't really the issue."[27] Again, he was unwelcome, forbidden to preach in the diocese.

To their Friends, they alluded to but did not divulge the full story, sharing the news in this way: "With two of us now over seventy, it is perhaps not surprising that we have wondered from time to time over the last year or so what future God might have in store for us. Members of communities don't really 'retire' in the normal way till they 'cross to the further shore,' but we do realise that living up this hill would become increasingly difficult, although until now we have been able to walk happily down and up with no ill effects!"[28]

Describing the dilemma of the approaching handover to China, they distanced themselves from the institutional church's position of "not rocking the boat" and spoke of their stand for human rights, political action, and increased democracy for the people of Hong Kong:

> For us Christians it is a question of "which Jesus do you believe in?"—the Jesus of the Gospels or a tamed version of Him? Perhaps you can guess which trend we support. The way of power and prestige, of being very impressive in terms of "bricks and

26. Ibid.
27. Ibid.
28. Letter #32.

mortar" and institutions, has, it seems to us, very little to do with the real Jesus of the Gospels. Some of us—and some of you, no doubt—were strongly influenced by Archbishop William Temple[29] and Pastor Dietrich Bonhoeffer. They in their day knew that a Gospel without a radical and costly call to social witness and action is not the Gospel of Christ. We sense the human and spiritual danger to which Hong Kong churches will be exposed if they yield to ideological and economic pressures.[30]

There had been another development as well, this one rife with the familiar sense of "coincidence," so often a theme in their discernment. A Canadian couple, Herbert and Susan Frizzell, had appeared at their door, they explained, initially "'by mistake,' as they were looking for another address, but we soon found ourselves to have much in common." Through the happenstance meeting, deeper sharing and friendship had developed. And now the Frizzells had invited them to come to live on one of their farms, where, "if it proved to be God's will," they would collaborate in creating a small center for "human and spiritual training."

Sharing a bit of their discernment process, they wrote: "We have thought and prayed, we have consulted and wondered." At one point as Murray questioned the wisdom of septuagenarians saying "yes" to this new adventure, a friend had queried, "Wasn't Abraham seventy-five before he began a considerable work?" Their still wondering response followed: "But are we Abraham? That's the question."[31]

Despite trepidation, they would be leaving Hong Kong, again to travel across the world to begin a new venture on a new continent, this time in Canada.

Rosmarie had left ahead of them. Emotionally depleted from her inner struggle between her loyalty and love for Jyotiniketan and her care for her mother, she had allowed Murray to decide for her. She would spend "an unspecified length of time in Switzerland before coming to Canada."[32]

Their departure, though unceremonious, was not without bittersweet leave-taking from friends. Early disappointments with the Tao Fong Shan Christian Centre long past, they bade farewell there with a gentle homily from Murray on the love of Jesus. Then at the Hong Kong airport they were surprised by a gathering of many of their closest friends in the airport

---

29. William Temple (1881–1944) became Archbishop of Canterbury. He was known for his social and political activism as well as for his preaching and teaching.
30. Letter #32.
31. Ibid.
32. Ibid.

chapel, where a service of prayerful gratitude was celebrated. As they told their Friends: "The words spoken, the silence kept and the written messages of blessing handed to us all live on in our memories . . . We left Hong Kong surrounded by strong reminders of love, both God's and people's."[33]

Heather, Murray, and Mary, together in the 'New World,' 1999.

33. Ibid.

16

Canada: A Geriatric Escapade?
1989–1994

> Laughter is immeasurable. Be joyful though you
> have considered all the facts.
>
> —WENDELL BERRY

BEFORE THEIR LEAP INTO the unknown of life in the New World, they had set aside three months for joyful reunions, a time of spiritual refueling. The first stop was Istanbul to reconnect with old and new friends, visit old haunts, and sense the spirit of their beloved Athenagoras in Orthodox worship. Then on they continued to Cyprus, renewing bonds with their Jerusalem neighbor Henry Selz.[1] Days in Greece with an elderly Indian Sister followed. Continuing by boat to Rome and Assisi—the latter, "still redolent with the spirit of St. Francis,"[2] they found shelter under the wings of the Little Sisters of Jesus. With the passing weeks, their very old friend, Don Michele, a Roman Catholic priest, welcomed them "home" for Easter in the Italian Alps, along with Rosmarie and Vroni Thurneysen—spiritual family all. More joy awaited in England, Scotland, and France as they reunited with their individual families. Only after all these reunions, "trusting God *and* taking a deep breath,"[3] did they board the plane for Montreal. Their apprehension lingered.

---

1. Henry Selz was an American Quaker who began his international career assisting refugees following the partition of India and Pakistan in 1948. As a professional relief organization administrator, he headed CARE operations in many countries; while in Jerusalem he served with American Near East Refugee Aid on the West Bank. A peripatetic citizen of the world, he maintained homes in the U.S., Cyprus, and India.

2. Letter #33.

3. Ibid.

Celebrating with family in England, c. 1989.

There, as they wrote in their first letter from Canada, they were met as promised by the Frizzells, "the good and generous friends who made this wonderful 'madness' possible!"[4] Yet more misgivings were bubbling up. Arriving at their house outside Montreal, they were taken aback. It was "very posh,"[5] complete with swimming pool and tennis court. Did that tennis court prompt memories for Murray of his own posh, yet unhappy childhood home? They wondered: had they misunderstood their hosts' dedication to a simple life? Pushing doubts aside, they continued on with them to their second house near the Bay of Quinte, Lake Ontario, in the pleasant, prosperous town of Napanee.

Jyotiniketan's home was to be the Frizzell's stable. It would be their own "dream house," spare and simple, renovated to their specifications. Recalling their adventurous days of building a simple, yet beautiful chapel in North India, Laurie Baker, their friend and designer of the original Jyotiniketan buildings, had provided the plan from afar, with local adaptations by an

4. Letter #33.
5. Interview with Trapnell.

architect friend from Greenwich, CT. Wouldn't life in a stable, they mused, be evocative of their call to live on the margins, even more gracefully, perhaps, than life in a garage? The chapel, at the heart of their new home, would be built around the original manger: "a daily reminder of the Incarnation."[6] It would sustain them, as it always had, with its icons of God's abiding presence and daily Eucharists. Such was their dream. Not until summer would work begin on the stable, but already their chapel was set up there, a refuge. In the meantime, the three remained awkwardly sheltered under Herb and Susan Frizzell's roof.

Characteristically, there was no waiting for new life to begin. After little more than a week, a day-long gathering for Christian meditation nearby spawned a meditation group under Murray's guidance. Word spread of their presence and new friends were drawn like bees to honey. A steady stream of visitors from Greenwich traversed the four hundred miles to bring supplies and provide labor and support for their project. Rosmarie too, still a part of the Jyotiniketan family, came for an extended visit from Switzerland. As construction proceeded, their chapel underwent frequent dislocations. But at last the work was done, the space was blessed, and, with gratitude, they moved in, again firmly anchored by their chapel with its treasured symbols of love and friendship. As they wrote in their Letter: "Each cherished thing in the chapel is full of vibrations of meaning, as is so much else in the house. Indeed, almost everything has been the gift of neighbors and friends, ranging from a refrigerator [from] some Salvation Army friends to gifts of skill and time given by so many people both here and from Greenwich ... tokens of their welcome and caring. We can turn in no direction without being reminded of this extraordinary generosity and friendship. We cannot thank God or our friends at all adequately for all this ..."[7]

They had quickly learned of their physical proximity to First Nations[8] people of the Tyendinaga Mohawk Territory. Already acquainted with Native American spirituality through their reading of *Black Elk Speaks* and their meeting with Black Elk's son in Japan, knowing too that the 'scent of God' could often be found in marginalized cultures, their curiosity was immediately piqued. Surely there would be much to learn from this ancient culture. The nearby Kanhiote Tyendinaga Library soon became not only a source of information, but a place to meet local Mohawks.

---

6. Letter #33.

7. Ibid.

8. "First Nations" refers to the various aboriginal people of Canada, similar to the way Native American refers to indigenous people in the United States.

Thus when Mary Valentine, a friend visiting from Greenwich, shared her knowledge of Native American spirituality, the group listened intently. For Native Americans, Mary said, "the Divine Spirit" often spoke through nature. She particularly referenced a belief that lightning striking a tree without killing it could be understood as a sign of blessing. That very night, as they all slept, a powerful thunderstorm enveloped their new home. Lightning hit an adjacent poplar, cleanly peeling off a strip of bark and wood, but with no visible burning. They were delighted. "For us," they wrote, "this was a clear Word from God, an assurance of His call to wake up and be ready for His Presence in our new little place. Are you surprised," they added, "that our cross in the new chapel is created from that wood, a reminder of 'Lighting East to West'"?[9]

They were grateful for the reassurance. Improbable as this new life had seemed to many and often to themselves, they longed to believe that their discernment process had not gone awry. As Murray later reflected: "We'd never dreamt of going to Canada, but, after all, we'd never dreamt of going to Hong Kong. We'd never dreamt of living in the Old City of Jerusalem. So, not dreaming about it didn't seem to be frightfully relevant. We just put it into our prayers, and wondered. We thought that they [the Frizzells] understood us so well, because they'd read our printed letters. We'd discussed time and again the way we lived and why we were as we were. We thought we understood one another. They did, I think, and we did, too."[10]

Settled uneasily into their new quarters, providence provided an unexpected and wonderful distraction from uncomfortable questions they faced. Before leaving Hong Kong, Mary and Murray had been asked to write a prayer—an ecological ode to nature—to be set to music and performed by the Hong Kong Children's Chorus and Symphony for the gala opening of the new Hong Kong Cultural Centre. And now came the news that airline tickets were being provided by sponsors of the event for them to attend the grand event! Delighted, off they flew to Hong Kong. Somewhat sheepishly, they reported to Friends: "You would have smiled to have seen us sitting in the V.I.P. box!"[11]

Such a welcome opportunity it was to reunite with Hong Kong friends. Now they could understand more deeply the implications of the world-shaking events of the past June (1989): the brave protests of Chinese students at Tiananmen Square and the brutal government crackdown. "Let us pray," they wrote, "that our courage and non-violence may be as strong as

9. Letter #33.
10. Interview with Trapnell.
11. Letter #33.

those of the Beijing students, that we may stand up for humanity, no matter what the cost. It is dangerous to be alive—which should be no surprise to the followers of Jesus."[12]

But if there were a signal event for the 'geriatric' trio during their Canada years, it happened, ironically, not in Canada but in Middlebury, Vermont, a day's drive from Deseronto. It was, as Murray said, an experience that would 'mark' them all—a *darshan*[13] with the Dalai Lama, infusing them with joy and perhaps courage too, for the road ahead. And what was *darshan*? Murray had learned, in India, that part of religious practice in Hinduism was to seek '*darshan*', a sharing the presence of a holy person, not just to talk to him or her, but "to draw some strength from [their] presence because of their worth as human beings, their spiritual depth, their reality, their genuineness."[14] It was to come "face to face with the Real." They had driven to Middlebury College with Vroni Thurneysen, their Swiss friend, and Adelaide Winstead, an old friend from the States, for an interfaith gathering with the Dalai Lama as the chief speaker. The theme was "Spirit and Nature," with Native American spirituality strongly represented. As the weekend long event neared its end, the group gathered in the College chapel for an interfaith service, then collected brown bag picnics and scattered onto the grass, which had been laid out with white ribbons in the shape of a Buddhist wheel of life. Once the crowd settled into various parts of the wheel, the Dalai Lama said grace in Tibetan. Then from the center, loaves of bread were distributed. Each participant tore off a small piece and passed it to the next, an interfaith sharing of the bread of life.

Then came another eucharistic moment. As they were about to enjoy their sandwiches, Murray looked up and realized the Dalai Lama had not yet begun eating. He was chatting and blessing children. Murray recalled: "I thought to myself, 'Well, Murray, what are you doing? Aren't you a child?'" Suddenly he found himself on his feet, standing right in front of the Dalai Lama. Years later, the memory of their encounter on that October day in 1990 was as vivid as if it had just happened. Here is his account:

> I stood in front of him, and quickly saw he was sitting down. I didn't want to talk down, or be higher than he was, so I went down onto one knee. He put out his hand and held onto mine. And then, this extraordinary little time happened. It was so little . . . yet it will last until my dying day. I had time to say

12. Ibid.
13. *Darshan*: a Sanscrit word used in Hinduism to refer to a spiritual experience of seeing a vision or of being in the presence of a holy person.
14. Rogers, "Who am I? The human question: one man's pilgrimage," 104 (87).

one sentence: "I just wanted to share my joy." Time stood still at that point. I couldn't tell you what happened. Everything did. He took my hand, drew me a bit nearer to him, and then looked intently into my eyes. I looked into his, and then he did the most marvelous thing. He *roared* with laughter ... And then we both laughed. You can't avoid laughing when you're near that man, and he's laughing a full laugh. When that ended, he pulled me closer still to him. Of course, he'd put down his bag by then, and the drink, the tin of something. And he pulled me to him, right close to him, and he put his face against mine, his right cheek against my left one, I think it was, or the other way around. And he held it there. I can still feel its warmth. I couldn't tell you what happened. Everything did. All I remember was how comfortable it was. I noticed nothing else. And then he let go—no, he let my hand go a bit, so I came back away from his face, and we looked at each other just for a second or two, and then we bowed. That was the end of that. I got up from my knee, and I bowed a tiny bit, and walked away. That is what the Indians call a *darshan*. I'd never experienced anything like that quite before. It was my deepest contact.[15]

Some might have seen two men enjoying a belly-laugh and imagined perhaps it was a private joke. But in that moment their laughter contained everything of human joy and, yes, human suffering: it was a soul-laugh. And while it may have seemed a private *darshan* for Murray, yet, even as the four women hung back, too shy to approach, they too partook of the sacred experience. Adelaide Winstead, who had driven them in her car the long miles from Napanee to Middlebury, recalled the image that lingers in her mind's eye, still touches her own soul: "I can still see those two precious faces pressed together,"[16] she said.

Murray's connection with the Dalai Lama, and perhaps to his courage and strength, was a touchstone for them as the frigid Canadian winter set in and they returned to the chill of their relationship with their benefactors. Murray recalled, "Little had we recognized, either they or we, the difficulties that would arise when a rich and generous couple, successful capitalists, and three elderly Gandhian Christians [tried] to live together. We should have known, I guess, but we didn't take it on board."[17] Susan and Herb Frizzell, it seemed, had envisioned a beautiful retreat center with Murray, Mary, and Heather serving as resident teachers of eastern spirituality. It would be,

15. Interview with Trapnell.
16. Interview with author.
17. Interview with Trapnell.

those prospective teachers belatedly learned, a place where large sums, at least from their perspective, could be spent for a weekend retreat. "Now how," Murray asked, "could we follow our vocation to be little and simple in those conditions? It was almost a non-starter, [which] we were terribly late in discovering."[18]

As the implications of their misjudgment became clear, they were once again face to face with their vulnerability. They had come to Canada as long-term residents, with minimal financial means. Though never pushed out by the Frizzells, they knew they could not stay in the Frizzell's stable. Suddenly they felt homeless. As their anxiety rose, they tried to let their faith sustain them. Going straight to their source, "tremblingly," they brought to mind the oft-repeated saying of Jesus to his disciples: "Don't worry, don't worry. Don't be anxious. God knows what you need." They needed to remind themselves; "It *must* apply for us, too. After all, it has for the preceding decades."[19]

In fact, it did apply. As Napanee friends learned of their dilemma, they guided the three to the town of Deseronto, less than twenty miles down the road. It was smaller and less fashionable with cheaper housing than Napanee. But still their resources were too limited, even for the most downscale market. On what seemed a fool's errand, they found a small and suitable house for around $57,000. Friends, trying to be helpful, suggested a mortgage. It was tempting, but they remembered Gandhi's admonition: "Never buy something you can't afford." So that was out. They were at an impasse.

Then Murray recalled: "God did it again! Who says God isn't a magician? I'm still staggered when I remember what happened." Almost to the week that they found the house, a letter arrived from their good friend Vroni, who continued to serve as pastor of a church in Switzerland. She had received an unexpected bequest from a parishioner. Not needing it herself, she wrote she'd be pleased and even grateful if they could find some use for it. It was $52,000. "Can you imagine!?" Murray exclaimed. They could manage the balance. But, still there was a glitch. How could an authentic ashram own property? Again, Vroni came to the rescue. She would own the property and allow them to live there, serving as their landlady as well as friend.[20]

Thus, after a bit less than a year in Canada, they trundled down the road to Deseronto, where they would make their home for nearly nine more years. It was a celebration of sorts, as moving day became, in Murray's words, "a 'fun-day' with friends rallying 'round with cars or trucks, [conveying]

18. Ibid.
19. Ibid.
20. Ibid.

us and our old tin trunks, bits and pieces. [Some] also came and spent a day or more with us, cleaning, scrubbing, painting, fixing, even inserting a partition-wall so that we could have once again a beautiful chapel."[21]

However simple the life they sought to live, their relationship with money remained complicated. They could accept gifts from benefactors, it seemed, as long as no strings were attached. There was, in fact, a little wooden box set in the back of their chapel where visitors could put free-will offerings. Because all three had been a part of the Christian Missionary Society, small pension checks arrived monthly for each of them from the Church of England. They were eligible too for Canadian government health cards, ensuring that most medical expenses were covered. They could accept these benefits. But when gifts seemed a form of payment for services, Murray drew the line. In a letter to Jack Bishop, Christ Church's Rector, just before their Lenten visit to Greenwich in 1992, he wrote:

> ... One other point I'd like to raise. Last time you gave me a great sum of money for which I was very grateful—it largely took me to Japan and to India, but this time will you let me decline such a kindness? Over all these years of a very much treasured relationship with Christ Church there has been no "pay" involved and I'd hate any commercialism to come in now; these have been for me times of joy and privilege, and the freedom of not being paid for ministry (which goes back to those days in India beginning in 1958!) is too precious to be lost, please. Of course I'm very grateful for the travel costs for me from here to you and back ...

Whenever the community coffers became a little too full for their spiritual comfort—or even if they were not so full—generous checks would be written: to the Canada Peace Alliance, the Jesuit Centre for Social Faith and Justice in Toronto, Amnesty International, the Hospice Movement, and to Jim Douglass's [the activist author of *Lightning East to West*] Catholic Worker House in Birmingham, Alabama. Always there were more interests, more gifts. To their amusement, in one tax-time meeting with an accountant, they were cautioned to stop giving away so much money. It looked suspicious!

Thus continued the delicate balance between the spiritual freedom of living somewhat off the economic 'grid' and the necessity of meeting basic human material needs. But now with a secure roof over their heads, their unencumbered life could resume. A sense of calm returned. In 1992 as winter melted into spring, they wrote of it this way:

---

21. Letter #35.

> Our particular style of life continues: up at 5 a.m. with silent meditation in our chapel from 5:30–6:00 a.m., followed by the Eucharist, the source and goal of everything, where the world is turned on its axis. Then comes work such as gardening and waterproofing the basement with cement (Heather's artistry is brought into play in both!), reading, writing letters, prayer, meeting people, food preparation, and, not least, laughter, until 8:30 or 9:00 p.m. when we are quite ready for bed. If you were to drop in at this chilly time of year, more than likely we'd offer you a shawl to put around you, for Gandhiji's call to control our wants—energy, water, comforts, paper, luxuries of all sorts—sounds in our hearts more strongly than ever, bidding us care, especially in this time of recession, for our environment before it is too late.[22]

Quickly they settled into their new surroundings, meeting neighbors on the street, in church, or over the back fence. Murray acquired a bike so he could get around town more efficiently, while Heather and Mary managed their errands on foot. Ruby Kells, a neighbor who became a lasting friend, recalled her own curiosity when first seeing a slender woman in a sari, seemingly lost on the streets of Deseronto. In such a small town, it didn't take long for another encounter: this time in church where the three were accompanied by a visiting contingent from Japan. But with warm invitations offered to visit Jyotiniketan, their seeming eccentricity dissolved into acceptance and welcome.

There were rare exceptions. One day when Mary answered a knock on the door, there stood a policeman. "There's been a report," he said sternly, "of a man walking along the road, wearing a dress. I'm told he lives here. I need to speak to him." It was but a small kerfuffle: another opportunity for Murray to engage, another chance for hilarious laughter, as the story circulated endlessly among family and friends.

Their call as always was to share their way of life with any who came their way. Their life was their message. Often that was enough. But on one occasion, to prepare Will Duncan, his young Greenwich friend, now in his late teens who aspired to come and live with them, Murray shared some no-nonsense words:

> How can I say something that may help you to be ready for this experience? I'd like to try. You know already that we've lived most of our lives among the very poor and oppressed who happen to be the majority of human beings; we've so many friends

---

22. Letter #35.

among them and appreciate and care for them very much. You'll never understand our life without remembering that again and again; it makes us want, as a joy, much more than as a duty, to live as simply, as inexpensively, as we possibly can. It makes us want to live like them as far as we possibly can. They have few choices, so do we especially in eating and our food is therefore more simple than the food of lots of well-off people. We have hot water for bathing (as so many of them don't) and therefore we use as little hot water as possible. We have found that consumer society, the one in which people are as rich as they are able to be, in which there is great competition, is very hard on the poor—it squeezes them out and many, especially children, die every day because of it. Of course because we now live in Canada we live in a consumer society also, but we try in every way we can to find another way to live. If you come to stay with us be a bit ready for this "other" way of life; it takes quite a bit of training to "control our wants," as Gandhi used to tell us.

From the outside our life may look a bit like a holiday! It isn't! It's a life in which we are asked willingly and happily, to be very disciplined in the use of our time, money and of our gifts.

Above all, our dream—our hope—is to learn to be more deeply human, not in words or ideas or on paper, but in the way the saints and masters teach us and show us. *If* we want to follow sincerely we simply have to die to our ego, and that isn't easy and quite often not very enjoyable, but it's the way to Love and Joy and Life.

Will arrived, as it happened, in the autumn—another chilly season. Eager and idealistic, he came by bus, peering from the window for a donkey, which Murray had said would signal his arrival. Scanning the passing fields in vain, he suddenly caught sight of a mailbox topped with a little wooden donkey. Stopping the bus, he jumped out, there to be greeted by Murray with a big hug and a mischievous grin. "Did you see the donkey?!" he asked. Then a bit confounded, but now, in retrospect comprehending, Will recalls, "It wasn't an outright practical joke, to imply that the donkey was alive, but it wasn't *not* a practical joke either. It was this space Murray often existed—just delighting in the cosmic joke of the universe. He was just always delighting."[23]

Like all guests, Will was allowed a full day to acclimate and rest before being fully integrated into household chores. Then as a serious student, he was assigned work. With the harvesting season for local farmers over,

---

23. William Duncan, reflection.

Will's job was to glean overlooked vegetables from fields [with the farmers' permission]. Some days were more fruitful than others. He recalls coming home after one full day's work, chilled to the bone, with only about half a pound of soybeans. A hot shower was not an option, as bathing was accomplished with a bucket of warm water, Indian-style. But, as he quickly learned, even with the heat in the house set very low, the bathroom could offer a modicum of comfort. Again, Will's recollections follow: "The only room they kept warm was a tiny bathroom. They would use it to dry their hand laundered robes and to let the heated milk with yogurt culture sit overnight to make fresh yogurt. One time I was sitting on the toilet again just reading when they called me for dinner. Slowly at the table questions started coming. How was my digestion? Was the food OK? Was my stomach OK? Suddenly it occurred to me they must have thought I had some 'real problems!' When I told them I was in the bathroom to keep warm, they all got a good laugh . . ."

Just as Murray had said, their life was not a holiday for Will. "I didn't last long," he said. "Maybe a month and a half." Only later did he come to understand he was not yet ready for the life they were living. "I remember when it dawned on me," he said "that their poverty was not a burden for them, that none of them was 'roughing it.' I was trying to *fight* the discomfort, [but] they were so surrendered that they no longer experienced discomfort in the same way I did."[24]

Friends and visitors were often confused by the apparent deprivation. Did they not have a taste for simple gustatory pleasures? As a teaching point, Murray told of a visitor in India who had come to the ashram bearing a gift of coffee. Imagining he might broaden their horizon of beverage options beyond their perennial tea, the kind visitor brewed a pot, and Murray partook of a small cup. The next day, he did so again. Again, Murray drank the coffee. By then, elated that his gift had been a success, he declared, "Murray, I do believe you're beginning to *like* coffee!"[25] The friend was not alone in missing the point of their limited diet. The idea their usual refraining from coffee, which Murray indeed loved, and other conveniences and treats was a free choice, was baffling to many.

Indeed, visitors were drawn into a world that threw many cultural assumptions into question. When the weather turned hot and humid and shawls were shed, windows were open to catch any breeze, but electric fans, offered by a concerned Greenwich guest, were quickly banished, likely a gift to the Salvation Army friends. This writer recalls one sultry summer night

24. Ibid.
25. Interview with author.

passed restlessly on a small cot in the guest room, dimly aware of the unaccustomed slipperiness of the sheet beneath her. As dawn broke and the call to meditation at 5:30 sounded, through bleary eyes she realized the sheets were not sheets at all, but well-worn silk saris, adapted to a new use.

She remembers too the stainless steel *thalis* on which heaping servings of nourishing vegetables, rice, and Indian spiced dal were served. Certainly no stinting on those servings, as hearty appetites were always brought to the table. And every plate was scraped clean. Nothing wasted. For breakfast there was porridge, sweetened with blackstrap molasses [for iron] and bread [never toasted, for there was no toaster]. But always jam. And all served on a variety of mismatched cups, bowls, and plates, all showing signs of long and active service to their previous owners. Around 4:00 there was tea, brewed according to one's preference, and biscuits. For those who preferred weaker tea, a tea bag from breakfast could be reused. For supper, Heather's renowned omelettes, prepared from farm fresh eggs, followed by carefully portioned nuggets of sharp cheese. And perhaps chocolate, again exactingly parsed into squares to be shared by the sweet-toothed family and their guests. All served up with plenty of lively conversation and laughter.

Discussions in those years were of local doings: hardships and joys of neighbors, solidarity with First Nation people in their continuing struggle with racism, mixed with happy anticipation of the annual Mohawk Pow-Wow. There was connection as well with the world at large, with an immediacy that made disturbing events in East Timor, El Salvador, or the Palestinian West Bank as close as those happening down the street. Each topic was enlivened with letters from friends that arrived almost daily in their ever-overflowing mailbox. Anticipation too, perhaps, of a coming family visit, pride and joy that their granddaughter, Victoria, was volunteering in Nepal with Tibetan children.

Rather than a life of deprivation, it was one of savoring and rich abundance. This visitor found a simple openness to join their daily life, authentic interest in what she brought to the table, concern for mutual friends, and, where there might have been condescension, patience. As the meal ended, in a sign of inclusion, there was the offer of a dish towel for washing up!

She recalls the daily Chinese exercises, meant to keep aging bodies limber and hearts pumping. Led now by Heather in Rosmarie's absence, they were practiced, weather permitting, in the small back yard amidst Heather's summer flowers—despite Mary's reluctance to be seen by neighbors in what seemed to her a private activity. And lots of visits from friends, calls from friends. Those who appeared with vehicles were quickly conscripted into providing a lift to the store, or, time permitting, a trip a little further afield to Frontenac Park, with its woods, lakes, and picnic grounds. There, an old blanket was spread, Marmite[26] sandwiches consumed, and the afternoon whiled away—Heather with her watercolor paints and brushes, Mary reading and napping, her face covered by a floppy sunhat, while Murray, suited up in threadbare swim trunks from Cambridge days, paddled about in the nearby lake. Then, amidst exclamations of what a lovely outing it had been, the drive home might conclude with a stop at the local market. There they could retrieve vegetable scraps collected and saved for them, like the tough outside leaves of cabbage that would otherwise be discarded, and purchase what few staples they required. Including, *if* it were on sale, a big carton of ice cream, or even two. Then home to 103 Brant Street, supper, lamp-lighting, night prayers and bed, usually by 8:30.

Heather painting.

There were, naturally, expectations for guests, articulated plainly in a printed letter.[27] It read in part: "Friends who join us . . . are asked to take a full part in our life, following our daily time-table with us. If you have some special need, kindly share about it with one of us; otherwise we expect you to join in our life and work and silence . . ."

---

26. Marmite: the traditional sticky brown vegetarian British spread.
27. See Appendix 9 for complete text of this document.

They were prepared to deal gently but firmly with spiritual freeloaders. Hilarious stories were told of an occasional close encounter with a n'er-do-well. Murray recalled one such learning experience from early India days: "Occasionally absolute varmints floated in, and then somebody sort of removed them, not quite physically, but . . . [laughs] I remember one swami who thought Mary and Heather were his servants. That splendid Indian fellow—Fidah Hussein—he said, '*I'll* look after *him*.' That swami decided God was calling him somewhere else and left before the next meal! He was left with no doubt he'd called at the wrong address! Dear old Fidah—[laughs] Oh, we had endless laughter!"[28]

Though indeed they did laugh, later at least, at the unfortunate swami, their laughter was usually at themselves—at their own naiveté, their own mistakes. "Endless laughter," he repeated before moving to a more existential observation: "Really, we're making such a ridiculous hash of it most of the time, if we take it too seriously, there's something seriously wrong with *us*. It is all so laughable."[29] More and more they could see that laughter was not simple frivolity but was tied up with their deep spiritual desire: to be small and weak. Laughter was reassurance that the ego was not running the show. Murray knew the tenacity of the ego was the biggest spiritual challenge, not least for himself. Often his teachings reflected his own struggles. In a 1992 Greenwich retreat, he remarked: "To be small and weak is a blessed thing to me. To be always that. When we feel strong, or frightfully successful, as we do sometimes, it's a terribly dangerous moment." He continued with a story of a church-goer offering congratulations to the preacher at the door of a church. "'Great sermon!' the church-goer said. To which the preacher thought to himself: 'Strange you should say that. When I came down from the pulpit, the devil said just the same!'"[30] Here was a glimpse, it seems, into his own inner life.

Thus, each morning, as they arose to their daily round, it was to a place of silence they returned, where God might help them notice new attempts of their egos to stay in charge. Only then could their activities begin. As always, Murray remained the face of Jyotiniketan, the gregarious spiritual leader, yet Mary and Heather remained the indispensable second and third legs of the sturdy community stool. Mary's literary gifts continued to link her to an international web of spiritual writers. Her translation from the French of their friend N. Shanta's 789 page *opus* on Jain nuns was complete; it would at last be published in 1997. She had consulted and contributed

---

28. Interview with Trapnell.
29. Ibid.
30. Rogers, audiotape of retreat.

translations to a lovely small volume entitled *Earth Prayers*, edited by Elias Amidon and Elizabeth Roberts, and published in 1991 in the United States.[31] Now she was collaborating with the same editors on *Life Prayers*, who later acknowledged her work: "Thanks to Mary Rogers for blessing this volume with her knowledge of the Vedas . . ."[32] Such achievements were celebrated quietly, within the family, without public fanfare. There was very little ego, it seemed, in her dedication, and she could just as easily quietly commit her time to ironing clothes for Betty, their over-the-fence neighbor, who was overwhelmed with raising six children.

As for Heather, who also could disappear into Murray's large shadow, her contributions were indispensable as well. Heather's niece Elizabeth, expressed it this way: "Where Murray was the visionary and Mary provided the intellectual backing which allowed the community theology to take shape, Heather created the practical space that enabled this life to be and allowed others the space to participate in it." It was the practical space of daily shopping and cooking, though shared by both Mary and Murray, that fell primarily on her shoulders. It was Heather who tended the chapel, gathered fresh flowers for the altar, trimmed the wicks and refilled the camphor so each evening the lamp could again be lighted. As Elizabeth recalled: "Where she couldn't help practically she lifted people up in daily prayer and stillness. The silent worship at Jyotiniketan which so many of us were privileged to share was a still space Heather helped to create. She had a deep listening stillness . . . a part of her being which she fed with regular retreats and pilgrimages . . . But also she sat quietly painting, allowing the beauty of the natural world to flow into and through her. She felt the presence of God in everything. To share her stillness was to become aware of stillness oneself. More than anywhere this was where Heather expressed and shared her love."[33]

From that common source their life continued as an indivisible threesome. No one could miss Heather and Mary's deep sisterly devotion to one another. The special bond between Murray and Heather remained, still tinged with longing. Though their chaste relationship as brother and sister in Christ was unquestioned, their hearts had refused to surrender. It was a reality—seldom spoken of—that even the most astute observer might fail to notice. Their children, of course, *had* noticed and had arrived, if not at peace on the subject, to a reluctant acceptance. Yet in 1990 they all warmly celebrated Mary and Murray's fiftieth wedding anniversary complete with

31. See Appendix 10 for two of her translations.
32. Roberts and Amidon, *Life Prayers*, xviii.
33. Robin, funeral tribute, 2010.

a holiday visit from Cheryl, André, and their three children, Marie-Hélène, Catherine and James. Later that summer they joined in a quiet observance of Murray's fifty years as a priest. There were more Lenten visits to Greenwich, often for all three, partaking in the "storehouse of friendship"[34] that awaited them there. That too was shared.

These early Canada years held two more heart-stirring trips to the East. The first was for Murray alone as he shared in a Retreat-Seminar in Rajpur, India on the mystical traditions of Christianity and Saivism, organized by the Abhishiktananda Society, and led by his close friends Raimon Panikkar and Bettina Bäumer. His official work was to present a paper on Julian of Norwich, entitled "Enclosed in God, the Joyful Surprise of 'One-ing.'"[35] It was a chance to share a spiritual treasure of the West in India and, in the process, to bolster his conviction that *advaita*—union with God—has always been experienced across geographical and religious boundaries. After the seminar, he traveled to Rishikesh with Raimon, nourishing his soul with deep friendship and communion with the land he most loved. Then with another visit back to the original Jyotiniketan on the Ganges Plain where, even without Swami Deenabandu, his hope again was buoyed. "Their life of simplicity and loving work is one of those small things, well out of reach of the media, upon which God builds a new world.[36] There followed a precious month with Minoru Kasai in Japan, culminating a time of renewal with two of the most influential men in his adult life.

The second journey was a visit to Hong Kong for all three in 1993. Though gifts offered for their personal comfort were often declined or simply passed along, travel to reunite with friends or family was a different matter altogether. And though averse to being "jet-setting tourists,"[37] when their dear octogenarian friend in Greenwich, Ellie Parker, gifted them with tickets to the East, they gratefully accepted. It was a monthlong visit, shared with wonderful friends. While Mary and Heather then returned to Canada, Murray again visited Minoru Kasai at the International Christian University in Tokyo where he was woven into student life.

There with Professor Kasai's students, Murray explored the great human question "Who am I?" It was a question the community had raised with its meditation group, with visitors who came for quiet days in Deseronto, with friends from Amnesty International—anyone who would explore

---

34. Letter #30.

35. "Enclosed in God, the Joyful Surprise of 'One-ing,'" published in 1997 in *Mysticism in Shaivism and Christianity*, ed. B. Bäumer.

36. Letter #34.

37. Murray Rogers, letter to Raimon Panikkar, 1993.

with them—along with its corollary: "What does it mean in practice to live a deeply human life?"[38] In his dialogue with Minoru's Japanese students, later published by the Institute of Asian Studies at the University, he asked students to set aside, temporarily, their logic and analysis and come "empty-handed." He told of his own gradual awareness that he was *not* the labels affixed to him—Christian priest, British citizen, son of his father, graduate of whatever school. Nor was his real identity about financial status. He described filling out a sixteen page bank form in Canada with the heading 'Personal Worth.' "All about money, not a word about anything else!" he exclaimed. "My personal worth was my bank balance." In his signature story-telling style, he continued,

> Is that who I am? Is that who you are? No . . . that can't be the answer. But when you hold that conviction, you are disagreeing with the vast majority of people in the so-called developed world, because for them my bank balance is the answer to who I am, who you are. So when, having filled up the form of my "personal worth" I was interviewed [by] a woman official on the other side of the desk, I couldn't resist and I said, "Excuse me, please, but I think you are worth so much more than your bank balance."
>
> She looked at me in amazement and said, "I hadn't ever thought about that."[39]

The talk continued: a vintage encounter with Murray. Drawing on his Buddhist experience, he told the students of special people in *his* life who had led him to understand, as the eastern *namaste* gesture indicates, that a divine mystery . . . a deeper 'being' dwells within each person, beyond what is seen on the outside, beyond what he called "the label level." People like Charles Raven, his Cambridge professor; C.F. Andrews, Gandhi's friend who had touched his soul, also at Cambridge; equally the illiterate Dalit woman they called 'Oldie-Oldie' who, back in Kareli, India, had come daily to sweep. "This old village woman was a real, deep human being. She had never been to school; she couldn't write her own name, but I swear she was a *real* person . . . She knew . . . how to live, how to be." Lastly he mentioned "dear old Swamiji," touching on the essence of their relationship: "Wherever Swamiji was there was much laughter and good humour. Here was a man who took himself lightly, even referring to himself as a clown . . . Yes, he was [a] man who listened; spiritually, humanly, he was a world ahead of me—if I can put it that way—yet never once did he make me feel inferior. Deep

38. Letter #35.
39. Rogers, "Who am I? The human question: one man's pilgrimage," 102.

human beings do not need to be impressive; they spend no time or effort being learned or cultured, in attempting to be a success. To live authentically is enough!"[40]

As Murray, now white-haired and slightly bent in his simple rough cassock, finished his soul-baring, very *un*academic talk to the young, eager university students, there was a pause before the first questioner spoke up. "Thank you very much," the student finally said. "I have listened and I believe that I've understood a little . . . but I have one question that requires an answer, yes or no." He paused, then continued: "May I give you a hug?"

The lively question and answer session ended with a forceful statement from Murray, summing up his message and his own personal call. He said:

> If you and I are training ourselves to see each other in this way . . . we will inevitably lay ourselves open to joy and to suffering, those two experiences that go very closely together. Society will try . . . to persuade us that certain people are more worthy of respect and honour than other people, but we must never give up hope in our attempts to honour and respect each and every one, especially the poor and oppressed, those who are looked down upon and despised. We must not allow ourselves to be deceived; in my experience it is often the rich and successful who are the saddest and most miserable of people . . . We can easily be tempted to be inhuman . . . especially when our countries and societies are rich and powerful . . . Dare we, you and I, no matter what the cost, change our style of life in order that we may say, in word and action, that the human being everywhere is of infinite worth? That is, I think, the challenge that faces us.[41]

It was a challenge that seemed ever more daunting. Perhaps some hope lay in sharing his lifetime experience with the young who would listen.

40. Ibid., 111–112.
41. Ibid., 115–116.

17

Young and Old Together in Canada
1995–1998

It is in the shelter of each other that the people live.

—Irish Proverb

IF HOPE FOR THE world lay in young people unwilling to 'buy into' the world of competition and consumerism, so too, back in Canada, did hope for the aging Jyotiniketan community lie in their friendship with young Kate and Adam Campbell.

Mary, Murray, and Heather first met the newly married couple in 1993. They lived in an apartment in Sydenham, about an hour's drive from Deseronto. Kate worked as a carpenter; Adam was employed by a local Christian group to work with high school students. Hearing of Jyotiniketan through a mutual friend, Adam had asked if he might bring his unchurched "guys' group" to a Maundy Thursday gathering to introduce them to the Easter story. Murray remembered: "I did my best to share about Holy Week and Easter, and . . . to let them see, a little bit, how central it is to the whole of human life, living and dying."[1] Kate and Adam recall that evening: not so much the teaching, but more the students' amazement that Mary, Murray, and Heather were so interested in *them*. Mostly though they recollected their own immediate affinity: "What we were thinking about God and couldn't express, they were speaking and *living!*"[2] Their shared anti-establishment leanings were immediately apparent, as Adam's experience as a novice monk in a Christian community in Uruguay had left him deeply bound to the Eucharist, if not to the established church. Indeed, the attraction was mutual. One of Kate's comments, as remembered by Murray, particularly

1. Interview with Trapnell.
2. Interview with author.

resonated: "Oh, yes," she had said. "I *love* receiving Holy Communion. The rest of it is just chit-chat."³ Kate and Adam, for their part, "fell in love right away." Not only did they find warm curiosity and openness, but they noticed many of their favorite writers on the shelves: Merton, Dostoevsky, Annie Dillard, de Chardin, de Foucauld. Mary, Murray, and Heather themselves were "luminous." But as much as anything else, it was the laughter, lots of laughter, that kept them coming back.⁴ Mary, Murray, and Heather sensed immediately that Kate and Adam were beautifully 'in sync' with their own way of life, not needing, as Murray put it, "talky-talks about anything. They knew," he said, "because they were already wanting to live lightly on the earth."⁵

Regularly, Kate and Adam would hitchhike the distance to Jyotinketan. Warmly welcomed, they would then be handed a little list of jobs: tasks in the garden too heavy for Heather, little fix-it projects. They would join in the liturgies and borrow books. Occasionally they spent the night. Little by little, they grew together in affection and respect, the physical energy of youth meeting the needs of old age; the encouraging wisdom of old age leading the way towards deeper spiritual maturity.

When, after about a year, Kate and Adam suggested they might move nearer, Mary, without a moment's hesitation, pointed at a space in the front yard and exclaimed, "You could live here!"⁶ And so it was that a room was added to the little house by Kate herself, trained at the hand of her architect father, along with an office for Murray and a downstairs bathroom with a shower. In April 1995, Kate and Adam moved in. "It might seem slightly crazy," they wrote to Friends, "for the 20s to live closely with the 70s, but all five of us agree it is fun and also a challenge. We join together in worship and in much else, while continuing to live our own lives . . . All we say so far is 'Thanks be to God.'"⁷ There was flexibility in the arrangement, no lifelong commitment as there had been for Rosmarie. Long gone were their prayers that Jyotinketan might grow, might live beyond them. Kate and Adam were simply a "marvelous couple . . . who paddled straight into our life"—an unexpected "bonus from God."⁸ Their Letter continued: "For how long? We don't ask, for the theory of relativity (which we are struggling to understand almost 100 years too late!) keeps us largely conscious of the present moment. So now we are five!"⁹

3. Interview with Trapnell.
4. Interview with author.
5. Interview with Trapnell.
6. Interview with author.
7. Letter #38.
8. Interview with Trapnell.
9. Letter #38.

Thus their lives became gracefully interwoven. "We were included," Adam wrote, "as much as we wanted to be. We were full-on participants, but with some autonomy." Kate and Adam maintained their outside work, doing farm and gardening jobs, tending animals, sometimes "farm-sitting" for a week. At home they all sat down together for lunch; for breakfast and supper, Kate and Adam usually shared a private meal. Old and young accommodated to one another: the elders gave them the emotional and physical space they needed; Kate learned not to practice her carpentry at nap time! As Adam recalled, "We'd co-ordinate work, their travel, our travel and all visitors to not clash or complicate. [It was] always very amicable."[10] They joined in Jyotiniketan's liturgies with Adam assuming responsibility for the mid-day readings, Kate leading the evening *arati*. They loved the silence and understood its deep importance. Knowing that Jyotiniketan referred to the "uncreated light" within each of them, they embraced it. Silence was, as Adam said, "our chance at photosynthesis."[11] Thus they grew in the shelter of one another.

Adam, Murray, Kate, Mary and Heather, with Jun Yasuda, visiting peace activist.

10. Interview with author.
11. Ibid.

As time passed and strength ebbed from aging bodies, Kate and Adam took on more chores—changing beds, lifting and fixing—in both house and garden. Even before they had arrived, there had been intimations of physical frailty. In Jyotiniketan's 1994 Letter, in the midst of the recounting of lively activities and joyous events, appeared a small announcement: "Murray discovered a couple of months ago that he is living with cancer. If you must have cancer, his type, i.e. of the prostate gland, is the best and slowest kind. We are thankful for two delightful doctors, our western medicine one near here, and our alternative medicine doctor in the States. Our experience with Chinese medicine has certainly marked us! As with everything else, how can we be simply western?! Actually he is extremely fit and the same goes, generally, for Mary and Heather. It is still very good to be alive and we are deeply thankful."[12]

Yes, they were fit, but the years were accumulating: Mary was seventy-eight, Murray seventy-seven, and Heather seventy-one. With each Letter their litany of loved ones passed "to the further shore" grew longer. In 1991, they had grieved the loss of Swami Deenabandu, Murray's successor at Jyotiniketan in India—"a shining example of love and Franciscan life." In 1992, while they were again visiting Greenwich, Murray's older sister Olive died, tended in her final days by Linda in England. And when in 1994, their beloved friend Ellie Parker passed to that further shore, Murray quickly departed for Greenwich to share in the joyful celebration of her life. In 1995 came the news their friend and neighbor from Jerusalem, Henry Selz, a recent visitor in Deseronto, had been killed in an automobile accident. Though the immanence of mortality touched them all, for Mary it intensified more than ever her longing to be with her children and grandchildren. At times the pain seemed more than she could bear, but with stalwart spirit, she awaited the next visit.

These visits now claimed higher priority. While in years past, news of extended family trips were often but a footnote in their Letters, now it was special news, marked with exclamation points. And well they might exclaim of a family Christmas in England—the first in thirty-eight years! But there they were in 1993, gathered round a table of eighteen with Linda and March, Richard and Alice, and a troop of children for Christmas dinner. While Heather celebrated with her family in Scotland, they traveled on to France for time with Cheryl and André and their family, including a two day trip to Brittany where André's widowed mother now lived. Then, incorporating Jyotiniketan family as well, Heather joined them to travel to Switzerland for time with Rosmarie and Vroni, their old friend and now landlady.

---

12. Letter #37.

But a dark cloud hovered over their time with Rosmarie. Having cared for her mother until her death, Rosmarie's darkness remained. Month after month, year after year, she remained engulfed in despair, feeling abandoned by God and by any sense of self-worth. Sheltered for a time in a psychiatric clinic, Rosmarie's diagnosis of cancer had only added to her sense that she was possessed by dark forces. Her dear friend Vroni was mystified: "What happened to Rosmarie is a great mystery for me."[13] When in her darkest days Murray flew to Switzerland to visit, Vroni recalls the light in Rosmarie's eyes, the sense that perhaps she was accepted. But Murray too was stymied and deeply saddened by her illness. Her name had quietly disappeared as a signer of their Letter to Friends. It was clear she would never return to the community, yet she remained a part of their spiritual family. Their life continued without her.

With Murray's involvement in interfaith dialogue now lessened and their family life firmly anchored in the West, they had never imagined they would see India again. When they did, it seemed almost a dream. "Did it really happen? We sometimes wonder," they wrote to Friends in 1996. The journey of nearly four months in 1995 for the three of them came as an unexpected gift, money bequeathed to them for that purpose by their devoted Greenwich friend, Ellie Parker. There were no meetings to attend, no sermons to preach, no papers to write. It was a marvelous gift, but one that gave them pause. Could they simply go for their own pleasure, like tourists? They were persuaded. "We already knew from first-hand experience the terrible power and danger of tourism to the poor, [yet] here we were leaving Toronto . . . to go round the world, certainly not feeling like tourists!"[14]

It was, as they said, "an endless feast of friendship"[15] to savor for their remaining years. There was more family time in Europe, visits to communities and friends throughout Europe, more friends in India, Hong Kong, and Vancouver. In Pokhara and Kathmandu, Nepal, and then in Delhi, they experienced a happy role-reversal, as Linda, along with Cheryl, led them to Tibetan friends and shared her work with Help Tibet, a small British nonprofit organization dedicated to self-sustainability for Tibetan refugees. Here was the little girl who had loved the mountains, now in her fifties, back in the Himalayas. And though Linda *hadn't* loved the discomforts of life in Kareli, a deep connection with the poor and displaced had seeped into her pores. Surely Mary and Murray could see within their own family visible hope for the world. Though all of their three children had cho-

---

13. Veronica Thurneysen, phone conversation with author, 2013.
14. Letter #39.
15. Ibid.

sen more conventional lives than theirs, traveling with them they caught "glimpses of awareness and consciousness, goodness and life, compassion and humanity."[16] Did it matter that none of them had patterned their life after theirs? Had they disappointed their parents? These were questions that sometimes crossed the minds of the younger generation.

Mary, Murray and Heather's journey continued on, as they wrote, for "an encounter with the heart of India [where we] contemplated the river above Rishikesh and scattered the ashes of our good friend Henry Selz in the Ganga, the overflowing grace of God, which takes us all to the ocean of his love." Then on they went to dwell in quiet and silence with their friend, the renowned scholar, Bettina Bäumer. Tucked away in her *kutiya* in the Himalayan foothills, they again found "just under the surface of India, with all its chaos and destitution, spiritual riches and experience which make it one of the richest of all human families."[17] Best of all, it wasn't a dream.

Back in their little house in Deseronto, Kate and Adam—their Canadian family—were there to welcome them home. Kate and Adam had missed them, though, admittedly, they had enjoyed 'sleeping in,' skipping the chilly pre-dawn silence in the chapel for their own prayers later in the day!

Their daily life, which they characterized as "full of nothing in particular but taking all our time"[18] was, for Kate and Adam, wonderfully full. Now resumed were the meditation group gatherings, studies of Lao Tzu's *Hua Hu Ching*, and trips to the Mohawk Library. And of course there were visitors, from far and wide or from just down the street. Kate and Adam's visitors equally were included. By now they knew almost everyone in town, at least by sight. A regular and always welcome face was that of Ruby Kells, a woman of First Nation heritage, mother of eight grown children, whose husband had been stricken with early Alzheimers. Now caring for him as well as a brain-injured son, she found moments of refuge at Jyotiniketan. She said, "They were there for me," offering reassurance, listening ears, and at times a small check. Often she would come just to listen. "I found such peace there,"[19] she added.

Family came too. Richard, however skeptical of his parents' choices and lifestyle, arrived with Alice and their children Miranda and Murray, now teenagers; so did Linda and her daughter Victoria. There too were Heather's step-brother Godfrey and his wife Honor Meynell and Mary's older sister Marjorie, just in time to celebrate Marjorie's eightieth birthday.

16. Ibid.
17. Ibid.
18. Ibid.
19. Interview with author.

Spiritual family members also made the journey. Mary, Murray, and Heather were thrilled when their Jerusalem neighbor and dumpster-diving cohort John Landgraf hitchhiked hundreds of miles across Canada to see them.[20] Minoru Kasai was welcomed again and again. And when Bo and Sita Lozoff of the Prison-Ashram Project came to visit, Murray had arranged visits at several local prisons where Bo was welcomed to share his inspiring talks and practice with Canadian convicts. All guests were made to feel special, yet Swami Nityananda Giri's[21] visit from the Thapovanam Ashram near Arunachala, India, deserved particular mention. His life, like Murray's, had been entwined with Abhishiktananda. Kate and Adam treasure the memory of Swami Nityananda and Murray sitting cross-legged holding hands, trading Swamiji stories. He was the "real deal," a man of such depth, they said. And they were "willing sponges" for the wonderful dialogue.[22]

Bishop Mar Chrystostom, senior bishop of the Mar Thoma Church of India and their old friend from Hindu-Christian dialogue days, regularly capped his annual pastoral visit to his Indian-Canadian flock centered in Toronto with a few days of spiritual camaraderie in Deseronto. Known as the "bishop with the golden tongue," conversation was lively and laughter-filled. Needless to say, Jyotiniketan was not a place where august titles were reason for kowtowing. Friends were simply friends. Ruby Kells remembers her repartee with him as they discussed the questionable legacy of Christopher Columbus for North America and especially, of course, for the Native populations. Learning she was of First Nation heritage, he quipped, "So *you're* one of those Columbus found when he landed in America!"

"Yes, indeed," Ruby responded, seldom at a loss for words, "And *you're* one of those he was looking for!"[23]

And how they all laughed, tears running down their cheeks, recalling an episode from long ago in India. Mar Chrystostom had been staying at their little ashram in Kareli, occupying a small room next to Murray and Mary's. The Bishop, whose spiritual practice included the yogic pose of standing on his head [*sirsha-asana*], was practicing alone in his room, stark naked as was his wont. Suddenly the flimsy wall against which he was leaning gave way, and there he was, just as he was, all jumbled up with them on their string beds!

---

20. Letter #36.

21. (1929-) A disciple of Gnanananda and yoga scholar, he is a frequent participant in inter-faith dialogues throughout the world.

22. Interview with author.

23. Ibid.

Kate and Adam loved being a part of community life. As Adam wrote. "I loved seeing them weep with mirth at the same old anecdotes, as well as new ones," laughing at their own foibles—Mary's habit of dissolving into giggles during certain solemn readings; Murray's tendency to doze off in meditation, betrayed by his nodding head with what they all came to teasingly call "the spiral and the jerk!" They absorbed what they called Jyotiniketan's "pragmatic mysticism—faith as a practical thing." As Adam reflected, "They supported and fostered our desire for a simple life; without debt, off-grid, somewhat self-sufficient and artistic in expression." With them there were "always new ways to look at old ways." Their faith was embodied in their hospitality, in their curiosity, in Murray's utter lack of fundamentalism, in Heather's special gift of listening, in Mary's learnedness and devotion, in their openness to the Spirit. Never to be forgotten was the Easter morning when they set out on foot together just before dawn to celebrate the Resurrection on Lake Ontario's nearby Bay of Quinte. Suddenly, they were caught up in what seemed a moment of mystical congruence. Looking east at the end of the street was the rising sun; looking west at the other end of the street was the setting full moon. For some moments, time stood still and they did too, "lost in wonder, love and praise.[24]" Proceeding to the shore for a contemplative reading of John Chrystostom's Easter Sermon, they shared his immortal words from the fifth century,[25] excerpted here:

> Are there any who are devout lovers of God?
>
> Let them enjoy this beautiful bright festival! . . .
>
> Let no one grieve at his poverty,
>
> for the universal kingdom has been revealed . . .
>
> Let no one mourn that he has fallen again and again;
>
> for forgiveness has risen from the grave . . .
>
> Let no one fear death, for the Death of our Savior has set us free . . . [26]

These were words that resonated: the universal kingdom, forgiveness, and facing death without fear.

If spiritual growth was happening for Kate and Adam, it is also true that for Mary, Murray, and Heather, their young friends brought them the spirit of Easter, of new life and hope. They marveled at their skills with their hands, their adaptability, their determination to live simply, their refusal to buy into

---

24. Quoted from John Wesley's words, immortalized in the hymn "Love Divine, All Loves Excelling."

25. Adam Campbell, Skype interview and written reflection, 2011.

26. http://anglicansonline.org/special/Easter/chrysostom_easter.html

conventional comforts. They treasured their honesty and authenticity. Just as Adam spoke of their "practical mysticism," so Murray observed, mirror-like: "They wanted to live out how God came through everything—the spiritual and the material were part of one another."[27] In Adam's recent words, "I hope we infused some youthful vigour, and encouraged them to know that their Gandhian way was successfully transmitted to a new generation."[28] That cannot be doubted. From Murray's perspective, their participation in Jyotiniketan could be explained only as God's great kindness.

Though Kate and Adam were an icon of hope, their presence did little to assuage Murray's growing despair for the world. Mary and Heather, of course, shared his outlook, but it was he who found it more and more difficult to parse his words with diplomacy. Increasingly their Letters were marked by a sense of desperation at the injustices they saw—the suffering inflicted by the rich and powerful on the poor and weak. The trend seemed to permeate not only secular life but religious affairs and institutions as well, and they registered their consternation with letters to leaders, protests, and marches and ever more outspoken verbal witness. They inveighed against certain corporations, practices of the World Bank, continued militarization, and the threat of consumerism. "Are you ever 'driven round the bend,' as we are," they wrote, "by the sad and dreadful situations prevailing in our beautiful and crazy world—*our* in the true sense, the *our* which accepts that we humans are one part of the creation, of the trees and water and sky and earth?"[29] Having painstakingly made the human family their own, now they could not turn away from the pain of its members. With time slipping through their fingers, their own pain increased with each new report of racism and injustice. Whether for the plight of refugees in Britain, Chinese villagers displaced by the building of the Three Gorges Dam, or oppressed Tibetans, they grieved. "Do [these people] mean nothing to us? Are we not all relatives?" they asked. "But who cares? Who objects? Seemingly, sad to say, very, very few."[30]

Nor did the organized church seem to offer hope. They wrote with sadness and more than a hint of bitterness: "At such a time how wonderful if there were a church really being Church! Where is it, we wonder? The narrowing of the churches' vision, concerned primarily for keeping themselves in existence, leads either to spiritual totalitarianism or to a predominant concern for money to maintain structures and clergy salaries. This vanishing

27. Interview with Trapnell.
28. Adam Campbell, reflection, 2011.
29. Letter #37.
30. Letter #38.

credibility for the churches and the trivialization of Jesus and the Gospel leaves us knowing at least where not at the moment to look for hope."[31]

Yet at the same time, there *was* hope they could not overlook. There was hope in Murray's collaboration with his friend Bill Lawlor, a professor of education at McGill University in Montreal. Just as he had done with his friend Minoru Kasai in Tokyo, Murray would visit Bill's classroom and interact with the students. "With the decline in universities so frequently into technical and business schools, it is remarkable to find students and staff ready to face issues of life and death and all set to 'cut off third leg of chicken!'"[32] he exclaimed. Bill's way of teaching inspired him. There was hope in many friends, who kept coming and writing.

But reminders of time slipping away were ever present. In 1997 word came that Raimon Panikkar had suffered a heart attack. Murray typed a letter to him—his friend, spiritual director, and teacher—transcending, at least in those moments, the tensions between hope and despair, sickness and health, moving and staying still, sorrow and joy, life and death. After some warm reminiscing, he wrote: "We were sorry indeed to hear that you had an infarct which has brought near for you the time of less moving and less talking, but how wonderful that you can now share your silent and invisible monastery with us all."

He continued, reflecting on his own vulnerability: "This news of cancer has been a blessing in that I was, and am, very much reminded of my mortality, of the impermanence of everybody and everything except the Eternal, and what a blessed freedom to begin to accept a little more deeply that truth of who I am! As with you, no doubt, we begin to be rather antique, but that is a bonus also in many ways."

Murray, it seemed, was glimpsing the unity beneath everything, allowing him a sense of peace and acceptance. He ended his letter with these words, a paean to their friendship: "It would be a beautiful moment if we were allowed to meet again, in our elderly bodies, but, of course, truly and deeply, we never un-meet! The Great Oneness has swallowed up time and space—on both sides of the great Ganga, on both shores ... Still God knows how good we would find it, to see you again, 'for from joy all beings have come, by joy they all live, and unto joy they all return.' (*Taittiriya Up.*) In that joy, with love, Murray"

Ironically, within weeks, Mary was penning another letter to Raimon with this news: "And now I must tell you a strange thing, a bit of a shock to us, as you can imagine, and very unexpected. Murray also had a small heart

---

31. Ibid.
32. Letter #40.

attack... just after Easter. He had to go into hospital—a friendly and caring small hospital in Napanee—for three or four days. He says he now feels very well... and we hope and pray he will continue that way. We are endeavoring to help him 'go slow' (not very easy!) and he is hoping very much to attend a conference of Sabeel [Palestinian Liberation Theology] in June along with our young friend Adam."

Despite the whiff of denial in Mary's words, she was correct in saying it was not easy to slow Murray down. As anticipated, he and Adam left Deseronto on schedule for the Sabeel Conference in Washington, D.C. More than almost any other concern, the ongoing Palestinian-Israeli conflict could trigger Murray's deepest despair, throwing him back into an unhappy dualistic state of no hope. Yet, to their surprise, the joy of meeting old Jerusalem friends—Elias Chacour, Jean Zaru, and Naim Ateek—all dedicated to the struggle for justice and peace, brought fresh inspiration. And, for Adam, to be at Murray's side as he engaged, no holds barred, in discussions where his still strong heart felt such passion, was an unforgettable experience.

This, in a sense, was "Real Church" for Murray and Adam. They, and the others, were moved by those who truly *lived* their faith in action. It was "Real Church" too that Murray discovered a few months later as he attended an international gathering in Thailand on "Alternatives to Consumerism," called by the Buddhist activist Sulak Sivaraksa. Their Letter reported: "As a member of the minority of westerners among a big majority of Asian friends, Murray came home full of hope for a more just and human world ... The way we lived together in those weeks, Murray sleeping in a 'glot'[33] on the ground among the trees, was an essential part of an unforgettable experience"[34] Here again were glimpses of oneness.

This then had become their *credo*: that contemplation and action needed to be a seamless garment, that beneath human divisions was deep unity. Their Letters to Friends in 1997 and 1998, couched in homely details, tried to make this clear. Their 1997 Letter began, "Earlier today when the five of us met in the chapel at 5:30 am. it was the prologue to the *Granth Sahib*[35] of the Sikhs that led us into silence: 'At the fragrant hour of early dawn, hold yourself in communion with the Divine Word and meditate on his glory. Only by his grace do we find salvation. Recognise the indwelling presence of the One Reality in all things.' Isn't it that Supreme Oneness, by

---

33. In the Thai forest tradition of Buddhism, a glot is a shelter for sleeping. Constructed somewhat like an umbrella of fabric similar to the monk's robes, it can be folded and carried during the day.

34. Letter #41.

35. *Granth Sahib:* Holy Scriptures of the Sikh religion.

whatever Name, which constitutes the path to justice and peace, if only we leave behind our lesser loyalties of race and class and religion . . . ?"[36]

Hope, they said, was to be found in small communities of people everywhere "discovering alternative ways of living their vision with joy and thankfulness." Of their own small community, they wrote, "Our hope and desire is to live beyond competition in a compassionate, responsible and sharing globalisation of human society, which for us the Kingdom of God is all about."[37] Longing to transmit their insights, they wove their inchoate spiritual awakenings from Sevagram so many years before—only very partially digested at the time—into their most recent learning from the Native American tradition, which itself seemed to vibrate with insights of their beloved St. Francis. It was all coming together. "We want to wake up more and more to sharing this universe as brothers and sisters of all, and that includes the earth and animals, trees and seas and sky," they wrote. "Some call it 'deep ecology.'"[38] Their own lack of worldly power came with the territory: "Only those with the power of the powerless, the sort that springs from weakness, will be able to free [the poor and the oppressed] everywhere." But their spiritual struggle continued; being powerless did not come easily. "Endeavoring to follow Mahatma Gandhi's way of simplicity was somewhat tough, though immensely worthwhile, in India; in the rich and comfortable west it is far more difficult." For that reason they turned, again and again, when despair darkened their doorway, to India: "India, our early love, still gives us enormous hope and strength. In spite of rampant corruption and the deep wound she has suffered from westernisation and from material 'achievements' she still guards and treasures a spiritual wisdom and practice which one day the West will, we believe, be thankful to share. When our materialistic 'civilization' comes nearer to destroying itself and the world, then perhaps we will be ready to learn from India's spiritual civilisation. We long for that moment."[39]

But there was no reason to wait: "The choice is open to each of us: either we bring our planet, by our greedy way of life, by our silence and indifference, nearer to destruction *or* we take our responsibility and dare to go what is sometimes called the "Integral Way,"[40] the way of simplicity

---

36. Letter #40.

37. Ibid.

38. Deep ecology is a term first used by Arne Naess, a Norwegian philosopher, in 1973.

39. Ibid.

40. The integral way is a Taoist-inspired way of being.

and compassion lived before us by Jesus, Buddha, Chuang Tzu and those of every age who have lived the Wisdom Way."[41]

And what was the "Integral Way?" Murray was delving into the writings of Ken Wilbur, the American philosopher who drew him back to the ancient wisdom of the East, back to the transcending of opposites, back to *advaita*. As he struggled with the "opposites" in his own being—despair and hope, life and death, East and West—Wilbur's words resonated: "In all the mystical traditions the world over, one who sees through the illusion of the opposites is called "liberated." Because he is "freed from the pairs" of opposites . . . he no longer manipulates the opposites one against the other in his search for peace, but instead transcends them both. Not good vs. evil but beyond good and evil. Not life against death but a center of awareness that transcends both. The point is not to separate the opposites and make "positive progress," but rather to unify and harmonize the opposites, both positive and negative, by discovering a ground which transcends and encompasses them both."[42] Wilbur quotes from the *Bhagavad Gita*, the Gospel of St. Thomas, the *Lankavatara Sutra* of Mahayana Buddhism, and Lao Tsu, all pointing to the truth he calls "not-two-ness" or *advaita:* that opposites are "only different aspects of the same thing."

Intimations of that "supreme oneness," never to be grasped, drew them on, even as they struggled with their own dualities.

Regarding life and death, it was hard not to prefer life. But certainly, with so many friends on "the further shore," they no longer seemed opposites. And the leavening of laughter could help bridge whatever gap remained. Death was growing nearer, this was clear. And though their decision that Kate would build a sturdy wooden coffin for whoever was the first to need it was serious, moments of mirth proceeded from the project. Before beginning the project, she measured Murray, as if for a new suit of clothes, to be sure he would fit. Once completed, they all gathered to admire her handiwork. Spontaneously, one by one, they climbed inside, checking the dimensions, the sturdiness and the view. Only when Adam, the tallest of the group, got in it did they see there was a problem: his legs were too long. But pragmatism prevailed, as one of them said, adding a bit of comic relief: "If Adam dies first, someone will have to bend his knees!"[43]

So would they die in Canada? To die in India had been their dream, not to die in Canada. But, with both Mary and Murray past eighty, perhaps that would happen. Murray seemed willing to lie in the Canadian coffin.

41. Letter #41.
42. Wilbur, *No Boundary,* 27–28.
43. Kate and Adam Campbell, interview and reflection.

Heather, for her part, had settled into life in Canada and had no particular desire to end her life anywhere else, save, of course, in her beloved India. What about England? Though rich with family and friends, it was also the place Murray wanted, spiritually at least, to leave behind, with its heavy legacy of history, tradition, and western mindset. No longer did he belong there. With regard to England, "supreme oneness" was elusive for Murray. As usual, Mary seemed willing to follow Murray's desires. And as usual, she masterfully hid the depth of her pain at being separated from her children and grandchildren and from England, the land where much of her heart remained.

It was Christmas Eve in Deseronto when her emotional dam broke. Daughter Cheryl had thoughtfully sent a tape of traditional Christmas music, sung by the choir of King's College, Cambridge. Gathered in their little chapel, wrapped in blankets and shawls against the chill of the winter night, awaiting the perennial new birth, they listened together. Suddenly Mary began to sob uncontrollably. And in Murray a depth of compassion he had never before experienced for her arose, as another stubborn piece of his ego fell away. No longer could he ignore the suffering right beside him.

There is a traditional Native American prayer Murray had shared at retreats, a favorite of the community. Now perhaps its power had touched his own soul. It reads:

> O Great Spirit
>
> Whose voice I hear in the winds, and whose breath gives life to all the world,
>
> hear me! I am small and weak, I need your strength and wisdom.
>
> Let me walk in beauty, and make my eyes ever behold the red and purple sunset.
>
> Make my hands respect the things you have made and my ears sharp to hear your voice.
>
> Make me wise so that I may understand the things you have taught my people.
>
> Let me learn the lessons you have hidden in every leaf and rock.
>
> I seek strength, not to be greater than my brother, but to fight my greatest enemy—myself.
>
> Make me always ready to come to you with clean hands and straight eyes.

So when life fades, as the fading sunset, my spirit may come to you without shame.[44]

Ever since they met as young Cambridge students, Mary had followed him. Now, at last, he would follow her back to England.

Mary and Murray, passing the peace, late '90s.

---

44. Roberts and Amidon, *Earth Prayers*, 188.

18

Complete Circle to England: "A Losing Victory"[1] 1998–2006

> With the help of the *Adityas*, the powers of my life,
> let my evening offering last until the end of a long life;
> and may not my sacrifice perish
> whilst the gods of light are the powers of my life.
>
> —Chandogya Upanisad 3:16

As in the past, this new transition was marked by the confluence of loss and a serendipitous invitation. First the loss. Just after the New Year 2007, word came from Switzerland that their treasured sister, the sensitive and devoted Rosmarie, who had shared their life for twelve years in Jerusalem and Hong Kong, had died at sixty-one. From the clinic where she had been treated, she had been able to move into an apartment with Vroni. Her sense of God's presence had returned. Though her cancer remained, the spiritual and emotional pain had abated and her creativity had bubbled anew. Together, she and Vroni had conspired in a surprise gift to celebrate Murray's eightieth birthday—three tickets for travel to Europe. And just two days before her death, she had written a new melody for Jyotiniketan's chapel worship. Mary, Murray, and Heather marked her "journey into Light" with a warm tribute: "These last months she was wonderfully free from her depression

---

1. "Losing victory": a phrase used by Mary in reference to a friend dying of cancer in 1972.

and she crossed to the further shore in great peace and contentment. May the same blessing come our way also!"[2]

As for the invitation, it had come from Michael Taylor, a Hong Kong friend and retired school principal, on the very day of Rosmarie's death. Would they, he wondered, consider sharing his house in the small village of Burgh on Bain in Lincolnshire? His wife had recently died, and he could offer space at a rate their pensions could afford.

Rosmarie and Vroni's birthday tribute to Murray ("What a gift!" they exclaimed.) had given them the chance to both grieve her loss and to experience her spiritual presence in a marvelous trip with Vroni to Switzerland, Italy, and France. Then in England, they had visited Michael Taylor at his Wold Cottage. Though there were aspects of the place that were not ideal, it was England, and that was where they had determined to be.

Even for them, this change had come as "a big surprise." In a letter to a few friends, they had written: "After a lot of pondering and prayer and consultation with the families, . . . we have decided 'yes,' trusting that we are doing the will of the Spirit. True, in our lives we are used to changes and moves but each one affects the heart very much as well as being an upheaval. We will miss very many friends and very much that has come our way during these just over nine years in Canada. It will be hard to go, however good it will be to complete the circle and return to live (and die!) in England for the first time since 1946. It surely will be a considerable change."

With heavy hearts, Kate and Adam had decided to stay in Canada. But they escorted them to Burgh on Bain, lugging all their worldly belongings up the long flight of stairs to their second floor flat. Safely arrived were the battered suitcases and old tin trunks that had gone with them to Sevagram, Kareli, Jerusalem, Hong Kong, and Canada and which would soon morph, as they always did, into pieces of furniture, draped with Indian textiles.

It was a small place, with little room for guests. The village, population c.100, boasted a combined bakery shop/post office and a picturesque old church. The cathedral town of Lincoln was a twenty minute bus ride away, London three and a half hours. As Mary cheerfully wrote in her clear, steady hand, "It's a very countrified area with small rolling hills (or 'wolds'). We of course miss our friends a lot, though the people around here seem very friendly."

But in Murray's more candid moments, he repeated the word "upheaval." England didn't really feel like home. Though they had always remained British, they were Britons of another era. Not having stayed abreast of

---

2. Letter #41.

contemporary culture for more than fifty years, they were returning to their native land like a crusty time capsule. It was, as he said, "a new/old world."

If not home, Burgh on Bain served as a stepping-stone from which they could satisfy their various yearnings for family. The Christmas holidays, last observed with brimming tears in the cold Canadian winter, became a sumptuous feast of family. While Heather joined her sister Armine and her nieces, Murray and Mary headed south to London. There the family converged for celebrations with Linda and March, Richard and Alice, and Cheryl and André ("the French," as they fondly called them), various grandchildren, and even a couple of fiancés of their granddaughters. Mary's older sister, Marjorie, still spritely in her mid-eighties, was there as well. And on Christmas Eve, the music was live—Mozart at the Royal Albert Hall. If Mary shed tears, they were of relief and joy.

Yearnings for spiritual family were fulfilled as well. Murray's longing to reunite with Raimon, so poignantly expressed in his letter from Canada ("It would be a beautiful moment if we were allowed to meet again, in our elderly bodies. . .") was next. Again, it was their faithful almost-sister Vroni, still living in Switzerland, who was their companion and driver for a weekend visit to Raimon's home in Tavertet, Spain. Their reunion with their old friend, their teacher, and spiritual director was all they had hoped: eucharist in the deepest sense. "Glorious" was Murray's word.

But if their return to England might have seemed a time to bask in family, their identity as "a community of resistance" was alive and kicking, especially in Murray. Like smoldering coals, his sense of outrage at the world's injustice could be instantly inflamed by a disheartening headline or dismal news from the BBC. It was fanned by his sense of time running out.

Some friends in Greenwich, Conn., noticed the shift. They had come to know Murray as the warmly engaging preacher and teacher who touched their souls with stories and humor. Yes, he challenged them and certainly he was countercultural, with his sandals and ascetic life-style. But his way was inviting, his focus on matters of the heart and soul. He brought alive the experience of community, the power of Eucharistic transformation, of prayer and self-giving love. Many remembered the gentle yet powerful Maundy Thursday sermon he had preached in 1996—an earthy meditation on bread. His critique to well-heeled listeners of a world where millions go hungry had been firm but non-confrontive. An excerpt follows:

> Real Church is a loaf of bread. We're the grains, ground up, which isn't altogether comfortable. God kneads us together— and those of you who make bread know just how to do it—God kneads us together that we be one loaf, and of course loaves of bread are made to be shared. And Real Church is where the folk are gathered, where we share our stories, and where we break

the bread. It's all so simple, so deep, and God's the wizard that makes it just that... We're somehow made to be nutrition—for each other... That's the judgment on our economic systems. But we've so arranged things that bread is for some people and less for other people. Some people have more than they need and other people are hunting for bread in garbage dumps. That can't be God's way. That can't be the church's way. Not *Real* Church. No, we're created to share ourselves with each other as nutrition for each other... Jesus invites us. "Will you let your grain be like my grain," he says, "to feed, to be nutrition for a hungry world"?[3]

His images evoked a warm communal table.

Murray celebrating the Eucharist.

3. Transcribed from audiotape. For complete text of this sermon, see Appendix 11.

But by 1999, when he paid a final visit—of nearly a dozen—to Greenwich, he could no longer contain his frustration. The time for patient invitation was past. Fully aware that many of the pews were filled with people wielding significant financial and political power, he preached a fiery Pentecost sermon. "Face it, Friends." he said, his voice crackling with urgency. "We have brought our human society to the brink of an enormous disaster. We don't know how it will happen, but we are near to the total destruction . . . of western civilization." Reciting a litany of injustices, rambling at times, he laid his views squarely on the table. Our system, he said, is built on greed. It is "a system of wealth for the wealthy and greater and greater poverty for the poor and hungry. We still kid ourselves. Our societies are full of lies and deceptions, from the top to the bottom. Much more at the top than the bottom. We deceive one another and we deceive ourselves by pretending that we do things for the good of people, when in fact, we do things for the good of our *own* wealth, our *own* income, our *own* bank balance."

He confronted his Greenwich friends with hard questions: "We believers. . .say we depend on the Eternal. We *say* that, but when it comes to the crunch, do we depend on what *Jesus* says to us *more* than we depend on our bank balances? *More* than we depend on being successful? *More* than we depend on people liking us? I just ask. I shiver to answer myself . . . I only hope to God that there's time to repent before we make a greater hell for the poor than we've made already."[4]

This was not a Murray many had seen before. He was angry. His voice rose and fell, shaking at times, growling, words tumbling out. No longer was he able or willing to soft-pedal the truth as he saw it. Aware that he was speaking directly to power, his inner prophet emerged as he loudly called for "the gift of repentance": "*Repent. Change* our attitudes. *Change* our way of life. *Change* the way we see people. Remember Pentecost. Remember what God says about his dear children at Pentecost: that they have a dignity beyond anything we can imagine because God himself dwells in them. How *is* it that we can make such a mess of this world?

"Repentance is the blessed way forward. Are we ready to grieve? *I wonder*. I notice that many of our predecessors as Christians grieved far more than we do. They seemed to take it excessively. They wept for their sins. Have *I* ever wept for mine? Have *you*? Have we really *felt* the enormity of what we do to God and his precious creation?"[5]

---

4. Transcribed from audiotape.
5. Ibid.

There was stunned silence. Was he a prophet, speaking a terrifying truth, or merely an old man, out of touch with real life, wading into deep waters where he simply didn't belong?

He closed with one more challenging question and an acknowledgement of the discomfort in which he was leaving them: "How ready, how firm is our resolve to follow Jesus? The answer to that question will go out and out all over. Pentecost brings us face to face, joyfully and profoundly uncomfortably, it seems to me, to who we are in the love of God today and tomorrow. Amen."[6]

It was not a comfortable good-bye to the people and place he had grown to love. But it was a good-bye.

Back in England, life was quiet but not quiescent. Burgh on Bain was a place from which Murray could connect, by telephone and by bus, and, as *we* might say, network with old friends and colleagues. But the flat in Lincolnshire was isolated. The winter months brought few visitors aside from immediate family. On one occasion Murray slipped and fell outside, twisting his ankle. Unable to get up, he called for help for what seemed a very long time before he was heard.

Thus in the spring of 2000, friends around the world received another letter—a harbinger of more last things: "We find your faithful friendship wonderful. Even after 41 letters, ever since our first in 1951, so many of you still follow us along with your caring thoughts and we are immensely grateful; we feel that No. 42 may be the last! Not the last personal letter, but the last printed one."[7]

Then came the main news of this final epistle: "We have now spent some 16 months in this village of Burgh on Bain in Lincolnshire, enriched enormously by the friendship and kindness of Michael Taylor in whose house we have lived, and by other friends in the area. This is now drawing to an end. Mary and Murray's "children"—now all three over 50!—sweetly wish us to be nearer to them and we certainly agree. The one village shop-cum post office closed on 1 January, and the stairs begin to be a challenge!"

And where would they go? Yet again, Murray's contacts had paid off. While they were living in Canada, Robert Runcie, then Archbishop of Canterbury had suggested to Sister Frances Dominica Ritchie of All Saints Sisters of the Poor in Oxford that she and Murray meet. She would be visiting Canada and the Archbishop thought she and Murray would enjoy one another's company. And indeed they did. She was a dynamic woman. Born in Scotland and trained as a nurse, she had joined the Anglican order

6. Ibid.
7. Letter #42.

located in Oxford as a young woman and by thirty-five had been named Mother Superior. Murray was taken by her story—her adoption of a tiny African orphan to raise as a single mother, her founding of Britain's first hospice for terminally ill children. Called Helen House, it was located on the grounds of All Saints Convent just off Cowley Road in East Oxford, and it was where Sister Frances Dominica continued her ministry to seriously ill children and their families. In the shadow of the big stone convent was St. Andrew's Lodge, a modest bungalow where her elderly parents had lived. Now both had moved next door to St. John's Home, where nursing care was provided by the order. Thus the sisters were wondering and praying what sort of people might be suitable to occupy the little dwelling in their midst. Just about that time Murray had called from Lincolnshire to see if Sister Frances Dominica might know of any places for them. Thus it was that the two praying communities—one with a need and one with a space to fill—connected, and it was soon decided: St. Andrew's Lodge would be their new home.

The door to Jyotiniketan, Oxford.

Ready and waiting with two small bedrooms, space for a living room/chapel and roomy office and cozy eat-in kitchen, and absolutely NO steps, St. Andrew's Lodge seemed another miracle come to pass. "Yet another of these wonders that leaves us spontaneously saying, 'Wow!'" they wrote in delight.

Spring was in full bloom when they arrived in Oxford in May 2000. Their spirits, too, seemed as young as the fresh green shoots. For a few short weeks, they settled into their new abode, meeting the Sisters of All Saints Convent and other neighbors, discovering the little shops of Cowley Road, finding bucolic walks along the Thames and the nearby Oxford Canal.

And despite their elderly bodies, weary from yet another move, there were invitations from America that beckoned. For nearly a year Murray had been in transatlantic correspondence with a young engaged couple,[8] agreeing to the "job-joy," as he said, of officiating at their wedding on a Maine island. And Maine was not so far from Nova Scotia, where Kate and Adam had resettled. Thus, at the end of June, barely unpacked, off they flew to Halifax. It was a joyous reunion for all young and old alike in the cozy off-the-grid house lovingly constructed by Kate's skilled hands. For Mary and Heather, it was a full month of time to relax and just *be*—together. Prayer happened, yes, but only once a day! Heather, ever-faithful steward of the Jyotiniketan kitchen, was off duty, delighted to leave all the cooking to Kate and Adam.

The month in Nova Scotia—pure blissful holiday for Mary and Heather—was happily multi-faceted for Murray, who flew off alone to tend to his wedding responsibilities. Arriving in Maine, he was primed not only for the job, but to share fully in the joy. Managing the next-to-impossible, he gently corralled the anxious bride and groom on their wedding day for some early morning silence. Inviting them and others gathered to set aside the frenetic preparations, however briefly, he offered the meditative "Salutation to the Dawn": "Look well to this day, for it is life, the very life of life."[9] And then, reveling in the festivities, his extroverted *joie de vivre* set free, he was as irrepressible ever. *Of course* he would go cruising on that old two-masted schooner with the wedding party! Never mind about that required siesta!

Even a potential disaster became fodder for another hilarious story. As the celebration following the lovely ceremony wore on and moonlight bathed the scene, Murray decided it was time for him to slip away to his little cabin, finally to rest. But stumbling on the dark path, he tumbled unseen into the underbrush. Only at breakfast the next morning did he reveal that he had been rescued by the most unlikely of good Samaritans, an inebriated wedding guest, who had gone to the woods to relieve himself. Murray described the scene that had ensued: "He was getting me up, and we almost both went down again. But finally we got back on the path. He wobbled one way; I wobbled the other way, and together we held each other up!"

---

8. The young couple happened to be the daughter and now son-in-law of the author.

9. See Appendix 13 for text.

Safely back in England after a month in America, the mood shifted as Mary and Murray celebrated their own partnership as wife and husband. Sixty years had passed since August 3, 1940 when they had shared their wedding vows in Cambridge. Thus on August 6, 2000, Mary donned a creamy linen sari and, together with Murray in his customary Indian cassock, welcomed friends and family to a garden party just outside their little bungalow on the beautiful grounds of All Saints Convent, Oxford. It was a happy day, honoring a union that had contained and survived so many joys and sorrows. The sun shone brightly in a blue sky as the Rt. Rev. John V. Taylor, former Secretary General of the Christian Missionary Society gave the blessing.

This was, of course, the same John Taylor who had been the target of Murray's angry tirade on western missions thirty years earlier. If it then appeared that reconciliation had been achieved by the two men, that was not entirely true. Murray, still feeling warm affection for his old boss, had been pleased to learn John Taylor was a resident of Oxford. But despite the Bishop's graceful blessing on their celebration, to Murray's distress, dark clouds remained over the relationship—clouds that lingered until John Taylor's death, only months later. Bishop Taylor, "a colossus of a man," known for his gentleness and humility and recognized as "one of the most gifted and widely admired churchmen of his time,"[10] had been deeply and lastingly wounded by Murray's words and actions. For him the angry and public departure of such a high profile missionary priest from the Missionary Society cast harsh judgment on his own life's work and devotion. The uneasy relationship between them seemed to carry echoes of other father-son relationships in Murray's life. He would not be close to him again. Perhaps John Taylor could forgive, but he could not forget.

Even more clouded was Murray's relationship with the Anglican hierarchy of Oxford. Rather than the customary welcome from the Bishop of Oxford to a newly arrived priest, there was stony silence. When Murray contacted the diocesan authorities, he was informed that a license to "exercise his orders"[11] would not be granted. And what did this mean? It was clear: he was being disciplined for his history of non-conformity and lack of obedience to church authorities. He had, after all, taken an Oath of Canonical Obedience in his ordination as a very young man. Technically, he was required to be licensed in a new diocese with a letter from his previous bishop attesting that he had served "in conformity to the doctrine,

---

10. Obituary of the Rt. Rev. John Taylor, *Telegraph*. Feb. 1, 2001.
11. Canons of the Church of England, 95.

discipline and worship of the Church of England."[12] Unsurprisingly, his well-earned reputation as a renegade had preceded him to Oxford. Thus, while retaining the "character of his order as a priest," he could not preach, minister, or celebrate the Eucharist in any Anglican Church. Even the Anglican sisters who lived next door were cool, seemingly having been warned that their new neighbor was a troublemaker. For Murray this was hardly the first time he had been 'banned' by irate authorities. Not surprised, his irreverent opinion of the office of bishop was reinforced, and he could dismiss the decision as yet another act of short-sighted rigidity. On a practical level, at age eighty-four he could forego invitations to preach or celebrate in local Anglican churches. Yet, at the heart-level, it was wounding. Years later, still unrepentant, he nursed disappointment and resentment. "Do you know that in six years, the Bishop [of Oxford] never phoned me up?" he commented.

Murray could dismiss the bishop and live with fading hope for the organized church more easily than he could abide the state of the world. The strife in their beloved India between Muslims and Hindus was heartbreaking. And the Middle East provoked utter despair. Early in 2001, in a letter to this author, he wrote, "I'm struggling to receive from God enough radical optimism to cope with public affairs day by day. It's difficult to be anything but appalled by your dear country's leadership in public affairs, right here because our Government is such a copy-cat of the States, and in the Middle East where the [United] States poisons the possibility of advance towards peace and away from violence. It remains tragic that its followers of Jesus are so devoted to power, money and control; no wonder people in other parts of the human family are not impressed with the Christian way.

"One longs for inspiration among leaders, both Arab and Jewish. It's so sad that both sides seem locked into violence. It must be awful to be a really believing Jew these days and terribly painful for Palestinian friends in all their suffering each day. God, who loves us all, must have a way forward, but how may we all repent and discover what His way is—and then find the courage to follow it?"

When, shortly after that letter, the World Trade Center in New York was bombed, Murray's sense of empathy for the West was strained. Nor was it much warmer when, in July 2005, coordinated terrorist bombings shocked the city of London. He was sorry, of course, but couldn't such happenings have been expected? Of deeper concern was the retribution the West would surely visit upon the Muslim world.

12. Ibid.

Yet, despite rejection by the Anglican Church and signs of the "destruction of western civilization" he had predicted to his Greenwich friends, life in Oxford was good for Mary and Murray and for Heather as well. The community of Jyotiniketan had been "church" for them for many years, and so it remained. Their familiar timetable, adjusted to a slightly later waking time, held them in its reliable predictability. The chapel, now tucked behind a removable curtain in one corner of their living room, reassured with its familiar icons: Melchizidek, their "patron saint," a wooden cross carved by a Russian monk, stones from a Tibetan monastery destroyed by the Chinese, another stone from a shepherd's field outside Bethlehem, and bamboo from Hong Kong. There too was the marvelous brass lamp, gifted to them by the students so many years ago in Kareli, along with smaller lamps. And tucked safely away in a little jade dish was the Blessed Sacrament, along with a tiny relic of St. Francis, given to them years before by a bishop in Assisi. "That's the heart and soul of everything," Murray said. Perched on a ledge across the room were what they laughingly called their "idols"—symbols of other faiths they held dear. There was a small Tibetan Buddha; a statue of Nataraja, the Hindu dancing god of creation; and a beautiful porcelain figure of a Chinese sage. At one end of the bookcase-lined room leaned a photograph of Abhishiktananda, looking nearly as wild and unkempt as that night they first met outside their North Indian chapel. And surveying the entire scene though his wire-rimmed glasses from the other end was Gandhi in a poster-sized likeness. Reading materials were stacked here and there: the latest copy of the *Guardian*, *Christian Century*, newsletters from Sabeel, and other favorite causes, and the latest crop of provocative books. It was a comfortable room with worn hand-me-down armchairs for reading, talking, and for partaking of tea and biscuits—a ritual nearly as central to their life as their prayers. For prayer times the curtain was pulled back to reveal the chapel, and meditation cushions, stowed under a table, were distributed around the floor. Though Murray had moved from his cushion to a small stool, Mary and Heather were still able to bend into their cross-legged position. Fresh flowers, procured by Heather, were in place; the lamp wicks were trimmed. Just as they held the cares of the world in their prayers, so too their prayers held them. Their chapel remained their anchor.

And, yes, at last they were closer to their families. From London Linda and Richard could easily drive to Oxford, and even Cheryl and André could drive from France. Now there were not only grandchildren; great-grandchildren were beginning to arrive. In 2000 little Freddie was born to Linda and March's Victoria, commencing a new generation. "Fancy that," exclaimed Murray. "Four generations!" Heather's nieces, Alison, Elizabeth and Jane, devoted to their aunt, were also available for visits, and her older sister Armine was within comfortable distance as well.

Yet Cheryl, Linda, and Richard were not of one accord on what their family roles might now be. Cheryl and Linda, resilient and accepting of their unusual upbringing, were genuinely happy to have their aging parents closer. As Richard noted, Linda had been endowed with a natural sense of caring, and, as far as Richard was concerned, all the problems that go with it. He was aghast that she would willingly fall into meeting their needs and, seemingly, their expectations of care and help in their old age. He challenged Linda. How, he wondered, after being foisted off all those years onto someone else's family, could she be willing to provide the services they seemed to expect? She was, in his view, "doing the most preposterous things," like changing beds and doing laundry. He was simply "not prepared to go along." In a candid moment, he shared his still simmering resentment. He had grown up feeling he didn't belong, and he found his parents' style of life "unacceptable." Unsurprisingly, he had found "benefits in a wholly opposite approach;" his path had been one of intellectual exploration, cultural enjoyment, and financial security. Families needed continuity; they needed to live under the same roof. That was what he and Alice had provided for their children, Miranda and Murray, the latter named, interestingly, for the father he did not admire. Richard had protected himself over the years by "keeping his distance." Now that they were in Oxford, he still had reservations about getting closer or resolving their differences. "I didn't have a huge appetite to get into it with him," Richard said, and so their emotional contacts were limited. His assessment of his mother was gentler. He saw her as an admirable woman, stoic in the acceptance of her life. He had felt her "emotional solidarity" with her children. But, still he wondered about her faith, "How can people be so sure about things that are manifestly uncertain?"[13]

Yet Richard was not uncaring. He and Alice did visit, and, demonstrating a bit of missionary spirit for his own lifestyle, arrived one day with a small television set. The conversion was not dramatic, but Murray did indeed join him, watching football matches with considerable enthusiasm, while nature shows and other cultural offerings were shared by all of them. Much of what they saw simply mystified them. Most days the TV, set in the corner of their living room, was draped discreetly with a swath of Indian fabric. Murray, from his side, felt the emotional distance with Richard and was laden with regret. "I'm afraid we failed Richard," he said. "We don't talk," he added. "It makes me very sad."[14] If he had noted the irony of being a

---

13. Richard Rogers, interview with author, Oxford, England, 2007.
14. Murray Rogers, interview with author, Oxford, England, 2006.

pioneer in interfaith dialogue who had difficulty talking to his son, he did not mention it.

Linda observed the same phenomenon in the family: "Isn't it extraordinary how we don't talk to each other in families?" Yet for her, their style of growing up was less a problem and more "a gift." She loved that her parents were "brilliant," yet she had never been allowed to feel "entitled." She continued, "It's given an unusual taint to my life . . . I'm exceedingly interested in Tibet and Nepal [and] I feel completely at home when I go there. You sort of gain things you didn't know you were gaining." Thus it seemed natural for her to be in Oxford, lending a hand; she didn't harbor resentments. It was true she had not embraced her parents' style of devotion; she and March belonged to a traditional Anglican church near their home in Barnes and occasionally attended. But, she admitted, coming to Oxford, "I try to escape the services." Murray was just her father, albeit an unusual one. "He's single-mindedly in love with God . . . I can't grasp it . . . I appreciate that people from far and wide appreciate him, but I don't really get it,"[15] she said. Nevertheless, she was there to do what she could—warm, cheerful and generous. March often joined her. They were a devoted and mutually supportive couple.

Cheryl too had emerged from her childhood with a nuanced sense of happy and painful memories, embracing a sense of independence that had come with her various experiences. More than either Richard or Linda, Cheryl had absorbed her parents' ideals. "The attitudes André and I have and the way we see things and the way we think follows very closely 'the Parents' attitudes," she said. She continued: "The way I want to live is surprisingly similar—without the additional prayer life—I'm not like them in that way, to that extent. But the way I want to live my life—and now I'm speaking for André and myself as a couple—is not very, very different. We don't *do* the way the Parents did, obviously. But I've picked up a lot without going out of my way to do so."[16]

André himself shared a long reflection on Mary and Murray; an excerpt follows: *"J'étais frappé par sa vision universelle, et donc oécuménique, de la mission de l'Eglise. Son expérience d'abord en Inde, ses contacts avec Abhishiktananda, lui avaient permis d'accéder à une vision proche de celle de Teilhard de Chardin, dans sa conception du cheminement religieux vers le Divin. Avant de le rencontrer, je dois admettre que je n'avais jamais pensé à cette dimension, dans la vie quotidienne. Les pensées de Teilhard restaient*

---

15. Linda Hancock, interview with author, Oxford, England, 2007.

16. Cheryl Poutier, telephone interview with Cheryl Poutier from Elancourt, France by author, 2007.

pour moi dans le domaine des concepts d'ordre intellectuel. L'expérience de Murray se situait au niveau du vécu religieux et spirituel, et à son contact, j'arrivais progressivement à pénétrer modestement dans son cheminement.[17]

In their retirement from paid careers, Cheryl and André remained dedicated to their life of service. Faithful Roman Catholics, Cheryl's continued teaching and André's work as a board member for a local ecumenical center were reflective of that ongoing influence. The effect had even trickled down to the next generation, as James, Cheryl, and André's red-haired son, then in his mid-twenties, had absorbed his grandparents' love of India. Already he and his wife Laurence had visited India twice, meeting up with old friends of his grandparents: Laurie and Kuni Baker and Mar Chrystostom, the delightful "bishop with the golden tongue." James and Murray had a special bond. Every few months, Cheryl and André made the trek from France to England. Being closer was deeply comforting, at least to Mary and Murray and their daughters. Regardless of lingering ambivalence about Heather's assimilation into the family, her presence had long since been accepted by all of them, Richard included. She too received their care and attention. Thus Mary and Murray's primary goal of leaving Canada and moving to England had been achieved. "Family-at-a-distance" had become a bit nearer.

Life in Oxford assumed a certain rhythm. Aside from elderly aches and pains and continued difficulty with Mary's eyes, their health remained fairly robust. Murray's prostate cancer remained dormant, and his heart was steady.

Financially, they could manage comfortably on their Church of England pensions of about £650 a month, which paid the rent and other basics. Their lifestyle remained as frugal as ever. Usually there was extra to give away to Amnesty International or perhaps to the Catholic Worker. Pensioners could ride free on the buses that plied Cowley Road to Oxford's High Street, offering access to the public library and the university. After a trip to the library, Murray might duck into the Oxford Union, the historic debating society, just off Cornmarket Street. He had his father to thank, he admitted, for his lifetime membership, established at the Cambridge Union when he was an undergraduate. For a pensioner there were no dues. Now he relished

17. André Poutier reflection. Translation: "I was impacted by his universal, thus ecumenical vision of the mission of the Church. His experience first in India, his contacts with Abhishiktananda, allowed him to reach a vision close to that of Teilhard de Chardin in his conception of the religious way to the Divine. Before meeting [Murray], I must admit I had never thought of this dimension in daily life. Teilhard's thoughts had remained for me in the intellectual domain. For Murray experience was the essence of the religious and spiritual life, and, influenced by him, I was little by little able to enter, however modestly, into that spiritual way."

the chance to sink into a big leather chair to rest and read the newspaper and, on occasion, indulge in a cup of coffee. Coach trips to London were readily accessible for special events. The telephone rang often, and there were frequent knocks on the door as visitors, expected and unexpected, dropped in. Heather, true to her nature, sometimes longed for more quiet time, but her efforts to rein in the gregarious Murray were fruitless. They were not lonely.

— 19 —

Following the Light: Living into Death

> As rivers flowing into the ocean find their final peace
> and their name and form disappear,
> even so the wise become free from name and form
> and enter into the radiance of the Supreme Spirit
> who is greater than all greatness.
> In truth who knows God becomes God.
>
> —Mundaka Upanishad

By 2001 it was clear to Murray and Heather that Mary needed more care. As Murray wrote in May of that year, "Mary is distinctly older and needs much more attention . . . I couldn't go away; it would be too much weight on Heather to care for her. Pray for her . . . and for me. I used to dream that I was patient but I now discover how wrong I was." His wings clipped, new challenges awaited.

Still, that summer they were able to travel back to Italy, Switzerland, and France again with Vroni. They all looked forward to visits with friends, culminated by the wedding of Cheryl's second daughter outside Paris. Murray jested wryly: "The old grandfather is being wheeled out to speak at the marriage service!" Alas, he spoke more truly than he intended. For arriving for the wedding from the Alps, he was beset with an unexplained weakness that left him hardly able to walk. As he slowly came back to his "old self" a few weeks later, he ruefully admitted, "I think the word 'old' must be the operative one!" The fragility of their little community was ever more apparent.

Yet for Murray, introspection and retrospection had led to renewed creativity. That same year marked the publication of his article for the

Hindu-Christian Studies Bulletin entitled "Grounds for Mutual Growth."[1] The topic—how his thinking had changed through interfaith dialogue—was dear to his heart, his passion apparent in the flowing words. Calling it his "swansong," and his "last testimony," he told how "what began as an academic exercise became [his] existence."[2] Such a powerful summary it was. Yet as he wrote, and even as he shared his finished work, Murray emphasized that he had been *asked to* write the article. The unspoken subtext seemed to be: "This article I'm writing about me and about my experience is *not* intended as self-aggrandizement." For despite urgings from countless friends, Murray had resisted writing any sort of memoir or autobiography that might appear as self promotion. The call of Jyotiniketan was to littleness. It remained the downward way.

But Murray *could* beat the drum for Abhishiktananda. And in David Barton, he found a kindred spirit and collaborator. David was an Anglican priest who lived just down the road from All Saints Convent. Years before, as a Cambridge seminarian, David had met Mary and Murray when they had come to share their Indian experiences. He recalled Murray's openness and the fun of meeting him, yet the most lasting impression on him was not Murray, but Mary in her sari. In the ensuing years, he had read their circular letters and encountered them from time to time. Independently of Murray, David had been introduced to the writing of Abhishiktananda and felt drawn to his spirituality. Thus, when he again encountered Mary and Murray in Oxford and came to know Heather as well, a deeper relationship was forged, and a joint project was hatched. Together they would create a small, accessible 'memoir' of Abhishiktananda. David wrote a short introduction and Murray, interviewed by David about his old friend, added the details that brought him to life: as David noted, "the attractiveness of the man, his love of company, and how totally he was given over to his inner life, driven by what Murray calls 'the smell of God.'"[3]

Oxford, it seemed, was full of Abhishiktananda followers and scholars. Even before the publication of David and Murray's booklet in 2003, Murray had heard of the writer Shirley du Boulay; her widely read spiritual biographies had come to his attention. Her latest book was a biography of Bede Griffiths,[4] the British Benedictine monk, who like Abhishiktananda and like Murray, had gone to India and become immersed in Hinduism.

---

1. For a complete text of "Grounds for Mutual Growth," see Appendix 12.
2. Rogers, "Grounds for Mutual Growth," 3.
3. Rogers and Barton, *Abhishiktananda*, 5.
4. Du Boulay's biography is titled *Beyond the Darkness*, published in 1998 by Doubleday.

Perhaps Murray had heard she had considered turning to the life of Abhishiktananda for her next work. Shirley too had been told of Murray and encouraged to meet him. Suddenly, there they both were being introduced at a benefit party for the Prison Phoenix Trust.[5] Shirley recalls how tall and impressive Murray seemed, and how, barely having said hello, he pulled out his diary and rather imperiously said she should come to Jyotiniketan at 9:00 the next morning. And so she did.

With her familiarity with the world of Abhishiktananda, she and Murray immediately hit it off. Not only, she recalls, was Murray charming and persuasive as they talked of her tackling another complex spiritual personage, but, kicking a big cardboard box under his desk, he piqued her interest when he said the box contained private letters and papers of Swamiji. Thus it was that she agreed to take on the task.

All of them—Mary, Murray, and Heather—were elated, for this was a project to which Murray could substantially contribute, not only with memories and documents, but with inspiration for Shirley to complete the formidable task. For the next few years, she was a frequent presence at Jyotiniketan, as she and Murray had long conversations about Abhishiktananda. Joining in their times of worship, Shirley came to know them well. As she delved into Swamiji's life, it was as if the great circle of their friendship with him was given new life. Old friends were available to help; new friends—scholars and members of Swamiji's family—were in touch. As *The Cave of the Heart: The Life of Abhishiktananda* took shape, the elderly members of Jyotiniketan were infused with joy, both in remembering and in knowing his life would be more widely shared.

When the topic turned to themselves, however, there was ambivalence. Yes, death was coming closer. For years now, the reality of death had been something of a preoccupation. Though they had left Kate's marvelously constructed coffin in Canada (later de-constructed and recycled as a part of a wall in their new cabin!), they had acquired a new coffin, inexpensive and earth-friendly, made of lightweight cardboard. It stood like an upright soldier at the end of their hallway, decorated with a cheerful tea towel, a constant reminder of their mortality. Mary and Heather seemed as much at ease with its presence as Murray. Often, along with the rest of the flat, it was shown matter-of-factly to visitors, who were left groping for words.

"My children think I talk too much about death," Murray remarked. But, as he explained, he remembered all too well how no one ever mentioned the word "cancer" when his mother was ill, let alone the word "death."

---

5. The Prison Phoenix Trust is based in Oxford and serves prisoners throughout the U.K. Like Bo Lozoff's Prison-Ashram Project in the United States, it "encourages prisoners in their spiritual lives through meditation and yoga" (www.theppt.org.uk/).

Away at university and oblivious to her condition, he had no chance to say good-bye to her. "That was exactly what I believe death *shouldn't* be," he exclaimed. "That's why there's nothing not to be talked about. It's silly to pretend you haven't got cancer when you've got it."

He hoped that at his own death friends would gather as the old worn-out overcoat of his body was laid aside. They would remember Swamiji's joyous affirmation that he loved to quote, "Mooray, is there anything but God?" They would know—"*not* that it's Rogers in the box with God floating around. Rather it's *all God*."[6]

He would be buried in his beige cassock, symbol of his priesthood "according to the order of Melchizidek." With him would be a Bible to symbolize Christ's resurrection. The Upanishads would be there too. They had obtained a plot, he said, beautifully located in a field at Wolvercote Cemetery in Oxford, in a "green area," unadorned with memorial stones. Three trees would mark the place where he, Mary and Heather would be buried. At his service, people could tell stories, and though they might "blub," it would be a time for thankfulness, "not because 'Murray's a lovely fellow,' but for all God has given to everyone and because Murray's been forgiven, along with everybody else." The service would include his favorite hymn: "There's a Wideness in God's Mercy," and would close with the blessing from the Jyotiniketan Liturgy. But, surprisingly perhaps, it would not include Eucharist. Rather than being overtly religious or even Christian, it would be "utterly ecumenical." All inclusive. All planned.[7]

So when fear and ambivalence arose, as they did, it was less about death itself and more about the possible death of their legacy. Yes, they did remember their heartfelt affirmation of life in the present moment, shared with friends from India in 1964. "Reminiscing about the past, or thinking ahead," they had written, "can so easily point to ourselves, to our supposed successes and to our more certain failures. God is not to be met in the past or in the future. It is more than enough that we may meet God in the present moment, with Him to fill completely, up to the brim, this moment, every moment."[8] Now, forty years later, they still found God in the present moment, but, at the same time, as friends died and their own memories faded, the thought of all those memories simply gone was unbearable. Somehow those past experiences needed to be captured for the future.

Serendipitously, another scholar appeared, namely Judson B. Trapnell. Judson, a professor at the University of Virginia, had, like Shirley du Boulay,

---

6. Interview with author, Oxford, England, 2006.
7. Ibid.
8. Letter #15.

written a biography of Bede Griffiths.[9] Interested in writing on Abhishiktananda, he had contacted Shirley, who, of course, brought him to meet Murray.

Murray and Judson quickly connected. Sharing Abhishiktananda stories with Murray, he was deeply engaged, not only with those stories, but with Murray's as well. Captivated by Jyotiniketan's journey, he was determined that their story be told. Judson did share a *caveat* with Murray: he was being treated for melanoma that had recently spread to his lungs. But he was optimistic and ready to forge ahead. And with Murray's PSA levels spiking ominously after a period of stability, indicating new activity in *his* cancer cells, it seemed Judson had appeared in the nick of time.

With Judson to write the story of Jyotiniketan, to vouchsafe that their experiences and insights not be lost, Murray gave himself permission to reflect openly on the past. Over nearly a week, with breaks only for meals, prayers, and sleep, he and Judson talked about his life's pilgrimage while the tape recorder ran. He found Judson's questions opening doors within himself. Focusing on the dramatic changes that had transpired in him, he seemed startled, almost as if he was appreciating his transformation from a new perspective. "What made this frightened boy, afraid to say 'boo to a goose' ready to say anything to anybody?" he wondered aloud. And again, he exclaimed, "I was an absolute fundamentalist! I'm amazed at what God's spirit can do with a simple fellow! Shoe-horning him out of one sort of life, into another." To which Judson replied, sagely, "Well, you had to be *willing* to be shoe-horned."[10] Judson, a skilled and sensitive interviewer, included Mary and Heather in his interviews as well. They trusted him and were deeply gratified that he would devote himself to this work. He had shared a bit of his own life with them, telling of his wife, Rosemarie, and their young twin daughters.

The news, just four months later, that Judson had died at the age of forty-eight hit them hard. Not only had they lost a respected friend with whom they had shared so much, but their hopes for his work were dashed.

Grieving for Judson, they grieved those lost hopes as well. They had come to believe in the importance of a written record of their work. Spiritually it seemed beautiful that Jyotiniketan and their lives, like a quintessential Indian ashram, would simply die and disappear, returning to the earth or to the mud, as Murray had expressed it. Murray himself had resisted writing about their lives, choosing instead to keep his ego on a tight leash in service

---

9. Trapnell's biography is entitled *Bede Griffiths: A Life in Dialogue*, published by SUNY Press in 2001.

10. Interview with Trapnell.

of becoming "little." They had imagined the wonderful "reality" of being consumed, like Anthony de Mello's Salt Doll in an infinite sea. Yet humanly, they did not want Jyotiniketan to disappear without a trace. With Judson gone, Murray, in a dark moment lamented: "I wish I'd written things down. I don't know what I did. I'm afraid it's all wasted; it's all gone."[11]

Other regrets from the distant past bubbled up as well. It was a time of self-questioning. "Why," he wondered, "didn't I visit Babs (his younger disabled sister) when I came to England? I feel very ashamed of that." And again, "I failed Richard. I remember him kicking angrily at me when he was about eleven. I couldn't understand, and now I wish I could." And about Mary: "Mum did a tremendous work, none of which is known." Referring to himself he said, "Sometimes men, so-called leaders, are like bulldozers. Pig-headed. Mary and Heather cautioned me, especially Heather. But sometimes I didn't listen, and then later I was sorry." Out tumbled regrets that he had hoped might be reconciled—perhaps with God, perhaps with his children, perhaps with himself. Regret was difficult; repentance was painful.

On brighter days, he still hoped that someone else might chronicle their lives. Perhaps writing could even be a way to heal pain, a way to reconciliation. Yes, he admitted, there would be the uncomfortable reality of pain and failure being uncovered. But he had learned over and again how God is "a conjurer, a magician" in being able to "make right" from failures. "Perhaps God needs our mistakes to work with," he observed.

Now, more than ever, often inadvertently, they wore their fragility on their sleeves. Mary's was revealed in her hand-writing that now staggered unevenly across the page, the words still clear and expressive, but difficult to decipher. Her eyesight had become very poor. As they gathered for worship, she could no longer be counted on to read the long list of intercessions without stumbling. Heather was visibly stressed with her companions, both so vulnerable. Deepening her pain was the loss of her sister Armine from cancer. Heather's painting had ceased and, reluctant to leave Mary, she had foregone the pleasure of her brisk walks. Only a quick trip to get eggs for the evening omelette or a fresh loaf of bread seemed safe, and her questions to Murray regarding daily plans were ever more frequent and anxious. More than ever Murray understood their dependence on him, and, in new ways, he was assuming management and care for the household. With his own aches and pains, he was concerned. How would Mary and Heather manage if something happened to him? Their relationships continued to evolve.

---

11. Interview with author, Oxford, England, 2006.

The devotion between the two women remained. In April 2003, Heather penned a card for Mary's 87th birthday. It was a retrospective tribute, spare but deep. It read:

Dearest Mary,

Just a little card, but with such thankfulness for all the years we have spent together and for all that you have shared with me of the things that really matter in life.

May this birthday be a very special and happy one for you, and the coming year bring joy.

With much love as ever,

Heather[12]

By the following year it was indisputable: not only were Mary's eyes failing; dementia was eroding her incisive mind. The adjustment for each of them was challenging. At one moment, Mary could seem fully present, recalling names and places from the past that eluded everyone else; then suddenly she was confused and disoriented. Mostly it was the present moment that boggled her. One afternoon, as their customary teatime was followed by a bit of reading, she suddenly jumped up and said, "Well, I *do* think it's time to get on with it, but what are we going to get on with?" What, indeed? Their need to focus simply on getting through the day was a difficult change. Yet what remained consistently intact and even augmented was Mary's gentle, agreeable nature. Indeed, as the urgency of the present moment slipped away from her, what lay beneath were remnants of a happy child, well-mannered, yet less inhibited than the woman she had become. A playful side emerged in little songs and ditties she remembered from long ago. Joining her after supper one evening to wash and dry the dishes, this writer found warm companionability as she chanted, "Here we are, here we are, happy as can be! Here we are, here we are, jolly good company!" Her childlike innocence was precious.

Mary's decline brought Murray to the realization again and again that his spiritual work was far from done. Having spent his life flying around the world, now he could go nowhere. "My old heart can still fly around, even though my old body is pretty decrepit," he admitted, on a transatlantic call. For a man dedicated to significant action for social justice, it was humbling. He himself felt ever closer to death, yet somehow there was still time. "And what am I doing with this extra time?" he asked, rhetorically. "I'm doing Mum's washing! I've never worked harder manually. It's very peculiar, you

---

12. Rogers personal papers.

know. Makes me wonder, what's God up to?" Again and again, he was faced with his shortcomings, mainly his impatience. He who had never bathed babies or tucked them into bed was now partnering with Heather in that very task, tending to Mary's bathing and dressing. The inefficiencies of the process and Mary's dawdling tested him. Finally, in abject frustration, he scheduled a consultation with a social worker provided by the British Health System to troubleshoot the problem. He ruefully reported the outcome. "Mary's all right," had been the response. "The problem is *you*."[13] Thus the hard work of cultivating patience and humility continued. After living for sixty plus years with an adaptable, pragmatic, no-nonsense woman, her *non sequiturs* could be disconcerting. But he would have to accommodate himself to her quirky retorts. "Now go to sleep, Mum," he said to her one night, having joined with Heather to recite the evening prayers around her bed. To which Mary replied, in a snappy but light-hearted comeback: "Sleep!—or forever after, hold your peace!!"

Yet Mary's dementia also brought unexpected joys and comforts to Murray. As he said, "In a way this illness has brought us closer; we need each other more."[14] He told of them awakening in the mornings, side by side in their narrow cots. Some days she would lie there, happily singing lullabies and childhood songs. Then, in a way that was unaccustomed but deeply welcome, she would reach for him across the small space, grasping his hand. Seldom had he felt so close to the woman he had married as in those moments. Here was the woman whom, in moments of tenderness, he would address as "Soul." This was a taste of the intimacy they both had longed for.

As for Murray and Heather, their special bond remained. Now they were partners in caretaking, working together and spelling one another. When Murray's patience ran short, he would call on Heather. He could learn from her gentleness and tenderness. When Heather's physical strength came up short, she would call Murray.

Yet Murray's physical strength was ebbing as cancer cells migrated to his back, triggering pain. Murray articulated the sense of helplessness they all felt. "We've always believed we must do whatever we can," he said, "and now we can do nothing. We are empty souls with nothing to give." At times he could orient himself to their situation from a wider perspective, as he had learned in Shigeto Oshida's "far away look." "I'm being asked to practice what I've preached." he observed. "I'm trying to be willing to accept what God is doing."[15] Standing framed on a table was a quotation from Swamiji.

13. Interview with author, 2006.
14. Ibid.
15. Ibid.

It read: "And then the Lord takes you seriously, removes every fine thought and leaves you there, capable of nothing more than simply being there! And that is what is most real." This was what they had called surrender. But could he truly embrace surrender?

He oscillated between hope and despair. He, who had so deftly talked of death, now turned to poetry, as his own words failed. In a steady voice, he read aloud a poem of Antonio Machado, allowing it to speak for his waking, clear-eyed soul, full of hope and anticipation:

> Last night, as I was sleeping,
> I dreamt—marvellous error!—
> That a spring was breaking
> Out in my heart.
> I said: Along which secret aqueduct,
> Oh water, are you coming to me,
> Water of a new life
> That I have never drunk?
> Last night, as I was sleeping,
>
> I dreamt—marvelous error!—
> That I had a beehive
> Here inside my heart.
> And the golden bees
> Were making white combs
> And sweet honey
> From my old failures.
>
> Last night, as I was sleeping,
> I dreamt—marvellous error!—
> That a fiery sun was giving
> Light inside my heart.
> It was fiery because I felt
> Warm as from a hearth,
> And sun because it gave light
> And brought tears to my eyes.
>
> Last night, as I slept,
> I dreamt—marvelous error!—
> That it was God I had
> Here inside my heart.
>
> Is my soul asleep?
> Have those beehives that labour

> At night stopped? And the water
> Wheel of thought,
> Is it dry, the cups empty,
> Wheeling, carrying only shadows?
>
> No my soul is not asleep.
> It is awake, wide awake.
> It neither sleeps nor dreams, but watches,
> Its clear eyes open,
> Far-off things, and listens
> At the shores of the great silence.[16]

The images were beautiful and brought both tears to his eyes and a smile to his lips. His soul was wide awake. Here buzzed the beehive of Jyotiniketan, with its failures redeemed into sweet honey, the "fiery sun" of God's inner light shining, even the water wheel—a Persian water wheel, surely!—flowing with the waters of new life, and the shores of the great silence beckoning.

But at other moments, despair and doubt could creep in like a dank, grey-skied England day. Then it might be the psalmist whose words Murray grasped for comfort. Reading Psalm 17 aloud one August 2006 afternoon, he wept openly:

> Lord, listen to my prayer;
> hear me in my hour of need.
> I am overwhelmed by my troubles
> and terrified by my thoughts.
> Guide my feet on your path;
> don't let me stop or falter.
> Teach me how powerful your love is
> and how insubstantial my fears.
> Like the pupil of the eye protect me;
> hide me in the shadow of your wings.
> Cover me with your mercy;
> rock me to sleep in the dark.
> And let me, when I awaken,
> see nothing but the light of your face.[17]

Surely God was there, but where?

They were not forsaken. They still had one another. They also had the steady resources of the National Health Service. They had the kind services

---

16. Machado, *Times Alone: Selected Poems of Antonio Machado*, 43.
17. Mitchell, *A Book of Psalms*, 9.

of Sobell House, a hospice day care facility where Murray now could go for emotional support. And, most of all, they had their children, often present—family-at-a-distance no more. Their prayers affirmed that God, as much as ever, was in their midst. Early morning prayers had, of course, disappeared, but the Eucharist, now a bit ragged, continued and visitors still came. The lamp from Kareli could no longer be lighted for the occasion; Heather said it was simply too worn. Perhaps she was just too weary. Nor did the words flow faultlessly from their lips; even Murray stumbled and lost his place from time to time. Yet despite the mistakes, participants were still moved, perhaps more than ever, by "the supreme quiet and wonder"[18] of his celebration. This writer recalls a Sunday Eucharist that same August. Once again, the elements, the prayers, and the peace were shared, the rhythm and beauty intact. With only the blessing remaining, Murray paused. Then, as if to transcend the impending limitations of earthly time, and, overtaken by the Spirit, his blessing became, however briefly, a mantram. Tears quietly flowing, he spoke the familiar words:

> The Compassionate Father bless you.
>
> The Son of God, the Real Man, bless you.
>
> The Giver of Life, true bliss, the breath of Life, the Supreme Spirit
>
> Bless you—again and again.[19]

Invoking the triune connection between God, himself, and all that he loved, all that was most essential, he repeated the treasured blessing, again and yet again. The prayer seemed meant for the entire world. The room fell into some moments of silence. Then, suddenly, the spell broken, cushions and prayer books were gathered up, curtains drawn around the little chapel. Heather scurried off to the kitchen to prepare lunch.

Overwhelmed as she was, Heather held tightly to the reins of household control. Murray himself was doing much of the cooking. Good friends and family might help with chores, but unfamiliar faces, however friendly and skilled, aroused her resistance. More and more, Linda's presence was needed, and Cheryl's sojourns from France became more frequent. They seemed to be holding on by a thread.

Cheryl recalls visiting in early October. They were having a companionable time, enjoying a television program on dolphins when the conversation turned to fish. Suddenly, to Cheryl's great surprise, Murray said, "I'd love to eat some fish." Thinking to herself: "Well, for heaven's sake, life's too short; let's go buy some fish,"[20] off she went down Cowley Road, returning

18. Shirley du Boulay's descriptors.
19. Blessing from Jyotiniketan's liturgy, see Appendix 14.
20. Cheryl Poutier, telephone conversation with author, 2006.

with a few filets, enough for all of them. When Heather and Mary demurred, preferring the usual omelette, Cheryl and Murray shared a last supper together. Never one to lose his gusto for eating and his hearty appetite, Murray savored every morsel.

About ten days later, October 16th, Murray had finally persuaded Heather they must get some household help. Together, with Linda present, they had interviewed "two ladies" for the position. The talk had gone well; Mary and Murray had sat together, holding hands. As reported by Linda and Cheryl, Murray had said, "You know my wife looks very ancient now, but she was a brilliant lady." It was, as they said, "Very sweet." At last they would have some relief. That evening, Heather and Mary having retired, Murray excused himself early and went to bed. He wished he could keep company with Linda, but he didn't feel well.

Suddenly death came with great intensity, like a clap of thunder in the night. Linda, reading quietly in the living room, was jolted. Responding to his cry, she ran to his side. Turning to her, he said simply, "I hope you'll all forgive me."

Linda's reply came from her heart: "Father, there's nothing to forgive you for."[21]

The medics came quickly, but by then Murray's great heart had stopped. He was gone.

In the days that followed, messages poured in. The cardboard coffin was brought from its place in the hallway and dusted off. Clad in his simple cassock, Murray was laid in the box, its flimsy sides now reinforced with good strong rope. David Barton, their neighbor, confidant, and priest, celebrated the Jyotiniketan Liturgy in All Saints Convent Chapel and led a simple graveside burial at Wovercote Cemetery. Mary's words, adapted from the Gaelic and published years before, were the blessing. While she stood quietly with her family and with Heather, David read:

> Deep peace of the Son of Peace to you,
>
> who, swift as the wave and pervasive as the air,
>
> quiet as the earth and shining like a star,
>
> breathes into us His Peace and His Spirit.
>
> Deep peace of the Son of Peace to you![22]

Later in December the remainder of Murray's vision for his memorial was realized. Friends and family from around the world gathered at the Friends

---

21. Linda Hancock, telephone conversation with author, 2006.
22. For the full text of Mary's adaptation, see Appendix 10.

Meeting House, St. Giles, Oxford, for the free-form remembrance he had imagined. There was solemnity, silence, tears, and many stories, reverent and irreverent. And, of course, lots of laughter.

Murray's departure seemed to have left a great emptiness. Blessedly, denial allowed Heather to continue to believe that he had simply gone out on one of his excursions. Day by day, she awaited his return. Mary grew weaker.

Cheryl, Linda, and Richard were as busy as ever, visiting and tending. Yet, at least for Cheryl, it was a strangely "exhilarating" time: a time of meeting their parents' friends, being in contact with people whose names she had heard for years but often had never met. However well-informed she had been of their doings, Cheryl was astounded. "I didn't realize," she said, "how *remarkable* everybody thought they were, including Mother, of course. The kind remarks, the fantastic messages, the compliments. A very strange thought hit me: 'How is it *possible* that *I* am the *daughter* of those two people?! It was absolutely overwhelming!'"23

As Christmas approached, Mary struggled with bronchitis. She had a fall. Right after New Years' she was hospitalized. Though Richard had departed for a time alone in Italy, Linda was already nearby, and Cheryl and André arrived as well. Mary, lucid and comfortable, was sharing a room with three others, including an elderly religious sister. Cheryl and André, chatting with other sisters from the order who had come to visit, told them who Mary was. They seemed to know of her and Murray. As they were leaving, they came to Mary's bed. One of the nuns put her cross on Mary's forehead and said, "Bless you. Have a good night. We'll see you tomorrow." Sweetly, Mary replied to her, "Good-bye."24 With that farewell, Cheryl and André departed as well.

The next morning, less than ten weeks after Murray's death, Mary too was gone. Peacefully, and discreetly as was her wont, she had slipped away in the night.

Again the calls and letters poured in. Among them was a message from Raimon Panikkar:

> Mary and Murray were two saintly persons. They were ordinary people with an extraordinary depth and intensity. They were really *authentic*, nothing more, but nothing less. They are among the saintly people who maintain the existence of the universe: *lokasamgraha*. I was also blessed by their friendship and confidence. *Amen, Alleluja.*

---

23. Telephone interview with Cheryl Poutier from Elancourt, France by author, 2007.

24. Ibid.

Epilogue

> Death is not extinguishing the light;
> it is only putting out the lamp
> because the dawn has come.
>
> —Tagore

For Murray and Mary the dawn had come. For Heather, the light was extinguished, but as yet there was no dawn. Her family was able to move her into St. John's Home, right next door to the little bungalow, on the grounds of All Saints Convent. There she lived for three more years, comforted by the loving care of her family and of Mary and Murray's family as well, yet lost in grief and dementia. She died peacefully on February 2, 2010. For her too, the dawn had come at last. Heather was laid to rest alongside Murray and Mary in Wolvercote Cemetery. Though Murray had planned for three birch trees to mark their places, in the end there was space for only two.

And what of Jyotiniketan? Having joined together for a sentimental sibling journey to their old haunts in India, Linda and Richard, along with March and Alice, confirmed what Mary and Murray had already heard from old friends in Kareli. After Deenabandu's death, the Franciscan authorities had decided to take Jyotiniketan in a very different direction. A big church was constructed with traditional pews. Electricity was brought in, a primary school built, and an imposing wall erected around the property. The Franciscans had written to Mary and Murray to share this good news. But the story heard from village friends was different. "We don't go there now, or, if we do we have to be very careful. They make us wait a long time . . . "[1] For Mary, Murray, and Heather, the news had been hard to take. Of all the details, it was hearing of the wall that had been most painful. Linda

1. Interview with Trapnell.

and Richard confirmed that everything they had known was gone, even the beautiful chapel.

Cheryl, Linda, and Richard had all returned to life with their families. Richard, retired from his government service job, could indulge his love of travel, to Italy in particular. But most of all, he loved his visits to Scotland where, in the spring of 2009, he had just completed the amazing feat of climbing all the highest mountains in Scotland. Called the Munros, there were nearly three hundred of them, all rising over 3000 feet. In the fall there would be a joyous celebration party for him and his climbing companions. But at the conclusion of another joyous occasion in late August, the wedding of his and Alice's son Murray, the news was shared. Richard was gravely ill. A metastasized melanoma had overtaken his body. On October 30, 2009 he died at the age of sixty-two, leaving a heartbroken family.

For our human selves, death is not easy, whether it is we who are dying, or we who are left. Yet through the ages, spiritual giants have shared their mystical knowing about death, a knowing that may sustain us. Raimon Panikkar, who himself died in 2010 at the age of ninety-one, offered this simple, clear reassurance: "Insofar as we are human beings, we might leave as individuals. Everyone has left, including Jesus. Insofar as we are divine, after we have left, the Spirit will remain. We do not leave reality deprived of our experience. We have been—forever."[2]

In a moment of such faith, Murray penned his own affirmation, a final note to Friends, to be shared when he was gone. Love is, after all, stronger than death.

> Friends, we know, don't we, that this is not the end. There are no oceans to separate us now. Remember the things we spoke of when we were together, show kindness to everyone you meet, and spread God's love throughout the world. Until we are together again, dear friends, live, live every day of your lives and be thankful. M.R.

---

2. Panikkar, *Christophany: The Fullness of Man*, 139.

Appendices

1. Map of Murray and Mary's India | 337

2. The Holy Eucharist Jyotiniketan Ashram, 1971
   (for the North India Liturgical Commission) | 338

3. C. Murray Rogers: Letter to the Editor, *Times* (London), 1973
   "Choice of Anglican bishop of Jerusalem" | 356

4. An Act of Commitment (Rosmarie's entrance into the community):
   Jerusalem, 1980 | 358

5. Sermon, C. Murray Rogers: Feast of the Transfiguration
   St. John's Cathedral, Hong Kong, August 9th, 1987 | 363

6. For Guests: The Jyotiniketan Community, Hong Kong, 1980s | 366

7. A Birthday Greeting to Rosmarie, Hong Kong, 1984 | 369

8. Night Prayers at One Bamboo Hermitage, Hong Kong, 1980s | 372

9. For Guests: Jyotiniketan Canada, 1990s | 376

10. Mary Rogers: "A Blessing," Adapted from the Gaelic for *Earth Prayers*,
    1991 | 379

11. Murray Rogers: Homily "It's All in a Loaf", Greenwich, CT, Maundy
    Thursday 1996 | 382

12. C. Murray Rogers: Article "Grounds for Mutual Growth"
    "Hindu-Christian Studies Bulletin," Vol. 14, Oxford, 2001 | 385

13. Homily for the Wedding of Laurence and James: Bourriot-Bergonce,
    France, June 28, 2003 | 390

14. Celebration of the Eucharist: Oxford, 2006 | 393

15. Favorite Prayers | 402

16. Last Prayer at Night: Oxford, 2006 | 408

Appendix 1
Mary and Murray's India

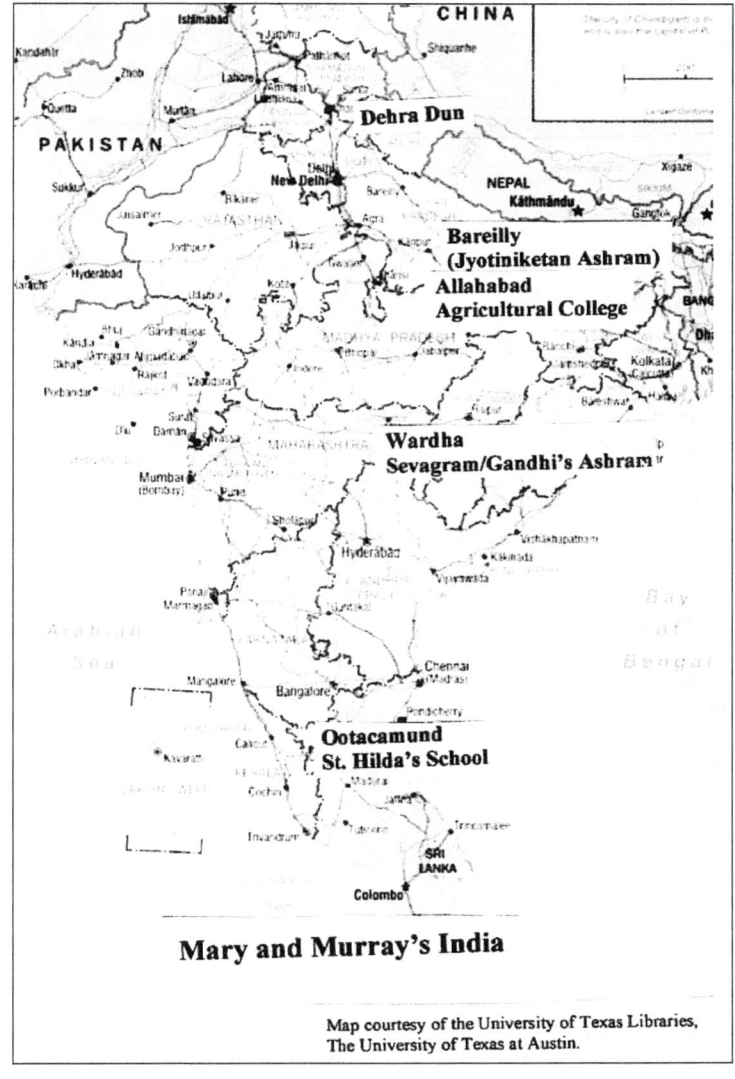

Map courtesy of the University of Texas Libraries, The University of Texas at Austin.

Appendix 2

The Holy Eucharist

Jyotiniketan Ashram

Church of North India
Liturgical Commission 1971

+ **Introduction to Silence** +

Leader: Blessed be God, both now and ever,
and unto the ages of ages.

Family: Amen.

Leader: Glory be to you, O Father everlasting

Family: Who sent your only begotten Son into the world, that we might live through him.

Leader: Glory be to you, O Lord Jesus Christ

Family: Who brought life and immortality to light through the Gospel.

Leader: Glory be to you, O Holy Spirit of God

Family: Who quicken us together with Christ
and shed abroad his love in our hearts.

+ *Holy Eucharist* +

Namo Janitre namaste' stu prabho,
devatmasakte namo namaste,
saccidanandaya namo namah,
paramevioman nihito guhayam yo virajate,

sada tasmai namo namah.

Glory to the Father;
glory to you, O Lord;
glory to you, divine Spirit;
glory, glory to Saccidananda,
to the one who dwells in the highest heaven
and is also hidden in the cave (of the heart);
ever glory, glory to you!

(or)

In the name of the Father, and of the Son,
and of the Holy Spirit. Amen.

The Preparation

Priest: I will come to the altar of God.

People: Praise the God of my joy.

Introit Psalm
(Gelineau numbers in brackets)

Sunday 62:1–8 [61:1-9]   Thursday –84 [83]
Monday 47 [46]   Friday –130 [129]
Tuesday 51:1–19 [50:1-19]   Saturday 138 [137]
Wednesday 43 [42]   Saints Days 48 [47]/66 [95] 147:12–20

Together: I will come to the altar of God.
Praise the God of my joy.

Priest: We have come together to hear God's most holy Word, and to receive the Body and Blood of the Lord. Let us therefore examine ourselves in silence, seeking God's grace that we may draw near to him with repentance and faith.

(short silence)

Together: Heavenly Father, we confess that we have sinned against you and our neighbour.
   We have walked in darkness rather than in light; we have named the name of Christ, but we have not departed from iniquity. Have mercy upon us, we beseech you, for the sake of Jesus Christ forgive us all our sins; cleanse us by your Holy Spirit; quicken our consciences; and enable us to forgive others, that we may henceforth serve you in newness of life, to the glory of your Holy Name. Amen.

Priest: Hear the gracious Word of God to all who truly turn to him through Jesus Christ:

"Come to me, all whose work is hard, whose load is heavy; and I will give you rest."

"God loved the world so much that he gave his only Son, that everyone who has faith in him may not die but have eternal life."

"Here are words you may trust, words that merit full acceptance: Christ Jesus came into the world to save sinners."

"Should anyone commit a sin, we have one to plead our cause with the Father, Jesus Christ, and he is just."

(short silence)

Priest: Almighty God, our heavenly Father, who of his great mercy has promised forgiveness of sins to all who forgive their brothers and with heartfelt repentance and true faith turn to him: Have mercy upon you; pardon and deliver you from all your sins; confirm and strengthen you in all goodness; and bring you to eternal life; through Jesus Christ our Lord.

People: Amen. Thanks be to God.

Priest: Turn us, O God, and bring us to life.

People: And your people will find their joy in you.

THE HOLY EUCHARIST

Priest: Show us, O God, your mercy.

People: And grant us your saving help.

Priest: O Lord, hear our prayer.

People: And let our cry come unto you.

Priest: The Lord be with you.

People: And with you also.

Priest: Let us pray:

Almighty God, unto whom all hearts are open, all desires known, and from whom no secrets are hidden: Cleanse the thoughts of our hearts by the inspiration of your Holy Spirit, that we may perfectly love you, and worthily magnify your holy name; through Jesus Christ our Lord.

People: Amen.
Lord, have mercy.
> *Lord, have mercy.*
Christ, have mercy.
> *Christ, have mercy.*
Lord, have mercy.
> *Lord, have mercy.*

(Prayers)

The Service of the Word

Liturgy of the Cosmic Covenant
(Before the reading of Hindu Scriptures)

> Purnam adah purnam idam
> purnat purnam udacyate
> purnasya purnam adaya
> purnam evavasisyate
> OM shanti shanti shanti

Fulness there, fulness here,
from fulness fulness proceeds.
Once fulness proceeded from fulness
Fulness remains.

(After the reading of Hindu Scriptures)

Asato ma sad gamaya	From the unreal lead us to the real
tamaso ma jyotir gamaya	from darkness lead us to light,
mrityor mamrtam gamaya	from death lead us to deathlessness.
OM shanti shanti shanti	OM, peace, peace, peace.

(a short silence follows each reading)

Priest: Let us pray:
O Lord almighty who has mysteriously revealed to the sages of old your ineffable presence in the depth of the heart, grant to us and also to those of our brothers who follow in their footsteps that being led by your Holy Spirit in this inward search we may discover therein the light incorruptible, your divine Son, Jesus Christ our Lord, to whom with you and the Holy Spirit be all honour and glory for ever and ever.

People: Amen.

(or another prayer)

Old Testament Reading

Together: Thanks be to you, O God.

Epistle

Together: Thanks be to you, O God.

First Intermediate Chant:

Refrain: Alleluia, Alleluia, Alleluia.
or (2) (during Lent)
Cleanse my heart, O Lord, teach me the wonders of your holy
 ~~law~~[1] word.
I love your ~~law~~ word, O Lord.
~~The livelong day I~~ Give me a heart to ponder it.
Open my eyes. Show me the wonder of your love.

Your ~~laws are~~ love is ~~songs~~ to me upon my pilgrimage.
Your word is a lamp to guide my feet along the path.

Second Intermediate Chant

People: Alleluia! Alleluia!
Wonderful and great are your works,
O Lord, God Almighty.

Just and true are our ways,
O King of all nations.

Who shall not revere you,
O Lord! Who shall not give glory to your name!
You alone are holy.

All nations shall come to worship you in your presence,
for your justice has been made known.

Gospel

Together: (before the reading)
Glory be to you, O Lord.
(after the reading)
Praise be to you, O Christ.

---

1. The strikethroughs indicate changes over time in the words of the liturgy.

Acclamations to Christ

Praise to Christ, the eternal Word of the living God;
    Praise to you, O Lord.
Praise to Christ, the eternal Truth of the living God;
    Praise to you, O Lord.
Praise to Christ, the eternal Light of the living God;
    Praise to you, O Lord.

(short address)

Creed

Priest: Let us proclaim our faith:
We believe in one God,

Together: The Father almighty, maker of heaven and earth, and of all things visible and invisible.

We believe in one Lord, Jesus Christ, the only begotten Son of God, begotten of his Father before all worlds. God of God, Light of Light, Very God of Very God, begotten not made, being of one substance the with Father, by whom all things were made: who for us men and our salvation came down from heaven and was incarnate by the Holy Spirit of the Virgin Mary and was made man. He was crucified also for us under Pontius Pilate, suffered and was buried. On the third day he rose again, according to the scriptures. He ascended into heaven and sits at the right hand of the Father. He will come again in glory to judge both the living and the dead; of his Kingdom there will be no end.

We believe in the Holy Spirit, the Lord and giver of life, who proceeds from the Father and the Son, who, together with the Father and the Son is worshipped and glorified: who spoke through the prophets.

We believe in one holy, catholic and apostolic church.
We acknowledge one baptism for the forgiveness of sins and we await the resurrection of the dead and the life of the world to come. Amen.

The Offertory

Priest: Let us present our offerings to the Lord with reverence and awe.

(then will follow words from the Bible according to the season and to the occasion)

The Singing of a Hymn

Together: (when the gifts are placed on the altar)

All things come from you, and of your own do we give to you, O creator of the world who are ever adored by the holy angels. We humbly beseech you to accept at our hands these (alms and) oblations, which we present at your holy table, and with them the offering of ourselves to the service of your divine majesty: through Jesus Christ our Lord. Amen.

(Sung at the offering of flowers)

OM Sri Yisubhagavate Namah
abhishiktaya Namah
devaputraya Namah
mariyasunave Namah
naraharaye Namah
sadgurave Namah
satpurusaya Namah

Glory to Jesus the Lord
    the Christ
    the Saviour
    the Son of God
    the Son of Mary
    the Man-God
    the True Master
    the True Person

The Thanksgiving

Priest: The Lord be with you.

People: And with you also.

Priest: Lift up your hearts.

People: We lift them up to the Lord.

Priest: Let us give thanks to the Lord our God.

People: It is right to give him thanks and praise.

Priest: It is not only right, it is our duty and our joy, at all times and in all places, to give you thanks and praise, holy Father, heavenly King, almighty and eternal God.

The Preface

Together: Therefore with angels and archangels, and with all the company of heaven, we praise and magnify your glorious name, ever more worshipping you and saying:

Holy, holy, holy, Lord God of hosts, heaven and earth are full of your glory. Glory be to you, O Lord most high. Amen.

Blessed is he who comes in the name of the Lord: hosanna in the highest.

Priest: You truly are holy, you truly are worthy of praise, O God our Father.

In your mercy you gave your Son Jesus Christ to assume our nature and to die upon the Cross for our redemption. He made there, by an offering for all time of himself to you, one perfect and sufficient sacrifice for the sin of the whole world. And he instituted for us a memorial of his life-bringing death, telling us to continue it again and again until he comes at the end of time.

> The night that he was betrayed he took bread, gave thanks to you and broke it. He gave it to his disciples saying: "Take this and eat it; this is my Body which is given for you. Do this in memory of me."
>
> Again, when supper was ended, he took the cup. He gave you thanks and gave the cup to his disciples, saying: "Drink of this, all of you. This is my Blood, the blood of the new covenant which is to be shed for you and for all people, so that sins may be forgiven. Whenever you do this, do it in memory of me."

People: Amen.

Priest: So now, Father, God of glory and majesty, we your people celebrate with humble hearts, through these holy things you have yourself given us, the memorial your Son gave to us. We recall his passion and death, his life-giving resurrection and his ascension into glory. We give you our heartfelt thanks for all that this means to us and look forward with joy to his return in power and great glory.

> Accept, Father, this sacrifice of praise and gratitude. Grant that we and all your church, relying upon your Son Jesus Christ and on his saving work may receive forgiveness of our sins and all the gifts of his grace.
>
> We ask you, merciful Father, to fill us and these your gifts with your own holy and life-giving Spirit that this bread may be truly to us the Body of Christ, and that this cup which we bless in your name may be truly to us his Blood. May all we who share in this sacrament be strengthened by your grace and bound together by your blessing in the unity of your Son our Saviour Jesus Christ.

People: Amen.

> esa sarvesvara esa sarvajna,
> eso'ntaryamy esa yonih sarvasya
> prabhavapyayau hi bhutanam.

Isano bhutabhavyasya,
sa evadya sa u svah,
OM tat sat

He Lord of all, he knower of all,
he the inner one, he source of all,
beginning and end of all creatures,
Lord of what was and what will be;
he both today and tomorrow.
OM tat sat.

Litany of Intercession

Priest: Let us pray to the Lord for his grace and mercy.
Let us pray for Christ's universal Church.
Let us pray for all men both living and departed.

(response after each intention)

People: Lord, have mercy.

Priest: Almighty God, your Son Jesus Christ taught us to intercede for all men.

We pray for the peace of the whole of creation and for the unity of all who seek after God.

We pray for your universal Church, that we may live together in unity and harmony; may the whole world be filled with Truth about You.

We pray you to enable our bishops, priests and deacons to teach your life-giving Truth, to live it out in their lives and reverently to administer the Holy Sacraments of your Church.

We pray for the nations, for peace and justice; for all rulers, especially . . ., that the whole world may be led in the ways of peace.

We pray for the poor and hungry, for those whose crops and livelihood are threatened, and we pray you to preserve those of us who have enough from hardness of heart and ingratitude.

We pray for all in sickness and trouble, for refugees, prisoners, victims of war, the mentally or physically handicapped, and for all outcasts from society.

We pray for all who abuse their position and power, for those who exploit the need and suffering of others to build up their own wealth and prosperity.

We pray for all who are lonely or erring, for all who do not seek God.

We pray for those who have passed on from this world in faith, asking you for grace to follow with them in the steps of your Son and by the merits of his passion.

We pray for ourselves that we may humbly and sincerely be open to your Word, and, recognising your glory in men and creation, may be enabled to serve you with joy and humility.

or

Priest: Look with favour, O God, upon this your family, the human race scattered throughout the earth. Deliver us from all evil, purify us, make us perfect. Gather us from all corners of the earth to the supreme meeting-place, your own abode which the glorious resurrection of your Son Jesus has opened for us.

We commend to your compassion, O Lord, all the churches of Christ among all peoples, races and cultures. Protect them; give strength and wisdom to those you have chosen to lead and guide them. Unite them in your love. Enable all the disciples of your Son Jesus to be sources of light and peace, of joy and reconciliation.

We pray also, O Lord, for all who are devoted to you everywhere on earth and who today adore you under the symbols received from their ancient traditions and through the experience of the Holy Spirit working in the depth of their hearts. Hasten the time when you will bring them to fulness of truth and inspire even now in their hearts that complete dedication to you that will lead them to salvation.

We pray you, O Lord, that all men may hear the message of your Risen Christ and, obeying the promptings of the Holy Spirit, come to know you, O Father almighty, and the one you have sent to earth, Jesus Christ, your beloved Son.

Have mercy, O Lord, on all who have the responsibility of ruling their brother men in our land of India and throughout the world. Give peace to the whole world, between all nations, all races and all human groups.

Look with compassion on all those who suffer in their bodies, or in their minds and hearts; remove their pain and give them joy, that joy which your Son has brought to earth and in which he desires us all to share.

Give food to the hungry by opening the hearts of those who have food so that with you they too become givers of food. Pour love into all hearts so that through all men your Son Jesus Christ may realise his work of love for the unity of mankind and the fulfilment of his Kingdom.

Behold in your love and mercy, O Lord, those to whom we are joined in a special way . . .

Bless, we pray you, all your family men and women, old people and children, married and single, rich and poor, employers and employees, gurus and disciples, learned and simple, for the sake of all creatures and for the joy of the whole world.

Priest: O God, our refuge and our strength,
it is you who always hear the prayers of your Church, and who alone put your love in our hearts, grant us these requests that we make in deep faith. Through our Lord Jesus Christ, your

Son, who lives and reigns with you in the unity of the Holy Spirit, God, for ever and ever.

People: Amen.

The Lord's Prayer

Our Father in heaven. Hallowed be your name. May your kingdom come. May your will be done on earth as in heaven. Give us this day the bread we need, and forgive us our sins and offenses as we have forgiven those who have offended us. Do not lead us into temptation but deliver us from the evil one. For yours is the kingdom, the power and the glory, for ever and ever. Amen. (Syrian Orthodox)

Priest: The peace of the Lord be always with you.

People: And with you also.
(short silence)

Priest: Let us pray.

Together: We do not venture to approach this your Table, O merciful Lord, relying on any goodness of our own but on the mercies you constantly show us. We are not worthy even to gather up the crumbs under your Table, but you remain always the same; you always show mercy. May we therefore, dear Lord, so eat the Body of your Son Jesus Christ and drink his Blood, that we may be made clean through and through from our sins by his Body and blood, and evermore dwell in him and he in us. Amen.

Together: O Lamb of God, you take away the sin of the world, have mercy on your people.

O Lamb of God, you take away the sin of the world, have mercy on your people.

O Lamb of God, you take away the sin of the world, have mercy on your people.

+

The Communion

Priest: Having now received the Body and the Blood of Christ let us give thanks.

Almighty and everliving God, we thank you with all our hearts that you graciously feed us, who have now received these holy mysteries, with the spiritual food of the most precious Body and Blood of your Son, our saviour Jesus Christ: you assure us by this that you love us and care for us, and that we are in truth members of your Son's mystical Body, the joyful company of all men of faith. By this, also, you affirm that we shall participate in your kingship for ever and ever, which was won for us by all that your dear Son did and suffered when he dwelt on this earth.

We humbly ask you, O heavenly Father, to help us by your grace that we may continue in that holy fellowship and that we may walk in love in all the ways you have planned for us, through Jesus Christ our Lord, to whom with you and the Holy Spirit, be all honour and glory, now and for ever.

People: Amen.

The Gloria

Priest: Glory be to God on high,

People: And on earth peace, good will towards men.
We praise you. We bless you. We worship you. We glorify you.
We give thanks to you for your great glory,
O Lord God, heavenly King, God the Father almighty.
O Lord Jesus Christ, only-begotten Son,
Lord God, Lamb of God, Son of the Father,
who take away the sin of the world, have mercy on us.
You who take away the sin of the world, receive our prayer.
You who sit at the right hand of God the Father,
    have mercy on us.
For you alone are holy.

You alone are Lord.
You alone, O Christ, with the Holy Spirit, are most high in the glory of God the Father.

Amen.

+

The Blessing

Svasti vo(no) dadhatu Pita mahesvarah
Svasti vo(no) dadhatu isaputrah satpurusah
Svasti vo(no) dadhatu jivandanandapranah
paramo devatma tatah punah.

May the Father almighty bless you (us).
May the Son of God, the real Purusa bless you (us).
May the Giver of life, True Bliss, the prana,
the Supreme Divine Spirit bless you (us)—again and again.

+

HYMNS

1. Namo Janitre namaste'stu prabho,
devatmasakte name namaste,
saccidanandaya namo namah,
paramevioman nihito guhayam yo virajate,
sada tasmai namo namah.

Glory to the Father;
glory to you, O Lord;
glory to you divine Sprit;
glory, glory to Saccidananda,
to the one who dwells in the highest heaven
and is also hidden in the cave (of the heart);
ever glory, glory to you!

2. Vande saccidanandam
Bhogi lanchita yogi vanchita carampadam

I bow to Him who is Being, Consciousness and Bliss.
I bow to Him whom worldly minds loathe, whom pure minds yearn for,
the Supreme abode.
Parama purana paratparam purnam akhanda paravaram
trisanga suddham asanga buddham durvedam

He is the Supreme, the Ancient of days, the Transcendent,
   Indivisible, Plenitude, Immanent, yet above all things.
Three-fold relation, pure, unrelated knowledge beyond
   knowledge.

Pitri savitri paramesham ajam bhavavriksha bijam
abijam akhila karanam ikshana srijana vishvesham.

The Father, "Sun", Supreme Lord, unborn, the seedless seed
of the tree of becoming, the cause of all, Creator, Lord of the
   Universe.

Anahata shabdam anantam prasuta purusa sumahantam
pitri svarupa cinmayarupa Yisu Khristam

The Infinite and perfect Word, the Supreme Person,
Begotten, sharing in the Father's nature, Conscious by essence,
Jesus Christ.

Saccidormelana saranam shuba shvasitandanda ghanam
pavanajavana vanivadana jivanadam.

He who proceeds from Being and Consciousness, replete with the breath
of perfect bliss, the Purifier, the Swift, the Revealer, the Life-giver.

3. Param jyotih prabho prabho, brihad jyotih sambho sambho,
atma jyotih prabho suno, pitur jyoti Yisu sambho.

Supreme Light, Lord, Lord; Great Light, Gracious, Gracious One; Light of the Soul, Lord the Son: Light of the Father, gracious Jesus.

Jagadjyotih prabho prabho, dyusadjyoti sambho sambho, atmajyotih prabo suno, piturjyoti Yisu sambho.

Light of the world, Lord, Lord; Light of Heaven, Gracious, Gracious One; Light of the soul, Lord of the Son; Light of the Father, gracious Jesus.
Yatra jyotir ajasram; yasmin loke suar hitam; tasmin mam dhehi maghavan;
amrite loke askhite

Where there is the unfailing Light in the world of the heavenly Light place me,
O bountiful One, in the world immortal, incorruptible.

Yatranandacca modacca; mudah premuda asate
kamasya yatrapta kamas; tatra mam amritam kridhi

Where are attained all bliss, all joys, all pleasures, all pleasing things,
all the best of desires, there place me immortal.

Appendix 3

Letter to the Editor, London *Times*, Dec. 24, 1973

Choice of Anglican bishop of Jerusalem

From the Reverend C. Murray Rogers

Sir, amid the events of universal concern taking place in the Middle East there is being lived out a smaller drama in the tiny Anglican community in the Holy Land, a drama which is heavy with foreboding and frustration.

For the last years it has been both implicitly and explicitly affirmed that on the retirement early next year of our Anglican Archbishop Appleton we would be given a bishop from this group of countries, from among Arab Anglican Christians in the reconstituted Jerusalem Diocese who make up over 90 per cent of Anglicans in this area. Along with this new Arab bishop the Anglican Church here was at long last to receive from Canterbury the freedom and autonomy to order its own life, a step which took place, for example, in India 43 years ago. These steps, for which we have been praying, planning and working, were confirmed by the Synod of Bishops (of the area Morocco to Iran) which met in Isfahan last January and later by the Anglican Consultative Council of the whole Anglican Communion meeting in Dublin in July of this year.

Now we hear that all these hopes and shared decisions are to be overridden: the Archbishop of Canterbury is appointing another English Bishop, a retired one, Bishop Stopford, with the title of Vicar-General, for a period of up to two years, in order evidently to choose and to train our new bishop.

Perhaps in England it is difficult even yet to sense the shock of such news. After 26 years in India, and two and a half spent in the Old City of

LETTER TO THE EDITOR, LONDON TIMES, DEC. 24, 1973

Jerusalem, it is difficult to hear still the sentiments, "we must not be precipitate" and "they are not ready". As was expressed with no mincing of words at the recent Assembly in Bangkok of the Commission on World Mission and Evangelism of the World Council of Churches our western ability to find reasons for continuing forms of spiritual colonialism through mission is utterly unacceptable and intolerable to our fellow Christians in Asia and Africa.

Such spiritual colonialism may be natural, and even unconscious, to many in England who lead the church and missionary societies, the greater part of whose active lives have been spent in the days of imperial glory and colonial rule; but to others of us who have lived many years in the East and have served, as in my case, under Indian leadership, and who sense our national fellow Christians' vital need for self-respect, living as they almost always do in minority situations, these presuppositions of paternalism and superiority are, and are increasingly felt to be, an insult to Asians and Africans.

The Jerusalem and the East Mission in London, which, living to a dangerous degree in that "colonial" past, firmly believes that only an Englishman can safeguard Christ's (Anglican) Church in the Middle East and whose chairman Bishop Stopford happens to be, may be able by its financial influence and scarcely veiled spiritual racism to control at present our future. The moment is surely coming—and how will we maintain good relations and mutual respect then?—when God's ability to guide his Church without the help of the Britisher, the white man, will through history become painfully clear. Is there nothing you—and we—can do to move into the present age before we are carried, moribund, into it?

Yours, etc,

C. MURRAY ROGERS

PO Box 1248
Jerusalem.

Appendix 4

An Act of Commitment

Rosmarie's entrance into the
community: Jerusalem, 1980

The Holy Eucharist.

The Collect: O Lord our God, Source, Guide, and Goal of all that is, we pray that Your blessing may rest upon us and especially upon Rosmarie as she offers her very self to You, a living sacrifice, in this act of worship and mind and heart, through Jesus Christ our Lord to whom with You and the Holy Spirit be all honour and glory for ever and ever. Amen.

Readings: "He comes to the thought of those who know him beyond thought, not to those who imagine he can be attained by thought. He is unknown to the learned and known to the simple. He is known in the ecstasy of an awakening which opens the door of life eternal.

"For a man who has known him, the light of truth shines; for one who has not known, there is darkness. The wise who have seen him in every being, on leaving this life, attain life immortal."

—Kena Upanishad, part II
—1 Corinthians 12:31b—13:end.
—St. John 20:10–18.

Priest: "Commitment is the gateway into a future given to God. The way ahead, as with Abraham, will be indicated by God and will lead through a 'nothing' known to God alone to the one goal of each one of His many and varied callings: participation in the life of God Himself, in His glory and love."

AN ACT OF COMMITMENT

Friend: "Complete abandonment to Love demands, then, an inner disposition of heart that keeps itself empty, receptive and eager before the boundless plenitude of God who gives us the gift of Himself; it demands a continual response in our deepest being, which will result in a state of absolute dependence upon the One who is Love. Since God's mercy is this Love in action ,to abandon oneself to this mercy is to entrust to Love the control of one's inner being and to open oneself fully to the divine initiative. It is, in short, to enthrone God in the place of one's 'me,' as the guiding principle of one's every activity."—St. Thérèse de Lisieux

"May you keep nothing of yourself for yourself so that you may receive to the full Him who gives Himself fully to you." —St. Francis of Assisi

Friend: "With what gladness and consolation have I handed over to Him my own will; Yes, I desire Him to take possession of my faculties in such a way that I no longer perform human actions that may be termed 'mine,' but actions that are wholly divine, inspired in me and directed by this Spirit of Love."—St. Thérèse de Lisieux

May you joyfully give yourself to Him, so that His Love may flow freely to all your brothers and sisters.

>Silence.

Friend: "No happening, however frustrating or calamitous it may appear to be, can constitute an obstacle to Love. Everything is given to us as a means of reaching Him.
Saved as we are by Love,
we shall only save by Love."

May you be ready to receive Him in all the details of your daily life and to dwell in Him.

>Silence.

Priest: "Love one another as I have loved you." —St. John 13:34.

> We are asked to love as Jesus loves, as God loves, which is obviously only possible if a divine love dwells in us. Then alone do we truly love. After this revelation John does not feel himself at all obliged to outline for us a 'rule of life' as individuals or as a group. If we believe that to

live is to be so united to Jesus as to love like Him, then we shall have every possible incentive for a brotherly way of life."

May you " . . . be all things to all men, with one single desire in your heart, that of giving Jesus to all." —Charles de Foucauld

Silence.

Rosmarie: "But this intimacy, this communion, this glowing ember of faith, of hope and of love, is ultimately only 'Christian' if there issues therefrom a life that desires to be open and to give itself to each and every creature. An intimacy which seals the heart is merely an illusion. It is simply an encounter with oneself. I can know whether or not I am a companion of the Risen Jesus by whether I dare to live to the uttermost, in relationship with each of my fellows."

Dearest Lord, teach me hour by hour, moment by moment, to receive Your forgiveness and to share it with all my brothers and sisters. Help me by Your Holy Spirit to receive You in everything—with a humble and deeply thankful heart—for Your love's sake. Amen.

All stand.

Priest: Rosmarie, that your decision to respond to Christ's call may be taken both in His presence and in the presence of your brothers and sisters of the Church, I would ask you the following questions:

Do you believe that Christ calls you for love of Him, to belong to Him with no limits and no reserve, to the end of your life and thereafter?

Rosmarie: By God's grace, I do.

Priest: Is it your will, freely and joyfully, to offer Him yourself, body and soul, to be wholly united with Him, your Bridegroom, your Beloved, and to offer Him your celibacy as a glad gift of space for Him alone to fill and dwell in?

Rosmarie: By God's help, it is.

Priest: Is it your intention to live out this resolve in this Community of Jyotiniketan, for as many years as God may give us, in simplicity of life and in mutual obedience?

Rosmarie: It is, with God's help.

Priest: Will you, again and again, whether in joy or sorrow, success or failure, return to the Lord for forgiveness and a new beginning, and to the sacrament of the Eucharist where He constantly renews us with His very own life?

Rosmarie: By God's grace, I will, and I ask you, my brother and sisters, by your love and your prayers, to help me to be faithful to this my commitment.

Others: By God's grace, we joyfully will.

Rosmarie: (holding in her right hand the Gospel)
I, Rosmarie Schönholzer, thankfully believing and trusting that God calls me to belong solely to Him, promise to Him, in freedom and joy, my self, my whole being, to be His for ever, for richer, for poorer, in sickness and in health, for this life and the next, in the name of the Father and of the Son and of the Holy Spirit. Amen.

> Silence.

> The ring is placed on the Gospel.

Priest: May this ring be the outward sign of your inward belonging to Christ Jesus your Lord in joy and fidelity until your life's end, in the name of the Father and of the Son and of the Holy Spirit. Amen.

> Rosmarie kneels and the group lay their hands on her head.

> The Blessing of Rosmarie:

May God the Father of our Lord Jesus Christ, from whom the whole family in heaven and on earth is named, grant you according to the riches of His glory, to be strengthened with might by His Spirit in the inner man; that Christ may dwell in your heart by faith; that you, being rooted and grounded in love, may be able to comprehend with all God's people what is the breadth, and length, and depth, and height; and to know the love of

Christ which passes knowledge, that you may be filled with all the fulness of God, and the blessing of God almighty, the Father, the Son and the Holy Spirit be with you and remain with you always.

All: Amen.

(the Holy Eucharist continues.)

30 April 1980 Jerusalem

Appendix 5

Sermon, C. Murray Rogers: Feast of Transfiguration

St. John's Cathedral, Hong Kong
August 9th 1987

2 Corinthians 3:12–4:2

Since we have such a hope, we are very bold, not like Moses, who put a veil over his face so that the Israelites might not see the end of the fading splendor. But their minds were hardened; for to this day, when they read the old covenant, that same veil remains unlifted, because only through Christ is it taken away. Yes, to this day whenever Moses is read a veil lies over their minds; but when a man turns to the Lord the veil is removed. Now the Lord is the Spirit, and where the Spirit of the Lord is, there is freedom. And we all, with unveiled face, beholding the glory of the Lord, are being changed into his likeness from one degree of glory to another; for this comes from the Lord who is the Spirit.

Therefore, having this ministry by the mercy of God, we do not lose heart. We have renounced disgraceful, underhanded ways; we refuse to practice cunning or to tamper with God's word, but by the open statement of the truth we would commend ourselves to every man's conscience in the sight of God.

. . . Dear Friends, do you see what this means for us? We must stop being in the kindergarten about glory. Of course people outside the Christian fellowship are free to think that gun-boat politics are glorious, that glory consists in being the head of the Hong Kong and Shanghai Bank, that glory is the possession of power to control other people, that glory is being on this important committee or that, that glory is being invited to tea with a

President, a Governor, a Pope or an Archbishop. But honestly, we ought to know better; we ought to behave better. We have no excuses, for our Lord and Master has shown us what real glory is, that it is being run through, inside, outside, with God's uncreated Light. Our glory is God's glory and never, never ours alone, no matter what our position, or status, our power in terms of money or prestige, our name and fame.

The second point is this: you notice, don't you, that the Transfiguration wasn't an exhibition of the glory or power of Jesus. He didn't bring it about; He wasn't advertising Himself (as sometimes we Christians try to do). It happened *to* Him. Glory, Light, God's Uncreated Light, flowed to him and from him; it still does. This is emphasized even more by the voice, the voice which the men clearly knew was God's voice, the voice which said who Jesus *is* and gave us human beings one simple, fundamental piece of advice: 'Listen to Him.'

That is who we Christian people are supposed to be: people who listen to Jesus. You'd hardly think it! Does your church, this church, behave in a way which would make people at once say: "O, they listen to Jesus"? In taking our decisions, in committees, in diocesan synods, at home, in business, are we listening to Jesus? Would we Christian people around the world support our governments' violence and racism and lying and deceit and love of money if we listened to Jesus?

You may say—and I wouldn't blame you—"Don't be absurd, Murray. People would say we were mad; people wouldn't respect us, if we didn't behave as they do in regards to money and power and status." "Good enough," I reply, but don't pretend then that this is a Christian church or that you and I are Christ's men and women. God says: "Listen to Him;" we are free to say, "Rubbish, God. You are unrealistic." Sad to say, we are not only free, but we do in fact take that freedom, and the condition of our human society today is to a very large extent the result of thus blocking our ears to God. It is not by chance but rather for our warning and our repentance that the first atomic bomb was dropped and killed more of God's children than had ever up till then been killed by a single bomb on the Feast of the Transfiguration, 1945—and dropped at the directions of a 'Christian' nation by an Air Force man whose conscience had been soothed by a 'Christian' chaplain. You and I, friends, daren't forget these things without being thorough humbugs.

Almost as astounding is this third and last fact about the Transfiguration. It surely give us a marvelous clue to who Jesus is; He was and is forever transfigured. And it gives us an almost unbelievable bit of information about ourselves—we too are transfigured! It sounds absurd, but precisely this is what the first Christians came to see. That the transfiguration of Jesus rubs off on every man and woman; it not only reveals who He is; it shows us who we human beings are. Extraordinary! It's just this that Paul is writing about to Christian people in Corinth—we heard it read just now. The splendour of God came off on Moses' face and, infinitely more so, the splendour of the Lord is reflected in you and me when we let Him make us who we, by God's creation and redemption, really are.

Listen once again to this—take it seriously, if you dare: "Thus we are transfigured into his likeness, from splendour to splendour." Mind you, if for a second we are stupid enough to think that his splendour of our Christian humanity is a qualification, if we claim it as our own, it's gone in a flash! It's all God and His light and His glory. Indeed, it is only ours in practice—though we are endowed with it at birth—when by God's grace we begin to see that the real me, the real you, is mysteriously hidden away in Christ, that we have no separate existence, no being in our own little selves. I am, only in the reality of Christ; you are, only in the reality of Christ.

The Transfiguration begins as the Lord's business, the Lord's life. Before we know where we are—as those first disciples discovered—it is very much our business, our way of life. Are you and I simple enough, honest enough, straight-forward enough, for the Lord's transfiguration to work in us, from splendour to splendour? His, not ours?

That is the question.

Appendix 6

For Guests: The Jyotiniketan Community

Hong Kong, 1980s

The *Tao Te Ching* says, "Shape clay into a vessel; it is the space within that makes it useful. Cut doors and windows for a room; it is the holes which make it useful." It might be speaking—or so we hope—about this 25-year-old Christian Community, which is, in a way, all about space.

Actually it began longer ago than that when Mary and Murray Rogers and a small group of friends knew inside themselves that they needed to discover another way of being Christian, of being human. Experience in the church in India had shown them that the Lord, Jesus Christ, was generally considered to be a western Lord, as much by Christians as by others—however little the West does what He says—and that Asian Christians tended to follow the West's almost exclusive preoccupation with material possessions and with "keeping up with the Joneses" in a thousand ways. As a part of their longing for a more real and down-to-earth experience of God, their Christian faith having been very much stimulated by a year's life with Mahatma Gandhi's followers, they decided to "jump over the wall," economically and in their way of life, and in terms of theological thinking and ways of worship. They wanted the Gentle Revolutionary, the Joyful/Suffering Jesus Christ, to lead them, in a 20th century way, to the Spirit of the life of the early Christians as reported in Acts 2.

1954 saw the beginning of the Community, in an ashram style, living mostly out of doors between two villages in north India. Ever since then four emphases have marked their life and work together:

1. Worship of God, prayer, silent meditation. Their daily life involves four times of return to this Centre, theirs and the world's, with the daily Eucharistic celebration being the inmost heart of it all.

2. Simplicity and a growing awareness that the poor and underprivileged have a great deal to teach the world about how to live. The fact that as a group they have no fixed or guaranteed income, depending upon God through those friends around the world who believe this experiment and "way" is a valid and worthwhile Christian pilgrimage, has led them to what some think is a hard life. They themselves think it is joy!

3. Obedience to Christ through the experience of shared living, with responsibility for one another, shared resources, shared decisions. They have discovered that one's area of freedom is increased as one's ever-demanding individualism is tamed.

4. The expanding awareness that harmony and unity are God's gift to humanity, between people of different Christian backgrounds, between Christians and members of other spiritual families, between human beings and nature, and, near the heart of it all, unity within each person.

These four "marks" are, they are convinced, to be lived out, in a continuing experiment in Christian growth into God, the Reality Who is the Source and Goal of us all. Their name, Jyotiniketan, Sanskrit for "Place of Uncreated Light", is a pointer to this radical dependence upon God, the One Uncreated Light.

India's Jyotiniketan continues, made up now of Indian men and women, chiefly members of the Roman Catholic Church. In order that the Community should be totally Indian, the original Europeans, Murray, Mary and Heather, left in 1971 for Jerusalem's Old City, where after a while they were joined by Rosmarie, who was already there living and working with handicapped people. After 9 years in Jerusalem they were invited to live this venture in Christian Community life in Hong Kong. Here they represent the Anglican and Reformed families of the Christian church and they wonder what the Spirit may have in store for the Community in this new setting.

Pray for them; maybe ask them to pray for you. If, as they have discovered, "the essential is the life deep inside" and if you too are called like them to live "in such a way that your life would not make sense if God did not exist", perhaps you and they are meant to strengthen each other and maybe . . . maybe . . . this tiny seed of life will not be hidden in Hong Kong society for nothing.

The normal daily time-table of the Community:

5 a.m.	get up.
5.30	meet in chapel for entering into silence, corporate silence (half an hour); celebration of the Holy Eucharist.
7.15	breakfast, followed by community chores and individual work.
12 noon	intercessions, followed by lunch and washing up.
1.30–2.30	rest.
2.30–4 p.m.	reading, prayer, study, letter-writing, etc.
4 p.m.	tea followed on certain days by Bible study, silent mediation or meditative reading of ancient Chinese writings.
6 p.m.	Lighting of the Lamp—evening worship.
7 p.m.	supper.
8 p.m.	time together, reading together, Community sharing.
8.45 p.m.	night prayers and to bed.

As a normal practice members have one day of silence and quiet a week, either together or individually; quite often when the weather permits they have this out of doors, walking and rejoicing in creation.

* * * * *

Their address is: Jyotiniketan Community, St. Francis House, P.O. Box 33, Tao Fong Shan, Shatin, N.T. Hong Kong. The group welcomes friends for a visit, for some hours of quiet, for sharing and for worship. They have no phone but a postcard will do instead!

Appendix 7
A Birthday Greeting to Rosmarie

Hong Kong, 1984

January 4th 1984

Dear Rosmarie, I'm sad to say
that without you our talents are
a little small for showing you~
in song or dance or exercise,
how much we wish you on this day
a Happy Birthday~much besides,
God's peace and joy and hope and love
and every blessing. We had planned
a long, long walk to Needle's tip
or down into a valley low,
but now disponibilité
is put to test, for Hari's down
with sad complaints; he huffs and puffs,
and certainly could not contrive
to drag his legs a mere ten yards,
while Heather (two-legged member) she
has only just recovered her voice
and still is snorting . . . As for me
(and Murray too) we'll do our best
but fear we cannot quite perform
to best effect without our teacher,
(you! but that's outside the metre!)
In Yat Juk Lonh
(words Chinese three)

we cannot prattle Cantonese.
    However, Rosmarie helps!

We cannot sing in harmony,
unless we're taught which notes are bass,
    However, Rosmarie helps!

To foot it featly in a dance
(Shakespearean phrase!) is not our métier.
    However, Rosmarie helps!

At Tai-Gik, though we're getting on,
although my memory has lapses,
    However, Rosmarie helps!!

We need a womble. Can I find
the pretty string or paper? No!
Nor fix it in a pleasing way.
    However, Rosmarie helps!

Good heavens, several hyperactive
children will soon be swarming round us.
What shall we do and how survive?
    No problem, Rosmarie helps

With neighbors to communicate
in deeper ways—a kind of sharing—
would be so good; you struggle on
with tones correct and words and phrases
(though sometimes we discount it all . . .),
So let me say, and please believe it,
in all our life on this hillside,
in Yat Juk Lonh, we'd be at loss
if it were not that Rosmarie's there,
to love the old ladies in the Home
the sixty-pluses at the Centre,
to talk and smile with those who sell
bean-curd and sprouts and fruit and veg,
In fact the same old phrase recurs:
    However, Rosmarie helps

A BIRTHDAY GREETING TO ROSMARIE

Please keep us, Rosmarie, thinking deep
on how to be and change and move.
Can we discern in our new name
the same four signposts for our life?
Unity, simplicity, worship, submission.
"One Bamboo Hermitage"—yes, "one" suffices,
"one" points to Unity, unity between us,
unity with all men, unity with creatures.
The bamboo, very straight and simple,
hollow within, bending and flexible,
free of self, submissive perhaps?
Selfless, empty, only such a one
can truly worship, be lost in God.

So, let us make of this your birthday
a joyful celebration of you and Yat Juk Lonh
together~together we'll all join in,

Murray and Mary, Heather and Rosmarie,
Hari and Ambie too, while from afar
Vroni will join and all your friends,
singing and dancing and chanting this song:
    Rosmarie, please keep on helping!

from Mary + Murray with love . . .

Appendix 8

Night Prayers at One Bamboo Hermitage

Hong Kong, 1980s

Leader: May the Lord almighty grant us rest and peace this night.

Family: Amen.

Leader: "Stay awake, and pray that you may be spared the test . . ."

"He found them asleep . . . The disciples all deserted him and ran away . . ."
"I do not know the man."

Short silence in preparation for confession.

All: We confess, O Lord, that we are often lazy and inattentive to your word, that we turn our backs on our brothers and sisters and thus desert and deny you. Forgive us, O Lord, raise us up when we have fallen and put your own courage and love in our hearts, for your name's sake. Amen.

Leader: Go in peace; your faith has made you whole.

Family: Thanks be to God.

Psalm or Night hymn.

Leader: You will keep him in perfect peace whose mind is stayed on you.

or

> He who waits upon the Lord shall renew his strength. He will rise up with wings like an eagle's. He will run and not be weary. He will walk and not faint.

Family: Thanks be to God.

Leader: Into your hands, O Lord, we commend our spirits,

Family: For you have redeemed us, O Lord, God of truth.

Leader: Glory be to the Father . . .

Family: As it was in the beginning . . .

Nunc Dimittis

Guard us, O Lord, while we sleep and keep us in peace.

At last, all-powerful Master,
you give leave to your servant to go in peace,
according to your promise. Guard us, O Lord.

For my eyes have seen your salvation
which you have prepared for all nations,
the light to enlighten the Gentiles
and give glory to Israel, your people. Guard us, O Lord.

Give praise to the Father Almighty,
to his Son, Jesus Christ the Lord,
to the Spirit who dwells in our hearts,
both now and for ever, Amen.

Guard us, O Lord, while we sleep and keep us in peace,
that awake we may watch with Christ and asleep rest in Him.

Leader: Turn us, O God, and restore us to life.

Family: May our hearts be ever conscious of your blessings.

Leader: In you, O God, do we place our trust.

Family:	It is you, Lord, who keep us from falling.
Leader:	O God, free our hearts from all fear,
Family:	For underneath are the everlasting arms.
Prayers:	We commend, Lord, to your love and protection this night all those who are near and dear to us . . . praying you to supply all their needs as you see best, to deliver them in the time of temptation, to guide them through this life and to bring them safely to life with you for ever, through Jesus Christ our Lord. Amen.

Extempore prayer

Together: Night is drawing nigh—
For all that has been—thanks!
To all that shall be—yes!
(Dag Hammerskjöld)

Three Refuges

With all my heart I take refuge in God, the Lord of all things,
the Creator of the universe,
the merciful Father and Source of all good.

With all my heart I take refuge in Christ,
the Remover of all sin, the One who re-establishes
man's pure nature within him,
the perfect Revelation of the Eternal Word of God.

With all my heart I take refuge in Him
who embraces the whole universe and
has myriad ways and means of influencing souls,
the pure and tranquil Holy Spirit. Amen.
(Karl Ludvig Reichelt)

Leader:	The Lord be with you
Family:	And with you also.

Leader: Let us bless the Lord.

Family: Thanks be to God.

Leader: The Almighty and Most Merciful God, the Father,
         the Son and the Holy Spirit, bless us and preserve us.

All: Amen.

The Peace.

Appendix 9

For Guests: Jyotiniketan Canada

1990s

Dear Friend, We hope you will enjoy your time here.

So that you may join in our life as whole-heartedly as possible we would like, briefly, to explain a thing or two about it.

1. From the beginning of this small Community in 1954 we have sensed that God gives us four marks, or signposts, to live by:

   A. the centrality of worship, prayer and silent meditation in human life if it is to be deep and genuine.

   B. simplicity and a growing awareness that we, the rich, owe a great debt of gratitude to the poor and oppressed.

   C. the gift of obedience to Christ through the experience of shared lives, shared resources, shared decisions.

   D. the expanding awareness that we are called to harmony, solidarity and unity as an essential response to God's creation.

2. From the beginning Jyotiniketan has been linked with the poor and underprivileged, first on the Ganges Plain in northern India, where Indian brothers and sisters still live the life, and later in Jerusalem and in Hong Kong, on the edge of China. This link with the poor, near and far, has been, from those early days, a part of our style of life for which we are very thankful.

    This means: we want, as a part of our love for God and people, to live as poorly as possible, even in Canada, this very rich country. So far as is possible we want to reduce our wants as regards food, clothing, way of life and attitudes of mind. The poor of the world, the vast majority of humanity, have few choices; we want, gladly, to reduce our choices. The poor suffer indignity, want, suffering, as a way of life; if these come our way because of what we believe true about God and about human beings, we too wish to be ready. Quite practically, this means never wasting food, using as little hot water for bathing as possible, bearing in mind that the telephone is used only for essential purposes, remembering the dying forests in the use of paper, for toilet or other purposes, keeping the heating as low as possible, even to the point of discomfort, and doing this joyfully with no grumbling, even inwardly!

3. Friends who join us, for a shorter or longer period, are asked to take a full part in our life, following our daily time-table with us. If you have some special need, kindly share about it with one of us; otherwise we expect you to join in our life and work and silence, etc.

Normal time-table in Jyotiniketan

5am we get up.

5:30 meet in chapel and entering into silence.

6am the Great Thanksgiving or Eucharist.

7am Chinese exercises followed by breakfast.

8am. and following: jobs, cleaning, gardening, prayer, study, meeting, etc.

12 midday approx. prayer for others in chapel.

12:20 lunch, and, after coping with dishes, siesta.

4pm. tea together;
more jobs of a mixed variety.

Lighting of the Lamp, shortly before or after supper.

8:30 pm. night prayers and to bed.

There are many changes in times, according to needs and occasions; the ringing of a bell tells you that something is happening!

We think you have already given us permission to ask for your help! So . . . please don't have a guilty conscience when you are not asked! Be thankful—either way!

We would like to provide all you need; we don't even try to provide all you want! Our motto (i.e. what we would *like* to live!) is:
> to be simple
> to be mindful
> to let go & be happy
> to Breathe deeply
> each day is 24 brand new hours
> in which to live.

Appendix 10

Mary Rogers: "A Blessing"

adapted from the Gaelic
for *Earth Prayers*, 1991

Gaelic version:

Deep peace of the running wave to you.
Deep peace of the flowing air to you.
Deep peace of the quiet earth to you.
Deep peace of the shining stars to you.
Deep peace of the infinite peace to you.

Mary's adaptation:

Deep peace of the running wave to you,
of water flowing, rising and falling,
sometimes advancing, sometimes receding . . .
May the stream of your life flow unimpeded!
Deep peace of the running wave to you!

Deep peace of the flowing air to you,
which fans your face on a sultry day,
the air which you breathe deeply, rhythmically,
which imparts to you energy, consciousness, life.
Deep peace of the flowing air to you!

Deep peace of the quiet earth to you,
who, herself unmoving, harbours the movements
and facilitates the life of the ten thousand creatures,
while resting contented, stable, tranquil.
Deep peace of the quiet earth to you!

Deep peace of the shining stars to you,
which stay invisible till darkness falls
and discloses their pure and shining presence
beaming down in compassion on our turning world.
Deep peace of the shining stars to you!

Deep peace of the watching shepherds to you,
of unpretentious folk who, watching and waiting,
spend long hours on the hillside,
expecting in simplicity some Coming of the Lord.
Deep peace of the watching shepherds to you!

Deep peace of the Son of Peace to you,
who, swift as the wave and pervasive as the air,
quiet as the earth and shining like a star,
breathes into us His Peace and His Spirit.
Deep peace of the Son of Peace to you!

A Blessing, translated from the French by Mary Rogers for *Earth Prayers*

May our corner of the earth join us
in blessing the Lord
fruit-laden papayas, fig-trees in bud . . .
You, guavas, replete with promise,
bougainvillaeas of every colour,
beans that twist and clamber,
tomatoes and all green vegetables,
and you, fields of rice in the valleys,
O praise the marvels of the Lord!

And you, Bamboo, who own neither flower
nor fruits, sing a song of praise to the Lord,
for you are rich in other ways:
supple and lively, hold your head high,
yield before the storm, but do not break.
Your shoots, hugging to one another all close,
will confront the hurricane.
Then, when it's passed,
lift up your head!
And if the typhoon sweeps you away,
let it carry you with it.
Someone will find you lying on the road
or maybe you will kindle a poor man's fire
or be made into a balance-pole
to ease men's burdens!

If need should arise, let yourself be split
into strips by the hand of a clever craftsman.
Thus you will become a mat or a basket,
a broom or a brush—again, on demand,
let yourself be used whole, without hesitation,
to support the sail of a sturdy junk
or enable a fisherman to cast his net.

In you, Bamboo, some will seek inspiration
to guide their brush towards lines of beauty,
or make of you a flute or a pipe.
Let yourself be emptied of self that you may
    sing a melody new.
Some may try to make of you a barrier
to separate people one from another.
Then let your leafage vibrate with the rustle
of a call which will resound near and far
and invite them to live in unity and love!

Appendix 11

Murray Rogers: Homily "It's All in a Loaf"

Greenwich, CT,
Maundy Thursday 1996

Friends, it's all in a loaf. God is a wizard. Somehow he gets himself into a loaf of bread and then gives us the bread to eat. And the result, the divine mystery who he is, becomes our divine mystery. He is in us. We are his divine mystery.

Real church is a loaf of bread. We're the grains, ground up, which isn't altogether comfortable. God kneads us together—and those of you who make bread know just how to do it—God kneads us together that we be one loaf, and of course loaves of bread are made to be shared. And real church is where the folk are gathered, where we share our stories, and where we break the bread. It's all so simple, so deep, and God's the wizard that makes it just that.

Of course a loaf of bread is food. Food, seldom for one person, for the family. And as this family doesn't have any boundaries, it's food, God's food, for everybody, because he doesn't want anybody to be without food. And because he must long, much more than we can imagine, that we are truly happy and truly strengthened by his divine mystery, his very own life. And of course, as *we're* the bread, mustn't it be true, that we are made for sharing? We're made for giving ourselves away. We're not made to draw in everything to ourselves—to be lovely or impressive or rich or poor or anything. We're somehow made to be nutrition—for each other. Oh, we're surely meant to share this sort of bread, made of wheat. That's the judgment on our economic systems. We've so arranged things that bread is for some people and less for other people. Some people have lots of it and more than they need and other people are hunting for bread in garbage dumps. That can't be

God's way. That can't be the church's way. Not real church. No, we're created to share ourselves with each other as nutrition for each other.

Sometime will you find somebody to make a loaf? It can be a little one and sit with it. Sit with it and just ask yourself, ask the Spirit that happens to live inside each of us, what's that loaf for me? How am I being a loaf of bread? Food for others?

You remember when Jesus spoke about grains of wheat. It was at a big moment, not long before he died for love of us all. It was a moment when Greeks, the cultured part of the society of his world, were just beginning to come and ask to see him. Before he'd been chiefly for his own people, or for people living there amongst his own people, or for Roman soldiers and civil servants, I suppose. But now Greeks came. They said, "We'd like to see Jesus." Two of his disciples heard that. I guess they were thrilled. Because where there's a little glory going, we are thrilled, you know? They take these two Greek gentlemen to Jesus. And Jesus, he's so surprising. He says, "Now is the moment of glory. If a grain of wheat doesn't fall into the ground and die, it remains a solitary grain." Very lonely. Good for very little. But if a grain of wheat falls into the ground and dies in the dark, ends its life as a grain of wheat—*then* there is a rich harvest.

And you and I, each of us, are grains of wheat. Grains of wheat that the cook—is God the great cook?—the cook waits patiently until the grain that is you and me falls into the ground and dies . . . disappears as a grain and comes up, yes, as a harvest that can be collected and cleaned and sieved, ground, and then into a loaf to be food. Food for our stomachs and food for our souls.

And of course the big question is, don't you agree, on a night like this when we are thrilled and deeply thankful for the bread that is the divine mystery, the big question is, What sort of grain are you, and what sort of grain am I? We're all grain, and we all have the terrifying freedom to either just be a grain that is looked at, *or* a grain that is given away to be food for others. It's what God does first in Jesus. He just invites us. Will you let your grain be like my grain, he says, to feed, to be nutrition for a hungry world?

Over there under the pulpit in a little basket there are some grains of wheat. I asked the Rector whether I could bring them along and have them there. And at the end of the service . . . the very end when the lights have gone very dim . . . I'm going to be standing there . . . and if anybody would care to come up, and without any words, I will put a grain of wheat into your hand. And maybe at the end of this Holy Week, you might take it home, hold it in your hand, and let it speak to you. Let it speak to you, the Spirit to help you, as I will myself. Listen to what God wants to share with us about grains and about bread. Thank you.

Appendix 12

C. Murray Rogers Article: "Grounds for Mutual Growth"

Hindu-Christian Studies Bulletin
14 (2001) 3–6

I was asked to share the way in which my view of Hindu-Christian dialogue has changed over the years and it is a joy to try to do so. Forgive me if, instead of a formal article, I write in a more personal vein as, maybe, a swan-song, a last testimony to what has become more and more central in my life. After all at 83 I am likely very soon to be singing my last song!

Naturally enough since moving to England after 52 years lived so largely in Asia and especially in India, I have less "official" dialogue with Hindu friends but that is no hindrance. What began as an academic exercise becomes one's existence. Notions are left behind and it is a question of everyday life, even of survival. I have only to go down any road here in East Oxford, or go to the Asian Cultural Club to which I belong, and I meet from India or elsewhere both Hindus and Muslims — not to mention the unique smells of their restaurants in Cowley Road! Their way, their presuppositions and perceptions, their scriptures and prayers, have reached so far inside me, into my mind and heart, that they are, I rather think, inseparable from "the little me". This is the gift of friendship and every year, certainly every ten years, since physically leaving the ashram in Kareli village, U.P., India, the distance between my close Hindu friends and myself, a disciple of Christ, grows less. We belong to one another; we see no need and have no intention of "becoming" the other; we even wonder what "other" means in the depth of our human and spiritual experience.

What happens to each of us is enrichment, augmentation. I used to think and to argue that becoming in any way a Hindu, sharing their presuppositions, would be a loss, almost a disaster, to me a Christian! Now, still in the same life on this plane, I sense that their Hindu way and experience is an immeasurable gift to me; they have added in countless ways to my life as a Christian human being. On the level of the mental, the conceptual, a gulf often remains, but deeper, when words fail, when in friendship and life we find ourselves to be as thankful for what we cannot fathom as for what we can, we find a positive strength and grounds for mutual growth. More sharing of silence between us, the end of defensiveness between us and our steady movement away from duality and any interest in comparison become a revelation of how far nonseparation and unity are built into life, into our shared human nature.

I wonder how long it will remain the perceived obligation of Christian people to engage in evangelism, if by this word one means to speak and act so as to encourage others to change their religion, be baptised and be officially named as Christian people, members of an organised church? Do we not all need to be converted, not to a different religious affiliation but, infinitely more deeply, in our inner being, to the spiritual way that we have received at birth? This does not, for one moment, mean that those of us who owe our life, our salvation and joy to the living and resurrected Lord Christ, should, or indeed could keep silent about the One to whom we owe so much. Our great hope is that by our life and word our very existence may point to him, to his love and presence.

My reading of the Gospel makes it very far from evident that Jesus had any intention of beginning a new religion or such institutions as present structures of power/control, prestige and money that are called churches. Am I the only one who would be appalled if the Dalai Lama or a saint of any spiritual way were to become a Roman Catholic, an Anglican, a Baptist or a member of any other Christian religious body? No, where the fruits of the Spirit, the fruits which were to be found so superlatively in Jesus himself, and described by Paul in his letter to the Galatians (5:22–23), are to be found, there for me is the catholic church, the universal family of God. In truth humanity is the church, coming into being, beyond every religious grouping. When Raimundo Panikkar says: "In Christ there is neither Hindu or Christian" my mind and heart echo his statement. Often most painfully—anguish was the word often on Swami Abhishiktanandaji's (Dom Le Saux) lips—our traditional mental categories are shattered and what Teilhard de Chardin called "the dimensions of God" are immeasurably widened. One's old intellectual position, described so accurately in Psalm 53 is blown away!

> "They think that they know;
> their minds move on the surface of things.
> They don't perceive the deep patterns
> or understand who they are"
>
> (Stephen Mitchell's version)

Then, when the old paradigm has "exploded", often in friendship with another person of faith, of "another" spiritual family, or indeed of no spiritual family, I am thankfully constrained to recognise it as a grace bringing joy and freedom from the narrowness in which we are so tragically educated in our so-called monotheistic families. This narrowness is always a short step from an intolerance and violence with which history is full, not least in our own time. This blessed and non-violent revolution in mental and spiritual outlook, owed in my own case to the friendship, patience and love of Hindu, Buddhist and Muslim friends, has left me with a respect and love for their scriptures and for the prayers of their spiritual masters. It was away back in the 1960s that Swami Abhishiktananda, himself a Roman Catholic monk and priest, led us sensitively and fearlessly to taste the marvellous gift of the Vedas, the Upanishads and the Gita, and to pray in our own "Christian" hearts prayers of the Sukla Yajur Veda, of Sri Sankaracarya, of Sri Yamunacarya, of Tulsidas, of the Skandapurana and of a host of others. A taste of such prayers follows:

> O Lord, thou art on the sandbanks
>   as well as in the midst of the current;
> I bow to thee.
> Thou art in the little pebbles
>   as well as in the calm expanse of the sea;
> I bow to thee.
> O all-pervading Lord,
> thou art in the barren soil and in crowded places,
> I bow to thee.
>
> Sukla Yajur Veda XVI, 43

> Thou art father, mother, husband and son.
> Thou art dear friend, relative and teacher,
> and the goal of the universe.
> I am thine own, thy servant and attendant.
> Thou art my only refuge.
> I have taken refuge in thee, and verily,
> O Lord, my burden rests wholly on thee.
>
> Sri Yamunacarya: Stotraratna 60

These do not for a minute take the place, either in our common worship or in our personal prayer, of the Bible and of the precious heritage of prayer in our Christian tradition. The one and the other flow together and increase greatly our joy and our understanding. In our daily celebration of the Eucharist, the high point of our life and work each day, it would now be unthinkable to omit a reading from Eastern scriptures, often with a commentary such as that of Eknath Easwaran, before we read from the Gospels in the New Testament of the Bible. The gifts of God are unbelievably lavish!

The question and challenge of interfaith dialogue confronts us in the West in many forms. Lately the intensely Hindu happening of the Maha Kumbh Mela in Allahabad has been brought vividly into homes in Britain through daily comments and photographs on radio and TV and in the press. For me personally it has been a strong reminder of changes in my own attitude. Just over 50 years ago I was on the staff of a Christian College in Allahabad, which was situated some two miles up the Yamuna river from its sacred confluence with the river Ganga and the mythical river, the Saraswati. It was then that I went as a spectator and mingled with the vast Kumbh Mela crowds, with the millions of people as they bathed in the river on the auspicious day and at the auspicious hour, led by the sages, holy men, ascetics, nagas and a host of simple people from the whole country. At that time it appeared to me to be a vast fair, an irrational explosion of religious fervour, a display of the human psyche, when Hindu human beings in their millions jostle together within an area of six square miles to bathe amid a furore of noise. How sadly superficial and false were my impressions at that time!

Owing to the great changes that have taken place over the years, in myself and in my relationship with Hindu friends and with the sanatana dharma, this year's great Kumbh Mela of some 70–90 million people (cp. this visit of the present Pope to Manila in 1995 of 5 million) brought forth to my surprise an extraordinarily different reaction.

The same vast and dense crowds of human beings were to be seen as fifty years ago but infinitely more numerous, the great organisational work of building a town, Kumbh Nagar, which will last for six weeks and house the millions of tents, not to mention the many miles of roads, the whole only to disappear within a few weeks to make way once more for sand and water ... Day and most of the night religious music is played on loud speakers and an endless variety of speakers, each preaching his own version of the good news of salvation, in ways that are often mutually contradictory according to our Western understanding. The sages and intellectual and spiritual giants, members of ashrams and matts coming from all over the subcontinent, sharing the same suffering and discomfort as the innumerable illiterate and poor majority of the Hindu family, and all together to celebrate faith. It is surely humanity's greatest festival of faith, the power of myth to bring unity out of the greatest intellectual, spiritual, social and educational diversity. There is in the air a glad willingness to live in uncertainty, even with the prospect of death, and an unspoken readiness to leave the others "space" and freedom to be utterly different from oneself; the word heretic is unknown! There is in that Kumbh world no claim to monopoly of truth, but a clear call from all, and to all, in their immense variety of expressions of the sanatana dharma, to celebrate faith, a festival of faith whose high moment of ecstasy is the plunge by each one into the sacred Ganga, the river of grace ever flowing from the silence of eternal snows to the ocean of God's love.

All this and more confronts me, a Christian, with many questions, with serious criticism of my own religious world and the self-understanding of us Christians. Is it indeed another example of the saying that "nothing is itself without everything else"? The fruits of interfaith life are, I am convinced, more essential than was ever conceived some years ago.

The Kumbh Mela experience leaves us, at least, with these insistent questions: Why is it that Christians search for unity so exclusively in intellectual and theological agreement on doctrinal and dogmatic matters? Why is it that hierarchy is so central to our life and to our conception of unity? Why is it that the "united" churches of south and north India, the fruits of many years of prayer and serious discussion of doctrines and order, show signs, many would agree, of results which are singularly disappointing? Are we being driven to the conclusion that, while our Christian leaders cling tenaciously to our intellectual structures to secure our very limited unity, our Hindu contemporaries entrust themselves to the Atman, the Spirit, and receive an infinitely greater measure of unity in unlimited diversity?

Until such questions find some answer a Christian festival of faith, parallel to the Kumbh Mela experience, will remain inconceivable because of our "Christian" disagreements on the intellectual and historical levels, not to mention the never very distant denominational vested interests and pride, would be insurmountable handicaps to such a Christian celebration. Dare we, who claim to have the mind of Christ, renounce our claims to the monopoly of faith, our claims of spiritual superiority and our inherent suspicion of uncertainty? How is it possible that we live, one might say, from our disunity while our Hindu brothers and sisters at the Kumbh Mela, show, for all the world to see, that their vast differences among themselves are not invincible barriers to celebrating faith, in fact that their great variety of spiritual and intellectual expressions is their glory? So many questions awaiting an answer, in life and experiences, and, later, in thought.

We remember, I am certain, Varuna's final word to his son Brigu in the Taittiriya Upanishad:[1]

> "For from joy all beings have come,
> by joy they all live,
> and unto joy they all return."

Isn't our whole search driven by joy? Joy together.

---

1. Mascaro, *The Upanishads*, 111.6.1

Appendix 13

Homily for the Wedding of Laurence and James

Bourriot-Bergonce, France, June 28, 2003
(please excuse my uniquely bad French!)

Friends, how blessed and fortunate we are to be here, a very special joy for my wife Mary and for me because James is a very dear grandson and we are rejoicing that from today onwards Laurence belongs to a second family. You won't think, I hope, that when I say, "friends" to you all, it is a sign of my being old-fashioned! No, we are friends because by our being born as human beings that is in fact our relationship; even before we meet one another, we belong together. What happens to you affects me and what happens to me affects you—even if, sadly, you and I are not often conscious about it.

Doesn't that mean that what James and Laurence do today in being married involves each of us also? There are no outsiders here. None of us is "looking on" as spectators. Each one of us has a part to play in this very special turning point of our lives, when, in the presence of God and of each of us, James and Laurence make promises to each other and accept, in front of us all, the joy and responsibility of being husband and wife. Knowing a little what is involved for them in this almost overwhelming action, they are the first, I know, to say how much they need our good wishes and prayers, as they set out on being a new family of our vast joint-family of humanity. We, their family members and friends, mustn't let them down.

The question arises: why come to church to be married? Why not be married by a river or in this marvelous forest that is all around us here in the Landes? Just as those of us who follow Jesus Christ in the church believe that the Compassionate Father of all humanity, the Unnamable Being upon whom this universe depends, wills marriage and family life for our happiness and growth into true humanness, so, with different symbols and signs, our brothers and sisters of other spiritual families—Hindu, Buddhist,

Taoist, Muslim, etc., experience the same mysterious depth and wonder of a Presence and Power of love and of joy. This beautiful old church stands for God's part in these two young people finding each other, on and on with no limit. This marriage is God's gift to them to which they have gladly said their "Yes" and we gladly echo that "Yes" as we send them on their way with our prayers and friendship.

As for me, an old grandpère, [addressing Laurence and James] I feel I know you too well and respect you both too much, to think that you will take this tremendous step of marriage, dreaming that it will be all easy and lovely. If you don't already know that love and suffering go closely together, you will discover it very soon; the two, love and suffering, travel together in you and between you, and every time you face them together your friendship will be strengthened and your courage and love will grow. Today it may seem unlikely, but you will sometimes hurt each other. You may, probably will, try to control each other and try to get the other to serve your ego and greed and pride. When any of that happens, don't please be too surprised, and come again to the other one and ask him, or her, for forgiveness. If, as will surely happen, you need to ask for forgiveness and give forgiveness, never wait until tomorrow; act at once and discover, again and again, how close forgiveness is to deeper, truer love.

A special request from me is that you may each give time and space for your friendship for each other to grow. Being too busy to listen, to be silent together, to share reading and longings and hopes, is a huge sadness and loss which I hope and pray may never be allowed to take hold in your family. You are given to each other to grow into unity, unity with all in its marvelous variety, and only by burning up time can that happen. And then, with compassion growing within you your home and life will always be open towards the poor ones in the human family, the "little people," the hungry and the broken-spirited, upon whom the future depends; they are waiting for you, for your compassion in love, wherever you may be, here in Europe or further afield.

In our tragic race to outdo the others, to be more useful, more productive than the others, to be rich in order to be happy, to look after our future, listen to the wise and ponder what their experience teaches them. One finds them, women and men, in the most unlikely places; they seldom advertise their wares, nor are they self-conscious of the gift they are for the world. One I have found, of all places, in the U.S.A., (the country whose government is now so devoted to killing that the rest may learn not to kill). There in Kentucky lives a farmer, a sage, a poet, Wendell Berry by name. To finish here are some words from him: ponder them if you will:

"So, friends, every day do something that won't compute.

Love the Lord. Love the world. Work for nothing.
Take all that you have and be poor.
Laugh. Laughter is immeasurable.
Be joyful though you have considered all the facts.
Practice resurrection."[1]

A vast and overwhelming programme, this, for "two people made one," and yet possible because of this blessing from India that I give you with all the love of my small heart.

The Compassionate Father bless you.
The Son of God, the Real Man, bless you.
The Giver of Life, true bliss, the breath of Life, the Supreme Spirit
Bless you—again and again.

---

1. An excerpt from Berry's "The Mad Farmer."

Appendix 14

Celebration of the Eucharist

Oxford, 2006

The Jyotiniketan Community

Priest: Blessed be God, both now and ever, and unto the ages of ages.

family: Amen.

priest: Glory be to you, O Father everlasting,

family: who sent your beloved Son into the world, that we might live through him.

priest: Glory be to you, O Lord Jesus Christ,

family: who brought life and immortality to light through the Gospel.

priest: Glory be to you, O Holy Spirit of God,

family: who quicken us together with Christ and shed abroad his love in our hearts.

priest: I will come to the altar of God,

family: Praise the God of my joy.

Reading of a Psalm

leader: Let us pause awhile to remember how often and in what ways we have failed to love God and our neighbor.

(short silence)

Together: We have forgotten who we are.
We have alienated ourselves from
 the unfolding of the cosmos.
We have become estranged from
 the movements of the earth.
We have turned our backs
 on the cycles of life.
We have forgotten who we are.

We have sought only our own security,
We have exploited simply for our own ends.
We have distorted our knowledge.
We have abused our power.
We have forgotten who we are.

Now the land is barren,
And the waters are poisoned,
And the air is polluted.
We have forgotten who we are.

Now the forests are dying
And the creatures are disappearing
And humans are despairing.
We have forgotten who we are.

We ask for forgiveness,
We ask for the gift of remembering.
We ask for the strength to change.
We have forgotten who we are.[1]

---

1. Roberts and Amidon, *Earth Prayers*, 70–71.

CELEBRATION OF THE EUCHARIST   395

Priest: The Lord is joy and compassion, patience and unchanging love.
   or
   When he was yet a long way off, the father saw him and ran to meet him.
   or
   As a father has compassion on his children, so the Lord has compassion on us all.

   or
   Our trust is in the Unnameable, the God who makes all things right.

Family: Thanks be to God.

The prayer for the day

Liturgy of the Cosmic Covenant

Chant   Asato ma sad gamaya   From the unreal lead us to the real
   tamaso ma jyotir gamaya   from darkness lead us to light,
   mrityor mamritam gamaya   from death lead us to life.
   OM, shanti shanti shantih

Reading from the Upanishads

Together: We thank you, Compassionate Lord, for those who today worship you
   through other symbols received from their ancient traditions and
   through the Holy Spirit working in the depths of their hearts.
   May we and they together find that salvation which is you.

Reading from the New Testament

Alleluia (chant)

The Gospel Reading

Chant   Purnam adah purnam idam   Fullness there, fullness here,
   purnat purnam udacyate   from fullness fullness proceeds.

purnasya purnam adaya	When fullness is taken from fullness
purnam evavasisyate	fullness remains.
OM shanti shanti shantih	OM, shanti, shanti, shantih.

The Offertory

Priest: Let us present our offerings to the Lord with reverence and joy.

This bread which symbolizes our work and the work of all people.

This wine—our celebration and also, strangely, our pains (the crushing of the grapes)

A little water which is no longer water.

These flowers, symbols of the whole of God's creation.
(Eight, in Indian thought, represents fullness and speaks also of the four points of the compass~and the four points in between.)

OM Sri Yesu	bhagavate namah	Glory to Jesus/the Lord
	abhishiktaya namah	the Christ
	tarkesaya namah	the Saviour
	devaputraya namah	the Son of God
	Mariamsunave namah	the Son of Mary
	naraharaye namah	the Man God
	sadgurave namah	the True Master
	satpurusaya namah	the True Person

This incense-the prayers and yearning of all humanity.

shantakaram bhujagavijayam
sarvanatham suresam
vande yesum bhavabhayaharam
sarvolokai kanatham

Giver of peace, victor of the serpent,
Lord of all, Lord of lords,
Remover of the world's fear, Lord of all worlds,
Jesus, I bow to you.

CELEBRATION OF THE EUCHARIST

The Great Thanksgiving

priest: The Lord be with you.
family: And also with you.
priest: Lift up your hearts.
family: We lift them up to the Lord.
priest: Let us give thanks to the Lord our God.
family: It is right to give him thanks and praise.

priest: How right it is, Lord, that Your praise
should move the world to joy and love.
The powers of evil flee in fear on every side
and all the hosts of good bow down to You.

(the Bhagavad Gita)
or some other preface

Together: Therefore with angels and archangels, and with all the
company of heaven, we praise and magnify your glorious
name, evermore worshipping you and saying:

Holy, holy, holy Lord God of hosts, heaven and earth
are full of your glory. Glory be to you, O Lord most high. Amen.

priest: You truly are holy, you truly are worthy of praise,
O God our Father. In your mercy you gave your son
Jesus Christ to assume our nature and to die upon
the cross for our redemption. He made there, by
an offering for all time of himself to you, one perfect
and sufficient sacrifice for the sin of the whole world.
And he instituted for us a memorial of his life-bringing
death, telling us to continue it again and again until he
comes at the end of time.

The night he was betrayed he took bread, gave thanks to
you and broke it. He gave it to his disciples saying,
"Take this and eat it; this is my Body which is given for you.
Do this in memory of me."

Again, when supper was ended, he took the cup. He gave
thanks and gave the cup to his disciples, saying,
"Drink of this, all of you. This is my Blood, the blood of the

new covenant, which is to be shed for you and for all people, so that sins may be forgiven. Whenever you do this, do it in memory of me."

family: Amen.

priest: So now, Father, God of glory and majesty, we your people celebrate with humble hearts, through these holy things you have yourself given us, the memorial your Son gave to us. We recall his passion and death, his life-giving resurrection and his ascension into glory. We give you our heartfelt thanks for all that this means to us and look forward with joy to his return in power and great glory.

Accept, Father, this sacrifice of praise and gratitude. Grant that we and all your church, relying upon your Son Jesus Christ and on his saving work, may receive forgiveness of our sins and all the gifts of his grace.

We ask you, merciful Father, to fill us and these your gifts with your own holy and life-giving Spirit, that this bread may be truly to us the Body of Christ, and that this cup which we bless in your name may be truly to us his Blood. May all we who share in this sacrament be strengthened by your grace and bound together in the unity of your Son our Saviour Jesus Christ.

family: Amen.

Together: We now offer to you, O Lord, unworthy as we are, ourselves, all that we have and are, to be a sincere spiritual offering to you. Do not look, O Lord, on our unworthiness, but pardon our offenses through Jesus Christ our Lord. For through him, in him, with him, in the unity of the Holy Spirit, all honour and glory is yours, compassionate Father, for ever and ever. Amen.

He the Lord and Knower of all,
He the inner one, the source of being,
The beginning and end of all things that are,
The Lord of what has been and what shall be,
OM tat sat

or

>Lord of the universe, O Eternal Light of lights,
>Lord of the universe, we bow to you.
>Most holy and supreme Spirit of creation,
>Again and again, we bow to you.

The Prayer that includes the whole of creation

>Our Father in heaven, hallowed be your name.
>May your kingdom come. May your will be done,
>on earth as it is in heaven. Give us this day the bread we need,
>and forgive us our sins and offenses, as we have forgiven
>those who have offended us. Do not lead us into temptation
>but deliver us from the evil one. For yours is the Kingdom,
>the power and the glory, for ever and ever. Amen.
>*(Syrian Orthodox)*

We share the peace

Prayer before communion

>Lord, I am not worthy to receive you. Say but the word, and I shall be healed.

Communion

A personal prayer in the silence after receiving communion

>I have carried you, Lord, in the hollow of my hand,
>you whom the whole universe cannot contain. I have
>placed you in my mouth, so that by the receiving of your
>Body and your Blood our sins may be forgiven
>both in this world and the other.

(Syrian liturgy)

Prayer after communion

Priest: Thanks be to God for his gift beyond all telling.

Together: We have received, Lord, your Body openly.
May your power now dwell in us secretly,
that we may go forth to meet you with gladness,
and praise you all the days of our life,
for your love's sake. Amen.

Priest: O Great Spirit, whose voice I hear in the winds,
and whose breath gives life to all the world,
hear me! I am small and weak, I need your
    strength and wisdom.
Let me walk in beauty, and make my eyes ever behold
    the red and purple sunset.
Make my hands respect the things you have made
    and my ears sharp to hear your voice.
Make me wise so that I may understand
    the things you have taught my people.
Let me learn the lessons you have hidden
    in every leaf and rock.
I seek strength, not to be greater than my brother
    but to fight my greatest enemy—myself.
Make me always ready to come to you
    with clean hands and straight eyes.
So when life fades, as the fading sunset,
My spirit may come to you without shame.[2]
(Prayers of First Nation people)

The Blessing: May the compassionate Father bless you.
May the Son of God, the Real Man, bless you.
May the Giver of Life, True Bliss, the Breath of Life,
the Supreme Divine Spirit,
bless you—again and again.

*This order for the celebration of the Eucharist,
as used in India, is published by*

*The Jyotiniketan Community
St Andrew's Lodge
St Mary's Road
Oxford OX 1RU
UK*

---

2. Roberts and Amidon, *Earth Prayers*, 188.

Appendix 15

Favorite Prayers

Salutation to the Dawn

Listen to the salutation to the dawn,
Look to this day for it is life, the very life of life.
In its brief course lie all the verities and realities of our existence—
The bliss of growth, the splendour of beauty,
For yesterday is but a dream, and tomorrow is only a vision,
But today well spent makes every yesterday a dream of happiness
And every tomorrow a vision of hope.
Look well therefore to this day.
Such is the salutation to the dawn.
—Kālidāsa, from the Sanskrit
first or second century, BCE

A Prayer for the Morning

We enter each day with
   the power of God to guide us,
   the might of God to uphold us,
   the wisdom of God to teach us,
   the eye of God to watch over us,
   the word of God to give us speech,
   the hand of God to protect us,
   the way of God to stretch before us,
   the love of God to teach us how to live.

Another Prayer for the Morning

Lord, when we awake and day begins,

Waken us to your Presence.
Waken us to your indwelling.
Waken us to inward sight of You
  and speech with You and strength from You,
that all our earthly walk may waken into song
and our spirits leap up to You, all day, always.

A Prayer to enter silence

Be silent, still, aware,
for there in your own heart
the Spirit is at prayer.
Listen and learn,
open and find
heart-wisdom
Christ.

In deep heart
a tiny room
with space for all
quiet filled
light filled
Christ filled
holding the universe
holding the ALL.

—Malling Abbey

Another Prayer to enter silence

O You who have come into the depth of my heart,
  enable me to concentrate solely
  on this depth of my heart.

O You, who are my guest in the depth of my heart,
  enable me also to penetrate
  into the depth of my heart.

O You, who are at home in the depth of my heart,
  enable me to sit peacefully
  in this depth of my heart.

O You, who alone belong in the depth of my heart,
    enable me to dive deep and lose myself
       in this deepest depth of my heart.

O You, who are quite alone in the depth of my heart,
    enable me to disappear into You
       in this depth of my heart.

—Tamil Lyric

Jesus, Master Carpenter

O Jesus, Master Carpenter of Nazareth
Who on the cross though wood and nails hath wrought our
    full salvation,
Wield well thy tools in this thy workshop,
That we who come to thee, roughhewn,
May, by thy hand, be fashioned to a truer beauty,
For thy love's sake. *Amen.*

Prayer of St. Francis

O Lord, make us instruments of your peace.
Where there is hatred, let us sow love; where there is injury, pardon.
Where there is discord, peace; where there is doubt, faith.
Where there is despair, hope; where there is darkness, light;
Where there is sadness, joy.
May we ourselves seek not so much to be consoled, as to console;
    to be understood, as to understand;
    to be loved, as to love.
For it is in giving that we receive;
It is in pardoning that we are pardoned;
It is in dying to self that we are born to life with you for ever.
In your blessed Son, Jesus Christ our Lord. *Amen.*

Hindu chant
(Pavamana Mantra)

Asoto ma sad gamaya
tamaso ma jyoti gamaya
mrityor mamritam gamaya
OM, shanti shanti shantih

From the unreal lead us to the real,
from darkness lead us to light,
from death lead us to immortality,
from death led us to life.

From delusion lead us to the truth,
from darkness lead us to light,
from death lead us to immortality,
from death lead us to life.

    OM, peace, peace, peace.

Hymn

Lord God transcendent immanent presence,
Fling wide all heart doors, unprison light.
In let your grace flow, in flow your glory,
Being resplendent, we bow before You.

Native American Prayer

O Great Spirit
Whose voice I hear in the winds,
and whose breath gives life to all the world,
Hear me! I am small and weak, I need your strength and wisdom.
Let me walk in beauty, and make my eyes
    ever behold the red and purple sunset.
Make my hands respect the things you have made,
    and my ears sharp to hear your voice.
Make me wise so that I may understand the things
    you have taught my people.
Let me learn the lessons you have hidden
    in every leaf and rock.

I seek strength, not to be greater than my brother,
>   but to fight my greatest enemy—myself.
> Make me always ready to come to you
>   with clean hands and straight eyes.
> So when life fades, as the fading sunset,
>   my spirit may come to you without shame.

Prayer of Cardinal Newman

Lord Jesus, I have the joy and the responsibility of believing that we are one. Don't extinguish the light of your presence within me. O Lord, look through my eyes, listen through my ears, speak though my lips, walk with my feet. Lord, may my poor human presence be a reminder, however weak, of your divine presence. For, to the degree that others notice me, it is a sign that I am, unfortunately, still opaque and not transparent.

Untitled

Lord, in your deep peace may our souls keep vigil, attentive only to the sight and sound of your love. Beloved, keep your steadfast watch within our hearts that in the stillness of your Presence we may turn from love of self to love of You.

Hymn to the Night

> O Night, you have filled this entire earth with your presence
>   in accordance with the Father's command.
> Outstretching your arms you reach to the highest heaven,
>   the twinkling darkness draws near.
>
> One cannot descry the opposite bank of her stream,
>   nor yet what lies in between.
> In her bosom reposes all that lives and stirs,
>   Grant, O wide darksome night,
> that we may safely attain your further shore,
>   attain, pray, your further shore!
> We make our dwelling in you. Our hearts crave sleep.
>   Keep watch then, O Night, we pray.
> Grant your protection to our homes, our goods, and our friends. Upanishads: Av. xix, 47

Appendix 16

Last Prayer at Night

Oxford, 2006

The sun, after journeying across the sky, has disappeared below the horizon. This day is coming to a close and with prayerful hearts we greet the approach of night. We pause now to thank God for all that has happened to each of us this day with its mixture of problems and joys, suffering and love. . .

(together) Lord of day and night, holy Creator of both light and darkness, we ask your loving care for all those who suffer tonight. You are the Companion of the lonely and the Physician of the sick. We seek your blessing also upon all those whom we as a praying community represent. Shed your light upon them and upon each of our family members. O Lord, Holy Father, guard us this night and grant us your gentle care. Amen.

(leader) And now with gladness and at peace with one another, we enter the Kingdom of God within our hearts as we wish each other God's peace.

Bibliography

Abhishiktananda, Swami. *Ascent to the Depth of the Heart: The Spiritual Diary*. Edited by Raimon Panikkar. Translation by David Fleming and James Stuart. Delhi: ISPCK, 1986.

———. *Swami Abhishiktananda: Essential Writings*. Selected and with an introduction by Shirley du Boulay. Modern Spiritual Masters Series. Maryknoll, NY: Orbis, 2006.

———. *Guru and Disciple*. Translated by Heather Sandeman. London: SPCK, 1974.

Almadas, Swami. "The Breath of God." *Monastic Interreligious Dialogue* 10 (February 1981). http://www.monasticinterreligiousdialogue.com/images/bulletins/1981-02%20Bulletin%2010.pdf.

Andrews, Charles Freer. *Mahatma Gandhi's Ideas*. London: Allen & Unwin, 1929.

———. *North India: Handbooks of English Church Expansion*. London: Mowbray, 1908.

Baker, Laurie. "India and Gandhiji." http://lauriebaker.net/index.php/life/india-and-gandhiji.

Balfour, Arthur. "Balfour Declaration." World War I Document Archive. http://wwi.lib.byu.edu/index.php/The_Proclamation_of_Baghdad.

Blackburn, J. "Frank Binford Hole," 1964. www.stempublishing.com/authors/Biographies/fbhole.html.

Book of Common Prayer 1929. (Anglican, Proposed). http://justus.anglican.org/resources/bcp/CofE1928/CofE1928.htm.

Canons of the Church of England. London: Church House, 2000. http://www.churchofengland.org/media/35588/complete.pdf.

Cardenal, Ernesto. *Abide in Love*. Maryknoll, NY: Orbis, 1995.

Chaturvedi, Benarsidas, and Marjorie Sykes. *Charles Freer Andrews*. New York: Harper & Brothers, 1950.

Churchill, Winston S. *Winston S. Churchill: His Complete Speeches*. Vol. 6. Edited by Robert Rhodes James. New York: Chelsea House, 1974.

Clarke, George Herbert. *A Treasury of War Poetry*. Boston: Houghton Mifflin, 1917. http://www.bartleby.com/266/.

Cort, Howard. "Martin Buber's Israel/Palestine Unity Movement." 1956. http://www.spiritualprogressives.org/article.php/20090810084113685.

Daniel, Monodeep. "Remembering Charles Murray Rogers." *Bulletin of the Abhishiktananda Society* 27 (April 2007).

Dart, Martha, ed. *Transcending Tradition: Excerpts from the Writings and Talks of Marjorie Sykes*. York, UK: William Sessions in association with Woodbrooke College, 1995.

Douglass, James W. *Lightning East to West: Jesus, Gandhi and the Nuclear Age*. New York: Crossroad, 1984.

Du Boulay, Shirley. "The Priest and the Swami." *The Tablet* (April 21, 2001).

———. *The Cave of the Heart: The Life of Swami Abhishiktananda*. Maryknoll, NY: Orbis, 2005.

Gandhi, M. *The Essential Gandhi*. Edited by Louis Fischer. New York: Vintage, 1962.

Gauthier, Paul. *Christ, the Church and the Poor*. London: Birchall, 1964.

Hole, Frank Binford. *Foundations of the Faith*. Plymouth, UK: Mayflower, 1922.

Kamat, Vikas. "Rashtriya Swayamsevak Sangh." 2015. http://www.kamat.com/indica/culture/sub-cultures/rss.htm.

Klostermaier, Klaus. "Meeting on 'Hindu and Christian Spirituality': Jyotiniketan." Unpublished paper, 1964.

———. "Jacques-Albert Cuttat, a Pioneer of Hindu-Christian Dialogue." *Journal of Hindu-Christian Studies* 2 (1989). http://dx.doi.org/10.7825/2164-6279.1015.

Machado, Antonio. *Times Alone: Selected Poems of Antonio Machado*. Translated by Robert Bly. Middletown, CT: Wesleyan University Press, 1983.

Mascaro, Juan, ed. and trans. *Upanishads*. London: Penguin, 1965.

Merton, Thomas. *Mystics and Zen Masters*. New York: Farrar, Straus & Giroux, 1961.

———. *The Way of Chuang Tzu*. New York: New Directions, 1969.

Mishra, Pankaj. *An End to Suffering: The Buddha in the World*. New York: Farrar, Straus & Giroux, 2004.

Mitchell, Stephen. *A Book of Psalms: Selected and Adapted from the Hebrew*. New York: Harper Collins, 1993.

Nehru, Jawaharlal. "A Tryst with Destiny." 1947. http://www.guardian.co.uk/theguardian/2007/may/01/greatspeeches.

———. "We must hold together." 1948. http://www.thehindu.com/opinion/op-ed/we-must-hold-together/article4358063.ece

Nouwen, Henri. *The Selfless Way of Christ: Downward Mobility and the Spiritual Life*. Maryknoll, NY: Orbis, 2007.

Oldham, J. H. *Life Is Commitment*. New York: Harper, 1952.

Oshida, Vincent Shigeto. "Zen: The Mystery of the Word and Reality." *Monastic Interreligious Dialogue* Bulletin 75 (October 2005). http://www.monasticdialog.com/au.php?id=491.

Overy, Richard. *The Twilight Years: The Paradox of Britain Between the Wars*. London: Viking, 2009.

Panikkar, Raimon. "Eruption of Truth: An Interview with Raimon Panikkar. *The Christian Century*, August 16–23, 2000, 834–36. Also at http://www.religion-online.org/showarticle.asp?title=2015.

———. *Christophany: The Fullness of Man*. Translated by Alfred DiLascia. Faith Meets Faith Series. Maryknoll, NY: Orbis, 2004.

———. *The Vedic Experience: Mantramanjari*. Delhi: Motilal Banarsidass, 1977.

Roberts, Elizabeth, and Elias Amidon, eds. *Earth Prayers from around the World*. San Francisco: HarperCollins, 1991.

———. *Life Prayers*. San Francisco: HarperCollins, 1996.

Robinson, Bob. *Christians Meeting Hindus: An Analysis and Theological Critique of the Hindu-Christian Encounter in India.* Oxford: Regnum, 2004.

Rogers, Murray, and David Barton. *Abhishiktananda: A Memoir of Dom Henri Le Saux.* Oxford: SLG, 2003.

Rogers, C. Murray, G. Clive Handford, Edward Every, Adela M. Every. "Human Rights in Jerusalem." Letters to the Editor, *Times* (London), Jan. 7, 1977.

Rogers, C. Murray. "An Anglican View of the Bombay Eucharistic Congress." *One in Christ: A Catholic Ecumenical Review* 1.3 (1965) 261–67.

———. "Choice of Anglican Bishop of Jerusalem." Letters to the Editor, *Times* (London), Dec. 24, 1973.

———. "The Far Way Look: Reflections on the Tao of Interfaith Dialogue." *Ecumenical Review of the World Council of Churches* (October 1985) 430–36.

———. "Grounds for Mutual Growth." *Journal of Hindu–Christian Studies* 14 (2001) 3–6.

———. "Hindu and Christian—A Moment Breaks." In *Inter-Religious Dialogue*, edited by Herbert Jai Singh, 104–17. Bangalore: Christian Institute for the Study of Religion and Society, 1967.

———. "Hindu Influence on Christian Spiritual Practice." *Asian Cultural Studies* 4 (1993) 137–44.

———. "The Joyful Surprise of One-ing: The Experience of Julian of Norwich." In *Mysticism in Shaivism and Christianity*, edited by Bettina Bäumer, 293–308. New Delhi: D.K. Printworld, 1997.

———. "Jyotiniketan Ashram." *Eastern Churches Quarterly* 16 (1964) 232–38.

———. "Jyotiniketan: A Community of the Church." *National Christian Council Review* (October 1963) 1–7.

———. "Missionary, Go Home?" *Asia Focus* (2nd Quarter, 1970) 47–53.

———. "A New Millennium—Nearly!" *Journal of Hindu–Christian Studies* 8 (1995) 36–41.

———. *'No More Humbug' Says the Fool: Some Sermons, Talks and Articles.* Selected and privately published by Michael Perrott, 2007.

———. "On the Pilgrim Path." *Asian Cultural Studies* 4 (1993) 145–49.

———. "Who Am I? The Human Question: One Man's Pilgrimage." *Asian Cultural Studies* 20 (1994) 101–16.

Sadhana Institute. http://www.sadhanainstitute.org/hist.htm.

Samartha, S. J. "Reflections on a Multilateral Dialogue." *Ecumenical Review* 26 (October 1974) 637–46.

Singh, Joginder, and Shrinivas Warkhandkar. "Laurie Baker's Creative Journey." *Frontline* 20.5 (March 1–14, 2003). http://arvindguptatoys.com/arvindgupta/bakerjogiatul.pdf.

Stock, E. *The History of the Church Missionary Society.* Vol. 3. London: Church Missionary Society. 1899. http://archive.org/stream/historyofthechur015639mbp#page/n3/mode/2up.

Student Christian Movement Hymnbook. 5th ed. Madras: Christian Literature Society, 1957.

Tagore, Rabindranath. *Gitanjali.* New York: Macmillan, 1913.

Taylor, John V. *The Primal Vision.* Philadelphia: Fortress, 1963.

Terricabras, Josep-Maria. "Laudatio of Raimon Panikkar Alemany." 2008. http://www.raimon-panikkar.org/english/laudatio.html.

Tuskegee University. "Legacy of Dr. George Washington Carver." No date. http://www.tuskegee.edu/about_us/legacy_of_fame/george_w_carver.asx.
Vatican: the Holy See http://www.vatican.va/roman_curia/congregations/cfaith/documents/rc_con_cfaith_doc_19980624.
Walmsley, Arthur E. "A Legacy of Leadership: A Reflection on Curtis Almquist's Years as Superior." *Cowley Magazine* (Summer 2010) 7–8.
Warren, Max. "Introduction." In John V. Taylor, *The Primal Vision*. Philadelphia: Fortress, 1963.
Weatherhead, Leslie D. *The Mastery of Sex through Psychology and Religion*. New York: Blue Ribbon, 1932.
Weber, Hans-Ruedi. *The Bible Comes Alive*. Valley Forge, PA: Judson, 1996.
Wilber, Ken. *No Boundary*. Boston: Shambala, 2001.
Wiser, William H., and Charlotte Wiser. *Behind Mud Walls: 1930–1960*. Berkeley: University of California Press, 1963.
Wiser, William H. *The Hindu Jajmani System* Lucknow, U.P. India: Lucknow, 1958.
World Council of Churches Archives. http://archives.oikoumene.org/en.

Letters from Mary Rogers and Murray Rogers to Raimon Panikkar were entrusted by Raimon Panikkar to Andrea Andriotto, Tymawr Convent, Lydart, Monmouth, Wales.

Index

Abhishiktananda (Henri le Saux/ Swamiji)
  advaita, sharing his quest for, 148–49
  his affirmation of God, (Murray quotes), 322
  anguish of, 386
  awakening and death; exchange of letters with Murray, 191–93, 259
  biographical writings on, 320–321, 323
  connection with Raimon Panikkar, 95
  dialogue with, 114–17
  Eucharist
    concelebration of, with Murray, 165, 166
    meaning of, for, 165–68
  grieving his death, 194
  Heather translates for, 162
  influence on Murray's spiritual evolution, 166, 197, 218–19, 237
  Jyotiniketan's introduction to, spiritual history of, 103–7
  keepsakes of, 314
  laughter and authenticity of, 287
  meetings and qualms about interfaith exploration, 120
  receives vows from Jyotiniketan members, 128
  remembering in India, 247–48
  Richard's memory of, 110
  Society, 286
  spiritual director, as, 134
  spiritual guide, as, 152–53
  spiritual influence on Jyotiniketan, 122, 131–32, 387
  stories of, 295
  strain in relationship with, 163, 164
  surrender, according to, 326–27
  visits to Jyotiniketan, 169
Addis Ababa, 161
advaita, 104, 105, 106n36, 131, 149, 168, 184, 246, 286, 301
Agricultural Institute (College), Allahabad University, 28
  contrasted by Murray with Sevagram, 35, 43
  decision to leave, 38
  Indian attitudes towards, 35
  Murray's reflections on, 86, 94
Ajaltoun, Lebanon, 197, 199
Allahabad, 30, 34, 39
  bishop from, 78, 145
  Kumbh Mela in, 108n46, 388
  Mary and Murray's return to, 57
  waiting and discernment in, 85
All Saints Convent, Oxford
  celebration of anniversary at, 312
  celebration of Jyotiniketan liturgy for Murray's funeral at, 330
  Helen House at, 310
  St. Andrew's Lodge at, 310–11
Almora
  first Cuttat Circle meeting at, 117
  insights on meeting at, 118
  return visit to, 247
Al Shak'a, Basam
  Nablus mayor controversy, 216
American Colony, Jerusalem, 173

Anabaptist, 6
Andrews, C.F. (Deenabandu)
    advice of, for missionaries, 31–32
    as inspiration for Murray, 287
    connection of, to Gandhi, 34
    friendship with Marjorie Sykes, 83–84
    ideas of, contrasted with Murray's, 57
    influence of, on G.W. Carver, 27
    letter to Gandhi, 51
    Murray's meetings with, impressions of, 15–16
    Murray learns of his death, 17
Appleton, George
    retirement triggers controversy, 202
    welcomes Jyotiniktan to Jerusalem, 172
arati, 150–51
Armenian Quarter, Old City of Jerusalem, 206, 207, 211
Arunachala, 104, 105, 106, 131, 165, 295
Aryanayakam, E.W.
    head of Sevagram, 35, 42
ashram(s)
    Christa Prema Seva Sangha, 162, 194
    Gandhi's, 3, 35, 38, 40–46, 78 (*see also* Sevagram)
    Hindu, 82–82, 133
    Jyotiniketan as, 82, 85, 88, 89, 90, 93, 94, 99, 114n55, 119–20, 125, 130, 133, 145–46, 148, 152, 156, 163, 227, 281, 295
    liturgy of, 168–69
    vows to, 128
    under Deenabandu, 176, 219, 247
    end of, 323
    Shantivanam, 103, 114, 131
Assisi
    Cheryl meets André in, 139
    Murray and Cheryl in, 138
    return visit to, 271
Ateek, Naim, 299
Athenagoras, Bishop
    Murray and Mary's meeting with, 115, 171
    remembering, 271
    story of his meeting with Pope Paul VI, 179–80
Augustine, Father, 163, 164, 170, 176 (*see also* Deenabandu)

Baker, Kuni (medical doctor and wife of Laurie), 64
    holidays with, 67, 110, 219, 247, 317
    Quakerism of, 83
    Trustee of Jyotiniketan, 100
Baker, Laurie (architect and husband of Kuni), 64
    meeting with Gandhi, creative genius of, 64
    Mary and Murray's friendship with, 67, 110, 166, 219, 247, 317
    plan of, for Jyotiniketan, 85
    plan of, for barn in Canada, 272
Banaras, 134 (*see also* Varanasi)
Banaras Hindu University, 95, 103
Bangalore, 114, 163
Bangkok, 114, 136, 176, 357
Bareilly, Uttar Pradesh, 59, 60, 69, 94, 96, 102, 136, 145
Barton, David, xvii, 320, 330
Bäumer, Bettina, 161, 247, 286, 294
Bath, England
    Mary's childhood home in, 12, 18, 22
    Monkton Combe School in, 70, 128
Berrigan, Daniel, 212
Bethany, 225 (*see also* Homes of Mercy in)
Bishop, Jack (John)
    invitation from, 253
    letter to, regarding money, 278
Bethlehem
    as a possible place to settle, 178
    cave of, 149
    conflict in, 208
    keepsake of, 314
    sesshin in, 183, 222
Bombay Eucharistic Congress, 116
Bonhoeffer, Dietrich
    community reading of his *Ethics*, 95
    miming of his ideas, 99–100
    Murray cites, 269

Murray visits home of, 71
Bossey, Switzerland, 114, 129 (*see* World Council of Churches in)
Buber, Martin, 63, 188n35, 197
Burgh on Bain, Lincolnshire, 305, 306, 309

Cambridge, England
  marriage and life in, 18–21, 24, 38
  Molesworth Peace Camp near, 264n17
Cambridge University
  Cheryl at, 129
  Mary and Murray at, 1–2, 12–14, 16–17
  Richard at, 140, 160
Campbell, Kate and Adam, xviii, 289–92, 294–97, 299, 301, 305, 311
Canada, xiv–xvi, xviii, 2
  decision to move to, 269
  Jyotiniketan in, 271–303, 376–78
  Murray's visit to Manitoba, 267
caste system, 30, 34n18, 41n6, 51–53, 57, 58
Ceylon (Sri Lanka)
  Heather in, 77
  students from, 28
Chacour, Elias, 209, 299
Chapel of St. Abraham, Church of the Holy Sepulcher, 192, 217, 226
Chidananda, Swami, 195–96
chowkidar, 60, 61
Christa Prema Seva Sangha, 162–63
Christ Church Greenwich, CT, xiii, 253–54, 278
  homily at, 382
Christian Missionary Society (C.M.S.)
  as entrée for Murray, 73, 94
  financial issues with, 46, 93–95, 110, 122, 140
  first assignment for, 28
  frustration with missionary life for, 30, 140
  Heather resists, 80
  Mary, as missionary for, 27
  Max Warren, head of, 26
  Murray's application to, 8

Murray ends relationship with, 142–44
  regulations on marriage of, 18
  reporting to, 48, 49, 72–72
  support of Murray by, 36, 73, 122
  teacher preparation for, 24
Christian Movement for Peace, 205
Chrysostom, Bishop Philipose Mar, 114, 118, 295, 317
Chuang Tzu, 235, 236, 237, 251, 301
Church of the Holy Sepulcher (Church of the Resurrection), 177, 179, 226
Churchill, Winston
  first radio address of, 21
Cole, John, 109, 115, 118, 122, 128, 130, 147, 155
Colombo, Sri Lanka, 194, 200
Coventry Cathedral, 158, 160
Cragg, Kenneth (Bishop)
  in interfaith dialogue, 199
Cunningham, B.K., 17, 18, 19
Cuttat Circle (Cuttat Group), 116–20, 122, 138, 197, 247
Cuttat, Jacques-Albert, 116, 118, 119, 138

Darbyites, 10
darshan
  with the Dalai Lama, 275–76
  defined, 275
David, Michael, xviii, 200–201
de Chardin, Teilhard, 121, 290, 316–17, 386
Deenabandu, Swami (Father Augustine), 163, 164, 170, 176, 247, 286, 292, 333
de Foucault, Charles, 73
Dehra Dun, 29
de Mello, Anthony, 227, 324
  on death, 258
  humor of, 259
  writings banned by Vatican, spirituality continues, 359n3
double-belonging, 120, 249, 255
Deng Xiaoping, 232, 257
Deseronto, Ontario, xvi, 275, 277, 279, 286, 289, 294, 295, 302

Douglass, James, 262–63, 278
dualism, 113, 184, 253, 262
du Boulay, Shirley, xvii, 102, 103, 104, 106, 116, 117, 118, 120, 165, 166, 191, 320, 322
Duncan, William, xviii, 254, 279–81

East Asia Christian Conference
    Murray chaplain of, 136, 161
Ecumenical Institute, World Council of Churches
    Ilse Friedeberg of, 114, 129
Ecumenical Theological Fraternity, 181
Eid al-Adha, 215
England
    children's education in, 39, 68, 70–71, 91, 94, 95, 111
    Gandhi on England, 32–33
    Jyotiniketan in, 304–21
    World War II years in, 5, 21–23, 29
    Mary and Murray's young life in, 1–27
England, Rita and John, 230
Eucharist
    Abhishiktananda's participation in, 106, 165–66, 192, 193
    banned by Bishop of Oxford from celebrating, 313
    Celebration of the Eucharist: Oxford (2006), 393–401
    centrality of, for Jyotiniketan, 135, 273, 279, 329
    Cuttat group's celebration of, 117
    development of Indian, 151, 165, 168–69
    experience of, 121–22, 123, 135
    interfaith readings in, 235
    Jerusalem celebrations of, 151, 185, 192, 200–201, 212, 217, 219, 223, 226
    Jyotiniketan's Holy Eucharist (1971), 338–55
    Murray celebrating, (photo) 307
    Murray's teaching and homily on, 306
    political flash-point, as, 201
    Raimon Panikkar's influence on Jyotiniketan's, 120–21
    theology of, 167–68
Exeter Cathedral, 18, 21, 24

Fairacres Community, Oxford, 139
Feuerbach, Ludwig, 63
First Nation
    people near Deseronto, Canada, 273
    heritage of Ruby Kells, 294–95
    prayer, 400
    solidarity with people of, 282
Friedeberg, Ilse
    at Ecumenical Institute, 129
    in Jerusalem, 115, 171
    tribute to, 114
Frizzell, Herbert and Susan, 269, 272–73, 274, 276–77

Galilee, 185, 200, 210, 261
Gandhi, Mahatma
    activism of, 3, 32–33
    as inspiration for Mary and Murray, 34, 44, 48–49, 108, 215, 221, 233, 244, 277, 279, 280, 297, 300, 314, 366
    C.F. Andrews, relationship with, 16, 27, 51, 83, 287
    death of, 33, 101
    educational system of, 38, 44–45, 46, 47
    Laurie Baker, meeting with, 64
    Marjorie Sykes and, 84
    Murray and Mary at the ashram of, 35, 37, 38, 43–44, 46, 78
    Murray struggles with, 47–49, 57
    quotation of, 37
    teaching of, 48, 51n34, 262–63
    Thakkar Bapa, friend of, 146n15
Gandhianism, 48
Ganga/Ganges River
    Abhishiktananda and, 165–66, 167, 247
    Kumbh Mela at, 108n46, 388–89
    misssionary bungalow near, 29
    scattering ashes in, 294
    source of, 107, 247
    spiritual invocation of, 126, 298
Ganges plain

Jyotiniketan located on, 58, 247, 67, 286
poverty of, 96, 108, 376
Gangotri
　pilgrimage to, 166
Garden of Gethsemane
　Eucharists in, 201
　stay at monastery in, 115, 171, 181
Gnanananda, Sri
　Abhishiktananda's encounter with, 105
Gordon, Charles (General), 173nn6-7
Greenwich, CT, viii, xiv
　friends from, 273-74, 279, 286, 292, 293, 306, 308
　Murray's first visit to, 220
　travels to, 253, 255, 286, 292, 308
Gyansu, 165

Hadassah Hospital, Jerusalem
　Verena Tschuden at, 187, 190, 203
Halifax, Nova Scotia, xviii, 311
Hall, Ronald (Bishop), 228
Ham Sok-Hon, Korean Quaker, 249-51, 262
Hancock, March, xvii, xix, 157-58
　life with Linda, 158, 160, 176, 292, 306, 314, 316, 333
Haridwar, 165, 169, 247
Harijan, 34, 58, 233
Hastings, Bradford, 219
Hawkhurst, 92, 94, 129
Higginbottom, Sam, 28
Himalayas, 107, 108, 162 183, 249, 293
　Eucharist in, 165, 167
　foothills of, 117, 293
Hindu(ism)
　Abhishiktananda and, 104-7
　beliefs, 43, 82-83
　holy sites, 29, 107
　joint families in, 49, 78
　Raimon Panaikkar and, 95
　worship and observances, 90, 108
　wedding, 53
Hole, Frank, 9-10, 25, 38, 136
Holy Trinity Anglican Church, Kowloon, 229

Homes of Mercy, Bethany, 176, 204, 205, 207
Hong Kong
　British Empire, as part of, 2, 231-32, 257
　decision to move to, 224
　Jyotiniketan in, 227-70
　Murray's travels to, 114, 136, 224
　transition to Chinese rule of, 257, 264, 267, 268
House of Isaiah, 182
Hussar, Bruno, 182, 187
Hussein, Fidah, 64, 88, 91, 115, 127, 170, 284

India
　adopting lifestyle of, 41, 50, 53-54, 61, 86-87, 89, 90-91
　desire of Murray to go to, 13, 16, 17, 24
　historical context of, 29, 30, 31-33, 141
　Jyotiniketan's decision to leave, 163, 164, 169
　Mary, Heather and Murray's love for, 125, 128, 152, 162, 164, 169
　Mary and Murray in, 28-170
　poverty in, 30, 31, 101, 108
Indo-Pakistani War, 125, 141
Islam [*see also* Muslim(s)]
　compared with other monotheistic religions, 174, 198
　holy mosques of, 180
　in interfaith dialogue, 199-200

jajmani system, 53
Japanese occupation of Hong Kong, 228, 232
Jerusalem, 171-226
　Anglican Diocese of, 199, 201-3, 205, 267, 356-57
　decision to leave, 223-26
　friends in, 174, 182, 188-89, 206, 271, 292, 295, 299
　history of life in, 367, 376
　invitation to, 171-72
　Rainbow Club controversy in, 209-12, 268

Jerusalem *(continued)*
  religious/political conflict in, 172, 178, 179–81, 185–86, 187, 190, 207–10, 213–14
  spiritual experience in, 200–201, 225, 226
John XXIII, Pope, 113, 116, 133
Jordan River, 201
Jumna River, 29
Jyotiniketan, xi–xix, 73
  Act of Commitment to, 358–62
  ashram described, 366–68, 376–78
  Cuttat Circle meeting at, 118–120
  demonstration against, 101–2
  governance and ownership of, 100
  in Canada (*see* Canada)
  in England (*see* England)
  in Hong Kong (*see* Hong Kong)
  in India, 81–170 (*see* India)
  in Jerusalem (*see* Jerusalem)
  liturgies of, 338–55, 393–400
  naming of ashram, 81–82
  physical layout of, 83, 64–65
  visitors to, 90, 96, 102–3, 109, 112, 114, 125, 134

Kareli, Uttar Pradesh
  historical/cultural context of, 58, 59–60
  life in, 55, 56, 61, 65, 73, 74, 79, 88, 91, 151, 169
  memories of, 186, 192, 266, 287, 293, 295, 314, 385
  visits to, 176, 219, 247
Kasai, Minoru, 109, 248–49, 251, 286, 287, 295, 298
Kedarnath, 107, 109
Kells, Ruby, 279, 294, 295
Klostermaier, Klaus, xviii, 119, 267
Kumbh Mela, 108–9, 113, 388–89
Kyoto, 266

Lamma Island, Hong Kong, 227–28, 259
Landgraf, John, xviii, 174, 175, 206, 207, 295
Lao Tzu, 236, 251, 294
Lawlor, William, 298

Lee, Peter, 223–24, 230
Le Saux, Henri, (*see* Abhishiktananda)
Little Brothers and Sisters of Jesus, 73, 114, 134
Lozoff, Bo and Sita, 255, 295, 321n5
Lunt, Evered, 14, 17, 158

Maharshi, Ramana Sri
  Abhishiktananda's encounter with, 104
  cited, 262
  spiritual influence of, on Abhishiktananda, 166
  teaching of, 104
Mahieu, Jean-Paul, 173
Mao Zedong, 232
Mar Thoma Church, 114, 118, 295
Martin, Clifford, 22
Maruki, Iri and Toshi, 251
Mejid, Sultan Abdul, 178
Melchisedech/Melchisedek
  Chapel of St. Abraham of, 226
  evoked in grief, 192
  identification with, 167, 322
  as patron saint, 314
Meynell, Honor and Godfrey, 294
Middlebury, VT, 275, 276
Miss-a-Meal, 26, 73
missionaries (*see also* Church Missionary Society)
  in Allahabad, 28, 34
  attitudes evolving towards role of, 56–57, 58, 85, 116
  C.F. Andrews, as model, 16, 32
  couple(s) as, xi, 18, 27, 30
  educational work, 28
  financial allowances, 73, 79, 80, 94, 100, 141–42
  Heather included as, 79–80
  Indian attitudes towards, 145
  lifestyle, 29, 30, 94
  Mary's father as, 13
  Murray's desire to be, 13, 14, 17
  quotation of, 37
  role of, questioned, 89
  separating from and disavowing role as, 140, 142, 143, 145–47, 148, 174, 189, 312, 357

Max Warren, as model, 26
  wife, role of, 29
  work of, for Mary and Murray, 37, 40
Mohawk
  people, 273
  pow-wow, 282
  Tyendinaga Territory, 273
Monchanin, Jules
  and Abhishiktananda, 95, 103, 131
Monkton Combe School
  Richard Rogers at, 70, 128, 138, 139
Monroe, Alice (Rogers)
  children born to, 222
  family reunions including, 292, 294, 306
  Richard Rogers' marriage to, 160, 315
  visit to Kareli, 333
Mount Tabor, 185, 201
Muslim(s), 59n8 (*see also* Islam)
  conflict with Hindus in India, 33, 101n13, 157n42, 313
  Feast of *Eid al-Adha*, 215
  holy sites in, 180–81
  interfaith relations with, 26, 80, 86, 90, 117, 127–28, 195, 199, 216, 387, 391
  in Sevagram, 43
  Jerusalem, managing conflict in, 179
  personal relationships with, 58, 64, 78, 81, 82, 102, 127, 385
  Quarter of Old City, living in, 173
Nagpur
  Cuttat Circle meeting in, 118
Nairobi, 200, 219
  "Nairobi 1975" (World Council of Churches meeting), 200
Napanee, Ontario, 272, 276, 277, 299
Nehru, Jawahar, 116, 124, 127
  speech of, 33
Neve Shalom/Wahat al-Salam, 182, 187
New Delhi Assembly (1963 World Council of Churches), 114–15, 141
Nilgiri Hills, 47, 67, 77

October War/Yom Kippur War/Ramadan War
  life during the, 185, 187, 203
Old City, Jerusalem
  life of Jyotiniketan in Armenian Quarter of, 206, 291, 225
  life of Jyotiniketan in Muslim Quarter of, 172, 173, 175–76, 181, 187, 206 (*see also* Jerusalem)
  Murray visits following Six Day War, 137
  Murray's letter re eviction in, 208
  Murray's talk on peace in, 215
  reflections on life in, 230, 274, 356–57, 367
Oldham, J.H., 62–63, 66
  quoted, 56
Ootacamund, Tamil Nadu, 46, 67
Opium War, 232
Oshida, Shigeto
  his integration of Zen Buddhism and Christianity, 183, 248–49
  friendship with, 169, 183, 192, 224, 248, 251
  spiritual teachings of, 184–85, 251–52, 326
Ottoman Empire, 178
Oxford, England, xv, xvii, xix, 139
  connection to Sister Frances Ritchie in, 309–10
  Jyotiniketan in, 310–31, 385

Panikkar, Raimon, xvii, 95–96
  affirmation for Jyotiniketan from, 96, 99
  beliefs of, 197, 386
  declining health of, 298
  double-belonging of, 120–21, 249
  introduction to Abhishiktanada by, 103
  Mary's literary collaboration with, 161–62, 164, 190, 214
  message from, at deaths of Murray and Mary, 331
  Murray seeks help from, 153, 163
  pilgrimage to Gangotri of, 166
  Richard's memory of, 110

Panikkar, Raimon *(continued)*
 spiritual director for Mary, as, 154–58, 160, 161, 178, 183, 184, 257
 spiritual mentor and friend of Jyotiniketan, 96, 121, 122, 152, 153, 166, 247, 267, 286, 298
 Tavertet, Murray, Mary and Heather's visit to, at, 306
 theological colonialism, Murray quotes re, 144
 his visit to Cheryl and André, 160
 his visit to Jyotiniketan in Jerusalem, 185, 201
 Visitor and confessor to Jyotiniketan, 134
pantheism, 113
Parker, Eleanor, 254, 286, 292
Paul VI, Pope, 116, 179–80
Pilkington, Hugh, 219
Plymouth Brethren, 9
 history and beliefs of, 10–11, 25
Plymouth, England, 10, 22
 life in, during Blitz of, 22–24, 185
Po Lin Buddhist Monastery, 136
Poona
 ashram in, 162, 164, 194
Poutier, André, xviii
 foregoes priestly vows, 158, 159
 life with Cheryl, 139, 159, 160, 233, 286, 292, 306, 314, 317, 331
 relationship with Murray, 217, 316–17
Rainbow Club (Group), 181, 190
 conflict within, 187, 189, 209, 210–11
 Murray and Mary's critique of, 188, 210
 Murray expelled from 211, 268
Raisalpur, Madhya Pradesh
 invitation to, 49
 life in, 52–55
Rajpur, 118, 286
Ramganga River, 69, 125, 126
Ranagal, 191, 219
Rashtriya Swayamsevak Sangh (RSS), 101n13
Raven, Charles, 17, 287
Reichelt, Karl Ludvig, 223, 374

Reisner, John, 26
Rishikesh, 107, 169, 191, 218, 247, 286, 294
Ritchie, Frances Dominica, xviii, 309–10
Robinson, Christopher (Bishop of Lucknow), 58, 60, 62, 66, 78, 153, 162
Rogers, Cheryl (Poutier), xv, xviii
 adult life of, 129, 138, 157, 333
 with André, 139, 157, 158–60, 176, 316, 317, 334
 relationship with parents, 45, 217, 222, 233, 286, 292, 293–94, 302, 306, 314, 315, 319, 329, 330, 331
 birth and early childhood, 25, 27
 photo, 46
 education of, 39, 45, 46, 67, 70, 71, 78, 94, 129
 life with parents, 53, 67, 91–92, 110–11, 115, 129–30
 life with surrogate families, 74, 92–93
Rogers, Linda (Hancock), xv, xix
 adult life of, 129, 157, 293–94, 316, 333
 with March, 157–58, 176, 334
 relationship with parents, 45, 222, 255, 292, 293–94, 306, 314, 315, 316, 319, 329, 330, 331
 birth and early childhood, 26, 27, 38
 photo, 46
 caretaker, as, 292
 education of, 39, 45, 46, 67, 70, 71, 78, 94, 115, 129
 life with parents, 53, 67, 72, 91–92, 110–11, 115, 129–30
 life with surrogate families, 74, 92–93, 111
 understanding of parents, 48–49, 316
Rogers, Richard, xv, xix
 adult life of, 160
 with Alice, 160, 222, 333, 334
 relationship with parents, 45, 111, 140, 255, 292, 294, 306, 314, 315–16, 331

birth and early childhood, 29, 37, 47, 78
photo, 46
education of, 47, 67, 70–71, 94, 128–29, 138, 139, 140
judgment of parents, 48–49, 316
life with parents, 67, 72, 91–92, 110–11, 115
at Sevagram, 41, 42, 45, 47, 52
life with surrogate families, 74, 92–93
Runcie, Robert, Archbishop, 309

Sabeel, 299, 314
Sadat, Anwar, 215
St. Andrews Lodge, Oxford, 310
St. George's Cathedral, Jerusalem, 172, 177, 190, 201, 208–9, 219
St. Hilda's School, 39, 47, 58, 67, 68, 77, 92
St. Francis of Assisi, 243, 271
Abhishiktananda and, 166
lifestyle of, 163, 164
love for, 138, 139, 300
Murray speaks on, 206
as patron saint of Jyotiniketan, 228
prayer of, 403
quoted, 359
relic of, 314
St. Francis House, Hong Kong, 228, 233
Sandeman, Heather, xv, xvii, 75–80
death of, 333
official status of, 80, 147
relationship with ashram (Jyotiniketan), 66, 67, 73, 74, 79–80, 91, 110, 112, 135, 173, 217
relationship with Mary, 47, 53, 58, 112, 135–36, 154, 285, 311, 325, 331
caretaker of, 319, 324, 326, 329
relationship with Murray, 112, 153, 154–56, 217, 285, 326
role in Jyotiniketan, 88, 89, 90, 102, 107, 109, 112, 115, 117, 124, 175, 176, 204, 229, 234, 254, 279, 289, 282, 284, 285, 296

spirituality of, 139, 156, 168, 176, 178, 183, 253, 289
takes vows to Jyotiniketan, 128
translation work for Abhishiktananda, 166
travels of, 196, 194, 206, 217, 247, 251, 254, 266, 286, 292, 294
Santiniketan, 83, 84
Samartha, S. J., 195, 197
Saraswati River, 108n46, 388
Schönholzer, Rosmarie, 205
"Birthday Greeting" to, 369–70
commitment to Jyotiniketan of, 216, 222–23, 224
"Act of Commitment" of, 358–62
gift to Jyotiniketan of, 305
illness and death of, 293, 304
role in Jyotiniketan of, 205, 212, 229, 234, 238, 256n70, 265, 367
spiritual/emotional crisis of, 255–56, 269, 271
travels of, 247, 251, 253, 273
Schütz, Roger, 73
Selz, Henry, 271, 292, 294
Sevagram
conflict with teaching of, 44, 47–48
decision to join, 38
decision to leave, 48–49
invitation to join staff of, 36
Murray's visit to, 35–36
Murray and Mary's life in, 41–49
Shanta, N., 266, 284
Shantivanam
Abhishiktananda and, 103, 104, 131, 165
Murray with, 114
Shenouda, Pope, 71
Sherborne School, Dorset
Cheryl and Linda at, 70, 71, 115, 129
Sivaraksa, Sulak, 299
Six Day War, 136–37, 182, 185, 225
Spafford, Horatio and Anna, 173
Spafford Children's Centre (Hospital), 173, 175, 211
spiritual colonialism, 357
Squire, Giles, 77

Sri Lanka (Ceylon), 28, 66, 114
   Heather's war work in, 77
   World Council of Churches
      meetings in, 191, 194
Status Quo, Jerusalem, 178–79, 180, 201
Strict and Particular Baptists, 6
Student Christian Movement (S.C.M.)
   at Cambridge University, 1, 14, 15,
      16, 129
   in India, 86, 94, 96
   1867 Hymnbook of, 21
swaraj, 51
Sykes, Marjorie
   friendship with, 44, 49, 55, 58
   Gandhian follower, 57, 83, 151n30
   Quakerism of, 83–84, 262
   supporter of Jyotiniketan, 10
syncretism, 51, 197, 200

Tagore, Rabindranath, 83, 84, 116, 180
   quotations from, 75, 124, 170, 333
Taizé, 73, 114, 219, 221
Tai Wai, N.T., Hong Kong, 228
Takamatsu
   Zen Temple at, 182–83
Takamori
   interfaith meeting at, 249
   Shigeto Oshida's community at, 249
Tantur Ecumenical Institute, 182, 207
Tao Fong Shan Centre, 223, 224, 228,
      230, 235, 239, 269
Taoism, 228n3, 235n24, 236, 237, 238
Tao Te Ching, 228n3, 366
Taylor, John V.
   Anglican priest and bishop, 94, 197,
      312
   Murray's resignation letter to,
      142–44
Taylor, Michael, 305, 309
Temple Mount, Jerusalem, 180
Thomas, M.M., 58, 100
Thich Nhat Hanh, 195–97, 212, 221
"third leg of chicken," 184–85, 195, 221,
   298
Thurneysen, Veronica (Vroni), xviii,
      205, 217, 222, 223, 224, 255,
      256, 271, 275, 277, 292, 293,
      304, 305, 306, 319, 371

Tiananmen Square, 274
Ticozzi, Sergio, xviii, 236
Trappist, 136
Tschudin, Verena, xviii, 187, 189, 190,
   194, 203–5
Tungnath, Temple of, 107
Tuskegee Institute
   Murray visits, 26–27

Upanisads (Upanishads)
   explorations of, 107, 197, 387, 119
   ideas in, 104, 130, 168, 198
   integrating into Christian worship,
      149, 150, 165, 168, 226, 358, 395
   learning to love, 107, 113, 117
   Murray buried with, 322
   quoted by Pope Paul VI, 116
   readings/quotations from, viii, 81,
      113–14, 149, 319, 358, 389, 405
Uttar Pradesh, 58, 130

Valentine, Mary, xviii, 274
Varanasi (Banaras), 134n35
   Bettina Bäumer in, 161, 247
   Heather at ashram in, 194
   Minoru Kasai in, 109, 248
   Raimon Panikkar in, 95, 96, 161,
      163
   Mary with, 161, 176, 285
Vaswani, Dada, 267
Vatican Council, Second, 116
Vedas
   integrating into Christian worship,
      149
   learning to love the, 107, 387
   Mary's collaboration with Raimon
      Panikkar on anthology of, ("the
      Elephant") 161, 176, 177, 183,
      190, 214–15, 285
   readings/quotations from, 149, 150,
      387
Verney, Stephen, 158
Villain, Maurice, 115, 140–41
Visitor, 134
Warren, Max
   Christian Missionary Society
      (C.M.S.) head of, 26, 36, 73, 94

missionary, on being, according to, 26
spiritual guidance and support for Murray from, 14, 36, 49, 94, 142
Watson, John, 73, 74, 90
Weber, Hans-Ruedi, 99, 150
Werblowsky, Zvi, 209, 210, 211
Westcott House, Cambridge University, 17, 18, 19, 83
Wilbur, Ken, 301
Winstead, Adelaide, xviii, 275, 276
Woodstock School, 30
World Council of Churches
    Assembly of, in Ataljoun (1970), 197–99
    Assembly of, in Colombo (1974), 194–97
    Assembly of, in Nairobi (1975), 200
    Assembly of, in New Delhi (1963), 114
    Athenagoras and, 115n61
    Ilse Friedeberg of Ecumenical Institute of, 114, 129
    Hans-Ruedi Weber of, 99
    interfaith dialogue through, 136
    Murray's role in, 161, 176, 191, 194, 197, 200, 266
wu wei, 236, 239

Yamuna River, 288
Yom Kippur War/October War, 185 (*see also* October War)

Zamindari system, 59, 61
Zaru, Jean, 299
Zen Buddhism
    practice in Jerusalem, 182
    Mary and retreat in Bethlehem, 183–84
    at Takamatsu, Murray and, 182–83, 249
    Thomas Merton and, 237n29
    Shigeto Oshida and, 183, 185n29, 248–49

www.ingramcontent.com/pod-product-compliance
Lightning Source LLC
Chambersburg PA
CBHW072117290426
44111CB00012B/1685